Indian Captivity in Spanish America

Indian Captivity in Spanish America

⚜ FRONTIER NARRATIVES ⚜

Fernando Operé

Translated by Gustavo Pellón

UNIVERSITY OF VIRGINIA PRESS *Charlottesville & London*

Publication of this translation was assisted by a grant from the Program for Cultural Cooperation between Spain's Ministry of Culture and United States Universities.

Originally published in Spanish as *Historias de la frontera: El cautiverio en la América hispánica,*
© 2001 Fondo de Cultura Económica de Argentina, S.A.

University of Virginia Press
Translation © 2008 by the Rector and Visitors
of the University of Virginia

First published 2008

1 3 5 7 9 8 6 4 2

Library of Congress Cataloging-in-Publication Data

Operé, Fernando, 1946–
    [Historias de la frontera. English]
    Indian captivity in Spanish America : frontier narratives /
Fernando Operé ; translated by Gustavo Pellón.
        p.   cm.
    Translation of: Historias de la frontera.
    Includes bibliographical references and index.
    ISBN 978-0-8139-2586-8 (cloth : alk. paper) — ISBN 978-0-
8139-2587-5 (pbk. : alk. paper)
    1. Indian captivities—Latin America. I. Title.
E59.C22O64 2008
970.004'97—dc22

                                                    2007016755

Contents

Acknowledgments

This book was the product of a long process that began at the John Carter Brown Library in Providence, Rhode Island. It grew slowly as my research proceeded from archive to archive and from library to library. In their shelves, little by little, I found histories, accounts, declarations, and letters that opened new avenues for my research, widened the horizon, and complicated any attempt at simplification in my approach to the topic. I therefore express my heartfelt thanks to the staff of the Archivo General de las Indias in Seville, the staff of the Archivo General de la Nación in Buenos Aires (who went to enormous lengths to help me), the staff of the Archivo Histórico de la Ciudad de Tucumán, and the staff of Alderman Library at the University of Virginia, whose professionalism and generosity were crucial.

The final product would not have been possible without the help of numerous friends, colleagues, and students. My students heard me work out my ideas in class, and their reactions and discussion were of unquestionable value. I am in great debt to Professor Javier Herrero, my mentor and guide, who has been a continuous inspiration. He has been one of the great teachers in my professional career. I am grateful to Professor David T. Gies, friend and colleague in the Department of Spanish, Italian, and Portuguese of the University of Virginia, who read the manuscript and various preliminary articles, made suggestions, and encouraged me continuously. The contributions of Herbert Tico Braun, professor of Latin American history at the University of Virginia, were fundamental. Tico, who is a rigorous reader, not only guided my research from the very beginning but also pointed out repetitions and incongruities in the manuscript. A fine historian, Tico read and reread several drafts, and his commentaries were implacable and lucid. My deepest gratitude to Mempo Giardinelli, Argentine novelist and essayist, who offered me his home in Buenos Aires during long research trips when I rummaged through the city's archives. Mempo, who has a deep knowledge of Argentine history and literature, found contradictions in the text, suggested lines of research, and helped to reduce the baroque style of certain passages. Carrie B. Douglass, my wife and companion of many years, and professor of anthropology at Mary Baldwin College, has my gratitude for her help, understanding, and sound judgment. Carrie pointed out some oversimplifications in my anthropological analysis, above all with regard to indigenous cultures. To this marvelous group of friends and exceptional intellectuals I owe, without question, the culmination of this project to which I have devoted the last six years. They have my infinite gratitude and my friendship.

Introduction

Spanish-American Frontiers

Some commemorations are like avalanches. As 1992 approached, interest in colonial America grew amid an intense debate among intellectuals in Europe and the Americas. Colonial America was discussed from political, historical, ethical, anthropological, and literary perspectives. Newspapers and magazines throughout the world published articles in which well-known as well as less qualified authors expounded freely on one of the richest and least known periods of Western history. From a scholar's point of view, the effect was positive because it led to the publication of chronicles and other documents of the colonial period that had not been printed in more than a hundred years and that were in urgent need of fresh critical study. New collections devoted to the period appeared and interest in general flourished, leading to new critical approaches. Among them, postmodern approaches stand out, with their focus on postcolonialism, frontier studies, and the construction of cultural identities.

My contribution to this ample debate is centered on a group of heterogeneous characters: practically unknown supporting actors who appear in the background of the historical scene. They barely have texts, they shout but are not heard—nor has there been much interest in hearing them—and they become silent almost as soon as we notice their presence. I am speaking of captives.

Captives were the silent victims of the problematic relationships of the frontier. They are the forgotten protagonists of the encounter in the New World. Their names and stories went unnoticed amid the turmoil of clashing cultures. Who today remembers the names of the first Taino Indians whom Christopher Columbus took from the island of Hispaniola and brought along on his return from the first trip to the Indies? We know, we have been told, that they reached Barcelona with Columbus, and that they knelt, decked out in feathers in order to impress the Spanish monarchs with their exotic garb.[1] And after that? What became of them? What room, street, or sewer became

ix

their final resting place? What do we know of the thirty Spaniards who reached the Yucatán peninsula together with Jerónimo de Aguilar and Gonzalo Guerrero and who disappeared into the vast greenness of the peninsula? Did they become slaves? Were they sacrificed to unknown stone gods, their dried-out hearts resting on rocks? Or did they marry Indian women and modify house construction by introducing masonry techniques unknown to Yucatán Indians? Where did the Chichimecas take the intrepid Castilian soldiers who penetrated the desolate deserts of northern Mexico? After they were stripped of their high boots and their heavy helmets, what rocky ground did their feet cover? How many Chilean criollos crossed the Bío-Bío River with their hands tied behind their backs, never to return? In the thick forest of Araucanía, did Mapuche youths, who learned horseback riding with the speed of those facing a daunting enemy, learn to ride, saddle, and tame horses from their Spanish captives? How many mestizo children did white Christian women bear in the cold lands of the pampas and Patagonia? What names did they give their children and what religion did they teach them? Did they continue to sew skirts, blouses, and shawls as they sang Spanish ballads in the shade of guanaco-skin tents? And the fugitives who never made it back to the longed-for border, to what God did they pray in their helplessness?

This book is an attempt to write a history of captivity in Spanish America. It is a first step, and it begins with the story of those captives (white, mestizo, mulatto, Creole, or other) who were captured by Indians somewhere in the vast continent and who lived for varying periods of time with their captors. This book seeks to fill a void, since, with rare exceptions, the history of captivity in Spanish America has yet to be written. There are numerous works devoted to two exceptional captives: Álvar Núñez Cabeza de Vaca, who was held captive for a few years on Malhado Island during his long trek through territories in the present United States,[2] and Francisco Núñez de Pineda y Bascuñán, the Chilean Creole.[3] But in both cases, their lives and experiences have not been approached from the perspective of the history of captivity. These men have attracted interest because of the fascination exercised by the voyages themselves and by the temperate tone of understanding toward the indigenous peoples evident in their accounts. They have also attracted attention because they are among the few ex-captives who left written accounts of their experiences in captivity. They were exceptional actors with scripts of their own. In Argentina, studies about captives have appeared in the past few years. Notable among them are the works of Carlos Mayo and Amalia Latrubesse; a couple of interesting articles, by Susan Socolow and Kristine J. Jones; and an anthology of captives' accounts.[4] Among Chileans, we must mention the publications of the Universidad de la Frontera en Temuco, in which the work of Leandro León Solís on frontier relations (rather than the history of captivity) and several articles by other Chilean historians have appeared.[5]

The Myth of the Frontier

Captivity is inseparably linked to the subject of the frontier. Hispanic historiography lacks a historian like Frederick Jackson Turner, who condensed in a theoretical fashion what the North American people felt about their experience of westward expansion. Turner, in 1893, expressed masterfully the dynamism of North American colonizers. He focused on a central idea, repeatedly elaborated through years of incessant expansionism, until it acquired mythical status: the myth of the North American frontier posits the infinite possibilities of a supposedly free and open frontier.[6] This frontier is subject to assimilation; it is a no-man's-land where, through the power of American genius, the cumulative expectations dreamt during the period of construction will come true. Turner's ideas were fundamental to the theoretical formulation of an American identity in which the spirit of individualism could grow without barriers, shaping expansive and progressive ways of life. Turner's frontier is a territory whose wealth awaits those men who can use and exploit it to the full. The fact that, in practice, the territories of the West, frontier land par excellence, were inhabited by indigenous peoples, and that in the Southwest the Spanish experience had for some time offered an alternative type of frontier, did not seem to hamper Turner's theories. His formula worked, and the North American myth of the frontier owes its existence to Turner's theoretical exposition.

In Spanish America it is not possible to speak of the frontier as a uniform experience. There were many frontiers, and they meant different things, although none of them ever had the dynamic and enterprising character of the North American frontier. The only possible exception might be the original Atlantic frontier created by European sixteenth-century expansionism. That century saw the greatest change in geographical and cultural space ever experienced in Western history. For Spain and the Spanish American world, it meant the creation of a new spatial frontier whose dynamics would exert a notable transforming influence on both sides of the frontier space. One side was intoxicated with creative vitality by the mythical promise of unknown territories, while the other felt that the recently experienced possibilities of conquest and prospects of wealth were a solution to a continent hemmed in by its limited borders. If remnants of an enterprising impulse have survived in Spanish American culture, they are due to another mythical frontier: El Dorado or Los Dorados, which spurred so many impossible journeys in the sixteenth century.[7] We must not forget, however, that the pursuit of those fantastical cities, while injecting energy into the process of discovery, also pushed the Spanish conquistador back into the attics of the Middle Ages, locking him into a framework that would keep him from recognizing the true possibilities of the New World. Many of the lands explored and repeatedly traversed by expeditions to the interior never became frontiers because their conquerors sought mythical cities, not lands to colonize. In the history of the continent, the frontier is associated with a vague idea of adventure and danger, savagery, and a descent into hell.

The particular characteristics of Spanish expansion in the Americas at specific places and times gave birth to various models of the frontier. Alistair Hennessy identifies eight kinds: Indian, mission, maroon, mining, cattle, agricultural, rubber, and political frontiers.[8] His work makes the case for the great complexity and diversity of Spanish American frontiers, embracing a span of time that extends from 1528, the date of Cabeza de Vaca's first trip, to 1956, the year of the return of Helena Valero, the last of the captives included in this book.

The first theoreticians of the frontier, if they can be called that, speculated about the legal right of the conquerors to take possession of the discovered lands. They debated the legality of the *encomienda* and other forms of vassalage. They expounded on the human condition of the natives while they sent missionaries and soldiers to regions that were far away from the foundational cities. In the eighteenth century, the term "civilization" came to the rescue of decadent Christian idealism, exchanging the Christian sense of ultimate perfection for the belief in reason as the only possible substitute. At the same time, other theorists put forth notions full of ambiguity, although in general, as David J. Weber and Jane M. Rausch have argued, "Latin American intellectuals have seldom considered their frontiers central to the formation of national identities or of national institutions."[9] The exception would be the apologetic version of the Argentine Domingo F. Sarmiento. His modernizing dream was condensed in a metaphor with numerous ramifications: civilization versus barbarism. In *Facundo: Civilización y barbarie* (1845), a text of and about the frontier, Sarmiento tries to bring order to the frontier and the interior (which he calls barbarism) through writing. His postulates and ideas are from the point of view of a witness who views the frontier from without, his impotent eyes lost in the vastness of the unknown.

> The immense expanse of land is entirely unpopulated at its extreme limits, and it possesses navigable rivers that no fragile little boat has yet plowed. The disease from which the Argentine Republic suffers is its own expanse: the desert wilderness surrounds it on all sides and insinuates into its bowels; solitude, a barren land with no human habitation, in general are the unquestionable borders between one province and another [. . .]. To the south and the north, savages lurk, waiting for moonlit nights to descend, like a pack of hyenas, on the herds that graze the countryside, and on the defenseless settlements. In the solitary caravan of wagons slowly traversing the Pampas that stops to rest for a few moments, the crew, gathered around a poor fire, mechanically turn their eyes [. . .], searching out the sinister bulks of savage hordes that from one moment to the next can surprise them unprepared.[10]

Sarmiento's frontier is an unavoidable evil whose negative influence will only be countered by a string of cities that will give birth to the civilizing dream. This paradigm of civilization and barbarism has given rise to so many interpretations that it is the most recurrent theme in Latin American thought. His vision of the pernicious nature of the Argentine frontier is the radical opposite of Turner's idea of the redemptive qualities of the North American experience. Despite the many critiques of Sarmiento's theory, his thesis found numerous adherents among nineteenth-century intellectuals and even some echoes among twentieth-century writers.[11] It could be argued that Sarmiento's ideas, especially the civilization and barbarism paradigm, fed the flames of the Hispanic bad conscience regarding its own accomplishments. Let's not forget that the creation of the black legend is the work of Hispanic writers and originated in this continent. E. Bradford Burns has called the nineteenth-century civilizing dream "the poverty of progress." Fernández Retamar reminds us that barbarism is the child of civilization; while Carlos Alonso thinks that, "despite its many discordant variations, the expression 'civilization and barbarism' is a hollow rhetorical figure, a trope that precisely because it is essentially empty, paradoxically has the capacity to enable and support a series of heterogeneous discourses."[12]

There is no doubt that while Turner's theoretical formulation was a gigantic simplification, it injected inventiveness and social dynamism into the North American frontier. In Latin America, the conflict between civilization and barbarism (even if one might argue that the presuppositions of the paradigm are not valid and never were) was resolved in favor of the former, muddying historical evaluation. Fundamental principles about the inaccessibility of the frontier, the concept of the hinterland as a journey to an inscrutable and menacing world, the failure of the plans to colonize the Amazonian and Andean interior, seem to support the view of those who postulated a frontier that divided rather than united. Latin American intellectuals, especially in the nineteenth century, thought of frontiers as zones that promoted violence, despotism over democracy, caudillos, and dictators rather than free men.

Frontiers and Captives

There were many frontiers in Spanish America, with multiple and disparate experiences. There were frontiers wherever Indians resisted European penetration and expansion. One could even argue that the whole continent was a gigantic frontier, since in practice the areas experiencing a quick process of integration, with consequent acculturation, assimilation, and synthesis, were the exception rather than the rule. Areas where the cultures in contact fused to a greater or lesser degree ceased to be frontiers. That was the case with the more densely populated zones of the central valley of Mexico, where a process of integration took place among the different cultures of the Aztec confederation; and the same was true for many neighboring provinces with which the Aztecs had maintained relations of vassalage. Likewise we can also include in this category ample areas of the Inca Empire, of the Maya and Quiché cultures, and some Indian pueblos of New Mexico.

The uprisings and sporadic rebellions of the inhabitants of these regions in the centuries that followed the arrival of Europeans were not sufficiently consistent to constitute frontier lines. Indians underwent integration with the newcomers through a slow process of assimilation. Rather, frontiers existed in places where different cultures contended with each other and with the environment, thus slowing the process of assimilation.

It is important to clarify that the frontier is not a dividing line that only separates peoples and cultures. This idea is the result of a historical, static Manichaeanism that has little or nothing to do with the evolution of the great majority of the Spanish American frontiers studied in this book. Frontiers produced a unique dynamics at a given time and place, and their effects underwent a ceaseless process of evolution. Simplistic theoretical formulations of the frontier have only clouded our understanding of its complex meaning and historical importance. Frontiers are not, simply, lines of demarcation between civilization and barbarism, nor are they peripheral areas of empires or nations. Frontiers are living entities that, as such, have a structure that changes according to the ebb and flow of their component subjects and elements. Fundamental aspects of the national imagery derive from persons, customs, idiosyncrasies, and folklore whose source is frontier life in all its elusive complexity. For example, national typologies have been constructed around the figure of the cowboy and his Latin American counterparts the gaucho, *huaso, charro, llanero,* and vaquero, typologies whose meaning has changed over time.[13]

I see the frontier as a zone of interaction, or "contested ground," to use the term coined by Donna Guy and Thomas Sheridan.[14] Even in those territories where constant warfare seemed to dominate frontier relations (as in the Araucanian frontier in Chile and the so-called Comanchería in northern Mexico), there was never an absence of cultural exchange. On the frontier, objects and social behavior filtered through in a process of sustained transculturation.[15] The introduction of cattle and its adaptation by Chichimeca tribes, otherwise so resistant to Spanish penetration, brought about a radical assimilation that would change their culture profoundly. It expanded their habitat and created new possibilities and needs that had previously been unthinkable. Much has been written about the great transformation brought about by the introduction of the horse and cattle among indigenous peoples. It substantially modified relations between neighboring tribes and fostered a new way of life in accordance with new possibilities of transportation and sources of food.[16] Nevertheless, my interest in this book is focused on other marginal agents who were key to the frontier scene. I am referring to captives, shadowy but fundamental characters in the transformative dynamics of the frontier. Captives were both protagonists and victims who suffered in their own flesh the rivalry, hostility, and rejection of the human groups who lived in a constant process of negotiation on the frontier.

The practice of captivity, or violent abduction, was common among numerous tribes of North America before 1492.[17] Upon their arrival, Europeans practiced abduction for different reasons, but fundamentally to take advantage of native labor. Many tribes that did not originally engage in captivity adopted it as a form of resistance, as a means of harassing the enemy, but also as a way of ensuring a supply of women and the birth of children, and enabling exchange and barter. As a result, countless numbers of women and children, and to a lesser extent adult men, were torn by force from their homes and inserted into the indigenous world. It is not possible to construct a uniform typology of captivity. But although exceptions confound any effort to generalize, as I suggest in several chapters of this book, we can perceive certain patterns with regard to age and sex. The fate of captives is also related to the circumstances of their capture, where it took place and other chance conditions. We know that many captives became part of the societies that forcibly adopted them, going native and contributing to the process of transculturation and *mestizaje*. Others never did and lived marginalized as prisoners or slaves, performing the lowest tasks and thinking constantly of an almost impossible return.

One of the historical explanations for captivity is the reproductive potential of the captive women. Captive women were the mothers of new generations of mestizos who grew up in the Indian camps. Recent studies about the Comanchería and the Indians of the North American prairies offer telling statistics about the magnitude of this process of *mestizaje*. James Brooks thinks that the number of Euro-American captives among the prairie tribes can be estimated at between 10 and 20 percent of their populations. Specifically among the Kiowas, according to the 1870 census, the number of captives and their descendants was between 200 and 400 out of a total population of 1,879.[18] The study published in 1933 by the Ethnographic Field Schools of Santa Fe calculated that 70 percent of the Comanche population had Mexican blood. An interesting case of cultural *mestizaje* brought about by captivity was that of the *genízaros* of New Mexico. *Genízaros* were former captives of different ethnic origins who lived between cultures and were obtained through barter with Comanches and Apaches. They were loosely organized groups of Indians whose integration was based on their ties of servitude to the Spanish administrative authorities and commercial centers. After the revolt and pacification of 1680, the territorial decree that required the ransoming of captives without regard to their origin or ethnicity increased the interest of prairie tribes in this type of activity.[19] The experience of the *genízaros* in New Mexico furnishes a valid analogy for the complex process of transculturation that took place in Spanish American frontiers as a result of captivity.

On the southern frontiers of Chile and in the Argentine pampas, the phenomenon of captivity was extensive and permanent. The mid-sixteenth-century Araucanian uprisings razed the precarious Chilean cities founded by the Spaniards and saw the development of the *maloca*. This type of rapid, sporadic attack of Christian settlements had as its goal the destabilization and weakening of the invader through theft and kidnapping.[20] The first references to Spanish captives in the Río de la Plata date from the seventeenth century, when the Chilean tribes began to spread to the open valleys on the other side of the Andes.[21] At the beginning of the eighteenth century, the tribes of the southern pampas were a kaleidoscope of people from different ethnic groups who lived in *toldos* (tents) and *rehues* (camps). The number of captives in this vast territory, which was practically unexplored from the pampas to Patagonia, is difficult to estimate. Nevertheless, many accounts of eighteenth- and nineteenth-century travelers mention the existence of more or less large communities of captives in the Indian settlements.[22] Representatives from 224 tribes attended the funeral of Calfucurá, the great cacique of the Pampa Indians in 1873. Pressured by the demands of high competition in the pampas, all these tribes practiced captivity.[23] In this world, whose natural resources were increasingly reduced by the southern expansion of cattle ranches, captives were greatly prized by the tribes for their labor and for their exchange value.[24] The expedition of Juan Manuel de Rosas to the southern part of the province of Buenos Aires in 1833, whose object was to negotiate with the tribes of the pampas, produced a total of 634 rescued captives, of which 389 were women. The accumulation of cattle and women obtained in invasions or *malones* (Indian raids) in Argentine territory made possible the formation of the Pampa empire of Cacique Calfucurá. In his empire, captive women had become a vital labor force in addition to their value as mothers of a new generation of mestizo Indians. The women tended the herds of cattle, they pitched and struck the tents, they wove blankets and ponchos that were used or exchanged for other goods, they produced a variety of craft items, and they plowed fields and cooked. Through their labor, a series of artisan and domestic techniques were introduced to the *toldos* which doubtless enriched indigenous procedures and means of production. It is safe to say that captive women and their families were crucial in the gradual but constant transformation of frontier societies.

The commerce in women and cattle, conducted through *conchabadores* (traders) with the tribes of the south, connected the territory adjacent to Buenos Aires with settlements in Chile and even with the Peruvian handicraft market. Leandro León Solís points out that "most likely a small percentage of the captives remained in the *toldos* of the pampas, while the majority continued their enforced exile to the Araucanian *rehues*."[25] Commenting on this commerce, Kristine J. Jones affirms that the Indian invasions (called *malocas* in Chile and *malones* in the Río de la Plata) were on balance favorable to exchange and commerce in the pampean region.[26] We also know that, in time, the taking of captives became a commercial practice based on the exchange of prisoners. Captivity as a by-product of warfare gave way to captivity as a lucrative endeavor.

The number of male captives was always smaller than that of female captives. Men offered more resistance during capture, tended to escape, and created more problems in the process of integration. Nevertheless, they were coveted now and then for their skills at various crafts, and the tribes considered them essential for the adaptation of valuable European techniques. The chronicler of the kingdom of Chile, Alonso González de Nájera, mentions the demand among Araucanians for captives adept in the arts and techniques they prized. Once the Indians had adopted certain Spanish military strategies and saw their benefit, they needed blacksmiths to make horseshoes and forge weapons, carpenters to make plows and other wooden implements, as well as artisans skilled at ceramics and leatherwork. Children, on the other hand, were more easily integrated into the culture of the captors and in time, depending on their attitudes and talents, became active members of the tribe. Racial distinctions did not make them marginal. The tribes of the pampas were solidly stratified, with caciques at the head of a pyramid made up of *loncos* or warriors and subalterns, but without apparent distinction by race or color. We know of important caciques who were the sons of captive women.[27]

Captivity was a personal experience in which there were two participants, a captor, the Indian who was assigned a prisoner under specific circumstances, and a captive. The personality of each of them and their ability to communicate were as important as the social, economic, and political circumstances of the captor group. It is true that in times of open hostility many prisoners of war were killed shortly after reaching the camps or even before. Some of the soldiers captured with Bascuñán were not as fortunate as he and were killed after crossing the demarcation line of the Bío-Bío River.[28] But we also have information about numerous captives who refused to return and of many who deserted to the Indians, especially on the Araucanian frontier, thus increasing the bad reputation of the Spanish administration in Chile.

Voices of the Captives: The Sources

The history of captivity, like any history, is fed by its sources. The recuperation of the voices of captives, whose echoes were erased by the distance of frontier settlements and Indian camps, has been the most difficult task in the construction of this history. Of the thousands of captives who swelled indigenous communities, the great majority either remained in forced captivity or integrated voluntarily, rejecting the possibility of any return to their homes. We know little or nothing about them. From time to time echoes of their voices reach us, sifted through the account of some traveler who interviewed or sketched them at a distance, speculating about their lot. It was common in the nineteenth century for traveling representatives of national governments to refer to captive women they had seen when visiting Indian *toldos* on diplomatic or topographical missions. Their comments betray the overwhelming feeling of superiority with which these representatives of so-called civilization viewed the indigenous communities and the captives' fate.

Of those who returned, either by escaping or by being exchanged, few wrote about their experiences, either because they did not consider it important or because their accounts were not well received. At military posts on the Buenos Aires frontier, captives who had fled or been ransomed were made to give their declarations to officials, who recorded them. These declarations are terse documents whose content is limited by the nature of the questions posed to the new arrivals. Government interest in returning captives did not lie in the human aspect of their experiences but rather in the military information they might furnish regarding the location and strength of enemy forces, and the imminence of future attacks. Ex-captives did not receive any special treatment upon their return. Rather than heroes, they were seen as marginal beings by the society from which they had been torn. Contact with the Indians left a stigma that marked them for life, especially in the case of women. For these and other reasons that I will discuss later, we have few firsthand accounts, testimonies, or sources. A notable exception is the case of foreign captives—French, German, and North American—who upon returning to their countries found that their exotic journeys and extraordinary adventures generated a great deal of interest in the scientific community and the public at large. The accounts of Hans Staden (1557), Auguste Guinnard (1864), and Benjamin F. Bourne (1880) were well received in their home countries.[29] The dissemination and popularity of captive literature in Great Britain and the United States is also well documented.[30]

Fundamental firsthand accounts are those of Álvar Núñez Cabeza de Vaca (captured by the Karankawa in the Gulf of Mexico), Hernando de Escalante Fontaneda (captured in Florida in the sixteenth century), Francisco Núñez de Pineda y Bascuñán and Juan Falcón (both captured in Araucanía at the beginning of the eighteenth century), Santiago Avendaño (captured in the pampas during the first half of the nineteenth century), and Helena Valero (captured by the Yanomamö Indians in 1932 at the age of thirteen), who is still living at a mission on the Orinoco River. Their voices are crucial for the construction of a history of captivity. In general, theirs are moderate voices that have the ring of those who have known the other in his own setting.

We know the stories of other captives through chroniclers, compilers, or scribes. The information they furnish needs to be handled with care because of their questionable impartiality. We know about some of the first instances of captivity that occurred in Florida during the sixteenth and seventeenth centuries from the writings of the Inca Garcilaso de la Vega (*La Florida del Inca*) and Father Luis Gerónimo de Oré (*Relación de los mártires que ha habido en las Provincias de la Florida* [An Account of the Martyrs in Florida]). The disappointing war in Arauco moved many chroniclers (Alonso González de Nájera, Alonso Góngora de Marmolejo, Pedro Mariño de Lobera, Diego de Rosales, and others) to take an interest in the fate of captives during this long conflict. In their accounts, the voices of the captives reach us through the partisan slant of the chroniclers, who regarded with horror the lot of Spanish women at the mercy of their "fierce captors."

In northern Mexico, ex-captives who found shelter on North American reservations were able to make their stories known through the work of Quakers and members of other Protestant denominations.[31] The work as a scribe of the Methodist minister J. J. Methvin was crucial to the recuperation of many voices of captives of the Comanchería and Apachería, at a time when the disappearance of the prairie Indians was imminent. For the earlier period, scattered sources can be found in reports by frontier commanders and governors, memoranda, religious narratives, notes, petitions, and letters written to the authorities of the viceroyalty or the Crown.

Comparative Systems, North and South

My biggest surprise in researching this book was to discover the scarcity of published sources. Captives in Spanish America did not write nor were they encouraged to write. Perhaps this is one of the most important aspects of the history of captivity, since it invites us to ask fundamental questions. If the history of captivity in Spanish America extends from the beginning of the sixteenth century to our own time, how is it possible that so few firsthand accounts have been published? Was there no interest in captives' stories? Wasn't the information these witnesses could furnish about Indian communities considered valuable? Weren't the Romantics, so fascinated by the exotic, attracted to these stories of captures and escapes?

The lack of interest in Spanish America is more glaring when we compare it to the situation in the United States, especially New England, where captivity literature (both factual accounts and fiction) was extraordinarily popular. According to Gary Ebersole, "Thousands of captive narratives, both factual and fictional were published over the years, enjoying a wide readership on both sides of the Atlantic; some were reprinted many times."[32] Chicago's Newberry Library houses approximately two thousand accounts by captives written before 1880. This figure includes just nonfiction accounts, but there was also a prolific output of fiction about captives. Thirty editions were published of Mary Rowlandson's *Sovereignty & Goodness of God* (1682), one of the classics of captivity literature in New England. It also met with success in Europe and went through several London editions. John Williams's *The Redeemed Captive Returning to Zion* (1707), another greatly popular captive narrative, sold more than a hundred thousand copies and was reedited under different titles until the twentieth edition, which dates from 1918.[33] Of the four best sellers between 1680 and 1720, three were books about captives. A hundred years later, between 1823 and 1837, four books reached sales of over a hundred thousand copies: three novels by James Fenimore Cooper in which captivity is an integral part of the plot (*The Pioneers, The Last of the Mohicans, and The Prairie*) and *A Narrative of the Life of Mrs. Jemison,* by James Everett Seaver, one of the classics of captivity literature.[34] There are thirty editions of the first account of captivity published in North America, *A True History of the Captivity and Restoration of Mrs. Mary Rowlandson.* (1682). Contemporary North American historiography and literary criticism have recognized its importance, and many books and articles have been written about it. Kathryn Derounian-Stodola has pointed out that "some critics believe that the Indian captivity narrative functions as the archetype of American culture."[35]

Why was there such interest in captives and their stories in Anglo-America but not in Spanish America? Many critics and historians (including Axtell, Cohen, Demos, Ebersole, Levernier, and VanDerBeets) have speculated about this phenomenon, and they argue that the key difference was the religious interpretation given by the Christian churches, principally by the Puritans, to the experience of captivity. Puritans were quick to compare captivity among the Indians with being held captive by sin, thus seeing Indians as incarnations of the devil: "To be taken captive, then, meant to fall into Satan's power. Indian captivity was an ordeal which had religious implications for both the captive and the Puritan community."[36] A captive's decision to remain with his captors was, in their eyes, an incomprehensible and catastrophic act. The drama of John Williams and his family, studied by John Demos, exemplifies the Puritan dilemma. The terrible anguish of the Williams family did not stem from the suffering inflicted on them by their captors for two years, but from the decision of their younger daughter, Eunice, to refuse to return and to stay instead with her Mohawk husband.[37] Not all Protestants shared the same beliefs. The hardships to which captivity exposed a Christian also had a salutary effect, the redemptive nature of suffering: "Captivity narratives were part of a spiritual regimen of self-examination and moral improvement."[38] Puritans made use of the experience by analyzing it as an act permitted by God from which important lessons could be drawn. Quotations of biblical passages are common in captive texts.

I should point out that the extensive production of captive narratives took on different forms according to the social group to which they were addressed, resulting in texts that were anti-Indian, anti-French, or anti-Catholic. Given these multiple audiences and functions, it is not surprising that captives were encouraged to write immediately upon their return by their relatives, friends, or editors. News of a return made its way quickly to the headlines of newspapers. If the protagonists themselves were unable to pen their own experiences, a scribe was appointed to carry out the project. These stories had a topical value and were published without delay. In time, "the infusion of melodrama and sensibility into the narratives, appropriately ornamented and stylistically embellished, capitalized on what became an increasingly profitable commercial market for properly 'literary' narratives of Indian captivity in the later eighteenth and early nineteenth centuries."[39]

Such was the popularity of these narratives that unscrupulous editors published fictional accounts as real experiences. One of the best sellers of the period was the fictional *An Account of the Beautiful Young Lady, Who was Taken by the Indians and Lived in the Woods Nine Years* (1787), written by Abraham Pantler, who passed it off as a true account. These abuses eventually hurt the prestige of the genre. In order to remedy this situation, some captivity narratives contained a sworn deposition that stated their authenticity.[40]

Nothing remotely similar occurred in Spanish America. The discovery and conquest were an enterprise of the Spanish monarchy under the banner of a universal Christian empire. A crucial part of the plan for the New World was the integration of Indians as vassals of the monarchy, once they accepted baptism. In the most densely populated areas, after their initial resistance was defeated by force of arms, Indians did integrate. Indians and Spaniards coexisted in the cities built by the New World Spanish society. Racial and cultural *mestizaje* was the norm. The Crown was interested in discoveries and conquests, not in failures associated with Indian resistance. Basically, the *crónicas de Indias* (chronicles of the Indies) were meant to be narratives of a civilization and its expansionist and civilizing energy, not an account of its failures.

In addition, the Spanish world never developed a personal code of conduct, but rather the opposite. Values, religion, and ideology sprang from a hierarchical and strictly regimented society. The Crown financed adventures and censored the chronicles.[41] A captive's story was a story of failure that contributed nothing to the glorious annals of expansionist Spain. Captivity narratives were stories produced in Florida, Nueva Galicia, Nuevo León, New Mexico, Araucania, Patagonia, and the Amazonian interior, the outer reaches of the empire, which were of little strategic value. In none of these places, with the exception of the silver mines in Zacatecas, Nueva Viscaya, were there appreciable riches. The Indians of these territories were not comparable, from a material point of view, to those of the zones controlled by the monarchy (the central valley of Mexico, the Maya and Quiché world, zones of the Inca and Aymara empires). The Spaniards felt that they had little to learn from the Chichimecas, Mapuches, or Patagonians, whom they considered primitive Indians in the most elemental stage of development. Furthermore, why take an interest in societies that resisted the triumphal advance of Christianity?

The apostolic plan of the Christian monarchy was to incorporate the Indians into the new order. After long debates about the nature of the Indians, it was decided that they were, not representatives of the devil, but *infantes en la fe* (infants in the faith) who had to be assimilated to the empire by way of baptism. It was necessary to give them a religious education by learning their languages and teaching them the catechism. In practice, missions were the vanguard on the most remote frontiers. Monks and missionaries were in daily contact with Indians and felt they knew them. Thus it was thought that a former captive had little relevant knowledge to contribute. The Mapuches, for example, had lived in the cities of the kingdom of Chile before the first Indian uprisings (1540). Their language and their social customs were known. What value then could there be in the story of a captive who returned from the other shore of the Bío-Bío River with his body covered with tattoos? It was better to silence his story, which was a story of failure. The Spanish Crown did have official chroniclers who from time to time took note of these stories and wove them as anecdotes into their voluminous account of events.

There were exceptions. Cabeza de Vaca had other ambitions besides being a notary (*escribano*). He wrote the account of his journey, *Naufragios* (*Shipwrecks*), hoping to dazzle the imperial authorities and obtain the position of *adelantado* on future expeditions. He was lucky; his narrative found favor with the king. Núñez de Pineda y Bascuñán, on the other hand, wrote his *Cautiverio feliz* (Happy Captivity) with reform in mind and freely criticized Spanish policies in Chile, blaming them for the long-lasting frontier wars. That is why his account, finished in 1673, was not published until the end of the nineteenth century. Spanish censorship strictly controlled the production of texts. Even the most innocuous accounts had difficulty obtaining permission to be published. Only those which answered the needs of the empire were printed, and certainly stories about captives were far from edifying. At best they were testimony to Spain's impotence to control all its territories and spread the religion of Rome.

Interest in returning captives was minimal. From a social perspective, they had difficulty adjusting to the obsessively stratified society. This was especially true for women. Contact with the Indians had marked them for life, and that stain was not easy to erase. One could almost say that their narratives were stories of shame rather than didactic texts as they were in New England. Probably the vast majority of those women, captured as girls, were illiterate and had very vague notions of the consequences and context of their adventures. If individuals or institutions did not express an interest in their stories, these would remain stories to tell at night in a whisper.

One notices the appearance, after independence, of a kind of fictive literature (both poetry and prose) on the theme of captives, especially in the Río de la Plata. It was a clearly programmatic literature, formulated according to the most simplistic Darwinism. The predominant notion was that the savagery of the Indians could be cured by neither religion nor diplomacy. It was thought that their hatred of Christians was innate and that their continuous acts of barbarism (the abduction of white women) justified their extermination as part of the project of civilization. A *malón* was a hard reality of daily life on the frontier, not an adventure story. Silence was the reward allotted to returning ex-captives. Rather than remembering their deeds and mentioning their names, Argentine society felt the urgent need to solve the Indian problem once and for all. Among the solutions considered was their forced relocation to the heart of Patagonia or their extinction.

To recover the voices of those silenced has been the major challenge of this research project. I am certain that in the archives of cities throughout the continent there must be other testimonies of captives waiting to be liberated by researchers.

Plan of the Book

Chapter 1 centers on a study of the first captives in an unexplored territory, at the time of the first encounters between Europeans and Indians, when no frontier had yet been established. Florida was the name given then to the vast territory that extended through what is now the southeastern United States from Key West to Texas. Those first encounters were full of surprise and novelty. Spanish expeditions were greeted by the native inhabitants with joy, or at least with expectation. The first Spanish captives in the area were the victims of shipwrecks. The inclement weather of the Caribbean Sea threw thousands of travelers on the coasts of the continent, where they were lost in the thick vegetation or taken in by local tribes. Such was the case of Álvar Núñez Cabeza de Vaca, Pánfilo de Narváez's *escribano* and a castaway of the catastrophic 1528 expedition. Held captive by Gulf of Mexico Indians, he later saved his neck by trading and practicing as a shaman. Seeking support for future expeditions, Álvar wrote a report addressed to the king of Spain which was published in 1542. It was the first text written by an ex-captive from the Indies.

The unusual narrative of another captive, Hernando de Escalante Fontaneda (1553–70), tells of the many Spaniards who, as captives or guests, swelled the native settlements of the Florida peninsula. Later in the sixteenth century, the recurrence of Spanish expeditions with explicit plans to conquer and take possession of land hurt relations with the native population. The frontiers were beginning to take shape. Juan Ortiz fell into the hands of the Timucuans, a victim of the first Indian revolts, provoked by the atrocities committed by another Spanish conquistador, Pánfilo de Narváez. The cacique of the Timucuans had sworn vengeance, and Ortiz paid for the crimes of others. His captivity lasted ten years. Hernando de Soto's great expedition, which found Ortiz, left captives and deserters in its wake. The desertions spoke eloquently of the soldiers' disenchantment with failed imperial enterprises. For some, like the Andalusian hidalgo Diego de Guzmán, who fell in love with a young Indian woman, desertion seemed the answer to the feeling of failure and futility felt by the members of many of the expeditions sent to conquer Florida.

Failure was equally prevalent on another of the most confrontational frontiers of the continent, Araucania. Chapter 2 explores this territory and the origins of the long conflict that began with the mid-sixteenth-century Mapuche uprisings. The firm resistance of the many tribes that formed the Mapuche coalition had its roots in the experiences that many of these Indians had had as *encomendados* and forced laborers of the Spanish colonists. The Araucanian wars produced thousands of victims and as many captives. During these wars a slow process of transculturation took place, beginning with the adoption of Spanish military tactics by the Mapuches and continuing through the silent work of the Spanish women and the criollo artisans who lived in the *rehues*. The partisan view of many of the chroniclers of the kingdom of Chile contrasts with the narrative of an exceptional captive, Francisco Núñez de Pineda y Bascuñán, author of *Cautiverio feliz y razón individual de las guer-*

ras dilatadas del Reino de Chile (Happy Captivity, and the Particular Reason for the Lengthy Wars of the Kingdom of Chile), one of the most complete firsthand sources for the study of captivity in Chile.

When the Araucanians spread to the pampas they continued their activities in the Río de la Plata region. Chapter 3 studies the phenomenon of transculturation known as the Araucanization of the pampas. In this migration Mapuche and Pehuenche tribes, feeling increasing pressure on their territories in southern Chile, moved gradually toward the vast territory of the eastern foothills of the Andes, Patagonia and the pampas. The greater abundance of grazing lands and wild cattle, as well as the relatively unprotected frontier settlements, made ideal targets for these warlike tribes, which had become stronger by adapting Spanish military tactics. Just as in the prairies of the North American Midwest, the recently arrived Araucanian tribes negotiated their predominance over the territory by making alliances with and wars on the original inhabitants. The Chilean experience, as well as the possibilities of a lucrative commerce in cattle and captives, led to the emergence of the Chilean *maloca* and the *malón* in the territory of the Río de la Plata. The first *malones* date from the beginning of the seventeenth century.[42] The last one took place in the Chaco in 1924.

During the eighteenth century, Indians grew stronger through increased commerce and alliances, which culminated in the confederation headed by Calfucurá in the nineteenth century. By then, trans-Andean commerce was regulated by the tribes and by the *conchabadores* who linked Creole frontier settlements throughout the south (Río Negro and Patagonia) and Chile. Captives were an integral part of this commerce. They were the shadowy protagonists of a permeable frontier inhabited by the marginal elements of the society of the Río de la Plata region.

Chapter 4 centers on the story of three nineteenth-century captives in the pampas and Patagonia whose adventures were fortunately published: the French adventurer Auguste Guinnard, the North American sailor Benjamin F. Bourne, and Santiago Avendaño, a resident of Buenos Aires. The first two accounts give detailed descriptions of different aspects of the life of the Pampa tribes. They take us on an exceptional journey to the heart of the other, the savage Indian, a figure as feared as he was unknown. Part of the uniqueness of these narratives lies in the fact that they were published owing to the enthusiasm of scientific and historical societies. The captives' adaptation process illustrates a conflict typical of this period: the dilemma between knowl-edge as the captives' instrument for survival, and knowledge as acquisition of scientific information. The narratives of Guinnard, Bourne, and Avendaño permit us to reflect on the reception of captive literature in the society of Buenos Aires, capital of the republic and formerly of the viceroyalty. The ex-istence of thousands of liberated captives who reached administrative or pro-cessing centers with an enormous number of unusual experiences and fasci-nating anecdotes contrasts with the lack of interest in their accounts evinced by the absence of publications.

It is hardly surprising, therefore, that Guinnard's and Bourne's accounts were published in Paris and Boston, respectively, where the scientific com-munity as well as the general reading public were interested in fantastic nar-ratives or adventures to exotic places. In Argentina, the image that the liberal administrations wanted to project—the construction of progressive societies based on European models—did not match the reality of a country inhabited by about two hundred tribes who challenged their program of civilization.

Chapter 5 investigates the slow formation of Mexico's northern frontier, the Spanish frontier in North America. The diversity and wide expanse of this territory, explored in the mid-sixteenth century by expeditions that ended in total failure (e.g., those of Cabeza de Vaca, Marcos de Niza, Francisco de Ulloa, and Vázquez de Coronado), force us to address the issue of juxtaposed fron-tiers. Even in the second half of the nineteenth century, these frontiers were still territories in dispute between their inhabitants—indigenous tribes, old Mexican inhabitants, and Anglo immigrants.

The discovery of silver deposits in the region of Zacatecas in 1540 drove colonists into the arid territories of northern Mexico. The first colonists ran into the inhabitants' hostile resistance, something to which the Spanish con-quistadores were not accustomed. The Pame, Guamare, Zacateco, and Guachi-chile Indians, usually embraced by the global term Chichimeca Indians, forced the Spanish administration to rethink its defensive tactics. The Indians harried the colonists without rest, tore up their vulnerable settlements, and seized cattle and women.

The difficulties inherent in the administration of such vast uninhabited territories forced the creation of the government districts of Nueva Galicia, Nuevo León, Nueva Vizcaya, and Nuevo México. Good and bad administra-tors had to face the difficulties caused by Indian resistance.

The massive arrival of Comanche and Apache tribes, starting in 1730, contributed further to the area's instability. The mobility of these diverse and unpredictable tribes affected both Spanish and Indian communities in the territory. Instability increased after Mexican independence and the North American advance from the east, which gradually reduced the tribes' ancient habitat. The Comanches, as well as the Apaches, Utes, Navajos, and Kiowas, lived partly off theft and the ransoming of captives.

The captives' traces are faint. Notes included in the reports of governors, administrators, and missionaries attest to the widespread nature of the phenomenon of captivity. The narratives of three captives in the New Mexico territory, however, furnish valuable information that allows us to sketch a map of the phenomenon on the northern frontier. These are the stories of Francisca Medrano and Tomassa, both captives of the Comanches, and Andrés Martínez, captured by an Apache patrol and traded to the Kiowas, with whom he lived as an adolescent and a man. These narratives are key sources for understanding the life of the Comanches, Apaches, and Kiowas during the last phases of intercultural transformation in the so-called Comanchería (Comancheland). They depict a time of growing insecurity and bear witness to the last gasps of the tribes of the prairies. These three Spanish captives wound up living in reservations created by the U.S. government to house the native population displaced by the advance of its army.

It is surprising to discover that there were captives in the twentieth century. These captives support Hennessy's opinion that "the majority of Latin American nations today are still in the frontier stage of development."[43] Hennessy points to the diffuse cultural frontiers that mark the borders of almost all southern cone countries and the great territory of Amazonia. With the exception of Chile and Uruguay, all South American countries have frontiers with Amazonian tropical forests. Amazonia, a territory the size of the United States, awaits the challenge of modernity. Millions of species and many Indian tribes live under the constant threat of the implacable advance of industrial civilization. The Yanomamö of the high Orinoco are among the many tribes who have seen their habitat reduced by the gold seekers, rich landowners, and impoverished farmers who have invaded the pristine territory where their ancestors have ranged from time immemorial. Helena Valero, captured by the Kohoroshitari Indians in 1932 at the age of thirteen, lived with the Yanomamö for twenty-four years.

Chapter 6 deals with the story of this extraordinary woman, who went from being Helena Valero to Napëyoma during her round-trip experience. The text, *Yo soy Napëyoma: Relato de una mujer raptada por los indígenas yanomami* (I Am Napëyoma: An Account of a Woman Captured by the Yanomami), published in 1984 after many vicissitudes, is an excellent autobiography that has many of the characteristics of the genre. Although reluctant at first, Helena finally decided to provide an oral testimony of her life when she learned of the various instances of plagiarism of which she was the victim.

Chapter 7 reviews the fictional literature about captives. My premise is that there were captives of the Indians and captives of literature. Especially in nineteenth-century Río de la Plata, fiction played an important role as an ideological instrument to promote specific political agendas. In other chapters we have seen that captivity narratives were archaeological objects of scarce interest to the greater public. Perhaps it is more accurate to say that makers of educational policy were not interested in associating the images of captivity with those of the liberal and progressive society they wanted to forge. Captives of the Indians said little, and their voices gathered dust in the shelves of the archives. The voices of literary captives, however, resonated in the urban centers, where their tragedies were seen through Romantic eyes. Romantic Marías, as in Esteban Echeverría's *La cautiva* (1837), made their appearance in literature. Captured by Indians, their lives and bodies came to symbolize the conflict of the frontier, simplified into the antagonism of civilization and barbarism. Romantic writers recovered stories from the colonial period and manipulated them to serve the needs of their own day. An example is the story of Lucía Miranda, told in Ruy Díaz de Guzmán's 1612 chronicle *La Argentina,* whose veracity was questioned by contemporary authors but which inspired several novels, poems, and plays in the nineteenth century.[44] Because it suits popular taste, fiction has a far greater impact than that of history.

A constant feature of fiction about captives, which partly explains its continuing popularity, is the symbolic representation of the body of the female captive. The controversial relationship between Europeans and Indians is represented by the victim's body. This is the case in pioneering seventeenth-century works like Diego de Saavedra's *Purén indómito,* or the already cited work by Díaz de Guzmán. The woman's body becomes the depository of virtues assigned to Christian society. Her rape is not only the greatest offense against its most sacred principles but also corroboration of the uncontrollable lust of the savage Indian aggressor. The civilizing discourse inverted the terms of the conflict by transforming the victims, the American Indians, into aggressors who usurped the most prized object of Christian civilization, the white woman.

The role of fictive works about captives can be traced with clarity in Argentine and Uruguayan literature since the nineteenth century. From Echeverría's vastly influential poem *La cautiva*, through the works of other poets of his generation, Juan Cruz Varela and Hilario Ascasubi, until the recent novels of the 1980s and 1990s, the literature of the Río de la Plata has continued to be interested in captives. The disappearance of Indians from the southern frontier of Buenos Aires at the end of the nineteenth century was a turning point in the process of representation. If nineteenth-century fiction justified radical solutions to the Indian problem, later literature sought to write a requiem for the vanished races.

Notes

1. Colón, *Historia del Almirante.*

2. I use Roberto Ferrando's edition of Cabeza de Vaca's *Naufragios y comentarios.* The bibliography on Cabeza de Vaca is quite extensive; works of special note are Adorno, "The Negotiation of Fear in Cabeza de Vaca's *Naufragios*"; Carreño, "Naufragios, de Álvar Núñez Cabeza de Vaca"; Howard, *Conquistador in Chains;* Lagmanovich, "Los naufragios de Álvar Núñez"; Molloy, "Alteridad y reconocimiento en los *Naufragios*"; Pastor, *Discursos narrativos de la conquista;* Pupo-Walker, "Pesquisas para una nueva lectura de los Naufragios"; Zubizarreta, *Capitanes de aventura.*

3. Of note on Núñez de Pineda y Bascuñán's *Cautiverio feliz* are Anadón, *Pineda y Bascuñán, defensor del araucano;* Armond, "Frontier Warfare in Colonial Chile"; Bauer, "Imperial History, Captivity, and Creole Identity"; Correa Bello, *El Cautiverio feliz en la vida política chilena;* Chang-Rodríguez, "Conocimiento, poder y escritura en el *Cautiverio feliz*"; Lancaster, "The Happy Captivity of Francisco Núñez de Pineda y Bascuñán."

4. Mayo and Latrubesse, *Terratenientes, soldados y cautivos;* Mayo, "El cautiverio y sus funciones"; Socolow, "Los cautivos españoles en las sociedades indígenas"; K. J. Jones, "*La Cautiva*"; Operé, *Cautivos.*

5. León Solís, *Maloqueros y conchavadores en Araucanía y las pampas;* also his "Las invasiones indígenas." See also works by Zapater Equioíz, Lázaro Ávila, and Guarda Geywitz.

6. Turner, *History, Frontier, and Section.*

7. See Gil, *Mitos y utopías del descubrimiento;* and Gandía, *Historia crítica de los mitos de la conquista americana.*

8. Hennessy, *The Frontier in Latin American History,* chap. 3.

9. Weber and Rausch, introduction to *Where Cultures Meet,* xiii.

10. Sarmiento, *Facundo,* 11 (Ross trans., 45–46).

11. See Sorensen, *Facundo and the Construction of Argentine Culture.*

12. Burns, *The Poverty of Progress;* Fernández Retamar, "Algunos usos de civilización y barbarie"; Alonso, "Civilización y barbarie."

13. See Slatta's *Comparing Cowboys and Frontiers* and *Cowboys of the Americas.*

14. Guy and Sheridan, *Contested Ground,* 3–15.

15. The Mexican historian Silvio Zavala has observed the similarity between the western frontier of the United States and those of Chile and northern Mexico ("The Frontier in Hispanic America").

16. See K. J. Jones, "Comparative Raiding Economies."

17. J. Norman Heard, who has studied the assimilation of captives, maintains that captivity was an established practice among North American Indians since prehistoric times. See his *White into Red.*

18. Brooks, introduction to Methvin, *Andele,* 5.

19. Russell M. Magnaghi, "The Genízaro Experience in Spanish New Mexico," in *Spain and the Plains,* ed. Vigil, Kaye, and Wunder, 117.

20. León Solís, *Maloqueros y conchavadores en Araucanía y las Pampas,* 32–33.

21. See Walther, *La conquista del desierto.*

22. Among the many travelers' accounts, of particular interest are those of Mansilla, Ebélot, Musters, and, in the collection by Pedro de Angelis, P. A. García, and José Cardiel, "Viajes y expediciones."

23. K. J. Jones, "Calfucurá y Namuncurá," 183.

24. See Mayo, *Estancia y sociedad en la Pampa;* and Puiggrós, *De la colonia a la revolución.*

25. León Solís, *Maloqueros y conchavadores en Araucanía y las Pampas,* 139.

26. K. J. Jones, "Comparative Raiding Economies," 102.

27. Ramón Platero, a cacique of the Tantum of Panghitruz, was the son of a Ranquel father and a captive mother. The Ranquel cacique, Baigorrita, grandson of Yanquetruz, was also the son of a white captive woman. Martínez Sarasola, *Nuestros paisanos los indios,* 227.

28. In chap. 10 of *Cautiverio feliz,* Nuñez de Pineda y Bascuñán describes the execution of a Spanish soldier who had been captured with him at the battle of Cangrejeras (37–41).

29. The accounts of Guinnard and Bourne are studied in chap. 4 below. Hans Staden, a German explorer captured by the Tupinambá of Brazil, wrote a sensationalistic account of the cannibalistic practices of his captors. The book was highly popular and went through many editions.

30. There are many studies about captives and the literature of captives in the United States, and I cite them in this book. Ebersole's *Captured by Texts* contains an up-to-date bibliography.

31. See Cutler, "Lawrie Tatum and the Kiowas Agency."

32. Ebersole, *Captured by Texts,* 10.

33. Namias, *White Captives,* 8.

34. Ibid., 10.

35. Derounian-Stodola, *Women's Indian Captivity Narratives,* xi.

36. Levernier and Cohen, introduction to *The Indians and Their Captives,* xvii.

37. Demos, *The Unredeemed Captive.*

38. Ebersole, *Captured by Texts,* 9.

39. VanDerBeets, *Held Captives by Indians,* xxviii.

40. Ibid., xxxi.

41. See Johnson, *Satire in Colonial Spanish America.*

42. In the meeting held on October 30, 1606, the *cabildo* (town council) of the city of Buenos Aires agreed that the Mercedarian monastic order would oversee the herds of wild cattle and stray oxen kept for the purpose of ransoming of captives. *Acuerdos del extinguido cabildo de Buenos Aires,* 17.

43. Hennessey, *The Frontier in Latin American History,* 3.

44. Lichtblau, "El tema de Lucía Miranda."

❦ ONE ❦

Álvar Núñez Cabeza de Vaca
and Florida Captives in the
Sixteenth Century

> In this manner we went up to their houses, where we found
> they had made a house for us, and many fires in it; and about an
> hour after we arrived they began to dance and to make a great
> party, which lasted all night, even though for us there was no
> pleasure, nor party nor sleep, as we were waiting to see when
> they were going to sacrifice us.
>
> —Álvar Núñez Cabeza de Vaca, 1555

The North American continent was not favorable to the great enterprise of conquest. Myths prevalent at the time of the conquest motivated many expeditions and consumed fortunes, but the expeditions failed to produce another Tenochtitlan. The Seven Cities of Cíbola, promised by the Franciscan Marcos de Niza in his expedition to the territory of New Mexico (1538), were but a fleeting preamble to the failed adventures of Hernando de Alarcón and Francisco Vázquez de Coronado (1540–42). Nor did the prairies of the Midwest yield anything to the conquistadores who lost their way amid the herds of bison, searching for the mythical Quivira. In the east, the Caribbean islands' nearness to the Florida peninsula made launching expeditions easy. The peninsula seemed to promise rich resources, which is why Juan Ponce de León gave it the enticing name of "Florida" during his first voyage of discovery (1513), although the name was suggested by the discovery of the peninsula on Easter Sunday (Pascua Florida).[1] Faced with marshlands, thick jungle, and the unpredictable climate in the Gulf of Mexico, expeditions to the vast

1

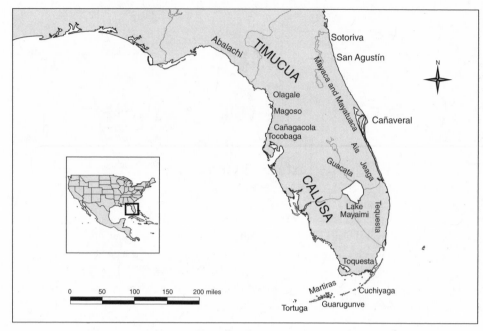

Map 1. Indigenous Populations of La Florida in the Sixteenth Century

unknown produced a story of failures and few quantifiable riches to justify further investment.

In 1536 slave-hunting Spaniards in northwestern Mexico found a pale-faced Indian together with an even stranger black-faced Indian. These tired, squalid men were a Spaniard from Seville, Álvar Núñez Cabeza de Vaca, and his companion, Estebanico, a black slave from North Africa, both of whom had been shipwrecked eight years before on the western shore of the Florida peninsula. They had lived for long stretches of time among the inhabitants of the southern coast. Part of their wanderings had been marked by the experience of captivity.

Still in their Indian garb, Cabeza de Vaca and Estebanico returned to the capital city of Mexico, where their lives took different courses. Estebanico, the slave, became an essential component of future expeditions. Like his companions in adventure, Estebanico had learned several languages, had traveled through previously unexplored lands, and swore that he had seen the wealth of the marvelous cities of the north. He was therefore a coveted guide. Eager to be hired, he was soon part of Father Niza's expedition to New

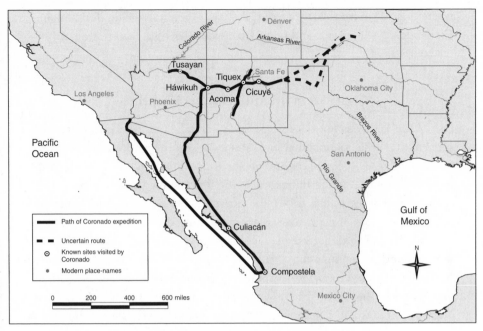

Map 2. Expedition of Francisco Vázquez de Coronado

Mexico, sponsored by Antonio de Mendoza, the viceroy of Mexico. Estebanico had assured the ambitious friar that there were cities with multistory buildings whose mineral wealth glittered in the rays of the setting sun. Estebanico's ambition cost him his life at the hands of the Zuñi Indians. Father Niza returned and told of Estebanico's sad end, but he did not refute the legend of the promised cities. That legend was responsible for one of the costliest incursions into that territory, the expedition commanded by Coronado. Furthermore, the priest added fuel to the fire by telling sensational stories of rich kingdoms with camels, elephants, and other exotic fauna.[2]

For his part, Cabeza de Vaca returned to Spain, where he wrote a report of his journey addressed to the king, which was published as a book in 1542 with the title of *La relación* (The Account).[3] A second edition, entitled *Naufragios* (Shipwrecks), was published in Valladolid in 1555. Cabeza de Vaca's adventure was included in the *Historia general y natural de las Indias* (General and Natural History of the Indies), by Gonzalo Fernández de Oviedo, who had interviewed him in Madrid in 1547.[4] Cabeza de Vaca was the first captive to write his story, but not the only one. References to captives in Florida are numerous. We have the stories of Cabeza de Vaca, Hernando de Escalante Fontaneda, Father Ávila, and Juan Ortiz, which have reached us from different sources.

Captives in a Land without Frontiers

Cabeza de Vaca was not the first person to be taken captive, but he gave us some of the most eloquent materials about the story of captives. It is interesting to ponder his vision of the Indian at a time when imperial policy regarding the inhabitants of the Indies was being formulated. Cabeza de Vaca's respect in describing Indian tribes, the care and understanding with which he presents his years of captivity or slavery, indicate that at this time relations with the Indians had not yet been spoiled. The only frontiers that Cabeza de Vaca and his companions Andrés Dorantes, Alonso del Castillo, and Estebanico crossed were those established by the region's tribes they visited or with whom they lived. The other frontiers, the lines of division or contact between Indians and Europeans, would be negotiated slowly during a long process marked by agreements, trade treaties, invasions, and resistance.[5]

In 1528 Cabeza de Vaca embarked on the expedition commanded by Pánfilo de Narváez, one of the unluckiest explorers of the continent. The expedition, generously financed, was made up of four hundred men and more than eighty horses. They landed on the western shore of the peninsula, in what is now Tampa Bay, and ran into the Timucuan tribes of the area. Narváez's conduct and its consequences were very unfortunate. The chronicle of El Inca Garcilaso de la Vega (*La Florida del Inca,* 1606)[6] notes that Narváez permitted the gruesome killing of Cacique Hirrihigua's mother. Furthermore, in an act of gratuitous violence, Narváez cut the cacique's nose. "However (since an injury knows no forgiveness), every time he remembered that his mother had been thrown to the dogs and eaten by them, and whenever he was going to blow his nose, he found no nose, he grew furious and yearned for vengeance."[7] Soon the bad reputation of the undesirable bearded men from the sea would spread among the tribes of the area. The cordial welcome of the first encounter gave way to hostile relations of mutual aggression.

One of the main reasons for the Florida expeditions was to capture Indians to supplement the dramatic decline in the Caribbean population, due pri-

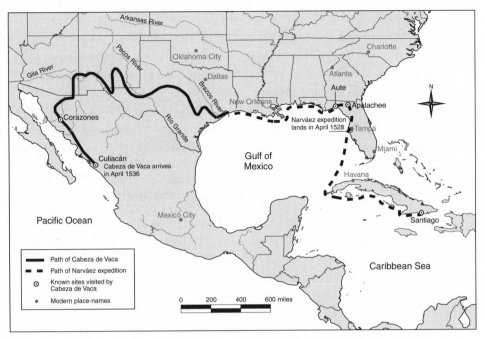

Map 3. Route of Cabeza de Vaca and the Expedition of Pánfilo Narváez

marily to epidemics. Spanish colonies urgently required manpower in order to meet the increasing demand of the mines, plantations, and ranches. The Spanish began to explore islands for the purpose of capturing Indians. Between 1514 and 1515, Captain Pedro de Salazar sailed from a point northeast of the Bahamas to South Carolina, where he captured Indians taller than those of the islands. This caused the rebirth of one of the most widespread legends of the time, the existence of a country peopled by giants.[8] Tales about men of colossal size stimulated other expeditions, commanded by Pedro de Quejo (1521), Francisco de Ayllón (1526), Pánfilo de Narváez (1528), Hernando de Soto (1539), and Pedro Menéndez de Avilés (1565). In 1570 a former captive, Hernando de Escalante Fontaneda, mentioned the great number and size of the Indians and recommended their use for commercial purposes.[9]

As they passed through Indian settlements, Spanish expeditions placed onerous burdens on the local economies. Fortunately for the natives, the expeditionaries were passing through and had no intention of founding permanent settlements. Their stays were temporary, perhaps for a winter or until the exhausted expeditionaries could recuperate from cold and hunger. Whenever the Indians perceived that the Spanish intended to remain, abusing the hospitality extended to them, they did not hesitate to react firmly. On the east coast several attempts had been made to establish cities and forts. They did not last long. The indigenous population on every occasion rejected the burdens and taxes imposed on them by the newcomers.

Juan Ortiz, Captive of the Timucuans

Juan Ortiz was one of the first captives in Florida. The ship on which he was traveling reached the mainland in 1528 after the bulk of Narváez's expedition (which included Cabeza de Vaca) had headed north. We know the story of Ortiz's captivity from El Inca Garcilaso, who met several of the survivors of the expedition and read some of their writings.[10]

> A few days after Pánfilo de Narváez left this cacique's land, having done the deeds we have recounted, a ship of Narváez's men, which had lagged behind, happened to reach that very bay looking for him, and when the cacique learned that they were with Narváez and were looking for him, he wanted to take all who were in the ship and burn them alive. And in order to make them feel safe he feigned to be a friend of Narváez and sent a message that their captain had been there and had left orders for the ship, if it reached that port.[11]

The ruse worked, and Juan Ortiz was captured together with three other Spaniards. This was the beginning of a ten-year-long captivity. Owing to the wrongs he had suffered at Narváez's hands, the Timucuan cacique made the captured Spaniards the objects of his vengeance.

> Cacique Hirrihigua had the four Spaniards kept safely under guard because he intended that their death would add to the solemnity of a great pagan feast he was going to celebrate in a few days. When the day of the feast arrived, he had them brought out naked to the plaza. One by one, they were made to run back and forth, and the Indians shot arrows at them as if they were beasts. They took care not fire too many arrows at a time so that it would take them longer to die. In that manner their suffering was greater, and thus increased and enhanced

the delight of the Indians and the solemnity of their celebration. This they did to three of the Spaniards, and the cacique took great joy and pleasure seeing them flee in every direction looking for help and finding succor nowhere but in death.[12]

Juan Ortiz was lucky in that the wife and the daughters of the cacique interceded for him, saying that he was "a boy worthy of pardon, because his youth freed him from guilt."[13] Nevertheless, his life was not easy during his year and half of captivity with Cacique Hirrihigua. "Many times he envied the fate of his dead companions, because the continuous work of fetching firewood and water was so much and he ate and slept so little, and they daily hit him with sticks, slapped and flogged him cruelly, not to mention the torture to which he was subjected from time to time according to their celebrations."[14] The situation worsened until the cacique decided to put an end to his life by burning him at the stake.

> One of their feast days, he ordered a large fire to be built in the middle of the plaza, and when he saw that there were a lot of embers, he had them spread out and over them they set a barbecue, which is a bed of wood in the form of a grill about a yard above the ground, and on it they placed Juan Ortiz, to roast him alive. This they did, and the poor Spaniard was for a long time stretched out on his side, tied to the barbecue.[15]

Those who knew Ortiz bore witness to the scars left by the grill on his body. For a second time, the women of the Timucuan cacique came to his rescue.

> When they heard the screams of the unfortunate man in the fire, the cacique's wife and daughters came to him and begged her husband, and even upbraided him for his cruelty. They took Ortiz from the fire, half-roasted. The blisters on that side of his body were like orange halves, and some had burst, and much blood ran from them, so that he was a piteous sight.[16]

The cacique's oldest daughter suggested that Ortiz run away to save his life. She gave him information and the means to escape to the domain of Mucozo, the neighboring cacique, where his fate changed radically. "Mucozo received him affably and heard with sympathy the account of the mistreatment and torments he had suffered, that were evident from the marks on his body [. . .]. Mucozo embraced him and kissed his face as a sign of peace."[17] With Cacique Mucozo, Juan spent eight years, about which we know little. Then one day he

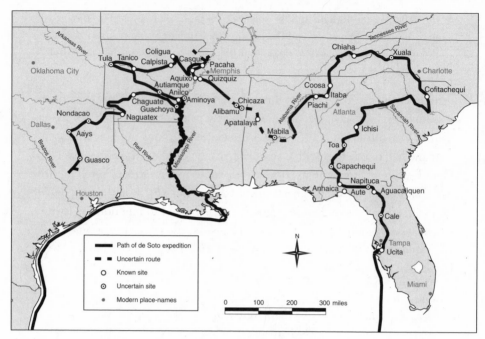

Map 4. Route of Hernando de Soto

received news that Spanish ships were approaching the coast. This was Hernando de Soto's expedition, which had left Havana in 1539. The Spaniards had heard of Juan Ortiz's fate from an Indian from Hirrihigua's tribe who had been captured by Juan de Añasco's expedition. For the purposes of de Soto's great expedition, the encounter with Juan Ortiz was a gift from heaven, since the Indianized Sevillian knew the region and spoke several local languages. Juan left with the expedition to serve as guide and interpreter. Unfortunately, he did not live to tell the tale. Like many of the other members of de Soto's expedition, he died during the fighting on the trek through the territory that is now the states of Georgia, South Carolina, North Carolina, Tennessee, Alabama, Arkansas, Mississippi, Texas, and Louisiana.

Cacique Hirrihigua's conduct is clearly justifiable. The chronicles of Cabeza de Vaca, Garcilaso de la Vega, Gonzalo Solís de Meras, and others make constant reference to the abusive burdens imposed by Spaniards. Their bad reputation had spread so quickly that often they arrived in towns and found them empty. "After seven days they reached the town of Naguatex and found it abandoned by its inhabitants, and lodged there, staying fifteen or sixteen days. They roamed everywhere in the vicinity and took whatever food they needed with little or no resistance from the Indians."[18] Hernando de Soto's expedition was accompanied by a great retinue made up of hundreds of Indians from the islands and others captured along the way. The cacique of the province of Acuera, through which the expedition passed, described the situation candidly, "saying that because other Castilians had passed through years before, he was well acquainted with them and knew well enough about their way of life and customs. That the way they made their living was to roam like vagrants from place to place living off whatever they could steal and sack, killing those who had done them no harm."[19] The undesirable guests not only finished off the Indians' precious reserves of food but also took their children to serve as guides and porters. "In four days that the Spanish rested in the town of Cofaqui, they brought together four thousand Indian servants to carry the food and clothes of the Christians, and another four thousand warriors to accompany and guide the army."[20]

Captives on the Peninsula

The vast majority of Spanish captives in sixteenth-century Florida were captured by chance. Some were shipwrecked or got lost and reached Indian settlements; others deserted and found refuge among the Indians. The minority were taken prisoner. For Indian communities on the continent, taking captives, both Spanish and Indian, was a common, institutionalized activity, and captives were desirable and a source of wealth. The captivity of children, women, and even adult males was widespread and has been widely documented.[21] In different passages of his chronicle, Garcilaso mentions Indian captives found in the settlements through which de Soto's expedition passed: "In the towns under the jurisdiction and vassalage of Colfachiqui, through which our Spaniards passed, they found many Indians from other provinces who had been enslaved."[22] Taking captives offered several rewards: potential ransoms, a labor force, and young bodies to increase the population. It is important to keep in mind that different tribes had varying attitudes toward captivity. "They used them to till the land and to perform other menial work."[23] Exchange and ransom were accepted practices in the conduct of war. "Prisoners captured by either side are easily ransomed and exchanged for others and eventually return to fight again. And this form of warfare is by now second nature among them."[24]

At bottom, captivity was a necessary mechanism, which enabled Indian communities to maintain the basic demographic level crucial for their survival. Captivity entailed a number of processes of acculturation and adaptation which varied according to the age and sex of the captives. A certain amount of proselytism was common, with a view to facilitating and speeding up the integration of the newcomers.[25] Assimilation was more difficult for adult captives, and they were a risky venture. Procedures used to keep adult captives from escaping varied: "In order to secure some of them and to keep them from escaping, they mutilated one foot, cutting the ligaments above the instep, where the foot joins the leg, or they cut the ligaments above the heel, and with these permanent and inhuman fetters they kept them in the interior."[26] The task of acculturation was easier in the case of children and women, as we shall see in other chapters of this book.

The experience of captivity also varied according to the circumstances in which it occurred. In sixteenth-century Florida, most captives were castaways who reached the shores of the peninsula or the keys after their ships had sunk or been beached by rough seas. The account of Gonzalo Solís de Meras, chronicler of the Florida expeditions of the *adelantado* (frontier mayor) Pedro Menéndez de Avilés, are illustrative in this respect: "Half a league from there was the town where there were some Spanish women and other Christians, and another two were farther inland, and another woman, because more than 200 Spaniards from ships of the Indies, were lost in the domain of this cacique now for twenty years, and his people took them all away."[27] Cabeza de Vaca and all his companions in the expedition, most of whom died or were taken prisoner and killed, were castaways. Also shipwrecked was Escalante de Fontaneda and the hundreds of captives mentioned by Solís de Meras.

Many chroniclers defined Florida as the land of captives, most of whom ended their lives anonymously among the Indians. Official documents, generally, make no mention of these brave Spaniards, who are counted as casualties of the expeditions of discovery and conquest. The conquistador Menéndez de Avilés was one of the few who showed an interest in redeeming captives. We must bear in mind that his son Juan had been shipwrecked years before and either lost his life in the wreck or was killed by Indians.[28] Menéndez de Avilés undertook several trips of discovery for the purpose of rescuing captives. On one of those trips, as the Spaniards approached the mainland they ran into a canoe in which was traveling a young man who turned out to be a longtime captive: "good-looking, of noble parents, the son of the late García Escalante, a conquistador from Cartagena."[29] As a child in 1545, Hernando de Escalante Fontaneda had been shipwrecked on the coast when the ship on which he was traveling sank near present-day Cape Canaveral.[30] He had spent seventeen years among different tribes of the peninsula.

Upon his return Escalante wrote *Memoria de las cosas y costa y indios de la Florida* (Memoir of Things and the Coast and Indians of Florida), a text that is very difficult to understand, since it is written in a disorganized manner and in an almost indecipherable style.[31] Nonetheless, a reading of his text allows us to make several conjectures, for example, that Escalante Fontaneda had a greater degree of liberty than other captives. He says that he spoke four languages (Calusa, Abalachean, Timucuan, and Tequesta), which makes one think that he was free to travel and live with different groups. Also, the recognizable details that he furnishes of the area's geography corroborate that he did indeed travel extensively throughout the peninsula. Escalante was thirteen when he was shipwrecked on the coast of Florida. At that age the possibility of assimilation is much greater. What is remarkable is that after seventeen years of captivity he wanted to return. On the other hand, it is possible that the Calusas negotiated his exchange and that of other prisoners without regard to his wishes. In his memoir, written many years after his return to Spain, possibly around 1580, Escalante makes no reference to this issue.[32]

The recommendations he makes at the end of his narrative are quite surprising. First, he suggests that Indians be brought into the fold of the Church: "I hold it certain that [they] never will be at peace, and [un]less they become Christians."[33] Later he recommends that the Indians be enslaved and points out the benefits.

> Let the Indians be taken in hand gently, inviting them to peace; then putting them under deck, husbands and wives together, send them among the Islands, and even upon Terra Firma for money, as some old nobles of Spain buy vassals of the king. In this way, there could be management of them, and their number become diminished.[34]

He feels that cleansing the peninsula of Indians will make the land more productive: "This I say would be proper policy; and the Spaniards might then make some stock-farms for the breeding of cattle, and be there to safeguard the many vessels that are wrecked all the way along from Carlos to the province of Sotoriva, where the port of Saint Augustine is."[35]

Although Solís de Meras mentions hundreds of captives, near or far from the Calusas, the negotiations carried out by Menéndez de Avilés to redeem captives produced the liberation of only thirty-two. Several women decided, at the last minute, to return to their captors "because they yearned for the children they were leaving behind."[36]

Proselytism and Assimilation

Juan Ortiz was not a castaway. His capture was planned as an act of vengeance by Hirrihigua, who enslaved and tortured him. The torture of captives was not an unusual Indian practice. In general, Indians chose their captives with a view toward increasing the likelihood of their total integration. If they were interested in captives because of their age, sex, or possibility of integration, they treated them with the deference necessary to make the process possible. Otherwise they killed and often tortured them. The first phase of the arrival of captives at the camps was marked by confusion and fear. Male captives were forced to run the gauntlet. The prisoners were made to pass between two long files of Indians of all ages who struck them with clubs, sticks, and sharp objects. Those who survived this ordeal and reached the finish line were treated benevolently. Those who failed were tortured and murdered.[37] Lewis Henry Morgan states that, among the Iroquois, "adoption and torture were the alternative chances of the captive."[38]

Father Ávila, captured around 1595, tells of being badly treated after his capture. The Indians mocked him and Christian religious practices, and tortured him during the first days of his stay.

> I was stark naked for they did not even let me have a poor coat. Another Indian came with a cord, the kind we use to gird ourselves, knotted and doubled, and gave me three or four strokes so hard that I was left like dead. While they were engaged in this, a cacique stood and carried a little bit of burning wood and threw it on my back. Since I was tied, I could not throw it from me very quickly. It left a deep mark on my body and caused me much pain. Soon the Indians began to dance around me as if they were passing in review before me, and if it struck someone's fancy, he gave me a heavy blow with a *macana*

[club]. In this manner they danced for three hours, while they made a thousand incantations.[39]

Finally they left him in peace. They planned to exchange him for a son of the cacique who was a prisoner in the fort in Saint Augustine. Meanwhile they set him to carrying firewood and other tasks of servitude. The abuse probably did not continue, since they proposed that he marry an Indian girl, a gesture that can only be interpreted as a sign of acceptance and integration. The proposal was not understood by Father Ávila, however, who considered it a trick of the devil, "who did not spare any occasion to tempt me."[40] The tendency to proselytize, common among most of the tribes of the continent and mentioned by many scholars, is obvious in Father Ávila's account, despite his reticence and religious prejudice. He writes that they would repeat:

> Leave your law and become an Indian and you will enjoy what we enjoy; you will have a wife or more, if you wish; furthermore, in the other life you will enjoy what you enjoy here, for we know that he who has been miserable and mean in this life, will be the same in the other, and as many wives as one had in this life, so many will he have in the other. This is our belief. Give up the things you teach us for they are foolish.[41]

Since 1573 Jesuits and Franciscans had established many missions in the territory of Florida, as far north as Jamestown and as far south as Saint Augustine. Their missionary labor was intense, and the natives responded to these intrusions with clear signs of rejection. They attacked and burned the missions, taking captives, among them Father Ávila and the so-called Martyrs of Florida, described in the narrative of Father Gerónimo de Oré. At the time of his capture, Father Ávila was a middle-aged man, a missionary by vocation, and he was unable to see the customs and religious practices of his captors without prejudice. Religious interpretations tended to justify the effects of captivity, especially in the context of redemptive suffering. The missionaries could not get away from the idea of captivity as a trial, a judgment, or a punishment from God. It was also justified as evidence of divine providence and the inscrutable wisdom of God.

We have seen that during the second phase of his captivity, Juan Ortiz enjoyed the benefits of Indian proselytism and cultural integration. Cacique Mucozo welcomed him, and in the words of the chronicler, "treated him as if

he were his own dear brother."[42] Garcilaso himself is surprised at the magna-
nimity and hospitality of the Indians, reflecting that their conduct was more
edifying than that of many "Christian princes who later have done such abom-
inable things here."[43] It can be deduced from the accounts that the treatment
meted out to captives varied case by case, and to a great degree it depended
on the characteristics of the captives.[44] Hernando Vintimilla and Diego Muñoz,
captured by the Timucuans, enjoyed great freedom: "These two Spaniards
were kept by the Indians of this province for ten years, and they let them roam
at liberty, as if they were masters of their own persons."[45]

As described above, Juan Ortiz lived for over eight years with Cacique
Mucozo. When he ran into de Soto's expedition, he was an Indian who had
adapted to his captors' way of life, having even forgotten the Spanish language, his native tongue. Garcilaso states that he "was not wearing more than
some rags for clothes, held a bow and arrows in his hands and wore a feather
headdress about half a yard high; this was all his regalia and adornment."[46]
The Spanish took him for an Indian warrior and made ready to attack him with
their spears. Seeing his predicament, Juan decided to hide in the forest, while
he shouted:

> "Shivil, Shivil," by which he meant "Seville, Seville." Juan Coles adds that since
> Juan Ortiz could not speak Spanish, he made the sign of the cross with his hand
> and the bow, so that the Spaniards could see that he was a Christian. Having
> little or no reason to employ the Spanish language among the Indians, he had
> even forgotten how to pronounce the name of his own country.[47]

Although Juan Ortiz did decide to return with the Spanish, this was not
always the case. In many instances, captives rejected the chance to return
when the opportunity arose, and there were others who voluntarily chose to
live among the Indians. This inclination was notable in other parts of the continent and has been studied extensively in the case of the northeastern English colonies. "Large numbers of Englishmen had chosen to become Indians
by running away from colonial society to join Indian society, by not trying to
escape after being captured, or by electing to remain with their Indian captors when treaties of peace periodically afforded them the opportunity to return home."[48]

As de Soto's great expedition advanced and faced greater hardships, the
number of those who chose to abandon the enterprise grew. Different rea-

sons led them to do so: exhaustion, depression, fear, insecurity, and relationships with Indian women. Garcilaso says that in the town of Coza two Christians stayed behind, Falco Herrado and "a sick black man who could not walk."[49] Such events provoked strong reactions from Spanish officials, who could not understand how a Christian vassal of the most powerful king on earth could want to live among savage Indians in material conditions that were extraordinarily precarious. The *adelantado* demanded that the cacique of Coza return the soldier who had deserted, but the cacique replied that, "since all of them had not wanted to remain in his land, he was very pleased that at least one had chosen to stay, and he begged his lordship to pardon the soldier."[50] Previously, the cacique of Coza had offered the Spanish land on which to settle. De Soto's expedition, however, was not after settlement and colonization; its objective was to find kingdoms and riches comparable to those of Mexico-Tenochtitlan and Peru.

Garcilaso tells in detail the anecdote of another Spaniard who, because of his social rank and the vicissitudes of his adventure, merits special attention. It is the story of Diego de Guzmán, an hidalgo from Seville, "who had gone on this conquest expedition like a rich nobleman with many costly and elegant clothes, with good weapons and three horses that he took to Florida, and behaved in every respect like a gentleman, except that he was a passionate gambler."[51] The year was 1542, and Hernando de Soto had just died "from very high fevers." The expedition had come to the region of Naguatex, in current-day Arkansas, where they spent five months waiting for good weather. When they were about to continue on their way, they got news that Diego de Guzmán had decided not to go with them. He was living with a young Indian woman, the daughter of the cacique. De Soto's successor, Luis de Moscoso, fearing that Guzmán was being held against his will, demanded that the cacique return the Andalusian nobleman and threatened to burn down the village. The cacique assured him that Diego de Guzmán was staying of his own free will, and to confirm this he suggested that the Spaniards write him a letter seeking an explanation "for his treason." On the third day, an Indian returned "with the same letter he had taken, and on it was written with charcoal the name of Diego de Guzmán, who wrote it so they could see he was alive and made no other reply. And the Indian said that Christian neither wanted nor thought of returning to his own people."[52]

What motives led an Andalusian nobleman to stay in an Indian settlement near the Mississippi River? Garcilaso's informants explained that Guzmán's passion for gambling had made him lose all his possessions, even the eighteen-year-old Indian girl with whom he had been living. Guzmán paid all his debts with his horse, clothes, and other property, but he refused to hand over the beautiful girl. Another reason could be the disillusion felt by the survivors about the failure of the expedition, as their numbers, energy, resources, and hope dwindled. It is also possible that the Spanish nobleman was attracted by the freedom of movement, living in nature, and other aspects of life in America that impressed Europeans. Factors such as these led to the repetition of cases like Guzmán's in the history of conquest and colonization.

The Story of Álvar Núñez Cabeza de Vaca

At a time when there were no frontiers, Cabeza de Vaca traveled through territories where a European had never trod.

> We traveled mute and tongueless, where we could be barely understood, not knowing what we wanted of the land, and we were entering a land we knew nothing about, what it was like, what was in it, what people lived there, what part of it we were in.[53]

Cabeza de Vaca was born in Seville around 1490. There he met Pánfilo de Narváez, with whom in 1527 he set sail from Sanlúcar de Barrameda to Florida on a voyage of exploration and conquest. When they reached the Caribbean, they went around Cuba, but before they could land, a storm hurled them on the coast near Tampa Bay. That is where Cabeza de Vaca's fantastic adventure as a castaway and captive began. "Since we left Castile we endured such hardships, so many storms, so many ships and men lost."[54]

Cabeza de Vaca spent a total of eight years among different tribes of the continent who had not yet experienced the trauma that Spanish expeditions left in their wake. His wanderings through unknown lands left behind a mythic aura, as members of Hernando de Soto's expedition found out ten years later. When they reached the province of Guancane, they observed many wooden crosses on top of the houses, and they asked the Indians how they came to put them there. "The reason, as they learned, was that these Indians had learned of the benefits and marvels that Álvar Núñez Cabeza de Vaca and Andrés Dorantes and his companions, through the virtue of our Lord Jesus Christ, had performed in the provinces where they lived in Florida during the years that the Indians kept them as slaves."[55]

The longest Cabeza de Vaca stayed with any tribe was a year and a half, his time of captivity on the island of Malhado. He was always with other Spaniards and never lost hope that his trek would eventually take him to Mexico. He had many different experiences: he was a castaway, a captive, a trader, a shaman, or healer, and a holy man. As a castaway, he suffered from the harshness of the climate and the vagaries of geopolitics. As a chronicler, he did not hesitate to criticize harshly the commander of the failed expedition, Narváez, whom he blamed for the disasters they endured.[56] The two men had had repeated confrontations with each other from the very beginning. What angered Cabeza de Vaca most was his commander's lack of solidarity. The last time they were in touch with each other was at sea. Cabeza de Vaca asked his captain for help because the boat in which he was sailing was taking in water. Narváez excused himself with words that Cabeza de Vaca could not comprehend:

> Since it was unlikely that we would be able to follow him and do as he had ordered, I asked him what new orders he had for me. He answered that it was no longer the time for commanding others. That each should do as he thought best to save his own life. That was what he intended to do, and saying this he left with his boat.[57]

Shipwrecked and lost, during the first months a number of incidents occurred among the Spanish troops that Cabeza de Vaca could not accept. The conduct of the Spaniards was certainly not exemplary. Their actions were marked by ambition and cruelty as each tried to save his own skin. For his part, Narváez did not hesitate to punish the Indians violently when they did not give him the information he wanted about cities and riches. Possibly the Indians did not understand why he wanted this information. Later, Hernando de Soto, too, was not a model of diplomacy. For his ambitious expedition he had brought with him Indians from the central valley of Mexico, although he used as porters principally Indians whom he captured along the way. For this purpose he had brought chains and iron collars to chain together the Indians who carried the large quantities of equipment for the expedition.[58]

What most alarmed Cabeza de Vaca, however, were the repeated instances where the Spanish castaways resorted to cannibalism. This is powerfully striking, since cannibalism is one of the great taboos of the West. The classical ac-

Indians torturing and eating Spaniards. Engraving by Theodor de Bry, from an edition of Bartolomé de las Casas published in Germany (1598).

counts of men devoured by men were made popular by encyclopedias and travel books about Asian barbarians. Anthony Pagden notes the European obsession with cannibalism, which seems to have reached its zenith in the fourteenth century.[59] Cannibalism is mentioned by the Greeks, Pliny, Saint Jerome, Saint Isidore of Seville, and others. They all associate cannibalism with people of exotic lands like the Tartars, Mongols, or inhabitants of unknown lands, including the Indians. Christopher Columbus, who chased after so many medieval myths, mentions encounters with the Caribs, who, according to him, ate human flesh. Columbus's belief is so strong that he confuses the term "Carib" with "cannibal" in his *Diary*.

The taboo against cannibalism had two basic consequences. First, the eating of human flesh was considered a sign of dehumanization. Second, it became the threat that followed conquistadores and travelers for centuries: the constant fear of being eaten. These fears surface with regularity in captivity narratives, as we shall see in the many cases of captivity studied in this volume. Myths about cannibal peoples included the belief that a consequence of cannibalism was the physical deformation of those who practiced it. Columbus registers his surprise at not finding any deformities among the Caribs despite their diet.

The first case of cannibalism mentioned by Cabeza de Vaca occurred just after his group separated from Narváez. Some of the survivors had decided to stay in a boat near the coast for fear of an Indian attack, and at night the sea swallowed them up. Lieutenant Pantoja, who tried to survive by eating crabs and other seafood, was now the head of the fragmented expedition. The situation of the expeditionaries was becoming more and more precarious. Cabeza de Vaca writes that Pantoja mistreated his subordinates, until Sotomayor, the shipmaster of the expedition, "turned on him and struck him with a stick, killing him, and that is how they wound up; the ones who died were turned into jerky by the survivors; and the last to die was Sotomayor, and Esquivel turned him into jerky, and eating his flesh kept alive until March 1."[60] Cabeza de Vaca does not omit the names of these unlucky Spaniards. By mentioning them, he no doubt sought to make his story more credible.

> When these four Christians had passed away, within a few days the weather turned so cold and stormy that the Indians could not harvest the roots, and from the canals where they finished they caught nothing, and since the houses offered such poor shelter, people began to die. Five Christians who were in a hut by the coast reached such an extremity that they ate each other, until there was only one left because there was no one left to eat him. Their names were: Sierra, Diego López Corral, Palacios, Gonzalo Ruiz.[61]

Cabeza de Vaca does not mention any acts of cannibalism among the Indians. On the contrary, he notes their horror at the Spaniards' cannibalism: "The Indians were so upset by this case and it created such a scandal among them, that had they been present when it happened they probably would have killed all of them. And all of us would have been at great risk."[62] The only reference to any type of cannibalism among the Indians is found in a passage that relates a burial rite in which the Indians drank the ashes of their dead: "It is their custom to bury their dead, except for the ones who are healers. These they burn, and as the fire blazes, they dance and have a great celebration. They grind the bones to dust, and when a year has passed, and they have a memorial and they all cut themselves; and the relatives of the dead are given their dust to drink in water."[63] This inversion of roles is surprising. Christians carry out acts of cannibalism that are culturally and religiously unjustifiable. The Indians, for their part, are shocked at the behavior of the Europeans.

On the other hand, Cabeza de Vaca makes it clear that the Indians ate disgusting things: "So great is their hunger that they eat spiders, and ant eggs, and worms and lizards and salamanders and snakes and vipers, which bite and kill men, and they eat earth and wood and anything they can find, and deer dung, and other things I will not mention."[64] In European mythology at that time there was a link between sexual excess and the consumption of unclean animals and things. Eating unclean animals was also an index of irrationality.[65] The indiscriminate consumption of animals, reptiles, and insects was considered proof of irrationality because it betokened an inability to recognize the place of each species in the animal kingdom. Aristotelian taxonomy divided the animal kingdom into high and low species, the latter including insects and reptiles unfit for consumption by rational men: "That men, who were so unselective in their food consumption as to fail to perceive this crucial division in the natural world, were equally prepared to eat their own kind was hardly surprising."[66]

Cabeza de Vaca, who distanced himself from the reprehensible behavior of his companions whenever he could, even refused to eat horse meat. "As for myself, I can say that since the past month of May I had not eaten anything except roasted corn, and sometimes I had to eat it raw, because even though the horses were slaughtered while the boats were being built, I was never able to eat of them."[67] In the context of the chronicle this is not a superfluous statement. Cabeza de Vaca, who as the omniscient narrator dominates the narrative, is conscious of the regression of his companions and tries to overcome chaos by establishing his distance from their behavior and adhering to the rule of reason. The expeditionaries eventually ate all the horses they had brought with them: "On September 22, they finished eating the horses, for there was only one left."[68] Cabeza de Vaca refused to take part because he considered the noble horse a fundamental instrument of conquest. He did not resort to cannibalism either and during his entire journey followed a pilgrim's diet. His conduct is interesting when we consider that a constant motif throughout the text of *Naufragios* is hunger. Hunger—whether the narrator's own, that of his companions, or even that suffered by the Indians—is an obsession in the narrative. The narrative is driven by the author's account of the strategies used to deal with hunger.

In the first chapters, when the shipwrecked men are traveling by land or by ship from the south of the peninsula across Mobile Bay and the delta of the Mississippi until they reach Galveston, the obsession is corn: "We traveled a distance of four leagues, took four Indians, and showed them some corn to see if they knew it, because up to that point we had seen no sign of it. They said they would take us where there was some corn, and they took us to their village, which is at the end of the bay, nearby, and they showed us some corn, which was still not fit to be picked."[69] The purpose of the expedition shifts from the conquest of rich worlds to the basic matter of survival in an alien environment. Nevertheless, gold still remains a goal and a motivation. "But seeing that we had arrived where we wished, and where they told us there was so much food and gold, we felt a great deal of our suffering and exhaustion vanish."[70]

Inquiries about food lead them along the coast in a pilgrimage that resembles the mythical search for El Dorado: "They said that following that trail, traveling toward the sea for nine days, there was a village called Aute, and the Indians there had a great deal of corn, beans and squash, and that being near the sea, they also caught fish."[71] When the reality of their shipwreck takes over the narrative, gold is relegated to a secondary status and corn becomes the principal object of their yearning. For the sake of corn they risk their lives, make war, and confront the natives. "And the solution we found so that we would have some food in the meantime was to make four forays into Aute [. . .] the raids were undertaken with the people and horses that could be spared. We brought back as many as four hundred bushels of corn, although not without some fighting with the Indians."[72]

The shortage of corn and the consequent hunger defeated the bulk of the expedition. Hunger was a worse enemy than the rough seas or sporadic Indian attacks. "And before we set sail, not counting those killed by the Indians, more than forty men died from illness and hunger."[73] During the first encounters, the Indians had courteously opened the doors of their larders: "They took us to their houses, which were at a distance of half a league. There we found a great deal of ripe corn, and we gave infinite thanks to our Lord for having come to our aid in such great need."[74] Indians continued to do this until relations deteriorated. No doubt, the unexpected bearded men became a terrible burden for the Indians, who lived from elementary agriculture, the harvesting of fruit, and hunting.

By mid-November 1528 Cabeza de Vaca and some of the survivors of the initial three hundred who had started on the expedition reached an island on the western part of the Gulf of Mexico which they named the island of Malhado (Bad Fate). This was possibly the island of Galveston or perhaps Follett Island. The island was inhabited by the Karankawa Indians, although Cabeza de Vaca lived with the Capoque subgroup.[75] There among the Indians they found protection from the cold and from hunger, although their greatest fear was to be sacrificed by those who "in our fear seemed like giants to us."[76] On this island, Cabeza de Vaca rejoined those who would become his companions in captivity and the last survivors of the expedition: Andrés Dorantes, Alonso del Castillo, and his Moorish slave Estebanico.

The beginning of Cabeza de Vaca's captivity on Malhado Island is marked by a change in the tone of the narrative. The life and customs of the Indians are described in much greater detail and with a certain degree of admiration: "Of all the people in the world they are the ones who love their children the most and treat them best."[77] Recent scholars have considered *Naufragios* one of the first documents of American ethnography.[78] The passage where he describes how the Indians received the Spaniards is eloquent: "When the Indians saw the disaster we had suffered and our present unfortunate and miserable condition, they sat among us, and all began to weep copiously with great pain and pity for our fate."[79]

One of the most interesting episodes of Cabeza de Vaca's captivity took place on this island when, according to him, the Indians insisted on teaching their curative practices to the Spaniards: "They made us doctors of medicine without subjecting us to exams or demanding to see our diplomas."[80] The author's irony can be interpreted as an attempt to distance and defend himself. In other words, Cabeza de Vaca makes it clear that they learned the Indians' healing arts against their will. We do not know what this apprenticeship entailed, or how long Cabeza de Vaca studied the curative practices of his protectors. But to judge from the many cures he accomplished throughout his adventures, he learned the craft and learned it well. From that moment on, the fate of the four captives changed. When they became healers or shamans the roles were inverted. Their reputation as holy men marked them and followed them on their long journey through the poor lands of southern Texas until they met the Spanish soldiers and returned to Mexico. By then, Cabeza de Vaca had become a sort of holy man, followed by hundreds of devotees who believed in his magic and special powers.

The episode is also important because it demonstrates the will to proselytize evident in many indigenous cultures of the continent and their capacity to convert and educate enemies and captives. Healers or shamans were persons chosen by their communities, and therefore their craft was held in high regard. If the Karankawas of Malhado Island chose Cabeza de Vaca, Dorantes, Castillo, and Estebanico as disciples with whom to share their medical-religious knowledge, this can be understood as a desire to integrate them into the tribe on the basis of their special talents. Cabeza de Vaca confirms that shamans were very highly regarded. They could have several wives, and they constantly received gifts for their services.

Castillo and Cabeza de Vaca learned the craft despite their initial resistance.

> During that period they sought us from many places, and said that we truly were the sons of the Sun. Dorantes and the Negro had not cured anyone yet, but because they importuned us so much coming from so many places, all of us became doctors. I, however, was the most daring in undertaking any cure and I was more highly regarded, and there was never anyone whom we treated who did not say that we had cured them.[81]

It is not clear why the Spaniards were initially reluctant to become healers. It is easy to imagine that, years after his adventure, writing in his home in southern Spain under the watchful eye of the Church, the chronicler was filled with doubt. Therefore, Cabeza de Vaca never fails to stress that the cures were due to divine intervention. "The very night we arrived, some Indians approached Castillo and told him they had very bad headaches and asked him to heal them. As soon as he made the sign of the cross over them and prayed to God on their behalf, the Indians immediately said that all pain had gone away."[82]

Against their will or not, Cabeza de Vaca and his companions were initiated into the healing practices of the Karankawas, which included the medicinal virtues of herbs and the curative power of the forces of nature. "An Indian said to me that I didn't know what I was talking about when I said that the cure he proposed would be worthless, [. . .] stones and other things that grow in the fields have virtue, and that by drawing a hot stone over the stomach, he could heal and take away pain."[83] In another passage he mentions it again: "They cauterize with fire, which is another thing they consider effective, and which I have used myself with success."[84] In the end, the curative arts learned by the four Spaniards allowed them to achieve amazing results: "We had a great deal of authority and standing among them."[85]

The continuous escalation of cures reaches a zenith in the passage where the author describes, not without some reticence, the surprising resurrection of a dead man. The episode is memorable. "When I got near their huts, I saw that the sick man we were going to cure was dead, because there were many people around him crying and his house was destroyed, which is a sign among them that the owner has died. Therefore when I got there I saw the Indian with his eyes turned up and no pulse, and every sign of being dead."[86] Dorantes becomes alarmed when it is clear that the patient is dead and when he realizes Cabeza de Vaca's boundless daring.

> I removed a straw mat that was covering him, and as best I could I prayed our Lord to give him health and all others in need of it. After I had made the sign of the cross and blown on him many times, they brought me his bow and gave it to me, and a basket of ground cactus, and took me to heal many others who were suffering from drowsiness.[87]

When they had finished their spells, Cabeza de Vaca and his companions retired to rest. They must have been very surprised when they were told that the alleged dead man had come back to life. "And they said that the one who was dead and whom I had cured in their presence, had gotten up healed and had strolled and eaten and spoken with them, and all the others whom I had cured were healthy and very happy."[88] News of this cure traveled faster than their wandering feet. "This caused a great deal of wonder and fear, and throughout the land this was all they talked about."[89]

The interesting thing about the episode is that the narrator refers clearly to two healing practices. He says, "What the doctor does is to make a few cuts where it hurts and they suck around them."[90] Further on, he reminds us of the crucial invocations that accompanied the healing. "The manner in which we cured was to make the sign of the cross and blow on them, and to pray the Lord's prayer and a Hail Mary and to pray to the Lord our God as best we could to give them health."[91]

Once their fame as healers began to spread, the captives became free men, who wandered in a long trek through part of what is now Texas, Arizona, and northern Mexico in search of a route to the capital of the viceroyalty. Their journey was marked by warm receptions and sad farewells. Hunger continued to dog them: "They [the Indians] are able to withstand great hunger and thirst and cold, since they are more used to it than others."[92] In almost every one of the remaining chapters there are references to cold and hunger. Chapter 31 is entitled "Of How We Followed the Maize Road." "After spending two days there, we decided to go in search of corn, and we decided not to follow the trail of the bison because it leads north, and this would mean a great detour for us [. . .] and we were not deterred in our decision even by the fear of the great hunger we would endure."[93]

Neal Salisbury has studied the importance of corn among the indigenous peoples of eastern North America, and he explains that for most natives of the continent corn was considered a sort of deity connected with the southern routes from which it had come to them.[94] Cabeza de Vaca's narrative makes repeated reference to the types of food that were available and their variety: "Because all day long we ate nothing but two handfuls of that fruit which was green and full of a kind of milk that burned our mouths. Since we had no water it made anyone who ate it very thirsty, and since we were so hungry we bought two dogs from them."[95] In fact, the most frequent episodes are those which tell of the Indians forms of subsistence, with large and detailed dissertations on their food, its preparation, and its ritual nature.

Literary Strategies

Cabeza de Vaca's account has several characteristics that make it unique in its genre. It is one of the most complete captivity narratives we have from a time when the new frontiers had not yet been established. The spontaneity of the journey, full of unexpected events, contributes to the impartial point of view of the text. Furthermore, read as a chronicle, *Naufragios* seems to invert the imperial project of the Spanish Crown, an aspect that has been noted by several authors.[96] Indeed Cabeza de Vaca appears as an innocuous castaway and captive, an impartial witness, although as a man of his time he is surprised or astonished by cultural behaviors that are foreign to him. In addition, it is a first-person captivity narrative, something unusual in Spanish America.

The many ambiguities of Cabeza de Vaca's manuscript are a result of his uncertainty regarding its reception at the viceroyalty and at the royal court. Cabeza de Vaca was saved because the first version of his chronicle found favor with the king. This permitted its publication at a time when the policy of the Crown was to discourage the production of maps and travel narratives of the Americas, thus restricting the dissemination of geographical information.[97] Cabeza de Vaca's adventure also captured the attention of the chronicler of the kingdom, Gonzalo Fernández de Oviedo, who included an account of it in his great work, *Historia general y natural de las Indias*.

Hernando de Escalante y Fontaneda, held captive for seventeen years by the Calusas, was another of the few captives who desired or was able to write memoirs of his experiences. His text, written in the first person a few years after his release, contains valuable information regarding the tribes of southern Florida and about the nature of captivity. According to his account, Escalante Fontaneda was captured when he was thirteen and freed when he was thirty.[98] He learned four indigenous languages and almost forgot Spanish, like his contemporary Juan Ortiz.

The story of Juan Ortiz was saved for posterity thanks to the pen of the great Peruvian writer El Inca Garcilaso de la Vega, who got it from several of the survivors of the expedition (see note 6). All of them knew the story of Ortiz's adventures, since they had traveled with him on Hernando de Soto's expedition. Since Ortiz died during the campaign, this account is necessarily at thirdhand. The work has been controversial for many years. Some have wondered whether the literariness of the work was achieved at the expense of factual accuracy.[99] There is no doubt that Garcilaso selected the materials that he found interesting or that served his purposes. He dwells in detail on the first phase of Ortiz's captivity and his suffering at the hands of Cacique Hirrihigua. He never fails to point out that the aggressive attitude of the Indians was provoked by the unwarranted conduct of the Spaniards, especially Pánfilo de Narváez.[100] The text also shares the premeditated ambiguity of Garcilaso's major work, the *Comentarios reales*. The narrative is sparse on the details of the eight and a half years that Ortiz lived with the tribe of Cacique Mucozo. We know that he was treated like a son, and that Ortiz gave evidence of acculturation on his return, having lost such basic cultural traits as his mother tongue.[101]

The narrative of Father Ávila has similar characteristics. It was recorded and expanded by Luis Gerónimo de Oré, another Franciscan who was a contemporary and compatriot of El Inca Garcilaso, whom he met in Cordoba. According to Maynard Geiger, Father Oré asked Garcilaso for several copies of his books *Comentarios reales* and *La Florida del Inca* so that Franciscan missionaries could familiarize themselves with the customs of the Florida Indians.[102] Curiously, unlike Garcilaso, Father Oré had visited Florida. Oré is the author of a collection of narratives published between 1604 and 1605 entitled *Relación de los mártires que ha habido en las Provincias de la Florida* (*The Martyrs of Florida [1513–1616]*). Chapter 28 contains a version of the captivity of Father Ávila, which Oré got from an original account of Father Ávila's kept in an archive in Havana. Father Oré kept the narrative in the first person, and it is difficult to tell which passages or commentaries were added to the original text and what was left out, despite certain allusions contained in the final version. In one of the passages he writes: "Father Ávila did not write this story about gunpowder and bullets in his *Relación* [a reference to the Indians' request that Father Ávila make gunpowder for the firearms they had captured from the Spaniards], I obtained it from a clergyman who knew Father Ávila before and after his captivity, and who spoke and had extensive conferences with him."[103] Religious orders frequently encouraged members who had been captives to set down their experiences to further missionary work. These ideologically charged texts, which include the stories of martyrs, seem suspicious to the contemporary reader.

Conclusion

Attempts to colonize the North American continent resulted in some of the most resounding failures of the great enterprise of discovery and conquest of the Spanish Crown. Expeditions lost in the vast expanse of unknown territory, ill-spent fortunes, shipwrecked vessels, devastated missions, were the norm for fifty years of effort. By the middle of the sixteenth century, the Fort of Saint Augustine stood out as one of the few tangible achievements in Florida. No colonies or cities had been founded, and the missions had short and precarious lives. The claiming of Florida in the name of the king by Menéndez de Avilés in 1565 was more the culmination of an incomplete process than the symbol of a practical reality. The history of exploration left an alarming balance of dead and missing men. The few captives who managed to return left a fascinating account from the human point of view, but one of scarce strategic value. Their stories furnished certain basic outlines of the physical and ethnic map of the unknown territory: wealth, topography, human population, languages, and customs.

Florida, defined as the extension of land that embraced the Florida peninsula and the lands adjacent to the Gulf of Mexico, was a land of captives. Many fell into the hands of Indians as a result of confrontations, others as a result of shipwrecks. Some who came into contact with the Indians chose to remain with them. Those who returned to write the account of their experiences were few. The great exception is the narrative of Álvar Núñez Cabeza de Vaca, a pioneer and chronicler, whose work has received ample attention of late.

⇥ TWO ⇤

Malocas on the Araucanian Frontier

The Happy Captivity of Francisco
Núñez de Pineda y Bascuñán

The deponent declares that he has seen many of the said Spanish women who have borne children to said Indians their masters in whose captivity they are and those children, he understood, they catechize and teach them our Catholic faith, which
they did secretly and clandestinely, not daring to do so in public
for fear that the Indians their masters might kill them or hurt
them, and he understood that some of the said Spanish women,
ashamed to find themselves pregnant and bearing children to
said Indians, they take their children and kill them.

— Fray Juan Falcón de los Ángeles

All you state is true, and I am and will all my life be grateful
for your favors, the love and the goodwill I have seen and experienced from all the principal caciques, your neighbors and
friends, principally from my *cuempo* and true friend Quilalebo,
whose attentions and inmost demonstrations of his soul have
conquered me and will be in my memory eternally carved.

— Francisco Núñez de Pineda y Bascuñán

Francisco Núñez de Pineda y Bascuñán was born in 1608 in the frontier city
of Chillán in Araucania, in the bosom of a military family. The family was
descended on both sides from illustrious and aristocratic military men with
careers of distinguished service to the Crown. His father, Álvaro Núñez de

Pineda, had reached Chile in 1583 during a time of great political conflict. Already the first Araucanian uprisings had taken place (1540), signaling the beginning of resistance to the Spanish advance on southern lands. During his first military engagement, in the battle of Cangrejeras (1628), the young Francisco was wounded and taken prisoner. He lived for a period of six months as a captive in different Indian *rehues* (camps). Several times he had to escape from mountain caciques who wanted to sacrifice him. Finally he was exchanged for caciques who were in Spanish hands. His account, published much later in 1863 by Diego Barros Arana, is the clear-thinking testimony of a Chilean criollo captive in Araucania.

The fact that he gave his account the title *Cautiverio feliz* (Happy Captivity), at a time of bitter confrontation with the Araucanian Indians, has caused heated controversy. The version he gives in *Cautiverio feliz* contrasts with many chronicles of the era, and with those of other captives from the same period, like Fray Juan Falcón. Almost all accounts, however, criticize the conduct of the Spanish administration in the kingdom of Chile. Using Bascuñán's account, this chapter analyzes the impact of the practice of captivity in Araucania. This practice became widespread through the mode of indigenous resistance known as *maloca*.

The Araucanian Frontier

During the first five years of the Spanish presence (1535–40), indigenous resistance in Chile was scarce. But starting in 1541 when the new governor of Chile, Pedro de Valdivia, initiated the advance into the heart of the Chilean territory, the Araucanian frontier became an area of extreme conflict with Indians whose belligerence surprised even the most seasoned veterans of the conquest. The Picunche caciques of the north, as well as the Huilliche and Tehuelche, met the Spanish advance with steady warfare. Several times, Pedro de Valdivia had to request reinforcements from Peru because the Spanish horsemen were unable to overcome the determined Araucanian resistance. The expeditions of Valdivia and his best men met with such resistance beyond the Bío-Bío River that this body of water became a legendary dividing line. In one of many letters he addressed to the Council of the Indies, dated October 15, 1550, Valdivia writes:

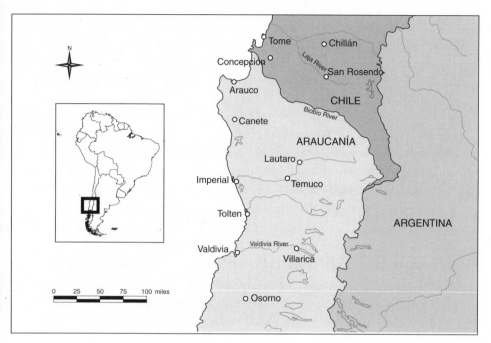

Map 5. Araucania

The second night, after midnight, three squadrons of more than twenty thousand Indians came against us, with such great clamor and impetus that it seemed the earth would sink, and they began to fight with us so fiercely that in the thirty years I have been fighting with many nations and peoples I have never encountered such resolve in fighting as they demonstrated against us.[1]

Despite this resistance, several forts and settlements were established beyond the line of the Bío-Bío: Arauco, Tucapel, Puren, Angalicán, Boroa, and Maquigua. They did not last long. Continual Indian attacks placed their precarious existence in constant danger. The first great Araucanian revolt took place in 1553. Several frontier cities were razed by the Indians. Pedro de Valdivia lost his life that year, fighting Mapuche warriors who charged the Spaniards in continuous, strategically orchestrated waves. The different versions of his last days all indicate the ferocity and desire for revenge that drove the Indians as they fought: The chronicler Pedro Mariño de Lobera tells that they made Valdivia drink molten gold to satiate his gold fever.[2] The chronicler and witness Alonso de Góngora y Marmolejo maintains that the Indians slowly amputated his arms with seashells and ate them in his presence while a friar preached resignation.[3] Diego de Rosales writes that the Indians hit Valdivia on the head with a mace and later took out his heart, which was shared among the caciques.[4]

The different versions of Valdivia's death corroborate the legendary courage and cruelty of the Araucanians. In the course of the dramatic resistance, two Mapuche names were raised to the pantheon of Indian heroes: Caupolicán and Lautaro. Caupolicán organized a coalition of Indian tribes with an army of thirteen thousand warriors, and Lautaro, Valdivia's former page, is given credit for the military strategies that permitted the Mapuche warriors to successfully confront the military might of the Spaniards.[5] The Spanish answer to the Indian uprisings was extremely harsh, to judge from the orders of the Spanish captains "to cut off their noses, their ears, and their right hands."[6] Miguel de Miranda Escobar in 1634 denounced Governor Melchor Portocarrero y Lasso de la Vega for ordering that the Indians captured in war should be branded on the face and sold as slaves, even after the decree abolishing the slavery of the Indians.[7] Far from intimidating the Indians, these violent reprisals filled them with a new resolve. Their opposition has gone down in history as one of the most remarkable examples of Indian resistance to conquest. Chilean historiography, especially in the nineteenth century, used this story of resistance to construct a nationalist ideology. More recent historiography, however, has revealed that Spanish–Indian relations were more complex. Historians now emphasize the flow of exchanges amid the cycle of war in Araucania.[8]

It is true that the serious and constant resistance encountered by the Spanish advance into Araucania in part serves to justify the myth of the Chilean Indians' skill in war and their will for independence. It is also possible that the chroniclers and governors of Chile found themselves in the difficult dilemma of explaining their inability to subdue the Araucanian tribes.[9] In order to justify Spanish failure, they stressed the warlike nature of the Indians, their courage, ability to adapt, and heroism. Indirectly this led to an interpretation of frontier relations in Araucania as an armed conflict that could not be won by force of arms.

Not all shared this opinion. Alonso González de Nájera's chronicle *Desengaño y reparo de la guerra del Reino de Chile* (Revelations and Objections to the War in the Kingdom of Chile) compares military tactics, studies the difficulties of the wars in the south, and seeks to dismantle the Araucanian myth. González de Nájera arrived in Chile in 1600 when the wars of Arauco had reached their greatest intensity. After a brief stay in Santiago, he was sent to a military garrison on the shores of the Bío-Bío, where he spent five years. He had ample opportunity to get to know the frontier in one of the most sensitive and conflict-ridden areas of the kingdom. When he returned to Spain, he wrote his chronicle, in which he advocated a policy of offensive warfare against the Araucanian resistance. The unpopularity of this view meant that the book was not published in his day.[10]

His insistence on destroying the Araucanian myth becomes a double-edged sword. He writes:

> Spain believes that the Indians of Chile have the advantage of extraordinary power, due to the Milonic, or rather Cyclopean strength attributed to them. It will, therefore, be difficult to believe whatever I can prove to the contrary about those barbarians. This is why I am forced to write of "revelations," although I believe it will suffice for me to certify that none of them have extraordinary powers.[11]

Another soldier who witnessed the first years of the Spanish penetration was Alonso de Góngora y Marmolejo, an Andalusian who served in the city of Concepción and on Valdivia's southern expedition. Like González de Nájera, who was also in Araucania, he had the opportunity to experience Araucania while stationed at Fort Tucapel in the heart of Mapuche territory. In 1575 he finished his *Historia de todas las cosas que han acaecido en el Reino de Chile y de los que han gobernado (1536–1575)* (A History of Things That Have Happened in the Kingdom of Chile and of Those Who Have Governed), where he describes in detail the warlike nature of the Indians.

> These healthy people, for the most part white, are well-prepared, and greatly inclined to give war and defend their land. In war they are greatly obedient to their elders and orderly when they prepare to fight [. . .]. Although they have fought the Spaniards infinite times, they have never done so without first sending messages to make it known. They are great enemies of the Spaniards and of all foreign people.[12]

But it was Alonso de Ercilla's long poem *La Araucana* (published in three parts, in 1569, 1578, and 1589) that exerted the greatest influence on the creation and diffusion of the myth of the greatness of the Araucanians, whose military prowess Ercilla compared to the greatest deeds of the classical epic.

> Beardless men, robust of gesture,
> Theirs are full-grown, shapely bodies,
> Lofty chests and massive shoulders,
> Stalwart limbs and steely sinews;
> They are confident, emboldened,
> Dauntless, gallant, and audacious,
> Firm inured to toil, and suffering
> Mortal cold and heat and hunger.[13]

Ercilla created the image of a people whose deeds merit epic glorification. He poeticized a culture that he described as governed democratically by senates, a people with a sense of cultural identity and strong political and military unity.[14] Nothing could be further from the reality of the scattered tribes that inhabited Araucania. But the myth created by Ercilla captured the popular imagination and obscured the real circumstances of political events. The belief that the Araucanians were a superior race of warriors became widespread and is accepted even today.[15] This vision of a heroically disputed land where the military glory of Spain met that of the Araucanians distorts the historical analysis of the frontier. The border was not solely a zone of conflict but also one of contact and exchange. During certain periods (1553–1622), war or guerrilla war predominated. There were even moments of Araucanian hegemony, or at least times when the military initiative was on their side (1598–1622).[16] After 1622, thanks to diminished belligerence, frontier relations began slowly to develop, permitting the growth of commerce and a fertile process of transculturation. However, it is true that peace was never general nor continuous. There were ruptures in the eighteenth century with the uprisings of 1766–70, but in general there was no repetition of the destructive Araucanian wars of the second half of the sixteenth and the first half of the seventeenth centuries.[17]

The pattern of open warfare was replaced by the fury of the *malocas*, which continued to plague frontier settlements until the end of the nineteenth century. The military objective of resistance to the Spanish invasion, with strategies of death and total destruction, gave way to the *malocas*, whose objectives were more commercial than military. The *maloca*'s plan of action entailed robbery, pillaging, destruction, and the taking of captives.

Bascuñán the Memorius

Francisco Núñez de Pineda y Bascuñán witnessed the first and most belligerent years of the Araucanian wars. As the son of a military family, he received a military education. What other choice was there for the son of soldiers on the battle-torn frontier? When he left Jesuit school, he entered the army at the age of eighteen (1626) and, following his father's wish, began military life as a buck private. His father, who did not believe in using the privileges associated with the family name, had held important positions in the Chilean government and enjoyed many of the prerogatives reserved for *Peninsulars* of his rank: he was a *maestre de campo* and an *encomendero* (a colonist granted control of land and Indians to work for him). Francisco served diligently. "Following my father's command I went to serve in the state of Arauco, where as a soldier I endeavored to learn quickly all that is necessary and desirable for a soldier to know."[18] The proximity of the Araucanian frontier was a draw for a young man eager to distinguish himself through merit. By 1628 Francisco had already been promoted to captain, and his first engagement was at the battle of Cangrejeras. On that occasion the Spanish army suffered a resounding defeat, and Francisco, who was wounded, was taken captive.

His six-month captivity allowed him to experience firsthand the other side of the frontier, which, though not far geographically from his native Chillán, was very far culturally. In contact with his captors, he asked questions, talked with them, and took an interest in learning about them. At a certain point he even wondered whether he should return or stay. His collected adventures and reflections appeared many years later in a magnificent autobiography. *Cautiverio feliz y razón individual de las guerras dilatadas del Reino de Chile* is an eyewitness account of the frontier and frontier relations that captures an entire era. It is also the testimony of a Creole captive.[19]

Of the many captives in Chile and other parts of the Americas, few memorialists had the ability or the desire to sit in front of blank pages and compose an account of their experiences. Núñez de Pineda y Bascuñán did. His written testimony captures the voice of a captive and his adventure; it is also a splendid ethnography of the Mapuche people. It must be noted that the violence of the wars in Arauco did not encourage the penetration of missionaries, travelers, or conquistadores beyond the Bío-Bío River. This affected the production of ethnographic works, especially in comparison with the abundance of such works in other parts of the continent. Resistance to Spanish penetration was so great that Spaniards and Creoles chose to settle far from the border zone. Before 1622 the image of Araucania was based on the perspective of soldiers assigned to forts in the interior and to some chaplains who served in these posts. I am referring to the chronicles of Diego de Rosales, Góngora Marmolejo, Mariño de Lobera, González de Nájera, and Alonso de Ercilla, all of whom were influenced by the fact that their experience occurred within the parameters of warfare. Thus Bascuñán's text is fundamental to gaining an understanding of Mapuche society from within.

The Happy Captivity

One of the first aspects that powerfully claim our attention in Bascuñán's account is its often jovial tone. Bascuñán is clearly a gifted storyteller adept at novelistic narration. The vocabulary is varied, and his lexical purism is softened by general or regional Americanisms.[20] At times, one has the impression that the author has only been on an excursion and is describing his amusing or exciting experiences. His account resembles a travelogue more than a captive's testimony. Bascuñán's propensity to describe celebrations and banquets contributes to this effect. In this respect, his text stands in stark contrast to Cabeza de Vaca's account. If Cabeza de Vaca's journey (studied in the previous chapter) is marked by the threat of hunger, Bascuñán's is full of gastronomic scenes in which great quantities of food are served and huge amounts of *chicha* (an alcoholic beverage) are consumed. Bascuñán describes, with a wealth of details, relations between families and between tribes seemingly characterized by continuous feasts and celebrations.

The first sequences after his captivity depict the group that captured him retreating to their *rehues* after crossing the barrier of the Bío-Bío River. Once in safe territory, the fugitive group paused for a few days in the camp of Cacique Colpoche, of whom Bascuñán says, "He was unsurpassed when it came to leisure and to the pursuit of pleasure, eating, drinking, and dancing."[21] Then our chronicler savors his account of a banquet which he still seems to remember fondly: "They brought me three jugs of chicha and some mutton, treating me with the same honor and courtesy they accord their principal guests." He continues, "They set before us, for our supper, some stews according to their manner with some cakes, potatoes, and wrapped packages of corn and beans, and at the campfire by us, they roasted fat meat."[22] The welcome dinner was followed by dancing, more food, and more drink, the party lasting until daybreak. When some of the guests were still deep in their chicha-induced stupor, a breakfast was served that surpassed expectations: "We ate and drank splendidly."[23] After several days of rest and dealing with the threat of the mountain caciques, the group of maloqueros, led by Cacique Maulicán, Bascuñán's captor and protector, reached their camp. There, awaiting them, was Maulicán's father, the old Llancareu,

> with a plate of *mote* [boiled corn] with many *achupallas* [bromeliads] and herbs of the fields which they use to season their stews, and the daughter of the old man into whose care I was entrusted brought me another dish of potatoes and some pieces of meat cured without salt, badly smoked. They had nothing else because they were frontier Indians, and they brought me a jug of chicha made of strawberries [*frutillas*], which the old man had saved for me the first night when I came to his camp.[24]

By the time of Bascuñán's contact with the Mapuche tribes, the process of transculturation was already under way, despite periods of intermittent warfare. We can deduce this from their meals, not only from the food they ate but also from its preparation. Bascuñán was served local products— beans, potatoes, chicha, the meat of a native sheep (that is to say, a llama), and so on—but he was also treated to mutton, lamb, veal, beef stews, fish seasoned in different ways, and a variety of pastries prepared the Castilian way. The arrival of European products, quickly adopted into the Indian diet, as well as the presence of captive European women, made its mark on their food (apparently not in short supply) and its preparation. Traditional Mapuche agriculture was precarious. The crops grown in the *chacras* (farms) was supplemented by the fruits and seeds they gathered. The staples of their original diet were fish and seafood, which they consumed in great quantities, and game from hunting, supplemented by the seasonal harvesting of crops.[25]

It is important to single out the impact captives, and principally female captives, had on the process of assimilation and cultural *mestizaje*. The opulent meals described by Bascuñán, which on occasion almost seem like orgies, included carefully seasoned meats followed by sweets and other treats in the Spanish tradition. Undoubtedly, the many Spanish and Creole women in the Indian camps, or those Indian women who had lived among Spaniards and Creoles, were responsible for the rich, varied diet. Spanish influence can also be seen in the improved agricultural practices mentioned by Bascuñán. "More than sixty Indians assembled with their plows and their tools which they call *hueuellos*, a kind of three-tined pitchfork with which they lift the soil. Other tools look like baker's paddles, about two yards long, and in this manner they dig in the soil, and they make the furrows in which the women sow the seeds."[26] From his observations we can deduce that planting was, by this date (1628), an important collective activity.

> These are days of rejoicing and amusement for them, because the owner of the *chacra* slaughters many calves, lambs, and sheep, and the fields where they are working, each according to his task, are provisioned with jugs of *chicha* and many campfires with meats roasting on spits, and stew pots, from which the women bring them food and drink frequently.[27]

Bascuñán took part in these labors as well as many of the other daily activities of the Indians.

Indian Parleys

Bascuñán also attended and described in detail the Indian parleys held to negotiate the precarious relations between the different Mapuche caciques and the Indians of the mountains. The first and most important of these parleys was held shortly after his capture. Maulicán was returning with his precious treasure when he ran into the mountain caciques, with whom he was forced to share his booty according to custom.

Chilean Indians and the Indians of Araucania had never been united politically. They formed entities that kept in touch principally through commerce.[28] Among Mapuche tribes commerce worked as a powerful mechanism of redistribution of surplus goods. Through commerce, tribes established relations among themselves and with other groups. In these relations there were continuous conflicts, which Chileans Indians resolved by means of parleys.

When the conqueror of Chile, Pedro de Valdivia, penetrated Araucania for the first time in 1550, he did so with little opposition on the part of the Indians, who lived in independent groups (*parcialidades*).[29] The lack of any kind of union or confederation allowed Valdivia to found a series of villages and to grant *encomiendas* to his companions in conquest. The Indians held in *encomiendas* would provide the labor for the exploitation of fluvial gold deposits. Three years later the Indians of Tucapel rose up against the oppression, starting a process of intermittent rebellions.[30] Besides the demographic factors that helped the Indians resist the Spanish war machine for a long time, an important part of the Araucanian success was the coordination of defensive strategies. This was their motive in organizing meetings and parleys, which were attended by great numbers of caciques and warriors. Father Valdivia records that the 1612 parley in Catiray was attended by five hundred *ulmens* (caciques or heads of bloodlines).[31] Later in the century, these meetings were organized by the Spanish-Creole authorities in an attempt to control frontier relations between Indians and Spanish-Creoles.[32]

By the time Bascuñán was captured in the battle of Cangrejeras, the Mapuches had acquired a vast knowledge of Spanish strategies and methods of warfare, and they were able to combat them with success.

> After they wounded my right wrist with a spear, rendering me unable to bear arms, they hit me with a *macana,* which is what these enemies call these strong, heavy wooden clubs, and they have been known to knock down even a horse with one fierce blow, and following up the first blow with others they knocked me off my horse, leaving me senseless, the backplate of my armor was jammed against my ribs and the breastplate pierced by a lance.[33]

Bascuñán woke up a captive surrounded by "furious and rabid" warriors. If the cacique Lientur had not intervened, the Araucanian warriors would have put an end to his life right there. Bascuñán's greatest worry in the first moments of his capture was that he would be recognized as the son of Don Álvaro, the *maestre de campo* of the Spanish army, who was hated by some and loved by others. Later that kinship acted in his favor. Unfortunately, a "miserable Spanish-speaking Indian," who had served as slave or servant among the Spaniards, recognized and betrayed him, shouting: "kill him, kill the captain now without a second thought, he is the son of Álvaro Maltincampo (for that is what they called my father), who has destroyed our lands, and has beaten and wiped us out." His tirade and shouts attracted many other Indians who were no less furious and rabid, and who lifting high their spears and *macanas* tried to discharge many blows on me and take my life.[34]

The role played by the Spanish-speaking Indian was not unusual. An important part of the process of transculturation which took place on both sides in Araucania was due to the traffic of fugitive Indians who fled the abuses of the *encomiendas* and the even worse conditions of slavery permitted in Chile after 1608.[35] There were many Indians who "due to humiliations and bad treatment"[36] fled and returned to their camps. This traffic created a flow of information through which the Mapuches not only got to know their enemy better in order to combat them but also adopted Spanish cultural elements in a constant process of assimilation.

Lientur's protection on that occasion was providential. Lientur was one of the caciques who during the first years of the Spanish incursion had served the Spanish forces as a friend and collaborator. The deterioration of relations between Indians and Spaniards due to the scarcity of resources in the kingdom of Chile and to the harsh policy of conquering the Indians led the Araucanians to change allegiance and abandon their former masters. The reference to Lientur's previous conduct illustrates this well.

> At the time this valuable leader collaborated with us, he was one of the best and most loyal friends we had in those times. That is why my father, the *maestre de campo general,* showered gifts and favors upon him while he governed this frontier. Later Lientur became a fierce enemy of other *ministros superiores* (government officials) whose deeds and conduct forced him to rebel.[37]

Bascuñán's text is full of long moral discourses about the well-deserved, bad reputation of Spanish administrators, and he denounces repeatedly the decree that legalized the slavery of the Indians. "I cannot justify slavery in this nation because it is responsible for great crimes and evil. The insatiable greed of our people has disturbed the peace this kingdom might have enjoyed otherwise."[38]

At that point Bascuñán's fate was in the balance. He was not just one more captive in the hands of Mapuche warriors. He was the son of Maestre de

Campo Álvar Núñez de Pineda, who was looked upon differently by those who had served him and knew his conduct and by those who saw him as an instrument of the Spanish Crown's repressive policy. At this difficult moment, Lientur came out in defense of the illustrious captive. In the captive's eyes, the cacique was "an angel of Divine Providence, sent to help me at a terrible moment of danger."[39] The negotiation was not an easy one. The mountain Indians demanded that the captive be handed over to them for immediate execution. Bascuñán remembered that moment with great clarity because he was a victim and a witness to the Indian parley a few days later that would decide the fate of captives and the preparation of future *malocas*.

> My master, who had friends and relatives in that lodging, learned from them that the previously mentioned caciques and *capitanejos* were planning to come to our lodge in order to buy me, kill me once they got to their land and use my head to recruit a large army to attack and destroy our frontier settlements.[40]

The caciques and *toques* (principal chiefs) who participated in this plot were what the chroniclers refer to as *indios de guerra* (hostile Indians). This term was used to refer to those Indians belonging to the different groups that after the first great uprising of 1550 had decreed war without truce against the *huincas* (Christians). They were chiefly from mountain tribes, Pehuenches and Huilliches, and their belligerence continued even in those years when peace otherwise prevailed. Chroniclers mention the different roles played by friendly Indians and by hostile Indians, especially the efforts of the latter to convince the former to join them. González de Nájera writes in his chronicle: "So the Indians seemed when the Governor and all those who were in charge of forts and frontier posts, went around, on the Governor's orders, asking information of the peace Indians and the prisoners taken in raids from the war Indians."[41] Bernardo de Vargas Machuca, a captain of the army in the kingdom of Chile and author of *Milicia y descripción de las Indias* (Army Service and Description of the Indies), published in Madrid in 1599, singles out two types of Indians who served the Spaniards, the ones he calls "indios de servicios" (service Indians) and the "indios amigos" (friendly Indians).[42] The former served as *peones de brega* doing chores indirectly related to the war: carrying water, firewood, and taking care of horses. The *indios amigos* were key as combat soldiers in the Christian armies.

In general the existence of these allied Indians was fundamental in many parts of the continent, since they made Spanish penetration easier. Much has been written on this topic, and there are many theories that inadequately explain this behavior. In this respect, the strategic importance of the Tlaxcalans in the destruction and conquest of the Aztec capital has often been stressed. This type of spontaneous alliance occurred repeatedly in many places during the Spanish conquest of America, but this feature of the conflict has not been analyzed in any depth. Álvaro Jara mentions that, given the choice of working in the mines, at other menial labor, or in the army, Indians preferred to serve as warriors. The great paradox of the war in Arauco, well noted by the chroniclers, was the great speed with which the *indios amigos* on the Christian side went over to the Indian side and became the fiercest enemies of the Spanish troops. Some of the mythical heroes of the Araucanian people, among them Lautaro, the indisputable hero of the epic *La Araucana,* had once lived in the Spanish-Creole settlements.[43] Service among the Spaniards provided them with an inside knowledge of Spanish strength, weapons, combat tactics, and strategic priorities. The violent and constant Indian uprisings after 1598 were seen as a justification for the decree legalizing slavery, which in turn exacerbated the conflict. The tribes, which previously had been dispersed across the vast Araucanian territory, found it necessary to enter into alliances in order to resist this new pressure. The number of treaties and parleys increased in an effort to coordinate *malocas* and invasions of the Spanish forts and settlements and to strengthen resistance.

Who could have imagined that Bascuñán would be the unwilling witness of a Mapuche parley to decide his fate? "And the truth is that in that predicament I was rather determined to die for the faith of our Lord and God as a brave martyr."[44] The parley was arranged according to the category of those attending. "Then they disposed themselves in order according to the customs of their lands and this group was larger than the head group which was made up of the principal cacique and most valuable captains."[45] Then Putapichun spoke, and in "parlas," the florid rhetoric used in Indian parleys, he addressed Maulicán to explain the reason why the parley had been called: "This war council and extraordinary parley has no other purpose than to come jointly to buy this captain whom you take [. . .] in order to sacrifice him to our Pillán."[46] The caciques present obviously knew the captive and his pecuniary and strategic value, and they set out to make Maulicán generous offers in exchange for his precious hostage: llamas (*ovejas de la tierra*), sheep of Castile, necklaces of rich stones, trained and outfitted horses, other Spanish captives, and one of Putapichun's own daughters. Maulicán resisted the exchange and justified his refusal on the grounds of the pleasure it would give him to arrive at his land and show the precious booty to his father and relatives. He promised that once he had done that, he would turn the captive over to them to be sacrificed to the great Pillán (an Araucanian divinity).

Given Maulicán's negative reply, and as part of the ritual that followed a *maloca,* they sacrificed one of the Spanish soldiers who was taken at the same battle as Bascuñán. During the period of the Mapuche uprisings and the wars of Arauco, these sacrifices or executions of prisoners were common, as were the cannibalistic practices associated with the ritual.[47] Bascuñán's narrative leaves out no detail and is very moving. The victim was brought with a rope around his neck and placed in the center of a circle. There followed a long ritual that ended with an offer to Maulicán to end the victim's life with his hands.[48] He was given "a heavy wooden club studded with horseshoe nails [. . .] and he drew near the place where that poor young man was or where they made him sit, shedding more tears from his eyes than I myself could not help shedding. Every time he looked at me, it pierced my soul."[49] Maulicán did not hesitate, but "struck his head such a blow that he dashed out his brains with that *macana* or nail-studded club. Immediately the acolytes who waited with knives in their hands, opened his chest and took out his beating heart, and gave it to my master."[50] Later Maulicán ate of the heart and passed it to the rest of the caciques and principal men, who continued the ceremonial communion.

Indian Factions

The parley concluded with Maulicán's promise to turn over the captive, and this appeased the impatient mountain caciques. Maulicán won his objective thanks to the support of the coastal caciques who accompanied him. Nonetheless, the mountain tribes did not desist in their demands and months later went to the camps of Maulicán and his father, Llancareu, in order to insist again that the precious captive be handed over to them. They felt that Maulicán had not kept his promise, and they were ready to take the captive by force.

The lack of political coherence among the various indigenous factions is made evident by Bascuñán's tale, as well as by that of his contemporary Juan Falcón, who was held captive for more than fourteen years in Araucania. Falcón writes: "Among the *indios de guerra* there is no head whom they obey nor follow, there is no sort of order in their republic, nor do they make an effort in any way."[51] Only the pressing needs of warfare led them to unite for a time under the command of a common chief or *toquí,* whose authority lasted usually for the duration of a campaign.[52] Especially in the region of Arauco, the abundance of natural resources and the high human density of the territory fostered greater rivalry among the different indigenous factions and the greed of the Spanish invaders. Bascuñán describes this aspect with great clarity: "[N]one of their nations have any chief head to hold them together, nor anyone whom they strictly fear or respect, and [. . .] each one in his faction and in his home is considered according to his wealth and the retinue of dependants and relatives who attend upon him."[53]

When he received news of the arrival of the mountain Indians, Maulicán feared not only for the life of his captive but also for the safety of his camp. This is why he hid the captive, and he himself also left. Bascuñán, together with two nephews of Maulicán, was taken to a refuge in the forest, where they spent several days in anxiety and fear. The sounds of the forest made them tremble: "That night, just before dawn, the mountain caciques, my enemies, arrived with more than two hundred armed Indians. Some headed to the camps of Maulicán and Llancareu, and others went to search the forest where the boys and I were sleeping."[54] They were not found, and the mountain caciques left without their prey. Nevertheless, the threat that the mountain Indians might again raid their camps made Maulicán resolve to send the captive to the domain of "Luacura, a highly respected cacique, who was powerful, rich and very favorable to Spaniards."[55] That was the last time Bascuñán had to deal with serious dangers darkening his happy captivity.

The Origin of *Malocas*

War was a fact of life from the first uprisings in 1550 until the peace treaties of 1652. It had two basic variants. The first was open warfare that devastated countryside and cities and established the frontier line of Araucania; the second was a type of intermittent warfare known by the name of *malocas,* whose objectives were not military but economic. These raids lasted until the end of the nineteenth century.

At first *malocas* were small military operations, swift incursions into enemy territory, carried out by small groups of soldiers or warriors whose aim was not exclusively to defeat the enemy but to cause as much damage as possible to his crops and property. During *malocas*, crops were burned, cattle were stolen, and captives were taken.[56] *Malocas* were a form of harassment practiced by Spaniards as well as by Indians. The word *maloca* is a Mapuche expression which came to exemplify the war in Araucania in the seventeenth and eighteenth centuries. From the act of carrying out *malocas* comes the verb *maloquear*, which is used by the earliest chroniclers. Bascuñán makes reference to Indian incursions into Spanish territory and also refers to the Spaniards who came to Indian camps to "maloquear."[57] He explains that *malocas* only took place when the weather was good because in winter the rising river waters made travel difficult and impeded quick getaways. González de Nájera uses the term "campeadas" and says their purpose was to steal cattle, burn the straw huts of the Indians, and rescue Spanish captives in their power.[58] This chronicler was a fervent proponent of offensive warfare and therefore justified *malocas* as necessary.

Malocas soon became the type of warfare used most by the Indians. *Malocas* differed from the early Spanish-Creole wars in the number of participants and the selective nature of their objectives. While open warfare had been directed against forts and frontier garrisons, *malocas* were aimed principally at small settlements, villages, and cattle ranches. The *maloca* suited the characteristics and strengths of the Indians, who did not have the military resources and weapons to confront Creole armies in open battle. *Malocas* were ideal for them because they entailed swift, intense, surprise attacks, during which the *conas* (warriors) stole, sacked, destroyed, and captured cattle, women, and children. They really were a form of guerrilla warfare without the prestige and epic aura of the wars of Arauco. León Solís maintains that *malocas* began owing to the rapid deployment of Indians from factions on the eastern side of the Andes who crossed the mountains in order to reinforce the Araucanian armies. "The flow of warriors across the Andean passes and the close military collaboration which was established between the tribes of Araucania and the pampas was, for more than a century, a factor on which anti-Spanish resistance in the southern cone of America depended."[59] The Indians of the southeastern band entered the territory south of the Bío-Bío through Andean passes and returned to their homes with part of the booty after the raids. Early *malocas* were marked by solidarity. In time they became more organized, the Andean passes were established, and *malocas* changed direction from west to east to the cattle ranches of the pampas. The Indians of Arauco and principally those of the mountains benefited from *malocas* and began a flourishing trade between Chile and settlements in the province of Buenos Aires that lasted until the end of the nineteenth century.

Captives

The captives were the human cost of the *malocas*. The decree legalizing slavery helped to establish the practice of the *maloca,* and the creation of an army further encouraged it. Thousands of Indian captives served in haciendas and in the Spanish army. Whenever relations worsened, or in the years following the legalization of slavery, Spanish *malocas* sought to take as captives Indian men, women, and children who were then sold as slaves to meet urgent manpower needs. The chronicler González de Nájera describes them:

> The whole jurisdiction of the city is full of slaves, especially a very fertile valley which is many leagues long and which they call Quillota. In the haciendas, farmhouses [*alquerías*] or farms [*cortijos*] and other rustic country houses belonging to the Spanish inhabitants of the city, there are many Indian slaves brought from the war, and they are mixed in with the peace Indians who are held in *encomiendas.* And in their attitude toward us, they are all of the same mind for they desire the victory of their people.[60]

The trade in Indian slaves brought significant profits to the military who participated in the wars.[61] Friendly Indians were even paid to procure slaves from among their own people. Scarcity of labor was a chronic problem in Chile. This scarcity together with the demands of the Peruvian market led to the increase in the commerce of native slaves.

The first time Christian captives were taken was during the native uprisings of 1550. The rebel Indians of Arauco razed the Chilean cities of Valdivia, La Imperial, Villarrica, Osorio, and Infantes de Angol and captured many prisoners, a great number of whom were killed. These first captives were prisoners of war, and their killing set a precedent. In 1553 Pedro de Valdivia and many of his officers and militiamen, as well as the priests captured in the destruction of Valdivia and other cities, were executed on the field of battle. As described above, Valdivia was tortured and killed: "They killed him and the chaplain, and they put his head on a lance as they had done with those of the other Christians, none of whom escaped."[62] The same fate befell Governor Martín García de Loyola in 1598. González de Nájera, who witnessed this first phase of war without quarter, relates, perhaps with too much passion, the tragic end of many of the captives taken in war:

> And the enjoyment and pleasure these barbarians derive from taking the lives of the miserable captives who fall into their hands are greatly enhanced by the cruel treatment they mete out, nor are they moved to pity by their heartrending cries, just as in our Spain when people enjoy fighting bulls which they lance and hamstring and even burn alive in many places with fireworks.[63]

The Dominican friar Juan Falcón de los Ángeles, in the declaration he made in 1614 when he was liberated, describes the murder of his brother friars after they were captured.

> Eight friars were captured by said enemies on that occasion and two of them were ransomed shortly after being captured, for which they took the boat which was in the river and port of said city of Valdivia [. . .] and six of them they took prisoner and among them their superior whose name was Friar Pedro Peroa, whom they killed by piercing him with lances with the greatest cruelty only because he reproved them for their deeds preaching the faith of Jesus Christ and pointing out their obligations as baptized Christians, for most of them were. The rest they killed using the same cruelty at different times and occasions and this deponent alone they spared.[64]

From 1623 to 1656 there was a clear decrease in belligerence, and at this time the *malocas* took on more of the character of harassment and captives acquired value as a commercial object of exchange. As the wars lost their virulence and the frontiers of the Indian territory were gradually defined, *malocas* settled into a pattern. They became part of commercial relations between Indian tribes as well as between Spanish and Indians. Indians continued to cross the mountains in both directions, but now their objectives were not military but commercial. What they sought was not military glory but products to exchange. The brave warriors of Arauco became hunters of

cattle and horses. In order to obtain them, they slowly penetrated the uninhabited eastern lands toward the dry pampa and the Buenos Aires cattle
ranches, where the great numbers of feral cattle and the wealth of frontier
farms made for easy prey. The Indians of Arauco and principally the mountain Pehuenche and Huilliche Indians began a flourishing commerce in the
promising ranches beyond the Andes which lasted until the end of the nineteenth century.

It is interesting to observe the double role played by the Pehuenche tribes.
They were, on the one hand, friendly Indians and principal allies of the Chilean
administration, and on the other, the most ferocious warriors on the other side
of the mountain range whose *malocas* fell on the estancias of Cuyo and sowed
terror and death wherever they went. Already at the end of the seventeenth
century, Chilean governors recorded holding parleys with the Indians in
which they addressed Pehuenche raids on the territory of the Río de la Plata.
By the middle of the eighteenth century, this trans-Andean commerce had
stabilized, and the Chilean market, always short of labor, acquired cattle,
horses, certain consumer products, and captives from the frontier of Buenos
Aires and Cuyo.

There were several reasons for the change in strategy: the growing pacification of the Chilean frontier, the lack of cattle-raising resources in southern
Chile and even in the central valleys, the abundance of wild cattle on the eastern side of the Andes, and the unprotected state of ranches and farms. In addition, the gradual pacification of Arauco had produced a surplus of warriors
who found an outlet for their activity on the other side of the mountain range.
The arrival in the pampas of growing numbers of Araucanian Indians deeply
affected the makeup of tribes on the eastern side of the Andes. They mixed
with them, made treaties, traded, and made war. This is the phenomenon
known as the Araucanization of the pampas, and it had a strong impact on the
composition and militarization of the territory of Río de la Plata.[65]

Voices of the Captives

Francisco Núñez de Pineda y Bascuñán was a Creole captive in a transitional
period in the kingdom of Chile. He was captured in 1628 when the first signs
of pacification were being seen in the region, although the causes that had

provoked the uprising of the Indians and the wars of extermination were still alive. He was a protagonist in the military confrontations, he witnessed *malocas* and the rivalries between the different Indian tribes, and he experienced daily life among the Mapuche more as a guest than as a prisoner. It is fair to say that his access to Mapuche society was privileged, especially when we consider that mendicant orders did not penetrate Araucania until the seventeenth century, although they had already reached other parts of the continent.[66] Bascuñán was an exceptional witness, and his testimony proves it. He was feted by most of the caciques with whom he dealt, with the exception of several instances of direct threats from the hostile mountain tribes who wanted his head. As his testimony states: "Great was the happiness and the good luck I had among these infidel barbarians. I was fortunate both in the love bestowed on me by the principal caciques and in the thwarting of the treachery of those who eagerly sought a disastrous end to my days."[67]

Several Indian chiefs offered him their daughters, but Bascuñán turned them down, alleging moral reasons. Some of these girls were captives or products of miscegenation. In the house of Cacique Quilalebo he was offered a girl, the cacique's goddaughter, who was the granddaughter of a Spanish conqueror of Valdivia. He declined for religious reasons, arguing that given his impending liberation such a compromising union was ill advised: "Because she was not a Christian and she professed a different faith from mine, because we Christians cannot break our laws without offending the Lord our God, and that this was the major reason for my qualms, and the other reason being that since I was awaiting the negotiation of my ransom that spring, I would regret falling in love with her if it were not to last."[68]

His privileged status allowed him to converse with caciques whose experience in wars, captures, and confrontations summed up the history of the Mapuche people since before the arrival of the Spanish, passed on with the fidelity of oral traditions among Amerindian peoples. Bascuñán showed an interest in learning more about the world of his captors and encouraged dialogue. In the voices of his interlocutors, he heard the other side of the story, the vision of the conflict expressed from the indigenous point of view. "Cacique Aremcheu (said this old man) will be able to give you a better account of the arrival of the Spanish to our land."[69] It was a story of injustice that, in Bascuñán's eyes, warranted the bellicose attitude of the Araucanians.

I don't remember the beginning well either, said Aremcheu; only the account I have from my parents is present to me. They said that when the Spaniards arrived, they began making war on us and fighting and that in the first battles they had, since our people were ignorant of the effects of harquebuses, many died in the first encounters, and the fearful survivors submitted easily.[70]

The Mapuche society of Arauco, despite the continuous state of alert and belligerence, had entered, beginning in the first half of the seventeenth century, into a slow but continuous process of change, which Bascuñán witnessed. Clothing, food, commerce, and language had filtered slowly through the narrow cracks of the frontier. Friendly Indian captains and the Indian commissaries had passports to enter either side, and their influence became stronger with the passing of time. The space of the frontier brought additional economic benefits, which justified its existence. Its value was unquestionable, and in those areas of the continent frontiers persisted for long periods of time. The frontier was also the place where déclassé Spaniards wound up. Among Indians, they could hide their penury or misery. In the frontier zone, these fugitives or deserters found a greater degree of freedom and greater opportunities to carry out semiclandestine trade or to live beyond established norms.

In Indian camps there were many who had experienced captivity among the Spaniards, whether as servants, as workers in the fields or mines, or as slaves. Bascuñán also mentions that he encountered many captives. The caciques with whom he talked stressed how the treatment meted out to their captives differed from the way the Spaniards treated theirs: "You see here, Captain, all the Spanish captives who live among us and how they are treated: they eat with us, they drink with us, they wear what we wear, and if they work, they work alongside us."[71]

Bascuñán's captivity ended after six months when he was exchanged for several principal caciques who were in Spanish hands. The emotional farewell he recounts underscores the friendly tone of the book, which insists repeatedly on the nobility of the "infidel barbarians," their right to their liberty, and the Spanish responsibility for drawing out the conflict.

These words, which I spoke with some tenderness, were answered by sorrowing old women with tears in their eyes and sighs on their lips, saying: "Ay! Ay!

our captain and companion is leaving us," and imitating them the rest of the girls, principally the mestiza with the boys who were my friends, began to weep and to raise their sorrowful voices so that I too was forced to weep with them and assure them that if I did not have a father, whom I loved dearly, and if I were not so sought after by my own people (as they had seen) who had sent so many messages, I would not leave their dear company, because they had obliged me with their welcome, their courtesy, their love and gifts, to reciprocate with goodwill and affection.[72]

Upon returning to Spain, Bascuñán wrote his extensive manuscript, which circulated widely but was not published until 1863.[73] Part of the book is devoted to narrating his captivity in a direct and jovial manner. There is an urgency on the part of the narrator to communicate his experiences. He writes with passion, and his account is a pleasure to read. Many critics have regarded the text as more of a novel than a chronicle.[74] The other part of the manuscript, which is more tedious, consists of a large political-moral treatise encompassing history, ethical-religious speculation, and lyric poetry. The author's purpose is made clear from the first pages: "The chief aim of my discourse is none other than to make the truth known. Thus we will start my *Cautiverio feliz*, where I will make known the reason for the drawn-out war in Chile, because the one and the other is the direct aim of this book."[75] It is equally clear throughout the book and in the final section, "Protestación y Resignación" (Protest and Resignation): "[M]y intention has not been driven by anything but reason, justice and the fervent zeal to make known and explain to His Royal Majesty, with clear and patent truths, the causes and reasons why he might lose his kingdom in Chile, and why they are wasting his royal patrimony fruitlessly and without any profit."[76]

In practice, the juxtaposition of both parts of the book helps neither of them. The excess of rhetoric and the recourse to juridical quotations cloud the author's purpose and have divided critics. It is not the purpose of this chapter to enter into that debate.[77] Nevertheless, it is interesting to contrast Bascuñán's text with the testimony of another contemporary captive. This testimony is the "Declaración que hizo el padre fray Juan Falcón en 18 de abril de 1614" (Declaration made by Father Juan Falcón on April 18, 1614), which upon first reading appears to contradict the idyllic panorama presented in *Cautiverio feliz*.

Juan Falcón's *Declaración*

Juan Falcón de los Ángeles, a Dominican priest, was captured in the Araucanian attack on the city of Valdivia in 1599 together with seven other friars. His
fifteen-year-long captivity coincided with the period of greatest Araucanian
belligerence along the frontier (1598–1622). After being liberated in a prisoner exchange, he was asked to make a declaration, in accordance with a new
policy implemented by the Crown in order to obtain information about Araucanian forces that might help to contain them. The text, which is of great testimonial value, at times takes on a strong emotional tone, owing to the dramatic
circumstances of his captivity. Of the eight Dominicans who were captured on
that occasion, two, the oldest, were ransomed immediately. Of the six who remained, only Falcón survived. His fellow Dominicans were brutally murdered
in his presence. He was a slave to four masters, "who treated him extremely
harshly, beating him with sticks and treating him badly by word and deed, despite the fact that the deponent, in order to save his life, tried to please them
by plowing, digging, and cultivating the earth and watching over their cattle
and horses."[78] He finally came to the cacique of Purén, Guenucuca, who employed him as an interpreter and "treated him with greater leniency."[79]

The accounts of Bascuñán and Falcón appear to contradict each other in
fundamental aspects, although on occasion the difference lies more in the
friar's totally negative tone. Obviously, this disparity in the accounts is the
result of the very different experiences and personalities of the captives. Bascuñán was a twenty-year-old Creole military officer who was born in the
frontier and used to Indians. His captivity lasted six months. Falcón was a
thirty-four-year-old clergyman who arrived in Chile as a missionary and spent
fourteen and a half years in captivity serving four masters. He witnessed the
brutal 1599 attack on the city of Valdivia and the violent murder of his fellow
friars. As a Dominican it was very difficult for him to overcome the religious
barrier that divided the two cultures.

One of the things that seemed to bother him most was the Indians' hereti-
cal mocking of the Christian religion. He writes that "in their banquets and
drunken bouts they dress in albs, chasubles, stoles and maniples in the manner of priests when they prepare to say mass, making a mockery of it all, and
even the ladino Indians who were Christians and born and raised among the
Spaniards participated in the mock masses."[80] He tells an anecdote that must

have spread among the Christian captives and that illustrates the gravity with which such acts of mockery were viewed by the clergy: "After they had laid waste the city of Valdivia, two of the aforementioned ladino Indians put on priestly vestments and made as if to say mass. They prepared the chalices to drink from them and it is known for a fact that their sides burst, by the will of the Lord."[81] For Fray Juan Falcón there was no room for understanding. Indians were apostates ("they hate the name of Christian") and vicious ("they are much too given to every manner of vice, especially those of the flesh, and therefore they have many women").[82] By contrast, think of the jovial and carefree manner in which Bascuñán describes the feasts and orgies of the Indians and the offers of women and marriage he received.

Every captive tends unconsciously to present his experiences in captivity in terms of a comparison with his own culture. The implicit antagonism of the situation may be modified by the experiences they undergo, and these can emphasize or minimize contrasts. If a captive feels that he is a member of a superior culture he is likely to stress that aspect. Bascuñán as well as Falcón belonged to the superior stratum of their society, one as a soldier, the other as a clergyman, and therefore they were special beneficiaries of their society. They had strong reasons to identify with their own culture and to reject the proposals to integrate into the society that held them by force. Christianity, as it expanded in the New World, preached the unity of doctrine and the irrefutable infallibility of Christian truths. Even Bascuñán, who has words of admiration for both cultures, unquestionably affirms the moral superiority of the Christian religion, and he makes it clear that one of the justifications for making war on the Indians and even for enslaving them is their apostasy. Nevertheless, he thinks that Indians cannot be heretics, since they never knew the true religion.

Falcón's testimony is very different. More than a question of superiority, his account synthesizes an infernal vision of captivity which justifies a war of aggression against the Indians. When asked how many captives there were, and how they were treated, he answers: "There are two hundred Spanish men and three hundred and fifty Spanish women, more or less, according to the reckoning of the enemy Indians in those provinces, and they use them as slaves, treating them very harshly in word and deed, selling them whenever it suits them and beating them with sticks and slapping them."[83] Falcón's declaration continues to dwell on the insecurity in which these wretched captives

live, in a state of extreme poverty and nakedness, and lacking any spiritual as-
sistance. He draws attention to the tragic situation of the Spanish women,
who are subjected to sexual abuse by their captors: "They abuse them, having
their way with them by force and against the will of the women who fear for
their lives."[84] He declares that captives live in total isolation, since the Indians do not allow them to communicate with each other, and many like
himself had forgotten how to speak Spanish: "[E]ven after he was no longer
in the enemy's power, even though he understood Spanish, he could not manage to speak it."[85]

Another difference between Falcón's text and Bascuñán's lies in the circumstances in which the accounts were produced. The former is a declaration
made according to the regulation of the *cabildo*, or town council, of Santiago,
and is limited to twenty-four questions included in a questionnaire. This no
doubt conditioned and limited the answers. It is not a text that has been
thought out, digested, and rewritten with the benefit of time and perspective,
but was produced immediately upon his return when the wounds of captivity
were still fresh for the friar. In addition, the wording of certain questions also
conditioned his response. For example, the question that asks whether Indians abused captives implies the existence of abuse and thus influences the
answer. By contrast, Bascuñán wrote his text many years after returning to
Spain, in 1673, and had the opportunity to correct it many times.[86] Distance
and time smoothed out the rough edges and clarified the author's priority in
writing his account: his fundamental concern with justice.

Nevertheless, despite the many differences that separate the two captives
and their experiences, it is possible to perceive a series of opinions implied in
Falcón's declaration which bring it closer to Bascuñán's account. Describing
how the Mapuches treated the mestizo children they had with Spanish captives, Falcón declares that "the children they have with said Spanish women
are treated the same as the others they have with their Indian women."[87] This
reveals the Indians's desire to integrate women and their bastard children into
Mapuche society. Moreover, despite his constant allusions to the Indians'
apostasies, dealings with the devil, and instinctive hatred of Christians, Falcón tells of three caciques from the coast of La Imperial who had accepted
Christianity and wished to "turn to our religion" despite being made the object of ridicule by other neighboring caciques. Both authors, one explicitly
and the other implicitly, coincide in assigning blame to the Spanish administration for the prolongation of the war in Arauco and its excesses.

During their captivity both men had occasion to speak to ladino Indians who had suffered harsh treatment during their Spanish captivity when they were forced to work on ranches and in mines. The Indian Ancanamón complains bitterly to Bascuñán about the betrayal and humiliation his people suffered when their women were carried off. Other passages reproduce the dialogue between caciques whose opinion was divided with respect to the behavior of Spaniards. Bascuñán opened his text to these caciques, whom we hear argue and justify themselves with extraordinary restraint.[88] Falcón finishes his declaration by presenting the reasons that he feels led the Indians to rise up against Spanish domination: "being forced to work in the Spanish ranches and being made to pay tribute, being forced to serve Spaniards, that they felt deeply these offenses and these are the grievances the deponent heard them state."[89] This is basically Bascuñán's thesis as well. Nevertheless, Falcón ends his declaration by concluding that the real reason for the Indian wars is "the hatred they bear us" and therefore proposes an offensive strategy to put an end to the Indian menace, "because they will in no way surrender nor give us peace if we do not make war on them with fire and blood."[90]

The Extent and Evolution of Captivity

It is not an easy task to reconstruct the history of captivity in Araucania over the years. The information we have is incomplete. Gabriel Guarda Geywitz has carried out a commendable task in identifying the documents by name, date of capture, and ransom (in the cases when there was a ransom).[91] The list is incomplete, however, and not very helpful for analyzing the phenomenon. He has managed to identify only eight captives before the uprisings of 1598; the chronicles mention hundreds. During the years of open warfare, the number of captives increased, although the official figures and those of various chroniclers vary. In the city of Valdivia, where Juan Falcón was captured, the official figure was 442. In Villarrica the number of captives was larger, possibly owing to the long siege. For the area encompassed by districts close to La Imperial, the chronicler González de Nájera indicates that there were more than 200 captive women. The men were fewer than the women, "because the rest had died in the defense of the cities."[92] Guarda Geywitz is surprised by the great number of mestizo children produced by slavery and wonders about their fate, since frequently these captives, the children of Spanish women, were sold or exchanged to tribes of the interior or on the other side of the

Andes with whom the Indians kept an active trade: "Because there are few captive women who have not been sold many times among them and therefore have had many masters."[93] In the 1614 memorandum to the king, Pedro Cortés proposes to take the necessary measures to "rescue from captivity the more than five hundred women, most of them important women, the daughters and granddaughters of conquistadores."[94] During the revolt of 1655 the figures apparently rose. The number of captives was estimated at 2,000, although other sources reduce the figure to 1,300.[95]

Captivity in this first period must have been a fearful scourge, as is evident in the concern of the administrators of Chile and Peru. One of the principal missions of Governor Alonso García Ramón upon his arrival in Chile in 1605 was the ransoming of captives, using, if necessary, "the royal forces." García Ramón crossed the frontier and headed for the devastated city of La Imperial, determined to accomplish his mission. He organized parleys and proposed to exchange the captives for the many Indian chiefs who were being held prisoner by the Spanish. To his surprise, some of the captive women refused to return. This is a phenomenon which recurs among women in the history of captivity. González de Nájera's description is rich in detail:

> On the one hand were the captive women, and on the other the mothers, daughters, sisters and other female relatives. All urgently applied to the governor presenting their petitions with heartfelt pleas, some alleging that these were their wives, others their sisters, and so on, as I said. Because the prisoners had been asked with what Indians they had been, and the governor sought to give satisfaction to those who merited it most. In these transactions of exchange and ransom, you saw things which moved you to not a little pity. The Indians would go to bring some of the female captives, who, although negotiations for their release had been concluded, did not want to come before our people because they were pregnant. Thus they preferred to remain condemned to perpetual slavery than to suffer such shame in the eyes of their husbands and all present. It did no good to tell them that they were exonerated from all blame because they were subject to violence and force as slaves. Others who had no such impediment, were not allowed to come by their masters, because they wanted them to raise the children they had together, and these women burst into floods of tears and begged them with tender words to accept the ransoms, but were left behind.[96]

It is no easy task to sketch out a sociology of captivity owing to the lack of sources, especially the lack of declarations or captive accounts. The hypothe-

ses would be as diverse as the different personal experiences and the different periods in which they took place. In times of open warfare many captives
were killed shortly after reaching the Indian camps. But in general the prag-
matism of Araucanian society imposed itself, and the Indians learned to integrate captives into their culture. The captives, masters of many agricultural
and cattle-raising skills, were made to work as slaves at these tasks, or in crafts
that the Indians appreciated for their usefulness: blacksmithing, carpentry,
hatmaking,[97] or the manufacture of gunpowder.[98] Women were valued for
their spinning and cooking. The awareness of the captives' commercial value
became widespread when Araucanian tribes began long trips to the other side
of the frontier to seek captives, and also cattle they could sell to the settlements of Araucania and the central valley of Chile. Toward 1647 the troops of
the *veedor general* (inspector general) in the far south ran into large groups of
captives who had been taken to distant southern lands in order to make their
escape impossible.[99]

As we saw above, Bascuñán had a luxurious captivity, so luxurious that he
called it a "cautiverio feliz." The sources we have allow us to conclude that his
experience was the exception, though by no means unique. There were captives who integrated perfectly, who "went native," or even went over to the
other side, choosing life among the Indians as more to their taste. Others lived
as slaves in abject conditions. Several accounts describe the sorry state in
which female captives arrived when they were rescued. There is also mention
of those who could not stand captivity and opted for the risks of escape.

> Doña Juana, the wife of a captain, by the name of Melchor de Herrera, who
> served with us, fled from the land of the enemy and came to a fort which I com-
> manded during the frontier wars. She was so virtuous that in order to return to
> her husband, she faced the greatest dangers and suffering, barefoot and poorly
> dressed, she crossed many rivers and harsh lands, coming from a great dis-
> tance, and with such spirit that I do not know what robust and spirited man
> would outdo her or even suffer what she experienced.[100]

The risks entailed by escaping were enormous, as the accounts of many
captives confirm. Shortly after being captured, Bascuñán had the opportunity
to escape by the shore of the Bío-Bío, when he was separated from his captors
when they were dragged by the violent currents of the river. The Spanish
captive with whom he was walking, Alonso Torres, urged him to take this

opportunity escape with him. Bascuñán hesitated, however, fearful of harsh reprisals if they were captured again. "Their rigor is well known among captives and there are few who will attempt to leave their servitude to these barbarians, at the evident risk of their lives, because all the fugitives they catch, they kill without exception."[101]

One of the curious stories that enrich the collection of captive anecdotes is that of the young Spaniard Juan García Tenorio. He was captured at Fort Paicavi, between Concepción and La Imperial, and spent two years in several Indian settlements. He had the opportunity to flee, and he took it, reaching Santiago after a hard and dangerous flight. In order to avoid being drafted into the army and being sent again to one of the forts on the other side of the frontier, he passed himself off as a Mapuche. He was greatly surprised when a Spanish soldier claimed his services as an *indio encomendado* (a Indian forced to work in mines or farms). The young man's protests and the declaration made in his favor by the chaplain of Fort Paicavi were to no avail. In vain he appealed his sentence of perpetual servitude. Embittered by the experience, after a two-year captivity and a hazardous escape, Juan García Tenorio, according to the chronicler Diego Rosales, "went on to that world ahead."[102] Since there were only two worlds, it is not certain but it can be deduced that García Tenorio returned to his previous captors.

Paleface Indians

It has been amply documented that hunger was the fundamental tool employed by Indians to overcome Christian resistance when besieging their cities. Chroniclers Diego Rosales and González de Nájera mention that when women could not stand the hunger, they went out to get food and were immediately captured, or they sent their children to the Indians rather than see them die of hunger. In the uprising of 1598, the devastation and the number of dead were so great that mothers "sent their maiden daughters to offer themselves to the enemy who was in plain sight, in order to spare them from certain death (their blind love compelled them to do so) believing that because of their beauty (because the Spanish women of that land are extremely beautiful) those barbarians would be satisfied to have them as slaves." Clearly, captivity was preferable to dying of hunger.[103]

The scarcity of food, especially in frontier forts, was also the major reason for desertions among Spanish soldiers. González de Nájera, who served as an officer in Fort Nacimiento on the frontier line, provides ample illustration of this. Captured deserters were executed by the garrote as soon as they were brought back, but the punishment did not keep the number of desertions from multiplying.

> [T]hey find themselves barefoot like Indians, as naked or badly dressed as Indians, working more than Indians, and eating, drinking and sleeping much less than Indians. As their nakedness, work, and hunger encourage them to take stock, they choose to go over to the enemy because they know their lot will be improved living among them.[104]

There are also many stories of deserters who were successful in captivity and rose to positions of power in Mapuche society. They don't fall strictly within the category of captives, since they acted of their own volition. Nevertheless, I include them here because, in many cases, these deserters lived as captives or in small captive communities. Furthermore, the existence of deserters helped to de-dramatize the idea of captivity, which was unimaginable to many contemporaries. Francisco Fris, for example, was a deserter who lived among the Mapuche for many years and was integrated perfectly. In 1645 he nonetheless decided to return of his own free will. He arrived accompanied by several of his wives and the numerous children he had had during captivity. He was forced to return to the Christian faith and to marry one of his wives.

One of the reasons mentioned by the Spanish administration to explain the impenetrability of the Araucanian defensive lines was the great number of fugitives who instructed the Indians and warned them about military strategies. "It is the case that there are among the Indians more than fifty Spanish fugitives who drill, teach and train them in all matters that exceed their capacity. Of these fugitives some are mestizo, some mulatto and others are legitimate Spaniards."[105]

The first known case of desertion to the Indian side is cited by Góngora Marmolejo. He recounts the story of Pedro Calvo, a Spaniard who was arrested for robbery in the Jauja Valley and punished by flogging and by having his ears cut off for being a thief. After his punishment he fled south, where he earned a reputation among the caciques of the Aconcagua Valley after several victories against other Indian groups. When Pedro de Almagro's 1536 expedition reached Chile, the ill-fated Pedro Calvo, now an Indian chief at the head of squadrons of Indians, greeted the Spanish *adelantado* (governor of a border province under Spanish colonial rule).[106] Another well-known case is that of the priest Joan Barba, who fled Fort La Imperial in the company of Gerónimo Bello, who had been accused of living with a woman without being married.[107] The story of Father Barba, told by Diego Rosales, attracted much attention because the renegade priest took part in the assault on the city of Osorno, where he entered all the churches he found and sacked them.

We have previously noted how Bascuñán's account of his captivity dwells on many moments of leisure among the Indians, characterized by an abundance of food, drink, and celebrations. Were Spanish soldiers, posted for long periods of time at badly supplied forts, attracted by the possibility of an easier life? It could be. References to fugitives are so numerous that it is clear they were a chronic problem that Chilean authorities had to sort out.[108]

After the last Araucanian revolt in 1655 and the subsequent peace treaties, frontier relations stabilized considerably. The number of *malocas* in Araucania decreased, although not the number of captives brought from the other side of the Andes by Indian traders. Continued references to *malocas* are possibly due more to fear and imagination than to the persistence of the phenomenon in Chilean lands.[109]

Conclusion

The dividing line of the Bío-Bío River in time became one of the most notorious symbols of continental resistance to the European invasion. The frontier persisted for so long because neither side was able to eliminate the resistance of the other, whether because of the numeric inferiority of the Spanish, the corruption of their administration, or the inability of Araucanian groups to form a united front when required.[110] In any case, the frontier, with its wars, conflicts, and truces, gave birth to a multitude of stories that, as time went by and they became part of the literature, acquired the force of myth. The Spanish, by way of their chroniclers, contributed fundamentally to that mythification, which excused their military ineptitude, while captive accounts repeated tales of Indian cruelty.

Over three centuries, the phenomenon of captivity produced continual changes on the Araucanian frontier, among them a widespread ethnic blend.

A letter Father Arizábalo sent King Philip IV around 1650 already noted this feature, speaking of the masses of mestizos who inhabited the frontier lands.[111] For his part, the Jesuit priest Miguel Olivares, in his 1874 work *Breves noticias de la Provincia de la Compañía de Jesús de Chile, desde que los religiosos entraron en este Reino, que fue el año 1593 hasta los años presentes* (Brief Notice of the Province of the Company of Jesus of Chile, from the Time the Priests Entered This Kingdom, Which Was the Year of 1593 until the Present Time), writes that "the majority of the people in this district of Boroa are mestizos, and also white as Spaniards, because on their father's or their mother's side many descend from the many captives who were taken when the cities were destroyed."[112]

There is no doubt that captives and mestizos played a important role in the transformation of Araucanian culture. The introduction of new methods of work and new crafts—among them agricultural techniques, methods of food preparation, the making of clothes, the construction of houses—led to a deep transformation, almost an acculturation, of the indigenous societies, especially those bordering on the frontier. Much has also been written about Araucanian military resistance to the Spanish invasion. Some have argued that the strength of this resistance was in large part due to Indian adoption of Spanish military tactics: the manufacture of arms (gunpowder) and strategies of attack and defense. In the Araucanian attack on Tucapel, in which the conquistador Pedro de Valdivia fell, the Indians showed the first signs of adaptation and alteration of their conventional strategies. Instead of the massive attacks formerly employed in intertribal conflicts, the Araucanians split into squadrons that attacked consecutively, until, overwhelmed, the Spanish resistance was forced to disperse.[113] Another skill that was rapidly assimilated was horsemanship, thanks to which the Indians were able to move with great speed from one side of the Bío-Bío to the other. They were also able to pass from one side of the Andes to the other and eventually to undertake the great treks to the territory of the pampas and the northern provinces of Argentina. It can be argued that the *huaso*, the Chilean version of the Argentine gaucho, is possibly the most genuine product of the Araucanian frontier and of the mutual influences in the region.

The declarations made by captives were the fundamental material used in the debate about the Indian policy. Those favoring offensive action were spurred by testimonies that spoke of the atrocities committed by the Araucanians against their prisoners. There were more testimonies that told of apostasy, impiety, murder, torture, sexual abuse, and so on, than there were accounts of happy captivity, and this discrepancy skews any attempt at balanced objectivity. Captivity was such an extraordinary phenomenon in colonial Chile that its study is indispensable to an understanding of the history of the frontier, and for three centuries that history was Chile's history.

⊰ THREE ⊱

Captives in the
Río de la Plata Region

Declaration received from the captive Luis Acevedo who has been rescued from the power of the cacique Chapingo. Asked what his name is, who his parents are, and where he was born. He said that his name is Luis Acevedo, his father Serafino, his mother Isidora, his sisters Pascuala and Silveria, a brother Severo and another whose name he does not know. That his father died before he was taken captive. That he does not know if the Indians left his mother at his house. That they also captured his brothers and sisters and that they have been rescued except for the brother whose name he does not know and among the Indians they call him Pulman, who is still in the interior. Asked how he came into the hands of the Indians, where he was captured and what year, he said that he and his brothers were captured near Luján at an estancia they had with a lot of property, that he was, as he explains, about seven or eight years old, and now must be about twenty-four.

—*Declaración*, May 21, 1797

María de la Concepción confined to the house of detention is a Pampa Indian belonging to the *toldería* of Cacique Tomás who died several years ago in the Luján Garrison, that when she was little she was captured there by the Teguelche Indians where she remained until she was found in Patagones that for that reason she is commonly called "the captive." She speaks some words of our language.

—*Declaración*, July 27, 1788

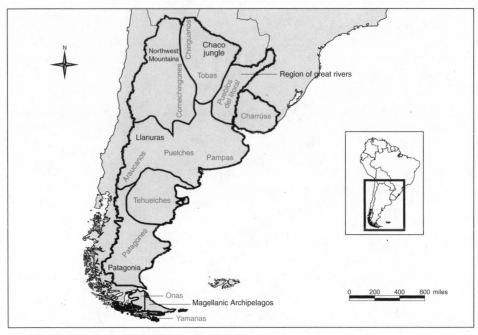

Map 6. Indian Tribes of Argentina

The eighteenth century witnessed profound changes on the pampa frontier and in all the territory extending from the limits of the province of Buenos Aires to the cold lands south of the Negro River. There were different causes for this. On the one hand, there was the ongoing process of Araucanization of the region and the adjacent territories. On the other, there was a parallel movement of criollo expansion from Buenos Aires in search of land suitable for crops and cattle raising. This constrained the area of the frontier and made relations among its inhabitants more problematic.

The process of Araucanization also spread irregularly by means of the rapid and violent attacks of the tribes. These attacks, which were known as *malocas* in Chile and *malones* in the Argentine pampas, were directed at the settlements and cattle ranches beyond the Andes. Livestock and captives were the principal objects of these swift incursions.

In the region of Buenos Aires and the pampas, as well as north of that territory toward Cuyo and south to Patagonia, captivity was a social, economic, and political phenomenon of extraordinary proportions whose impact gradually shaped evolving frontier relationships.[1] Although the role of livestock in the province of Buenos Aires is beginning to be understood thanks to important studies, little or nothing is known about captives.[2] Who were they? What was their lot once they reached the *toldos* (tents)? Did they manage to integrate? What role did they play in frontier society? How did they adapt once they were liberated? This chapter seeks to answer some of these questions and to establish a foundation for constructing a history of captivity in the Río de la Plata region.

The Araucanization of the Pampas

The Araucanization of the pampas was a gradual movement that began at the end of the seventeenth century. The series of political and social changes in Araucania, studied in the previous chapter, and the lure of rich lands on the other side of the Andes encouraged the progressive transfer of Mapuche tribes and their Pehuenche and Huilliche relatives from the foothills of the mountain range to the flatlands east of the Andes. The Araucanians had not only defended themselves well during the centuries of Inca and later Spanish invasions but had also adopted the military tactics of their enemies. They developed solid tribal lineages that in the eighteenth century extended their dominion to the deserts of the south, the lands to the north, from Cuyo up to the humid pampas and Patagonia.

This process, which began toward the end of the seventeenth century, was consolidated during the eighteenth. Its major expansion was in the nineteenth century when the great Mapuche chief Calfucurá settled in the Salinas Grandes and established the first Indian confederation. This confederation dominated frontier relations for the rest of the century.[3] Araucanization was felt in all aspects of intertribal relations: the seasonal movement of herds to winter or summer pastures; the Indians' adaptation to tents made of skin, which replaced the heavier *rucas* or traditional huts; their increased use of textiles instead of guanaco skins; the introduction of Mapuche crafts and agricultural methods; and finally increased trade with the criollo population.[4] By 1740 the Araucanians were permanently established in the pampas, and Araucanian (*Mapudungun*) was the lingua franca used in trade by most of the tribes that traversed this vast territory.[5] Under the impact of the Araucanians, the existing tribes of the pampas, or those that evolved from the fusion that took place, acquired a cultural unity and an organizational dynamism that they had previously lacked.[6]

As long as there was an abundance of wild cattle, the arrival of tribes from the other side of the mountain range did not constitute a great economic problem. But when increased demand affected the number of existing cattle, the human groups living in proximity to this wealth of livestock entered into conflict. The expansion of hunting parties on the eastern slopes gradually constrained the wild cattle at a time when Buenos Aires was considering the need to expand its sphere of action, fencing lands that had previously remained open. The decrease of wild cattle and the expansion of the ranches, promoted by the government after independence, worsened the situation and drove Indians to search for livestock on the estancias. The final stage of Araucanization (1830–79) is associated with the rise of Cacique Calfucurá. In 1875 his son and successor, Namuncurá, organized sizable invasions of several frontier settlements which resulted in many deaths, numerous captives, and the massive taking of cattle.[7] This long and difficult frontier conflict came to an end with the expeditions of Generals Adolfo Alsina in 1877 and Julio Argentino Roca between 1878 and 1879. The triumphantly dubbed "Conquest of the Desert" effectively brought to an end the Indian menace. What remained was its cultural impact.[8]

Frontier Conflict

One of the primary objectives of Indian attacks on the criollo-Spanish settlements and estancias was to capture women and children. This was a recurrent practice in periods of greatest conflict. Travelers in the interior, the increasingly frequent military and scientific expeditions, and the declarations of captives who had been liberated or escaped bore witness to the existence of large groups of captives in Indian camps. In effect, cattle and captives were the valuable spoils through which frontier tribes negotiated their antagonistic relationship with criollo society. In the years of greatest conflict (1737–85 and 1858–73),[9] there was not a single family among the inhabitants of the rural frontier areas unaffected by the *malones*. The first antecedents of these raids are found in the seventeenth century. In 1606 there is notice of an Indian raid on the scattered settlements of the province of Mendoza provoked by the mistreatment of Indians.[10] Years later, in 1620, a message from the governor of

Chile to the *corregidor* (mayor) of Cuyo announced that "he had notice from the army that Indians on the warpath had formed two large groups to attack certain Spanish settlements and that the Indians are on the other side of the mountain range making *malocas*."[11] In 1658 the governor of Chile reports a movement of Mapuche Indians whose object is to steal cattle and take captives on the eastern slope of the Andes.[12] *Malones* became more frequent after the middle of the eighteenth century. In 1740, in the region of Magdalena, the hosts of the Pampa chief Cangapol o Bravo carried out a sudden raid in which they killed some two hundred settlers and withdrew with many captives and some twenty thousand head of cattle.[13] Such raids were carried out not only by Araucanian and Pampa Indians. That same year, 1740, Father Lozano, a Jesuit missionary in Paraguay, in a letter addressed to the general of the Jesuits in that province, told of the continuous attacks on the missions by "barbarous Indians." He mentioned Abipón, Mocoví, Charrúa, Toba, and Chiriguano Indians who had killed Spaniards and hung their corpses near the cities. He also referred to numerous captives and cattle stolen in these raids.[14]

Taking captives was not exclusively an activity of Chilean Indians. Tribes in the Chaco and north of the Chaco had practiced it since time immemorial. Chiriguanos, as well as Tobas, Chanes, and Matacos, took captives from other tribes and peoples and continued to do so until the end of the nineteenth century. Some captives were used as slaves, others were sacrificed and devoured as part of the man-eating tradition of Tupi-Guaraní tribes. The last Chiriguano uprisings in the northern Chaco date from 1875 and 1892.[15]

Missions, forts, and garrisons, mining towns and ranches, were the traditional institutions of Spanish territorial expansion on the continent and were used as instruments of pacification and control. The choice in the use of these vanguard institutions depended on the characteristics of the terrain and the level of resistance of the native peoples. In the northern zones of the Chaco and the government of Paraguay, the Jesuit missions had offered an almost ideal solution for the pacification of the disperse Tupi-Guaraní tribes. In the decade of the 1740s, the town of Nuestra Señora de la Concepción was founded on the banks of the Río Salado. This was the first Jesuit *reducción* (a mission where Indians lived and worked under the authority and protection of a religious order) north of Buenos Aires.[16] On the other hand, the estancia, like the ranch in northern Mexico, was the civilizing institution used for the flatlands. Nevertheless, the growing hostility and number of Indian invasions from the south and the east required a complete restructuring of defensive strategies. To this purpose a chain of frontier forts was constructed, not far from the settlements, in order to ease their isolation and facilitate their supply. The militarization of the pampas was the inevitable result. The foundation of the first frontier fort of Arrecifes in 1736 was followed by a series of Indian invasions targeting the frontier settlements of Fontezuelas, Luján, and Matanza.[17]

The traditional Spanish answer to Indian raids was the formation of military punitive expeditions, despite their dubious success. The colonial authorities tried to alleviate the problem through diplomacy. In 1778 the first expedition was sent to Sierra de la Ventana to negotiate a peace treaty with Indian chiefs in exchange for their control of the great salt deposits of Salinas Grandes. After the establishment of the viceroyalty of the Río de la Plata in 1776, the policy of the Bourbon monarchy, in its search for unity of ideology and purpose, was to negotiate in order to eliminate the threat of hostile and aggressive elements.[18] At the same time, a chain of forts was built near frontier settlements.

By 1781 colonial authorities had reinforced the frontier through the renovation of a line of forts along the Río Salado which the Viceroy Vértiz called "the frontier line of civilization."[19] This line of forts was intended to protect the varied rural frontier population: pioneer settlers, farmers, ranchers, and soldiers, but also other less orderly members of the frontier: vagabonds, deserters from either side, escaped convicts, gauchos, and poachers. The fort-building strategy had some positive results. There was an increase in trade with the Indians, who from time to time approached the frontier settlements of the province with their woven goods, bolas, feathers, and lassos.

Nevertheless, the unstable situation persisted owing to demographic pressures on either side of the frontier, whose inhabitants were competing for the same resources: land and cattle. The so-called defensive policy of Spanish authorities was in truth a long-term offensive strategy dressed in sheep's clothing. It advanced slowly with the establishment of forts; the mobilization of militias; the creation of a specific frontier corps of gaucho cavalry, *los blandengues*,[20] founded in 1751; and the organization of the war department (*ramo de guerra*) in order to finance the costs of defense against the Indians.[21] The frontier, which in practice had been open up to this period, now became a militarized zone.

Malones

From the first decades of the eighteenth century until well into the nineteenth, great *malones* fell on the Buenos Aires corridor, laying waste its frontier settlements. Their principal objective was to steal livestock for consumption and for resale to Chilean and Patagonian tribes, and to take an additional booty in captives. The *malones* were not a continuous phenomenon. The numbers varied according to periods of greater or lesser conflict until the final stages of the desert campaign carried out by Generals Adolfo Alsina and Julio Argentino Roca put an end to them.[22]

Malones were the greatest menace of the frontier. Their fame had expanded, creating legends of terror about the Indians of *tierra adentro* (the hinterland). The *malón* caused an atavistic fear among the frontier settlers and the soldiers who guarded the forts. *Tierra adentro* was the name given to the extensive territory of the pampas and Patagonia inhabited by Indians and traversed seasonally by nomadic tribes. The term came into use early in the first expeditions south of the Río Colorado to Patagonia. Properly speaking, "the hinterland" did not denote the frontier but the unknown territory beyond it. As Martínez Sarasola has remarked: "The frontier and the hinterland are two distinct spaces confused in the same cultural energy. Beyond what they tell us of the indigenous population and its identity, these spaces show us the existential disorder of a unique daily life."[23]

Malones were both part of a longstanding tribal ritual and a form of guerrilla warfare that kept white settlements in a state of uncertainty and insecurity. For Indians, the *malón* had traditionally been a type of reprisal and a ritual way to obtain a wife. The traditional ceremonial abduction, with or without the consent of all parties involved, could be peaceful or involve some violence and bloodshed. The *malón* also implied a kind of reparation or vengeance. It was understood that any harm would receive double or quadruple retribution.[24] The people of the pampas brought the same attitude to their relationship with the *huinca* (Christians), whose original aggression had deprived them of grazing lands and threatened their traditional way of life.

Some *malones* were sudden attacks carried out by a few warriors equipped with traditional weapons (bolas and spears), and they were limited to the stealing of livestock and property. If the attackers encountered resistance, there could be bloodshed. On other occasions, the *malón* was the effort of

A group of Tehuelche Indians, from the region known as "tierra adentro." Drawing
by Bayot. From the book *Voyage au Pole Sud et dans l'Oceanie sur les corvettes*,
by J. C. Dumont-d'Urville (1846).

several tribes, even from different ethnic groups. Thousands would take
part, including women and youths, great numbers of horses, and auxiliary
personnel who were charged with taking victims from the field and trans-
porting the booty. In Buenos Aires *malones* had been known since the beginning of the seventeenth century. In 1606 a ruling of the *cabildo* or town
council of Buenos Aires specifically set aside wild cattle for the ransom of
captives.[25] In 1636 edicts were made to prevent the thefts carried out by
Indians in the haciendas which by then dotted the Buenos Aires countryside.[26] But it is from 1737 to 1785 that one can observe a substantial increase
in Indian raids.

Although the product of an organized and directed strategy, the execution
of a *malón* entailed solving a great number of unforeseen problems, which
called for improvisation. This factor contributed to the feeling of disorien-
tation and chaos that seemed to go with them. *Malones* began with night
marches preceded by scouting parties of Indians called *bomberos* (firemen).[27]
The *bomberos* sent back detailed information about the lay of the land and

activity in white settlements by using *chasquis* (runners) or smoke and fire signals. They traveled on horseback at night, resting during the day and taking care not to spook the wild cattle. Attack came simultaneously on several fronts, with a feint on one front and the final blow on another, to confuse defenders. The final attack consisted of skirmishes by Indian riders who stampeded the extra cattle. All of this was punctuated by a great deal of shouting, which further confused victims. The attackers took as many goods as they could carry, as well as women and children. The men they killed on the spot. Besides the horses themselves, which the Indians handled with great skill, the weapons they used were spears, knives, bolas, and the *bola perdida* (a single ball attached to a leather thong).[28] Not until 1830 did some tribes begin to gradually adopt the use of firearms. These they acquired in Chile, where most of the booty of the raids wound up.[29]

Blas Pedrosa, a Spaniard from La Coruña, was captured by Pampa Indians in 1776. He escaped ten years later. His declaration contains a vivid account of a *malón*.

> That he cannot say for certain how many Indians participated in these invasions because the number varied according to the occasions, that sometimes there were five hundred men, at other times seven hundred, and sometimes up to two thousand. That they carry out their raids, from what he has heard the Indians say, since he affirms that he has never accompanied them on a raid, at daybreak with a scouting party in the vanguard. That the center is made up of warriors in formation, and the vanguard are boys, who are in charge of the horses. Once the scouting party has gathered information about the lay of the land and the advantages it offers, it returns to inform the one who acts as the head of the raid and he orders the boys and the horses forward so that they can begin herding the livestock. The warriors, deployed in wings, take captives and whatever is useful. If the people are not useful because of their great age, or because they are weak, they kill them, reserving only the young boys whom they use for breaking horses and for carrying water and firewood.[30]

Retreats were effected at full speed, changing horses frequently. The principal booty (captives, goods, and horses) went first; behind came the scattered cattle. As they retreated, they set fields on fire in order to hinder pursuit. No time was wasted in eating, or in any distraction that would delay their return. Blas Pedrosa continues his declaration with a description of the retreat:

[W]hen they retreat they do not go the way they came. They advance at a distance of half a league taking care to reconnoiter the terrain ahead and to their flanks; the boys, the horses and booty, follow the scouts with the captives, accompanied by a few warriors and the rearguard is covered by the remaining small groups until they reach their camp.[31]

Nicolás Romero, in a declaration taken by the Guardia del Monte, January 15, 1781, says that when he was taken captive "it took six days to get to the Monte de los Algarrobos beyond the Salinas."[32] María Paula Santana declares, in December of 1781, that immediately after the attack on the hacienda where she was taken captive, "they set fire to the fields, driving the captives and what little booty they had, and at a trot and gallop they reached another lake where that night they changed horses and traveled all the following day."[33] The bands of Indians spread out gradually in search of their camps or trade routes. María Paula's description is very precise on this aspect:

After four and a half days they reached the mountains, always traveling at a trot or a gallop, never lighting a fire until then, even at night because whenever they stopped they had the horses hobbled. When they reached the mountains they spread out in different directions, and the ones who took her and her younger daughter (because since the day of the attack she never saw her married daughter again, that she asked some of them about her, and some told her that she had escaped with her goods and others said that the Christians had taken her away) traveled another five days always at a trot or gallop until they reached the bank of a stream, where there was a camp of about thirteen or fourteen *toldos*. There they spent eight days and following the bank of the stream they made other stops, always taking their *toldos* [. . .]. At the last stop they received news that the main body of Indians was returning with booty and livestock; and the *china ladina* [a Spanish-speaking Indian woman] advised her and urged her to flee to Buenos Aires because otherwise when the rest of the Indians arrived they would sell her farther inland.[34]

In general, Indians avoided confrontations with troops. If they had no choice, however, they dispersed in small bands and attacked alternately, reuniting afterward in order to offer resistance.

Captives were apportioned according to the number of horses that each Indian brought to the *malón*. Chiefs or captains, who had contributed many horses and their Indian dependents, kept the larger portion of the captives.

Many of the captives were quickly bartered for food at Christian stores or sold to tribes in the hinterland. They were taken to the frontier camps in the south or to the other side of the mountain range, into Chilean territory. Horses in particular went into Chile, since they were much valued by the Mapuches.

The pillaging during a *malón* was the fundamental commercial activity of the Pampa tribes. Their economy depended on these raids. The ransom of captives was such a common commercial practice that it helped establish relations between the tribes and criollo society. Kristine Jones argues that although they were hard on the settlers, Indian raids were not intrinsically harmful, since they presented new trade opportunities for the different groups involved.[35]

Thanks in part to the *malones,* the tribes and factions had adopted a more complex military organization within an increasingly hierarchical social structure. This stratification led to the appearance of *cacicazgos* (chieftainships) and large territorial political units. Noteworthy are the great chieftainships of Calfucurá and his son Namuncurá among the Mapuche, Yanquetruz and Painé among the Ranqueles (a coalition of Mapuches and Pehuenches), Mariano Rondeau among the Voroganos (bands of Mapuches and Pampa Indians), and Cacique Catriel of the Pampa Indians.[36] Meanwhile, the increasingly warlike tribes developed a more segmented hierarchy made up of caciques, *caciques segundos* (secondary chiefs), *caciquillos* (little chiefs), *capitanejos* (little captains), and *indios de lanza* (lance carrying warriors).

The participation of captives in *malones* was not infrequent, although it depended on their degree of integration and the favor of the caciques. Most often they were left behind in the camps because it was feared that they would attempt to escape when they came near the frontier. However, when captives showed they had adapted to the Indian life, they were included in *malones* as members of the lance corps.[37]

A Portrait of the Captives

The practice of taking captives affected many aspects of Río de la Plata society in this period, but more than a military or economic problem, captivity was the barometer of a growing frontier problem.

There are several sources for studying this subject: (1) declarations of captives taken shortly after they crossed the frontier and came in contact with military authorities, usually the commandant or *capitán de fronteras* (frontier captain); (2) the account made of captives liberated during Governor Juan Manuel Rosas's 1829 *Expedición del desierto* (Expedition of the Desert), and (3) references to captives in the diaries of the military and scientific expeditions sponsored by the government.

Captives' declarations are unpublished documents dated between 1752 and 1803. They are preserved in the historical archives in Buenos Aires and other Argentine cities. I have found no declarations made after 1803. Either the practice of taking declarations was discontinued owing to lack of interest, or they have not survived. In most cases these documents were written immediately upon the arrival of liberated or escaped captives at frontier outposts. Their format is a series of questions about the age of the person making the declaration, the date and place of captivity, the names of the tribes and caciques, the ethnic groups, the existence of other captives, and plans for future invasions. These declarations were affected by the haste in which they were made. In general, they are succinct and not very eloquent. Unfortunately, they were not written with the intention of describing the experience of the captives.

After analyzing these documents, I conclude that generally captives were not interested in narrating their experiences during captivity. They do so reluctantly, forced by circumstances, revealing only what the interrogation elicits. Maybe they were ashamed of their situation and felt manipulated by frontier authorities. Perhaps captivity had become such a common occurrence that it no longer attracted attention. This does not mean that criollo society was uninterested in the problem. It is clear that any project of territorial expansion had to deal with the existence of the *toldos* and *malones*. Captives' accounts were of interest insofar as they provided information about the movement of tribes and their possible invasion plans. The human dimension was secondary.[38]

Most captives were born on the frontier and had grown up in constant direct contact with indigenous populations. In general, captives belonged to the lower strata of society, and primarily of rural society. They were slaves or servants on the estancias and *chacras* (small farms). They were farmhands, rural workers, mule drivers, or travelers, and most of them were illiterate. They were the marginal settlers of criollo society. Santiago Avendaño, a captive for seven years, writes that captives came generally from the poor among the settlers in the countryside. "There was a large number of captives of all ages, but as a rule they were the wretched of the frontier, people who had little contact with urban centers, as stupid almost as the Indians themselves."[39] The declarations we have were taken down by frontier commandants or officials assigned to this task. Once finished, the declarations were read back to the deponents so that they would ratify the content and sign them. Almost all deponents signed with a cross, to which was appended the following note: "The deponent does not know how to sign and signed with a cross."

Few are the declarations that reveal some eloquence or the ability to articulate the dimensions of the experience of captivity. One of the exceptions is the declaration of the Spaniard Blas Pedrosa, a clerk, who came to Buenos Aires in 1776 seeking a career in trade. He was the protégé of a Chilean cleric and decided to accompany him on a trip from Buenos Aires to Chile. "In the vicinity of Córdoba they were ambushed by a group of Indians in the passage known as Ruy Díaz and although all the members of the wagon train sought to defend themselves as much as possible, they killed said clergyman together with forty others and wounded the deponent in the back."[40] They left him for dead, but later they took him, along with two other survivors who were black slaves of the priest. "The caciques Anzemán and Canevayan took me captive to their *tolderías* [Indian villages or camps], which at that time were in the salt marshes of the Theraco and about a thousand Indians were there."[41]

Why did the Indians take the two black slaves and kill the rest of the travelers? What were their criteria for selection? Age, physical strength? Was it a question of racial preference? Sebastián González was a mulatto married to a Pampa Indian woman. Indians killed his companions but left him alive.[42] Juan Mateo was a black slave belonging to Captain Carlos Tadeo Romero.[43] He was taken captive while he was performing chores on his master's estancia. The black man Antonio was fifteen years old when he was taken (1777) and had been a captive for two years when he decided to escape.[44] Rafael Soto declares that he was taken captive by the Pehuenches, as were an Indian, a black slave, a mulatto, and a *tape* (meaning dirty or miserable) Indian; the rest were killed. Other captives claim to be ladino (Spanish-speaking) Indians or to belong to other Indian nations. The human composition of the *toldos*, as described by numerous travelers, was a kaleidoscope of races in a constant process of acculturation and assimilation. I have not found, in any of the references I consulted, any information to support the thesis that Indians discriminated racially in choosing captives.

The Indians did have preferences with regard to age and sex. In 1832 Juan Manuel de Rosas, shortly after his first governorship of Buenos Aires, carried out a large military expedition for the purpose of negotiating with the Indians over the distribution of disputed lands. In that expedition, 634 captives were liberated from the Indians. The information pertaining to these captives was compiled in the *Relación de los cristianos salvados del cautiverio por la División Izquierda del Ejército Expedicionario contra los bárbaros al mando del Señor Brigadier General D. Juan Manuel de Rosas* (The Account of the Christians Saved from Captivity by the Left Division of the Expeditionary Army against the Barbarians under the Command of Brigadier General Don Juan Manuel de Rosas), a document published in Buenos Aires by the state press in 1835.[45] This account contains information about the 634 freed captives, not counting the 63 children born in captivity.

These data are of great value for reconstructing a demography of captivity. The freed captives were subjected to an interrogation based on a standard questionnaire that asked for name, age, family background, distinguishing physical characteristics, years of captivity, whether they spoke Spanish, and other pertinent facts that would facilitate the captives' identification. They were not asked their opinions nor were they asked about personal aspects of their captivity.[46] Most of them, over 600, came from Pampa, Tehuelche, and Araucanian tribes. Some were liberated in the course of military operations, others in the negotiations carried out by Rosas with caciques of friendly tribes. Upon their return, they were turned over to justices of the peace who tried to locate their relatives. An indeterminate number of ex-captives were returned to their families.[47] Others were assigned to charitable organizations, or were sent to Jesuit *reducciones,* or were handed over to criollo families as servants. The reintegration of captives was a thorny problem, which I will address later.

The exact number of captives recovered in the expedition was 707, of which 389 were women, 245 men, and 63 children born in captivity. That is to say, 61.36 percent of those liberated were women. If one considers their ages, the numbers are more significant. The average age of the women was 21.26 years, while that of the men was 13.07. The majority of male captives were

Tehuelche Indians wearing guanaco skins.

children or had only reached puberty. Many could not remember how old they were when they were captured. Exactly 62.7 percent of the men were unable to furnish this information. About those who did remember their age at the time of their capture, we have the following information: 69 were less than 9 years old; 19 were between 10 and 19 years old; 2 were between 20 and 29 years old; and only 1 was older than 40 years old. On the other hand, 63 percent of the women could estimate their age at the time of capture. For them we have the following data: 88 were captured when they were less than 9 years old; 63 between 10 and 19 years old; 40 between 20 and 29 years old; 39 between 30 and 40 years old; and only 5 women were older than 40.[48]

These figures coincide roughly with those in most references I consulted, including declarations by captives, the accounts of travelers who visited the *toldos,* and reports on the liberation of captives at different dates. In 1764 the outgoing governor of Tucumán made reference to thirty-three incursions carried out by Spaniards in the zone of the Chaco, which resulted in the liberation of "20 Christian men and 240 women and children."[49] In his expedition to the Sierra de la Ventana in 1821, Colonel Pedro Andrés García visited different Indian *toldos.* He writes: "We found 10 captives, six young males, and four white women."[50]

Female Captives

Women were the preferred booty of *malones.* Indians were interested in taking young women and children, while men and the elderly were usually discarded, killed, or abandoned. In March 1780 an invasion took place in the jurisdiction of Córdoba, near the Cuarto River, during which Indians carried off forty women and killed many men.[51] Manuel García was a youth when he was taken, together with his boss and his wife, Petrona. His boss was killed right there.[52] Juan Luis Bariola was fifteen when he was taken captive, together with his mother, grandfather, and grandmother. His grandfather was set free and his grandmother was allowed to escape. Bariola explains that the Indians saw that she was escaping but did nothing to pursue her. His father, who managed to escape when he sensed the approaching *malón,* came back the next day and traded *aguardiente* (brandy) for Bariola's mother. Bariola himself was taken to the *toldos,* where he saw many captive women.[53]

Most sources I consulted noted the existence in the *toldos* of communities of female captives who lived together and spoke in Spanish. Many captives say they spoke Spanish during captivity or even that they learned it from groups of female captives. In his 1806 expedition to explore possible routes between Buenos Aires and Chile, Captain Luis de la Cruz met the ex-captive Petronila Pérez, who had lived since she was a girl with the Pehuenche Indians and had married Cacique Carrilón. When the Spanish captain was surprised that she spoke Spanish so fluently, Petronila answered: "I dealt with other female captives who taught me to speak like them."[54] It is clear from the accounts of many females captives that they were conscious of their cultural and linguistic differences from their captors. Nevertheless, there is no reference to the women acting as *lenguaraces* (interpreters). This task was reserved for men and was an occupation held in esteem by caciques.

If captives were prized as labor and as valuable commodities in the trade among tribes and with Christians, female captives were doubly valued because they could also be wives and mothers. The Araucanized tribes of the pampas were highly hierarchical, and social differences were marked by two closely related factors, wealth and military power.[55] Women were property and a mark of power and status. Although polygamy was an accepted practice, only caciques and *capitanejos* could afford the luxury of supporting more than one wife.[56] Concentration of power was one of the distinctive features of the Araucanization of the Pampa which in time led to the great nineteenth-century *cacicazgos* previously mentioned. For many lower-status Indians, without the means to buy a wife, capturing a white woman was a way of obtaining a spouse without paying the price of a bride.

Female captives also carried out a series of important tasks within the tribal economy. In the gender division of labor among Pampa societies, besides the domestic work of child care and cooking, women also had to construct *toldos,* pitch them, take them down, and keep them in good repair. They were also employed in the herding and care of livestock, tanning of hides, extraction of grease, and the manufacture of feather, wood, and bone objects and of textiles.[57] One must also add the role that white female captives played in the improvement of the diet. The diet of the Pampa tribes consisted fundamentally of beef, horsemeat, lamb, and yerba maté, when there was any. González Arili maintains that the diet of the Indians was complemented by "white female captives who spread their culinary art among the Araucanian *toldos.*"[58]

One aspect that is difficult to study is sexual relations and the Indian preference, if it existed, for white women. Although Kristine J. Jones asserts that "Araucanians believed that white captives were endowed with a special erotic talent lacking in Araucanian women,"[59] I have not found references to support this statement. While it is true that some important caciques had white captives among their wives, the alleged sexual attraction of white captives has its origin in fiction. It is through firmly established legends like that of Lucía Miranda (discussed in chap. 7), which appeared first in the chronicle *La Argentina* (1612), that this belief gained currency.

Female captives were taken to the *toldos* as slaves and concubines. They were expected to fulfill a series of vital roles in the indigenous economy, among them sexual reproduction. Their lot depended on unpredictable factors, such as marriage to a principal Indian, their favorable or unfavorable reception among the Indian women, or the wealth or scarcity of resources of the group to which they were taken. We know that there were many important caciques who had among their wives white captives who were the object of special deference. The Ranquel cacique Painé was married to the Cordobesa María and considered her among his favorites until his death.[60] Several important caciques were sons of chiefs by white captives, for example, Ramón Platero, famous cacique of the Tantum of Panghitruz Guor, and the Ranquel cacique Baigorrita, grandson of Yanquetruz.[61] The powerful Araucanian cacique Calfucurá, creator of the first panindigenous confederation of the pampas, had dozens of white captives among his concubines. González Arili maintains that, at the beginning of the nineteenth century, the great abundance of sons and daughters of captives resulted in a mestizo population in the *toldos* that outnumbered the aborigines.[62] This is almost certainly an exaggeration, but it indicates the great process of miscegenation taking place among the aboriginal population and the great dimension of the captivity phenomenon.

It was not infrequent for captives to change owners several times. María de la Concepción lived in the *toldería* of cacique Tomás until he died. Later she was taken to Patagonia by Tehuelche Indians, which is why the Indians "commonly called her 'the captive.'"[63] It is not clear whether María de la Concepción was a white captive or a captive pampean Indian from another tribe. At the first *toldo* where she was taken, María Paula Santana was advised by an Indian woman who spoke Spanish to try to escape as soon as possible because soon "they would sell her inland," possibly to southern tribes of the foothills of the Andes, from where it would be impossible to escape.[64]

Life in Captivity

It is no easy task to generalize about the treatment of captives in the *tolderías*, since references to both good and bad treatment abound. Andrés was taken by Toba Indians from the estancia of Santos Cornejo on the Chaco frontier. He was held captive for a year and a half. In his declaration of 1804 he says "that twice they wanted to kill him and would have done so the last time if the *chinas* [the Indian women] had not defended him, for he was treated badly and suffered much hunger."[65] Juan Joseph González was taken captive as a child. At the time of his declaration, December 16, 1788, he said that "he does not know his age, but he must be about 22." While living at the *toldos* he fell ill. His cacique must have been very worried about him because he took him to a Christian hospital in Patagones so that he would receive the care he needed. Once he was released from the hospital, the rumor spread that he was planning to escape with his fellow captive Bernardo Rojas, and both were punished. This induced them to escape and cross the frontier.[66]

There are also numerous references that suggest that there was an affectionate relationship between captives and captors. The youth Avendaño decided to escape in the autumn of 1849, although he had been planning to do so for a long time, principally because of his contact with other captives and *capitanejos criollos* who frequented the *toldos* as allies of the Indians. In his account, written several years after his escape, he includes many passages in which he mentions "the paternal affection" with which he was treated and his adoptive father's many expressions of love. "Caniú-Calquín esteemed me and treated me well. He spoke of the hope he placed in me. In moments of familiarity my adoptive father would say, and not just one time: —Son, you will be great man. When you are grown, you will have us in the palm of your hand. Our fate will depend on you."[67]

There are also repeated cases of female captives who refused to return when they had a chance. The report of Bartolomé Aráoz of February 17, 1749, given in the city of Jujuy, illustrates the difficulties in rescuing female captives, as well as the resistance offered by ex-captives on the reservations and in the charitable institutions where they were taken after their rescue. He writes:

> The male and female captives entrusted to me were eight and a little boy a few months old, son of an Avipón Indian and a captive whom I have brought under guard because they tried to escape. Another time I brought others and thus by guile I will tear them all away because it is incredible the resistance they put up about leaving. This is more on the part of the captives than the Indians. Against the will of the captives, the Indians hand them over to me, searching for them in the hills where they hide and it is for this reason that I have not brought many others and I left Alayquin in charge of bringing them all to the *reducción*.[68]

Aráoz also indicates the problems they faced when they tried to convert Indians, and he blames the captives as the chief obstacle in this endeavor. Luis de la Cruz relates in his *Diary and Report* of 1806 the story of Petronila Pérez, a captive of the Pehuenches and married first to the Indian Carrilón, and upon his death to his brother Mariñán. This Spanish official interviewed her in the *toldos* and offered to ransom her, bribing her with gifts. Petronila refused. She said she had been in contact over the years with Spaniards who came to the nearby salt flats and offered to rescue her. Her firm reply serves as a model of the attitude of many captives who were married, had children, and were used to the life of the *toldos:* "I didn't want to leave because I love my children very much."[69]

One of the most intriguing captivity stories is that of Juana María Sánchez, who in December of 1777 was being held under house arrest together with her fifteen-year-old daughter, accused of having tried to go over to the Indians with her husband and a criollo boy. As a child, Juana María had been abducted by Indians. "Having been taken captive by the Pampas when she was two or four years old, she was raised among them where she joined with an Indian with whom she had nine children."[70] At a certain point in their lives, and for reasons not specified in the declaration, the family decided to return among Christians. "Given religious instruction in the camp of San Francisco, they were baptized in due course, and were legitimately married."[71] Time passed, and for reasons that are also not made clear, the family decided to return to the *toldos.* They were apprehended as they tried to cross the frontier on their way back "to infidelity" accompanied by a young ex-captive. Juana declares that the captive persuaded them, but that the main reason was that she wanted to return to find another daughter she had from a previous marriage. The mother and daughter were kept under house arrest, the father and one son were jailed; the other children were parceled out. After five months they were transferred to the convent of San Francisco "because they have given signs of being good Christians."

The story of Juana María Sánchez and her family reaffirms the existence of an ample zone traveled by persons who were familiar with frontier culture. The frontier culture with one foot in criollo society and another in the society of the *toldos* was shaped by a web of interrelations. This culture of forts, *pulperías* (trading posts), and other meeting points made it possible for a Pampa family to seek a place in criollo society only to change its mind later and decide that it was better to continue to live in the *toldos.* Clearly the two worlds were not as isolated as certain (particularly Argentine) historians of the frontier have maintained.

The versions of captivity and captives that emerge from the accounts of military and other officials in charge of negotiating or reconnoitering expeditions to Indian lands are very revealing. In the diary of his travels to Tehuelche territory in 1770, Captain Juan Antonio Hernández writes: "Each one has the women he can buy, and when he gets bored of them sells them to others, and if they take female captives, when they reach the *toldos* they marry them, and if said captives, even if they are Indian, go unwillingly, they spear them and throw them from the horses, and even if they are only half-dead, they leave them."[72] Comandante Pedro Andrés García, who later carried out important expeditions to the interior at the behest of the government, expressed similar opinions with respect to the situation of female captives.

> Apparently, she, as well as her companions in disgrace, were of good family, and certainly brought up to a very different life. How difficult, how painful it was for us to be cold spectators of the misfortunes of these wretches, victims of misery, without being able to run to their aid! They begged us several times to secure their freedom legally by means of a pact with the caciques, their masters, and to take them away from that harsh slavery, but despite the repeated efforts of the commission to effect that business, the results were none or insignificant.[73]

Alfred Ebélot was a French engineer who traveled to the pampas on a commission from the government of Avellaneda to survey a line of defensive trenches along the frontier. To that purpose he traveled extensively in the territory, and even accompanied Adolfo Alsina in 1875 on the first Campaign of the Desert. He favored an offensive war in order to solve the Indian question, which was so debated in his day.[74] He saw captives as victims of the unredeemed savagery of the Indians and held that captivity was an unnecessary evil which it would be easy to eliminate. On occasion he wrote interesting passages about the frontier, while at other times he fell into coarse generalizations.[75]

Colonel Lucio V. Mansilla was a perfect representative of the Buenos Aires society of his time and its contradictions regarding the Indian question. Commissioned by the government, in 1870 he undertook an eighteen-day trip to the Ranquel *tolderías* with the object of negotiating a solution to the problem of the frontier. He was aware of the historical nature of his mission and of the inevitable triumph of civilization. "I have already told you that the barbarians respect Christians, recognizing their moral superiority, although as Indians they like to live the *dolce far niente,* to have the greatest number of women, as many as they can support."[76] On his expedition he talked to caciques and many captives in the *toldos.* His commentaries fluctuate according to his mood at the moment, since at each *toldo* he encountered a different situation.

At one point on the trip, when he was a guest in the *toldo* of the Ranquel cacique Mariano Rosas, he comments:

> The female captives were the servants. Some were dressed like Indians and were painted like them. Others hid their nakedness in rags and dirty dresses. How these poor women looked at me! What badly dissimulated resignation their faces betrayed! The one who seemed most at ease was the nurse of Mariano's youngest daughter: she had been raised in the house of Juan Manuel Rosas. She was captured in Mulitas, in the famous invasion of the Indian Cristo.[77]

On another occasion, as a guest of Cacique Epumer, he once more came in contact with the female captives of the *toldo*.

> Epumer introduced me to his wife, whose name was Quintuiner, his daughters, who were two, and even to the female captives, whose air of contentment and health greatly drew my attention.
>
> "How are you?" I asked them.
>
> "Very well, sir," they answered.
>
> "Don't you want to leave?"
>
> They didn't answer and blushed.
>
> Epumer said to me:
>
> "Yes, they have children, and they do not lack a man."
>
> The captives added:
>
> "He loves us very much."
>
> "I'm glad," I replied.
>
> One of them exclaimed:
>
> "I wish all female captives could say the same, your Excellency."[78]

Without wishing to invalidate the testimony of these documents, it must be borne in mind that they were written by representatives of the Spanish or Argentine government, and that they project on the female captives a deep feeling of superiority typical of the Spanish-criollo culture. The *tolderías* were for these military men, García, Ebélot, and Mansilla, as foreign as life on the frontier. The frontier was an ethnic mosaic made up of soldiers forced to serve in the forts, *blandengues,* renegades, deserters, gauchos, rustlers, scouts, field hands, rural officials, vagabonds, black slaves, mulattos, converted Indians and those in reservations and missions, the marginal elements of society. For many of these people, to live on one side or the other of the frontier was a question of convenience and happenstance. We have already pointed out how many captives, after being liberated, returned to the *toldos* of their own accord. They complained that they had to work too hard or that they felt restricted by a code of behavior that was more rigid than that of the *toldos*. A feeling shared by those who had lived in the interior was a feeling of freedom. Some captives had integrated to life in the *tolderías* to such a degree that they worked as spies for their masters, returning to frontier settlements and pretending to be escaped captives in order to obtain information or steal.

In the *toldos* of Mariano Rosas, Colonel Mansilla ran into Dr. Macías, a captive of the Ranquel Indians for two years. Macías was forty years old, the son of a Spanish merchant of Buenos Aires. He had studied at the university and obtained his doctorate in medicine. He had lived a life of adventure as a doctor on the high Paraná River and as a lumber industrialist in the Chaco, among whose Indians he had lived for some time. Later he participated in the peace negotiations with the Pampa tribes headed by Colonel Elía.

When these failed, Macías went from being a negotiator to being a prisoner. He tried to negotiate his freedom. He wrote letters that were intercepted, and appealed to friends without success. Cacique Mariano Rosas took a liking to him and made him his secretary. As a result, his lot improved for some time. This was one of the tasks for which the Indians employed some of their captives. The major caciques of the Pampa Indians, certainly those who exercised notable influence and carried out considerable political and commercial negotiations, needed educated secretaries to handle their diplomatic correspondence. For example, the French captive Auguste Guinnard, in 1851, was sold to different tribes of Puelche, Mamuelche, and Pampa Indians. Finally, he arrived at the *toldo* of Calfucurá, who employed him as his personal secretary.[79] Guinnard then enjoyed a greater degree of freedom and certain prerogatives that went with his new condition. Macías was not as fortunate. His friends spoke ill of him, and Mansilla admitted that he himself had done so. As a result he fell into disgrace. When Mansilla ran into him in Mariano Rosas's *toldo,* Dr. Macías was one of many marginal beings of the *toldería:* renegades, gauchos, and captives who were not part of a family. Mansilla negotiated his release and even included a clause to secure it as part of the treaties signed with the Ranqueles.

Male Captives

Dr. Macías did not come to the *toldos* as a result of a *malón.* He was more a political prisoner than a captive. Seldom did the Indians capture grown men in *malones*. Such a capture entailed many risks. Men offered more resistance, they tended to escape at the least opportunity, and they made the return trips difficult. Furthermore, they did not integrate well in the *toldos* and were a constant threat. In the highly hierarchical societies of the pampas, male captives increased the hosts of "poor Indians" who made up the dependent clientele of any cacique.[80] Caciques provided them with food and horses, when needed, especially for *malones,* in which they participated, although infrequently.

The vast majority of male captives lived in conditions of semislavery, denied the privileges of warriors and condemned to sexual abstinence. Women were expensive prizes that captives could not obtain easily. There were exceptions. Luis Acevedo was twenty-four when he was rescued from the Auca Indians in a treaty negotiated in 1792.[81] He declared that he had been married and had a son by an Indian woman who had died. He had paid a very high price for his wife, who was the sister of his master, the cacique Chapingo.[82] An interesting case is that of the cacique called El Padre, about whom we know from the declaration of Felipe Barquero, who professed to be "a criollo, Christian, Catholic and Apostolic Indian." He relates that when he was with some Indians of his area near the Cañadas del Tigre, they were approached by ten Indians of another nation at whose head was a white-skinned cacique whom the Indians called "El Padre," a Spanish Jesuit "whom the Indians loved and had made cacique."[83] It is not clear whether "El Padre" had joined the Indians as a captive or as a renegade.

Male captives carried out important tasks that made them valuable prizes, although they were always subject to suspicion. Besides serving as secretaries, they represented caciques in trade or peace negotiations. They also served as scouts, especially in white territory, and as *lenguaraces.* On August 20, 1783, Pedro Pablo Maldonado was taken from the *chacra* of Matías Santana, where he and his family were employed. In his declaration he says that when the Indians attacked, the settlers initially offered resistance, using the protection of the fort, "but the Indians attacked on all sides, jumped the wall and all came in at once. In the ensuing confusion, the deponent was wounded by a blow from a bola and several Indians jumped on him. As one of them was about to cut his throat, the Indian Capitán Bravo shouted, 'let him live; he will serve as a scout.'"[84] Before they left, Santana saw his eight comrades dead, including the owner of the farm. The Indians asked him to lead them to the *chacra* of

Juan Leal and then, on the way back, to the frontier of Luján. Pedro Maldonado was also used as a negotiator in order to attempt the liberation of the Indian Petronila in exchange for a son of Capitán Bravo.

Another task assigned to male captives, especially to those who had lived for several years in the *toldos* and had learned the language of their captors, was that of interpreter. José Ignacio Ricaldes was saved from death in a *malón* by a Spanish interpreter in the service of the Indians who advised him "to stop fighting that there weren't enough of them to resist so many Indians," and took him along.[85] Many captives in the *tolderías* served as interpreters and translators. The Indians never trusted them totally, and so caciques had several *lenguaraces* to reread and check letters. Nevertheless, *lenguaraces* and secretaries enjoyed more prestige and liberty than other captives whose labors were limited to herding cattle and carrying firewood.

The great majority of male captives reached the *toldos* as children and grew up integrated into an Indian family. Referring to an old captive of Cacique Mandano, Ebélot describes him in these terms:

> He was still a suckling babe when the Indians captured him. Thus he is proud to be a "raw Indian," a perfect Indian. He is proud to be one, but his beauty is notable. His black beard attracts attention among the hairless faces of his comrades. During the Guaminí expedition he wore a wide-brimmed hat whose crown, in tatters, was replaced by a piece of ostrich skin tied with horsehide strips, which gave him the air of a rather distinguished bandit. Valiant and clever, he is influential and firmly advocates an alliance with civilized people, on condition that they do not impose their customs on him, which he finds hateful.[86]

A smaller number of male captives came to the *toldos* under varied circumstances and not necessarily as a result of a *malón*. Many had been captured while traveling, while lost in frontier territory, or while on a hunting party.

Renegades

It was common to find renegade Christians among the Indians of the pampas. The mistreatment to which frontier troops stationed in forts were subjected (unpaid salaries, terrible living conditions, obligatory military service) generated a constant flow of renegade soldiers who went over to the side of the Indians.[87] Desertion was individual or collective. In 1777 the head of the Luján garrison reported that, of the 150 militiamen called up, only 30 came, "and the captains say that they cannot send more because they all have fled."[88] Martín Fierro, the eponymous protagonist of the poem by José Hernández, is torn by force from the daily life of the frontier. He deserts from the army and goes to the interior in order to escape the injustices suffered at the hands of military and administrative authorities. Mansilla as well as Ebélot tells of the great number of gauchos (dark-skinned Martín Fierros) whom they found in the *toldos*. Referring to the gaucho Chañilao, Mansilla paints a vivid portrait:

> Chañilao is the famous Cordobés gaucho Manuel Alonso, a former settler of the Cuarto River frontier. For years he has lived among the Indians. There is no scout more expert or braver than he. He has the topographical map of the frontier provinces in his head. He has crossed the pampas in every direction thousands of times, from the mountains of Córdoba to Patagones, from the Andes to the shores of the Río del Plata. [. . .]
>
> He speaks the language of the Indians as well as they. He has his own wife and lives with them. He is a horse breaker, expert with the lasso, and bolas. He has all the skills of an *estanciero* [ranch owner]. He has met Rosas and Urquiza. He has been captured several times and has escaped always thanks to his cunning or his boldness. [. . .]
>
> He is the oracle of the Indians when they invade and when they retreat. He lives with mistrust with [the cacique] *Inché,* thirty leagues or more to the south than Baigorrita, to whose Indian group he belongs. He has followers and is a *capitanejo,* and that is all there is to say about this man, a true native plant of the soil of Argentina. Chañilao is not bloodthirsty and has lived alternatively among Christians and Indians.[89]

Returning from his expedition to the salt flats on November 24, 1803, the captain of the *blandengues,* Miguel de Tejedor, has nothing new to report except the ransoming of two captives and the desertion to the Indians of an artilleryman, two *blandengues,* and six *peones de carreras* (auxiliaries).[90] References to desertions are numerous despite the severity of the punishment meted out to deserters. In 1779 the administrative instructions for the viceroyalty gave the punishment for desertion as imprisonment in the Malvinas Islands for a period of ten years, and even the death penalty was considered for very serious cases.[91] In 1788 the *blandengue* Juan de la Cruz

Córdoba "was sentenced to a year in prison with shackles."[92] Josef Almada, also of the company of *blandengues* on the Luján frontier, was sentenced to "running the gauntlet."[93]

Farmhands and rural workers also deserted for many and varied reasons. The black man Josef Antonio declares that he went over to the Indians because of the mistreatment he received on his estancia. For a year he was with the cacique Catrué. There he says he knew another Christian, Tadeo Silva, who also had gone over to the Indians.[94] The black slave Pedro was found in the fields of Guardia del Monte on September 18, 1788. He had run away with the Indians because his master, Juan Ferrada, would not let him marry a woman with whom he was living, and his confessors would not absolve him unless he married her. He declares that he decided to go over to the Indians because of his master's stubbornness and because his master mistreated him and locked him up at night.[95] Blas Pedrosa declares that in the *toldos* where he was taken, besides an infinite number of captives, there was a Spaniard married to an Indian who was there of his own free will and who served the cacique as a spy. He visited white settlements dressed in Spanish style and informed the cacique about possible army attacks, and about routes and locations appropriate for Indian incursions.[96]

The life of Colonel Manuel Baigorria (1809–75) exemplifies the permeability of the frontier. According to the official civilizing discourse, the frontier was a limit, a line of containment, but this concept does not match the social reality of the frontier in practice. Baigorria deserted to the *toldos* after the defeat of the *unitarios* by the *federales* in 1831. Fearing Governor Juan Manuel de Rosas, lacking the resources to support himself, or perhaps not trusting the peace promises of the Buenos Aires government, this military man chose self-imposed exile to the *toldos,* where he remained until 1852. He was yet one more renegade who lived as a *capitanejo,* surrounded by women and the community of captives. He had four wives: three captives and an Indian.[97] He participated in *malones* and in time acquired great ascendancy among certain caciques of the pampas who respected him. Through negotiations he was able to dissuade the powerful cacique Calfucurá from carrying out a *malón* that was about to attack Buenos Aires. Baigorria's purpose was political, to discredit the leader of the Argentine Confederation, Urquiza, to whom Baigorria had promised his services after the fall of Rosas in 1852.

Crossing the frontier offered the possibility of liberty. For those who lived on the frontier, the hinterland beyond offered an escape from their tormented lives. In the dangerous and unpredictable life of the interior, dominated by Indian tribes, there was even the possibility of acquiring land, which was difficult to do in areas adjacent to cities. It was no easy task to prevent the numerous desertions that undermined frontier settlements. The population of the province of Buenos Aires in the decade of 1740 did not exceed 6,000 inhabitants.[98] By 1820 it had grown to 56,300, which is very small considering the vast territory that extended from the shores of the Río Salado to the shores of the Río de la Plata. Labor was scarce and criollos and Indians competed for it. On occasion, officers in forts paid friendly Indians to search for deserters. An oxherd, José Gabriel Zorina, who abandoned his drove of oxen and escaped to the Indians, was apprehended and brought back by a Ranquel Indian at the behest of the captain of *blandengues* Miguel de Tejedor, who paid him for his services with "a small barrel of fourteen bottles of brandy and ten pounds of yerba maté."[99]

The ransoming and exchange of captives were important commercial transactions for the acquisition of consumer items in demand in the *toldos*. The commander of Fort Carmen in Río Negro writes in 1790 that the Auca Indians who passed by had offered him the opportunity to pay the ransom of a four- or five-year-old captive girl, the daughter of Christians, for whom they wanted brandy, bolts of baize cloth, yerba maté, sheets of brass, and several barber's bowls.[100] In Río Negro, Joaquín Maestre describes the arrival at the fort of Cacique Capitán Chiquito, offering to ransom back a Christian woman of thirty years of age, captive since she was twenty, who had nine children, four with Cacique Capitán Chiquito himself. He asked in exchange for four silver-plated bits, four pairs of silver spurs, four woolen blankets (two blue and two red), ten cows, forty cascabels, four ponchos de pala [a kind of textile], four pack mule sacks of yerba maté, and a barrel of brandy.[101] The ransom was considered too high, and the negotiation did not go forward. The response was an administrative report that argued against paying high ransoms, since in the long run they would be an incentive to take more captives. On the other hand, the report also noted that this female captive was already too adapted to the customs of the Indians because of the long time she had lived among them, and that her reintegration to white culture would thus be too difficult.

Ransoms were not always so high. The commander of the Mendoza frontier, José Francisco Amigorena, asked to be reimbursed a real and a half which he had paid to ransom five female captives in Chilean territory. He added that these captives, used to the life of the *toldos* after eight years, no longer knew how to work.[102] Francisco Antonio Rico requests reimbursement for the price paid for the ransom of a captive named Isabel and a ten-month-old boy. He had exchanged them for red woolen blankets, a poncho, twenty cascabels, ten bottles of *aguardiente* brandy, two bits, yerba maté, and three bunches of beads.[103] The information we have shows that the ransoming of captives was a common practice in Indian-Christian relations. During the annual expeditions to the salt flats, Indian parties would approach the expeditions to offer captives in exchange for the consumer items they greatly prized.

The ransoming of captives was of concern to the Spanish administrative authorities. In 1686 a *cédula real* (royal decree) established the prerogatives of the Orden de la Merced (a religious order that ransomed captives) for the collection of alms and the establishment of convents for this order in the Indies. In 1790 a *cédula real* confirmed the mission of the monks of the Orden de la Merced "to go into the towns and cities and solicit alms to this end [. . .] the which they are to remit from time to time to their bishop so that he may send them to the principal convent of la Merced situated in his diocese, with the reminder that the product of these alms is to be allocated to the liberation of many slaves."[104] Thus the Orden de la Merced was in charge of collecting alms which were to be used to free captives, whose ransoms, as we have seen, could be very high.

Another form of ransoming was the exchange of captives. Captives could be used as hostages and exchanged for Indians held in prison. The captive Pedro Zamora was sent in 1781 as representative of the cacique Lorenzo to negotiate the ransom of several Indian women held in a convent who were related to the cacique and to negotiate peace treaties with the authorities. If he succeeded, he would win his liberty and that of his wife and daughters, who were also captives, and the Indians undertook to negotiate the ransom of all male and female captives in their power. If after a month Pedro Zamora did not return with the peace treaties and the two Indian women, the Indians would withdraw farther into the hinterland, taking the captives with them, and threatened future attacks on frontier settlements in the province of Buenos Aires. They also threatened to kill his wife and daughters if he did not return within the allotted time.[105] There were many Indians held in prisons or in convents, and caciques were always ready to negotiate their exchange. In

1793 José Francisco Amigorena, commander of the Mendoza frontier, said that in various expeditions carried out "against those savage Indians who devastated those lands," he had apprehended more than three hundred Pehuenches and confined them in appropriate places. Rafael de Soto reported that the Indians in the *reducciones* were the agents through whom an active trade with the *toldos* was maintained.[106]

The ransoming of captives also was a mark of goodwill. It was a gesture that anticipated a desire for peace. Pólito Burgos escaped and arrived at a frontier fort. His declaration states that he was able to escape without difficulty because the Indians did not watch him much, since they were interested in negotiating peace treaties.[107] An Indian named Juan, of the Pampa nation, declared at a frontier fort on October 10, 1784, that he had come of his own free will accompanied by an Indian woman and two Auca Indians to sue for peace, and as a token of goodwill he was handing over "a four-year-old captive by name Ramón, whom they had captured at the age of two in the Cañada de la Pala together with his mother who remains a captive."[108] The Indians promised the prompt liberation of the mother and other captives in their power. Theodoro Flores tells of the constant trade between Indians and some Spaniards who acquired captives in exchange for *aguardiente* and yerba maté. He declares that the Indians wanted to sue for peace and would hand over three captives as a token of goodwill.[109]

Reintegration

We know little about the fate of the male and female captives who were rescued. I have pointed out already that some women returned to their former captors, especially those who had left families in the *toldos*, or who were older and more adapted and so for whom the return to white culture would entail a second process of acculturation. Moreover, it is easy to imagine that for many women the return would be psychologically traumatic, especially in the case of the married ones, who could expect to meet their former husbands and families. Women who had lived in the *toldos* for a long time were Pampa in their dress, customs, and appearance. However, the lack of information allows us only to speculate on this subject. There were significantly few women who escaped captivity. There is scant information on escaped female captives, and what there is normally deals with those who had been captured recently.

An interesting case because of the epic aspect of the escape is that of María Paula Santana, referred to above. Her story seems to be taken from fiction. She made her declaration on March 3, 1781. She had reached a frontier fort on February 23 after traveling on foot for twenty-eight days. "She says her name is María Paula Santana, a resident of Arrecife, married to José Ortellao. She lived with her husband and two daughters on a *chacra*."[110] Very early one morning, a group of Auca Indians attacked the *chacra* and took her and her two daughters. Her husband escaped, and she never saw him again. "That same day they spent the night on the shore of a lake, and the next day shortly after sunrise when the Indians were rounding up the horses in order to trade, they spied the Christians, and they put her and her daughters together with other female captives while the fight lasted."[111] At that point she lost track of her married daughter, whom she also never saw again. It is not known if her daughter escaped or if she was rescued by the attacking soldiers. Finally the Indians set out on the long march to the hinterland. On their way they set fields on fire in order to cover their escape. The withdrawal to the *toldos* was long and hard, typical of retreats after *malones,* when the Indians traveled for days without stopping for fear of being followed. María Paula managed to befriend a Spanish-speaking Indian woman who advised and encouraged her to escape before the last *malón* came back. Then they would begin their definitive march to the south, where almost certainly they would sell or exchange her to other tribes of the interior. The possibility of escaping would then be remote.

After several days of uncertainty and fear, María Paula decided to escape on foot, without any help. She was afraid of getting lost on the way back or being found by an Indian patrol, in which case she would in all likelihood be punished severely or murdered. "The night she escaped, she lost her way and never found it again and she guided herself by the sun." Even expert scouts could get lost in the pampas. "After eight days of walking, she saw a group of Indians leading a herd of horses and as soon as she saw them she lay down behind some grass and they passed very near her without seeing her." After twenty-eight days of walking, without food, dogged by thirst and fatigue, she found a party of *blandengues* who escorted her to Fort Areco. Hers was an exceptional case.

It can also be argued that women had fewer opportunities to escape and that escaping from the interior of the pampas was an adventure that required extraordinary resistance and some knowledge of the land. Once they became part of a family, many women grew used to or resigned to life in the *toldos*. To return, moreover, was no easy task owing to the many difficulties of re-integration. It is significant that many freed female captives refused to make declarations, as if they did not want to talk or as if they had something to hide. In fact, of all the declarations I have found in the archives, and those provided by the researcher Carlos Mayo, only two are by women. Many reports mention the freeing of female captives, but the women either did not make declarations or were not asked to make them.

At noted elsewhere, we know that many of the female captives brought back by Juan Manuel de Rosas's desert expedition were handed over to their relatives. If these could not be found, captives, especially those stigmatized by their intimate cohabitation with Indians, were made to live in convents or handed over to criollo families as servants. Female captives had better luck as a source of inspiration for fiction and engravings than they did in real life.[112] In fiction, the virtues of Christian morality were projected onto the body of these women, and they were raised to the altar of heroism, a subject treated in chapter 7.

Freed male captives had fewer problems adapting. Men did not have to be ashamed of intimate cohabitation with Indians. Upon their return, they could be employed as scouts or interpreters and thus serve criollo society in its fight against the Indians. Although they made declarations, very few were inclined to write in greater detail the account of their experiences in captivity, a subject taken up in the next chapter.

Conclusion

The captivity of white settlers reflects the territorial conflict and the cultural diversity of the frontier in the Río de la Plata region. Taking captives was part of the resistance strategy of the Indians. The Indian tribes of the pampas and Patagonia, even those who at given moments joined confederations, never undertook offensive warfare with the aim of restoring the precolonial order. When they had the opportunity to do so, especially at the time of Calfucurá's confederation, they did not attempt it. *Malones* were a kind of "small war"[113] whose objectives were not military and therefore did not have any of the epic characteristics associated with offensive warfare. The objective was theft and the sacking and destruction of estancias or frontier settlements. *Malones* began with the migration of Mapuche tribes to the other side of the Andean range, although in areas like the Chaco captivity had been practiced before, especially among the Chiriguanos.[114] In fact, the peaceful coexistence observable in eighteenth-century Chile contrasts with the growing conflict in the areas of Cuyo and the pampas.

At the end of the nineteenth century, conflict had become a chronic situation. The relative worth of livestock in tribal or local economy, where only the hides had some value, turned the vast expanse of the pampas and the plains of the south into what amounted to a semi-uninhabited hunting preserve. When the tribes of the interior adapted to horses, they found themselves in a privileged position to compete for wild cattle. Other items that were increasingly consumed in the *toldos* could be obtained through trade or by sacking frontier settlements. Thus the Indian *malón* became widespread as a form of military resistance and as a modus vivendi. Captivity was always associated with this intermittent "small war." Captives were the sacrificial victims of a society in constant negotiation for its existence. They were also the source of the ethnic and cultural blend bred by these frontier societies.

⊰ FOUR ⊱

Accounts of Captives
in the Pampas and Patagonia

During the eight days we were moving in a north-west direction, through a wooded country that appeared to me delightful compared with the spots I had hitherto lived in, I was continually the object of conversation among the Indians, who exhibited toward me a kindness to which I was little accustomed. The name of my country appeared to me to have reached their ears for the first time.

Some of their questions convinced me of their intelligence. They inquired with marks of great interest as to the form of our government.

—Auguste Guinnard, *Three Years' Slavery*
among the Patagonians

One of the most striking features of studying captivity in Spanish America is the captives' lack of interest in writing their stories or the lack any incentive to do so. Indeed, if one compares the number of captives in the cultural area of the Río de la Plata, especially in the eighteenth and nineteenth centuries, with the scarcity of firsthand accounts, the imbalance is thought-provoking. We have no trustworthy statistics, but to judge from the accounts of expeditions to the interior and the letters and reports of governors, we can conjecture that many thousands of captives were taken by the Indians in the geographic area of the Río de la Plata in the eighteenth and nineteenth centuries. Nonetheless, for reasons that will be discussed in this chapter, published accounts by captives can be counted on the fingers of one hand. Why didn't former captives write? Was there no religious, political, or scientific value to their experiences? Even just as reading matter, wouldn't a genre so close to adventure literature be of interest?

Through the reading of three captive narratives, those of Auguste Guinnard, Benjamin F. Bourne, and Santiago Avendaño, this chapter proposes a series of conjectures in an attempt to answer these questions. At the same time, the chapter reflects on three related themes: (a) the Western vision of America, still dominated by foundational myths, (b) the hostile relations of the Argentine Republic with the indigenous population, and (c) the construction of a literary text.

Anglo-Saxon America

We know that in Anglo America thousands of captivity narratives were published, and they were extraordinarily popular.[1] This immense output was obviously a response to public demand, or perhaps indicates the usefulness of the genre as an educational and propaganda tool. James Levernier and Hennig Cohen maintain that captivity narratives, appropriately edited, were used as children's literature, to teach reading, to instruct, or to preach moral virtues.[2] Obviously, hidden under different pretexts lay the implicit notion of the endemic evil of the Indian and the moral superiority of the white man. Richard VanDerBeets, who has also studied this subject in the United States, corroborates the extraordinary popularity of captivity literature in certain periods. He singles out several contributing factors to account for this popularity, among them the fact that these publications stressed the image of a white, Christian hero immersed in a voyage of initiation, "a variation of the Death-Rebirth archetype."[3]

The popularity of female captivity narratives, as numerous as those of male captives, can be interpreted as a response to the myth of the white adventurer in the unknown lands of the West, where there was barely room for women. "The resentment and anger women felt toward the husbands who risked their futures in an inhospitable environment were displaced onto the figure of the Indian, a projection of the husband's darker nature."[4] In some way, captivity was an intimate and personal experience that women could share with each other that did not include their husbands. There were more female than male captives, which made the problem of captivity especially pertinent to women. Many women shared the experience of the unexplored interior, and they identified with the trauma suffered by female captives.

Levernier and Cohen add that captivity literature in some way compensated for the Anglo-Saxon public's general lack of knowledge about Indians. What little they knew was based, not on observation or on living beside them, but on the abstract formulations of philosophers, theologians, and historians.[5] This ideological apparatus, drawn mainly from medieval imaginary, shaped a Manichaean vision of relations with the Indians who lived in the same territories that the Anglo-Saxon pioneers chose as the site for their religious utopia. Puritans and Quakers interpreted the experiences of captives as divine messages, and they were ready to draw appropriate lessons: "Puritan ministers incorporated captivity exempla into their sermons and ecclesiastical histories."[6] The Indian menace was an intervention from the Most High, who could permit New England to fall again into the hands of savages and thus into the realm of darkness.

Later on, in the mid-eighteenth century, during the French and Indian wars, captivity narratives also played the role of corroborating not only the image of Indians as savages but also the idea of the French as agitators who encouraged them.[7] It is important to underscore this propaganda aspect. Of the captives who expressed favorable opinions of the Indians, very few wrote narratives or were given the opportunity to do so.

Some key works of captivity literature became best sellers, reaching as many as thirty editions.[8] They were also published in England, Germany, and France.

Captivity Narratives in the Río de la Plata

Captivity narratives were not written or at least were not published during the eighteenth and nineteenth centuries in the viceroyalty of the Río de la Plata and then in the United Provinces of the Río de la Plata. From that period, when captivity was a daily occurrence on the frontier, we know of only three narratives of significant length. In the national archives and in the archives of provincial capitals in Argentina there are many declarations made by captives, which we studied in the previous chapter. The majority of them have yet to be discovered. They appear amid dusty, timeworn piles of papers and have rarely been published. Most of these descriptions are raw material for researchers, but they are certainly not pleasure reading. Two collections that have been published are Professor Carlos A. Mayo's facsimile edition *Fuentes para la historia de la frontera: Declaraciones de cautivos* (Sources for the History of the Frontier: Declarations of Captives), and a recent anthology of mine entitled *Cautivos*.

The three significant narratives that I am referring to are *Tres años de esclavitud entre los patagones: Relato de mi cautiverio* (Three Years of Slavery among the Patagonians: An Account of My Captivity), by the Frenchman Auguste Guinnard; *Captive in Patagonia; or, Life among the Giants: A Personal Narrative*, by Benjamin Franklin Bourne; and "La fuga de un cautivo de los indios" (A Captive's Escape from the Indians), by Santiago Avendaño.

Auguste Guinnard was born in 1832. At the age of twenty-three he traveled to Montevideo, and from there, for the sake of adventure, he made his way on foot through the frontier settlements of the pampas. On one of his trips he was captured by Poyuche Indians, and he remained their captive for three years. Upon his return to France, he was encouraged to write about his adventure by Jonnard, a French scientist, who also advised him on how to carry out the project. The first edition, written in French, *Trois ans d'esclavage chez les Patagons (1856–1859)*, appeared shortly thereafter as part of the collection "Around the World: A Collection of Voyages Undertaken to the Five Parts of the Universe during the Nineteenth Century," directed by Eduard Charton.[9] In a short space of time, there were three editions of the book. The third French edition was translated into English and published in London as *Three Years' Slavery among the Patagonians: An Account of His Captivity* (1871). The first Spanish version, translated by Mariano Urrabieta, was published in France the same year. Not until 1941 was the work published in Buenos Aires, by Espasa-Calpe.

The second narrative is that of Benjamin Franklin Bourne, whose three-month-long captivity among the Patagonians in 1848 was published in Boston in 1853, with the title *Captive in Patagonia; or, Life among the Giants: A Personal Narrative*. The first translation into Spanish was published in 1998.

The third is the work of Santiago Avendaño. With the title "La fuga de un cautivo de los indios," it appeared in 1867 in *La Revista de Buenos Aires: Historia Americana, Literatura y Derecho*, volumes 14 and 15.

It is interesting to pause and consider that only three narratives managed to take shape and reach publication. Of the three, two are by foreign captives, a Frenchman and a North American, who published in French and English when they returned home, no doubt encouraged by the interest their narratives aroused in those countries. Only one of the stories, Santiago Avendaño's, was published in Argentina and in incomplete form, since it only described his escape.

Auguste Guinnard returned to France after his captivity and a long period of time in Chile, which he reached by crossing the Andes on foot, driven by the fear of being recaptured by one of the Indian tribes that roamed the interior of the country. When he returned to France, he was received with goodwill by the scientific community, who urged him to publish what they considered a fascinating experience in exotic America. In the introduction to the second edition, Guinnard makes clear the circumstances and reasons that moved him to write.

> Urged on by numerous expressions of encouragement, as well as by the benevolent advice I have been honored to receive from some of the most distinguished persons, whether it be for their knowledge or their high rank, I have decided to relate the horrible sufferings that I bore during my long captivity, and to describe the customs and habits of the different peoples whose slave I was. [...]
>
> I have not tried to imitate, like so many others; I have limited myself, pure and simply, to providing a scrupulous account of my adventures and of the customs and habits of the Patagonians, Puelches, Pampas, and Mamuelches, with whom, due to an unfortunate chain of circumstances, I was forced to live during three and a half years. My knowledge of their language and the long time that I participated in their way of life, place me in the condition of being able to consider them from their own point of view, and thus the reader will be able to compare my various observations with those of certain other writers, who shall remain nameless.
>
> I have been inclined more to literature than to science, but since I am the only person who, up to the present day, has been able to penetrate so deeply into the interior of Patagonia, I find, for that very reason more than any other, that I am in a position to exactly inform the reader about its nomadic inhabitants.[10]

Guinnard was furnished with financial support to carry out his project. He wrote a first draft based more on the vicissitudes and intrigues of his adventure than on the ethnographic aspects of his experiences. In the second edition he added descriptions of such things as the Indians' customs, their way of life, and religious practices. In the introductory note to the second edition, he writes: "A few months ago, I published in *Around the World,* a summary of my adventures in Patagonia. The bad state of my health was the only cause which kept me from giving a complete account from the start. Nevertheless, I did not give up on the execution of this project which only today I am able accomplish."[11] Guinnard had the support of distinguished intellectuals who considered the information in an adventure told from the point of view of the eyewitness to be very valuable. He was nominated for membership in the Paris Geographical Society.

The nineteenth century was experiencing an effervescence of the expansionist spirit of the Enlightenment. The Americas were being rediscovered as a new frontier, a European frontier, a zone of contact open to capitalist expansionism. The obstacles to scientific knowledge created by Spanish colonial protectionism began to break down during the eighteenth century, and more notably by the nineteenth century. The doors were opened to neocolonial expansionism. Travelers and men of science put on their exploring boots; and bearing instruments that could measure and classify with greater precision than ever before, they set out to rediscover and reconceive the planet and—of course—that as yet unknown or badly interpreted world. "One by one the planet's life forms were to be drawn out of the tangled threads of their life surroundings and rewoven into European-based patterns of global unity and order."[12]

Auguste Guinnard, Memoirs of a Captivity

Auguste Guinnard did not travel to the Río de la Plata for scientific reasons. He was motivated by many other things, including ambition and financial need.

> In 1855 I was no more than twenty-three years old, had limited experience, some ambition, and, above all, a love of travel. From my earliest childhood I had been thrilled by the accounts of his travels of my maternal grandfather, Ulliac de Kvallant, a naval officer who, by the age of twenty-two, had three times made the passage to the Great Indies.[13]

Nevertheless, on Guinnard's return, when he came into contact with the French scientific community, he became aware of the importance of his experiences and of the value of the knowledge he had acquired. Guinnard's text is more than the narrative of a captive. It aspires to be scientific, as can be seen from the author's carefully detailed descriptions of different tribes, his ability to pick out their cultural and ethnic differences, and the addition of a map, which he slowly drew during his hazardous journey and which he included in the second edition of his book. Mapmaking can be understood as an attempt to invoke the spatial and temporal presence of subjects previously separated by geographical and historical circumstances, and was the basis for the first manuals of exploration. Guinnard writes:

> In the eastern zone, which runs from the Río Salado to the Río Colorado, live the Pampeans, properly so-called, divided into seven tribes. The wooded region, which extends between Lake Bevadero and Couron-Lafquène (Black Lake), as well as the watercourses, which run from this lake to the Río Diamante, belong to the Mamouelches (inhabitants of the woods), who form eight important tribes, called by the Indians, Ranquel-tchets, Angneco-tchets, Catrulé-Mamouel-tchets, Quinié-Quinié-Ouitrou-tchets, Renangne-Cochets, Epougnam-tchets, Motchitoué-tchets.[14]

Despite this descriptive scientific tone, useful in many places, the narrative contains elements typical of the viewpoint of the captive who desperately struggles against a destiny plagued with evil omens. Occasionally he presents his captors in the stereotypical savage mold common to his time.

> I never saw anything more dreary and weird-looking than the aspect of these half-naked beings, mounted on spirited horses, which they managed with surprising dexterity. Their robust bodies were bistre-coloured, their thick and uncombed hair hung over their faces, and revealed at every abrupt movement a set of hideous features, to which the addition of glaring colours gave an expression of diabolical ferocity.[15]

In some ways the experience of Auguste Guinnard with the inhabitants of the Patagonian lands was not the happiest of encounters. He was their captive and treated as a slave. Captivity was a by-product of a frontier where the elements in interaction were still subject to a system of distrust and rejection. Nevertheless, the mood that predominates in his narrative is not that of a frontier dweller who lives in a situation of chronic insecurity and who understands his relation with the other in terms of defense. Rather, his position is

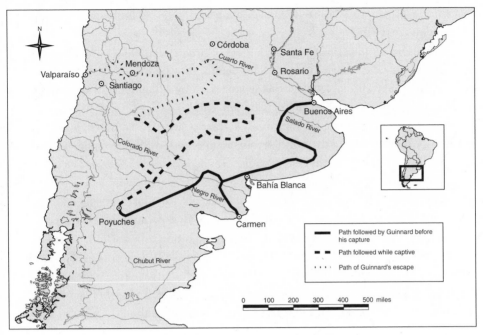

Map 7. Route of Auguste Guinnard

that of a traveler surprised by the magic of the unexpected, although in his case, captivity caused deep trauma as a result of the dangers to which he was exposed. On more than one occasion, his life was seriously threatened, and like so many other accidental travelers, he might have ended his days in the unknown interior of the pampas. The thought of suicide never left him.

Guinnard embarked in 1855 from the port of Le Havre bound for the Río de la Plata. From there he went to Buenos Aires, which in those days was in the midst of a civil war. It is not clear why Guinnard decided to explore the territories of the south, possibly he was motivated by a combination of a spirit of adventure, scientific curiosity, and the desire to make a fortune. The Americas embodied, in the European imagination, a combination of all those elements, with the possibility of becoming rich being preeminent. In early 1856 Guinnard traveled to the settlements near Carmen de Patagones on the Negro River, and to Fort Argentino and Bahía Blanca bordering on Patagonia. On his way back he spent some time wandering through certain settlements on the Buenos Aires frontier, Tandil, Azul, and Quequén. In Quequén he met an Italian traveler, Pedrito, who like him was wandering in the area without any known destination.

Without supplies, horses, or a compass to guide them, the two travelers lost their way in the untamed plains. The pampa showed them its crudest face. Unfordable rivers, wild grasses that made their way difficult, the coming of the pampean winter, and their lack of geographical knowledge turned the pleasure trip into a hard struggle for survival. "On the day after the commencement of our journey, indeed, a torrent-like rain, augmented by a violent and icy wind whistling from the depths of Patagonia, cruelly assailed us. This bad weather continued for four mortal days, during which we were compelled to rest stretched upon the wet ground, without being able to hunt or to light a fire."[16] Their lost steps led them away from the city of Rosario and, unbeknownst to them, toward territory inhabited by Poyuche hunting tribes, whom Martínez Sarasola has described as "gangs that wander in search of cattle, or follow the retreat of a fortuitous *malón*."[17] In the midst of their desperate plight, Guinnard and his companion were discovered by a party of Indians. "The Indians . . . rushed as by enchantment from all the hollows of the ground, and surrounded us with demonstrations of ferocious joy, uttering guttural cries, and brandishing their lances, their *boleadoras*, their bolas—in Indian, *locayos*— and their lassos."[18] They tried to defend themselves. Guinnard even shot and wounded an Indian. In vain. In the fight, Pedrito fell mortally wounded. Guinnard was hit on the head by a bola, and this saved him from death.

The party began a long southerly march toward the homeland of the Poyuches, western Patagonians, who were his first captors. Later he was exchanged to a group of Puelche Indians for an ox and a horse. He spent six months with the Puelches, but they were disappointed with their captive's lack of equestrian skills and sold him "out of a spirit of speculation" to a party of eastern Patagonians. Herding cattle by night and carrying firewood and heavy utensils were his first chores. The eastern Patagonians, in turn, got rid of him. They didn't know how to make use of him and sold him for "some horses and a few *pilkènes*, pieces of common red or black cloth."[19]

The Pampa Indians, who were used to maintaining frequent correspondence with frontier settlements and even with the military authorities, employed him as a scribe. Nevertheless, he was accused of treason by the Indians, who had never come to trust him. They concluded that a letter, written by Guinnard in his own hand, contained equivocal information about the Indians and for that reason their messengers had been jailed in the frontier fort. Guinnard understood that this could cost him his life. He wasn't wrong. He had to flee and did so that night, without much preparation. Early in the morning, he was lucky to run into the camp of Cacique Calfucurá, who offered him protection. Integrated into the life of this tribe, he spent the most pleasant days of his captivity. He had conversations with the Mapuche cacique, and Calfucurá put him in charge of his diplomatic correspondence. With regard to Calfucurá, Guinnard's testimony is of great value, because he was one of the few Europeans who lived with this legendary cacique. "He was a man already more than a hundred years of age, though appearing to be sixty at most; his still black hair covered a vast unwrinkled forehead, which bright and scrutinizing eyes rendered highly intelligent."[20]

Guinnard's desire to escape never left him, though. He says he tried to escape fourteen times. Spurred by a growing depression, he also tried to commit suicide. Finally, taking advantage of the aftermath of a great feast in the camp, he decided to escape. His flight lasted thirteen days, until he reached the first frontier settlements on the Quinto River, where he was helped by a Spanish family. After a long convalescence, he decided to cross the Andes on foot and regain his liberty in Chilean territory. In March of 1861 the traveler returned to France with an empty suitcase and an exhausted body, but with a great cargo of experiences and observations that would earn him a place in the French scientific community. His narrative deserves our attention.

The Captivity of Benjamin F. Bourne

Seven years separate the adventure of Auguste Guinnard from that of Benjamin Franklin Bourne, who on February 13, 1848, set sail as a pilot on the schooner *John Allyne* from the port of New Bedford, Massachusetts, westbound toward promising California. These were the years of gold fever on the Pacific Coast. The schooner on which he was traveling had to make the difficult passage through the Strait of Magellan, in Tierra del Fuego, a mythical place in the history of navigation until our century. Nightly stops were unavoidable because of the difficult passages of the strait. In the heart of Tierra del Fuego, Bourne's schooner made such a forced stop. The captain, A. Bronwell, suggested that Bourne and a group of sailors go ashore to get the food they needed—meat, fowl, eggs—from a group of Patagonian Indians who were watching them from the coast. Not without fear and caution, Bourne approached the coast, although he refused to get off the boat for fear of the "black-looking giants" who were observing them impassively from the beach. "A recollection of the many ugly stories current about the Patagonians, their barbarous and cruel character, did not greatly fortify our confidence, or make us especially anxious for a personal acquaintance with them."[21] Nevertheless, his more daring companions followed the so-called giants on the beach and suddenly disappeared. His premonitions soon became true. The Patagonians invaded Bourne's boat, and he wound up disembarking to search for the sailors, who were long in returning. On the way back, he was forcibly taken, and in exchange for his liberty the Indians demanded huge quantities of rum which were never enough. The negotiations came to nothing, and Bourne found himself in the hands of the Patagonians, in the midst of the southern night and assailed by the legendary fear that he would inevitably be devoured by his captors. This took place on April 30, 1848.

Benjamin Bourne's journey through the Patagonian interior lasted until August 7 of the same year, three long months. Although the obsessive fear of being sacrificed never left him, Bourne had time to observe the customs of the Indians, take notes, participate extensively in their hunting activities, and set these experiences down in a diary that became the basis of his narrative. His flight, less dramatic than most captive escapes in the pampas and the southern lands, gave him his longed-for liberty, but did not free him from his fears until he was picked up by Captain Morton's schooner, which was making its way from New Orleans to California. When they reached the port of Callao, in Peru, Bourne was overjoyed to learn what happened after his disappearance. The news of his capture in Patagonia had reached Boston, and some of his friends and neighbors pressured the navy into undertaking a search expedition, for which purpose the sloop *Sarah* was sent out to find and rescue him. Inclement weather thwarted the mission, however, and the *Sarah* never reached its destination. Nonetheless, the attempt itself is of great interest. The disappearance of a North American sailor in Patagonian territory prompted the organization of a rescue effort of great operational complexity and obvious expense. It is not surprising that the account of his final rescue would be considered newsworthy and publishable, as is proved by the swiftness with which his narrative saw print and the unexpected fame Bourne acquired in a short time.

The manner in which the news reached his native Boston was peculiar. During the long crossing through the narrow channels of Tierra del Fuego, both Morton, the schooner's captain, and Bourne decided to write diaries of their adventures. Morton thought that his own voyage and vicissitudes deserved publication, and he encouraged Bourne to revise the diary of his captivity. Both manuscripts were put into a bottle, which was hung on a tree near Sea-Lion Island in the hope that if someone found them, they would be taken to the United States. According to Bourne's account in the definitive version of his book, the manuscripts "first fell into the hands of an Indian, who sold it to some passing trader, by whom the soiled writing was deciphered, and kindly forwarded to Smith's News-room, in Boston and was published in the Boston Atlas."[22]

The story of his trip and captivity appeared in its only edition in the *Boston Atlas* in 1880. It is a long and tedious account, with only a few passages of interest dealing with Bourne's daily life among the Patagonians, hunting guanacos in the barren steppes. As with many other travelers and captives, his preconceived notions of the Patagonians, beginning with their supposed gigantism and inherent cannibalism, kept him from developing a dialogue with this captors. Bourne consistently misinterpreted the tokens of goodwill and protection given by the cacique with whom he lived. The book's interest lies in its being one of the few captivity narratives published in the nineteenth century.

Like Auguste Guinnard's text, Benjamin Bourne's *The Captive in Patagonia* was published because its subject was of interest to the scientific and geographical societies of the time, immersed as they were in the cataloging of the planet and avid for stories that would satisfy their growing passion for the exotic. Patagonian Indians were considered one of the most exotic peoples of the Americas, and their fame was accompanied by the legends of their gigantism and their innate aggressivity. Bourne's text endorses these preconceptions. Furthermore, there was in Europe a reading public eager for stories of impossible voyages, risky adventures, shipwrecked people in unknown islands, or captives of fierce tribes. The popularity of captivity narratives in New England has already been mentioned.

There were many other texts of voyages and expeditions to Patagonia which are of greater geographic and ethnographic interest and which had a warm reception. A few years before, one of the most interesting books about travelers in Patagonia was published in London. It is the narrative of George Chaworth Musters, *A Year in Patagonia,* of which several versions and summaries were published in 1871, 1872, and 1875, sponsored by the Royal Geographic Society. The first Spanish version, *Vida entre los patagones: Un año de excursiones por tierras no frecuentadas desde el estrecho de Magallanes hasta el Río Negro,* dates from 1911.

Publications about Captives in Argentina

Unlike in New England and Europe, in the liberal Argentina that had emerged from independence the stories of captives were of no interest. When Benjamin Bourne was traveling through Patagonia in 1848, the United Provinces of the Río de la Plata were not so united. They were going through a long political conflict that divided the country into *unitarios* and *federales.* Between 1845 and 1848 the port of Buenos Aires was subject to a blockade by the British and French navies, which permitted no entries or departures. While the opposition to the government conspired in Montevideo, the provinces of the interior were being bled to death by partisan conflicts. The indigenous tribes of the pampas did not remain uninvolved in these conflicts. Both *unitarios* and *federales,* while they resented the constant threat of the *malones* on the frontier, were quick to establish alliances with caciques. In 1806, some years before independence, in light of the menace of a British invasion, several Tehuelche, Ranquel, and Pampa caciques offered their services to the *cabildo* of Buenos Aires.[23] Their participation was never worked out, but their initiative was a sign that the frontier tribes counted or wanted to count in the political life of the United Provinces.[24] Calfucurá was an ally of Juan Manuel de Rosas and a fundamental bulwark against the tribes that supported the interests of the *unitarios.* Calfucurá and Rosas remained in constant negotiation with each other, which brought a degree of tranquillity to the frontier and neighboring settlements.[25] Calfucurá mentioned that on one occasion Rosas called him over to the other side of the frontier to upset the balance of power of the Ranqueles and their cacique, Yanquetruz.[26] Wars, alliances with frontier tribes, expeditions to the interior to negotiate or trade, *malones* and captives, were constants in the political practice of the period.

Auguste Guinnard became Calfucurá's secretary for the confederation located in Salinas Grandes. By this time, Rosas had left for exile in Southampton, England (1852), having been replaced by the caudillo from the province of Entrerríos, Justo José Urquiza, who managed to approve a constitution in the federalist mold which was not accepted by the *unitarios*, who drafted their own constitution in 1853. With this act, the province of Buenos Aires separated itself from the rest of the country. Political problems and the problem of economic expansion continued with unabated virulence, and so did frontier conflicts, which in fact became worse. Without Rosa's diplomatic control, the tribes of the interior entered a period of direct aggression.

> To the Creoles in Argentina, the arrival of Calfucurá heralded a new epoch, an era in which old treaty and alliance networks with the indigenous Pampas and Tehuelche Indians broke down, organized raids threatened the livestock and property of frontier settlers, captives were carried away by hundreds, and Argentina society turned to gaucho soldiers for help.[27]

The instability of the society seemed to spread to intertribal relations. These were also strained by the decrease in the numbers of wild cattle in the pampas, which was their mainstay for survival. The threat of Calfucurá's confederation continued after his death in 1873, at the age of a 101. He was succeeded by his son Namuncurá, who for the five years he directed the confederation organized attacks on frontier settlements that took hundreds of captives and head of cattle.[28] For Creole society, the "Indian question" was not resolved until General Roca's definitive expedition to the desert (1878–79)— if the extermination of Indians which it effected can be considered a solution.

The image that the Argentine Confederation wanted to project to the exterior was not that of a country inhabited by turncoat Indians whose tents were raised in the proximity of frontier settlements. Some of the first works of the most talented writers of the period clearly reject any relation with indigenous peoples, especially with the tribes dwelling in the pampas and Patagonia. The poem "La cautiva," written by the young Esteban Echeverría, is a passionate and violent diatribe against life in the Indian camps. His fundamental metaphor is that the barbarous savagery of the Indians is a cancer that must be eradicated without hesitation. In his writings, President Domingo Faustino Sarmiento, as passionate at times as he is lucid at others, points out the harm that caudillos and gauchos can bring to the future of Argentina, but nevertheless finds a way to integrate them into his regenerative plan for the nation. Not so with the Indians; they are the other, those who are outside and can in no way be included in the national plan. In Sarmiento's plan no regeneration is possible for the Indian, and he repeats this numerous times in his writings. "For us, Colocolo, Lautaro and Caupolicán, despite the noble and civilized garb in which Ercilla clothed them, are nothing but a bunch of disgusting Indians, whom we would have hanged today."[29] His position with respect to the indigenous population leaves no room for doubt.

> It may be very unjust to exterminate savages, to suffocate civilizations in the process of being born, to conquer peoples who are in possession of privileged territories; but thanks to that injustice, America, instead of remaining in the hands of savages, who are incapable of progress, is occupied today by the Caucasian race, the most perfect, the most intelligent, the most beautiful, and the most progressive that lives on Earth.[30]

Who can doubt the great ideological influence that Sarmiento had in his day? David Viñas affirms that "no one can challenge Sarmiento's role as the major theorist of the Argentine bourgeoisie."[31]

The poet José Hernández, who saved the gaucho from ostracism and reinvented his culture, which had been so badly treated by Romantic intellectuals, also had no compassion for Indians.[32] His Martín Fierro, a frontier character who hides in the *tolderías,* the Indian camps, to escape the yoke of civilization, returns horrified at the savage dehumanization of the Indian. The passages that take place in the *tolderías* are the hardest and most partisan criticism of pampean cultures. His bottom line favors the radical thesis: the savage must be exterminated.

In this ideological context, of what interest were captivity narratives that on occasion sympathized with the Indians or humanized them? Even accounts that are openly tendentious, like Benjamin Bourne's, can be read as incomplete ethnographies in which the culture of the Patagonians is seen in its natural context. Bourne doesn't hide his prejudices. "I observed the savages, like a horde of half-starved dogs, devouring their portions with the greatest relish."[33] Nevertheless, his own observations sometimes betray him, moments when he lowers his cultural defenses and becomes involved in the hunt, or takes part in an open dialogue with his captors. Captivity narratives bring us closer rather than farther apart. They humanize, even in the midst of surprise and incomprehension. As we shall see in chapter 7, in terms of furthering an ideological program, fiction offered more freedom for invention and for manipulation. Transported to tragedies and adventure stories, Indians and female captives became symbolic figures.

Travelers' Diaries: The Other Side of the Coin

The diaries of trips of discovery or of geographical and scientific expeditions had a different purpose and were addressed to another public. Descriptions of the national territory and its inhabitants fit within a national plan of exploration and delimitation of the frontier. The Indians who emerge from these diaries appear as museum pieces or items in a catalog. They belong to the past, although their tepees, settlements, and *toldos* may still rise next to large cities.

> More than 30 people lived in the *toldo:* eight or ten young men in a circle, playing dice or cards, and the women who prepared the food and roasts for them. It is impossible to understand the laziness of these men and their repugnance for work. It is the women who do the work the men should do, in addition to all the burdens imposed on them by their large families.[34]

This is what Colonel Pedro Andrés García wrote in 1821 in his "Diario de la Expedición a la Sierra de la Ventana" (Diary of the Expedition to the Sierra de la Ventana). Travelers at this time were superficial chroniclers of an alien environment in which natives, flora, and fauna constituted a coherent, exotic habitat worthy of study. The publication of travelers' observations and diaries was of practical interest and helped to integrate the new republics into the international scientific community. In the United Provinces of Río de la Plata this job remained to be done. Bourbon policy in the eighteenth century had begun the task by sending Captains Antonio de Ulloa and Jorge Juan on a mission to explore and catalog. Their work, collected under the title *Noticias Americanas: Entretenimientos phisicos-históricos sobre la América Meridional y la Septentrional Oriental* (American Notes: Physical-Historical Considerations about North America and Eastern South America), is a compendium of information about many aspects of geography and colonial life which earned them the recognition of French and British academies of science.[35] Their observations were published in Madrid in 1747 and reprinted in

1772 and 1792. Later, the Spanish Crown also sponsored the trips of Alexander von Humboldt and Aimé Bonpland, who would become famous.[36]

The viceroyalty recognized the importance of these explorations. They were useful not just for tracing routes, acquiring knowledge of natural resources and means of communications, but also for counting settlements and their inhabitants, becoming familiar with their customs, and establishing the limits of the frontier. Antonio de Viedma, in 1780, was one of the first Creoles to travel to Patagonia, following the steps of famous English travelers.[37] Two years later, Basilio Villarino, a navy captain, undertook a similar voyage.[38] Of great interest are the first expeditions to the Gran Chaco, made by Jerónimo Matamorras in 1774 and by Juan Adrián Hernández Cornejo in 1780.[39] Even toward the end of the colonial period, these trips continued to elicit a great deal of interest. Noteworthy among these for its wealth of information is the expedition to the pampas of a Chilean captain, Luis de la Cruz.[40]

After independence there was renewed interest, which resulted in the expeditions of Colonel Pedro Andrés García—*Navegación del Tercero* (Navigation of the Tercero) (1813), *Diario de un viaje a Salinas Grandes* (Diary of a Trip to Salinas Grandes) (1810), and *Expedición a la Sierra de la Ventana* (1820–23)—and that of Félix de Azara in 1815.[41] Of great importance, without doubt, was the expedition to the southern frontier led by Juan Manuel de Rosas in 1828,[42] in the company of the scholars Félix de Senillosa and Juan Gallo Lavalle, who gathered a great quantity of cartographical and even astronomical information. Interest in these expeditions must have been deep, since even in the midst of the civil wars that wreaked havoc in the newly minted Provinces of Río de la Plata, the government of Buenos Aires subsidized the publication of *Colección de obras y documentos relativos a la historia antigua y moderna de las Provincias del Río de la Plata* (Collection of Works and Documents Relative to the Ancient and Modern History of the Provinces of the Río de la Plata), edited by the diligent Pedro de Angelis, an Italian in the service of Governor Juan Manuel de Rosas and director of the *Gazeta de Buenos Aires,* the official newspaper of the *federal* party and its weapon in the ideological battle against the *unitarios.*

In the majority of these travel diaries and notebooks we find commentaries regarding captives found in the *toldos* or Indian settlements. They are snapshotlike comments made by a partial observer, without the benefit of factual analysis, which project personal impressions about the scene. In "Viaje a la

Sierra de la Ventana," Colonel García, while he was at a Ranquel *toldería*, set down his observations of the Indians' deeply rooted custom of bathing every morning in rivers and lakes, regardless of inclement weather.

> We have not seen or suffered a greater freeze, nor a crueler night, but we could not help wondering at the inhabitants of this small settlement, principally those of the feminine sex, who at first light left their dwellings in order to bathe at the shore of the lake. Mothers, more diligent than the fathers, went out with all their children and servants to take part in this exercise, which is generally practiced every day, even on the cruelest winter days. Not a half hour had gone by and yet we saw at the lake all the people of the village bathing, and the husbands and young men still luxuriating in sloth and laziness in their loathsome quarters. We were also surprised that together with the Indian women, among whom this custom is not strange, some captive girls who served as slaves also bathed. We witnessed and observed that they were truly not compelled to do so but did it out of habit and found some moments of pleasure in this practice. Nevertheless we saw that a good-looking girl found the bitter moment that was forced on her unbearable. It seems that she and some of her companions in misery, were of high birth and certainly brought up to quite a different life. How painful, how sad, it was for us to be cold spectators of the misfortune of these poor wretches, victims of misery, unable to run to their aid![43]

The distance that separates the arrogant superiority of the Creole colonel from the monotonous routine of the *tolderías* forms a barrier that does not allow him to see beyond these snapshot scenes, which as a distant observer he set down in his diary. This is a general characteristic of expedition diaries. A traveler catalogs according to preestablished categories and, in doing so, negates the specificity of the person cataloged.

The epitome of this kind of traveler is Colonel Lucio V. Mansilla, a dandy of the generation of '80. Saúl Sosnowski writes: "Mansilla never stopped talking about himself, even when he was purportedly speaking of others,"[44] capturing well the self-absorption and prejudices typical of a social class that had already historically closed the chapter on indigenous contributions to the country at large. In that sense, *Una excursión a los indios ranqueles* (An Excursion to the Ranquel Indians) is the perfect model of an expedition to the interior of the Creole fin-de-siècle generation. Mansilla made the best of the opportunity to express his personal viewpoint about many of the problems that affected the republic.

His observations about the life style of the Ranqueles have something of the amateur anthropologist about them. He wastes no opportunity to devote a large number of his pages to a reflection on the broadest issues of civilization and barbarism, the "Indian question," his view of the country's progress and future. [. . .] *Una excursión a los indios ranqueles* is, above all a "travel book."[45]

On his trip to the *tolderías* of the Ranqueles, Mansilla spoke with many male and female captives. His descriptions fluctuate between compassion and incomprehension. Some captives are portrayed as sorrowful mothers or sacrificial victims, as if against a theatrical backdrop. Mansilla comments on their situation with a tone of compassion proper to the plenipotentiary representative of Western civilization who observes and renders judgment, coloring all he sees with exoticism, verbosity, and adventure. Whatever his state of mind at the moment, he projects it onto the captives. Sometimes they seem to him sad victims resigned to their fate, far from the unquestionable advantages of civilization, and other times they are happy, perfectly adapted beings.[46] "They had painted their lips and fingernails, they had put on many beauty marks on their cheeks and they had put shadow on their lower eyelids and eyelashes. They looked very pretty."[47] By that date, the future of the Indians communities of the frontier was already decided. There only remained to adopt the final strategy.

Following the expeditions he made between 1870 and 1875, commissioned by the government of Buenos Aires, the French engineer Alfred Ebélot left a series of written impressions in which he describes and evaluates the human problem of the Río de Plata frontier. As a good positivist, he was moved by his confidence in the infinite possibilities of progress and understood the radical social changes the country would have to undergo. His notes about the Indians and captives he met need no commentary.

> The first thing an Indian does when he returns from an expedition, before embracing his sons and beating his wives, is to set aside his share of the stolen horses [. . .]. Depending on circumstances, they slit the throats of their prisoners. Usually they slit their throats because they are troublesome; but they are interested in Christian women and make an effort to take them to the *tolderías*, where the wretches, exposed on the one hand to the brutality of their masters and to their perhaps even more repulsive caresses, and on the other to the fierce jealousy of the other wives, suffer a horrific fate.[48]

Back in France, Ebélot published between 1876 and 1880 a series of articles in the *Revue des deux mondes* which drew on his observations and the work he did in Argentina. The first of these articles, entitled "An Indian Invasion of the Province of Buenos Aires," opens with the following clarification:

> A very unusual feeling takes hold of a Frenchman of our century, of our critical, rational and slightly pedantic century, when he finds himself in the presence of authentic savages and catches them in the flagrant act of committing savagery, in the full flush of slaughter, robbery, and devastation. Unquestionably, it is a feeling of horror or rather of repugnance, since primitive bestiality seen at close range is prosaically ugly. But at the same time, one feels interested and moved, a kind of curiosity mixed with pity. Pity for those brutal and fierce savages, for those so-called degenerate races. Wouldn't it be more accurate to say that they are fully developed and that their greatest crime is not so much that they are savages but that they are anachronisms?[49]

For Europe at the end of the nineteenth century, South America was still a vast promised land waiting to be used. Europeans always felt themselves to be the beneficiaries of the natural world, and from the first great voyages of the fifteenth century they had not ceased in their efforts. The Spanish and Portuguese empires had explored the continent, subjugated its native inhabitants, and despoiled their wealth. The new Europeans, feeling that they were heirs to an as yet undiscovered world, were ready to contribute to a new order, not with service but with civilization. America was of interest to Europeans as a task to be undertaken and as a field for experimentation, but also because of its exoticism and mystery. There was nothing new in this, although in the nineteenth century the possibilities of travel and exploration had grown. The new discoverers were making breaches through which the first flow of immigrants would seep. Anthony Pagden defines a traveler as a mediator whose voyage serves to separate one universe from another.[50] Travelers were the avant-garde of that exploratory and predatory civilization. In this sense, the captive is also a traveler, but a traveler sui generis, since his knowledge is the result of a traumatic experience.

The Captive as Traveler

Auguste Guinnard and Benjamin F. Bourne had begun their voyages of exploration with different purposes. The former wanted to experience and emulate the exploits of his grandfather and, while he was at it, to make his fortune. The latter sailed to Patagonia as part of his journey to California, the new promised land, where gold fever was reaching its zenith at mid-century. The plans of both men were cut short by their unexpected capture and servitude. They experienced the lives of their captors at close range and with an unwanted intensity. From interested, distant observers, they became victims of their own curiosity. To what degree are their observations more valid than those of other travelers, whether scientists or diplomats?

Since the previous century, life on the southern frontier had generated constant contacts among its inhabitants. Indians, Spaniards, and Creoles traded, negotiated, and made war on each other. In the course of these exchanges, frontier inhabitants had numerous opportunities to become acquainted with each other as neighbors or mediators. However, the journey of the captive is one that goes beyond the frontier, to the heart of the other, whose culture ceases to be a piece of information and becomes an inclusive or exclusive daily reality. For captives, Indians cease to be characters in a local color scene, notes in a traveler's notebook, and instead become human beings from a different culture with whom they must learn to live, or die. Knowledge in their case was a survival mechanism that allowed the traveler to adapt to an alien daily environment. The bottom line depended to a great degree on the captive's ability to adapt. Those who resisted by constantly raising cultural defenses suffered loneliness and alienation. The stereotypical image of the savage neither disappears nor becomes hazy, it acquires sharpness. Benjamin Bourne, for one, was barely able to cross the barrier erected by his bigotry, and Guinnard too first saw his captors in a stereotypical way. But through daily contact with their captors, captives' first impressions modified according to their experiences, the passage of time, their captors' character, and their own adaptability.

Cannibalism

It is remarkable, however, that some preconceived notions, part of the collective imagination, persisted, constantly altering the perceptions of personal experience. I refer, for example, to Western belief in the innate cannibalism of all Amerindians. From the early days of the discovery, chroniclers and officials had corroborated the conviction that the Indians were cannibals. Columbus writes that cannibalism is practiced not far from where he is, while Bernal Díaz del Castillo and other chroniclers of the conquest of Tenochtitlan give abundant descriptions of the cannibalism that followed human sacrifices. But it was the German Hans Staden who gave the definitive descrip-

The captive Hans Staden exhibited by Tupi Inwa women.
Engraving by Theodor de Bry, published in *America* (1563).

tion, rich in morbid details, of the cannibalistic practices of the Tupinambá. In 1553 Staden was held captive for a year by this tribe of the Tupi-Guaraní people. His account was published in 1557, upon his return to Germany. This first edition was followed by many others, with translations into Latin, French, and Dutch. More than three centuries later, the first Portuguese edition appeared in 1892.[51] His account was accompanied by engravings showing in detail the man-eating activities that so impressed Staden. The drawings were prepared under his supervision, and the bearded Staden appears in them, bound and awaiting sacrifice. The book enjoyed wide dissemination in Europe and served to reaffirm belief in the chronic cannibalism of Amerindians.

Forever after, one of the risks feared by European discoverers and travelers was the imminent possibility of being sacrificed and devoured. Everyone in the sixteenth century accepted this belief, including persons who had lived among Indians and traveled extensively in the continent, like Father Bartolomé de las Casas.[52] Cannibalism was in fact practiced among the Tupi-

Guaraní peoples, and more specifically among the Tupinambá, who sacrificed their enemies as a sign of restitution.[53] But the inhabitants of the pampa's southern frontier knew very well that cannibalism was not practiced by any tribe in the area. They worried about being captured and murdered, but not about being eaten.

Benjamin Bourne lived three months in captivity with the Patagonians obsessed by the idea that they were going to eat him the next day. This fear is expressed in the most pressing manner in the first moments of his captivity.

> I looked round on a bleak and cheerless region, and forward on a life as barren of human joy, made up of every species of suffering—hunger, cold, fatigue, insult, torture—liable to be cut short by the caprice of my tormentors, and so wretched that death itself, with all the enormities of cannibalism, lost its terrors by comparison.[54]

His firm belief that he was going to be sacrificed kept him from reading the signals of his captors, who always treated him with respect and consideration. There is no mention of any abuse in the whole of his narrative. The Indians fed him; they invited him to hunt guanacos, a principal activity of men; they communicated with him as best they could, considering the language barrier; and they took an interest in his stories.

> They would sit around me for hours, as eager as so many children, their eyes and ears all intent, while in broken Spanish, mixed with a few Indian phrases that had been grafted into my speech through the ear, aided by abundant gesticulations, that shadowed forth and illustrated whatever was obscure in expression, I spun yarns of no common length, strength and elasticity. Sometimes, in response to a general call from the company, the old chief at the end of some marvelous tale, would command me to tell it again.[55]

On one occasion, when he was resting in the tepee he shared with the cacique's family, he heard a large group of Indians approaching the tent in an aggressive and demanding manner. They held a long and hard discussion with the cacique, which Bourne interpreted as the cacique's resistance to hand over his prized captive. Terror-stricken and exasperated, "clasping my arms about his dirty neck, patting his breast, and looking (with as confiding an air as I could assume) into his dull eyes, I begged him to speak to me, to tell me what these men wanted. 'Do they want to break my head?'"[56] The cacique's reply broke the spell: "'The men don't want to hurt you,' he said; 'Indian wants a girl for his wife; poor Indian, very poor, got no horses nor anything else. I won't give him the woman.'"[57] His constant apprehension made him interpret every tribal conflict as if his person were the only subject of discussion. The obsession did not leave him. Days later, he writes that he heard a young Indian say that three whites, captured previously, had been sacrificed and eaten.[58]

Auguste Guinnard was not exempt from fears arising from his prejudice. During his first night of captivity, his fears would not let him sleep. "All through the night which followed, a crowd of thoughts oppressed me. In my sleeplessness, the remembrance of my companion's death was always present to me. I formed a thousand conjectures as to the destiny which the Indians were reserving for me. What appeared most probable to me was, that they were reserving me for some solemn sacrifice."[59] His first comments about the Poyuches, the Patagonian group that captured him, are colored by his previous beliefs. "Their intelligence is limited, their character grave, their physiognomy stamped with a wild ferocity and incredible hardihood. . . . They are very courageous and daring in the infrequent wars in which they have occasion to take part, but most barbarous toward their Christian enemies, whom they torture and kill without pity."[60]

In time, his opinions became more nuanced as he became familiar with his captors. Guinnard spent more time in captivity than Bourne, which allowed him to discard unfounded prejudices and identify cultural traits with greater subtlety. His narrative is of extraordinary ethnographical value. He spent three years with three different groups of captors versus Bourne's three-month captivity. Time is unquestionably a defining element in a captive's experience. It allows him to learn the language of his captors, opening the door to communication. Bourne and the Patagonians communicated by signs and a few random Spanish words. The Patagonians answered him in their rudimentary Spanish. When he overcame the language barrier, Guinnard was able to work as Calfucurá's secretary and translator.

Gigantism

Another universally accepted myth about the inhabitants of Patagonia was their gigantism. The legends about giants and pygmies come from the popular imagination of the Middle Ages. Cantino's map, drawn in Lisbon in 1502, shows the Island of the Giants in the vicinity of the recently discovered but as yet unmapped Indies. Amerigo Vespucci refers to the same island in his second voyage and locates it in present-day Curaçao. For his part, Pedro Mártir de Anglería, ready to accept any dubious information as good, points to the many comments conquistadores made about the great height of Indians.[61] In his chronicle *La Argentina,* Ruy Díaz de Guzmán mentions Magellan's circumnavigation of the globe and his original contact with the inhabitants of the strait: "After they explored the Río de la Plata, they followed the coast until they were about 50 degrees from the Strait, where seven harquebusiers jumped ashore and found giants of a monstrous magnitude."[62] Belief in the gigantism of Patagonians extended until the nineteenth century, and it was corroborated by travelers and sailors who went near the southern lands.

In many other parts of the continent, chroniclers and travelers also seem inclined to see giants everywhere, whether from fear, the power of suggestion, or the desire to enhance the value of their deeds. Hernando Escalante Fontaneda mentions the gigantic stature of the Florida Indians. Before even touching land, Bourne refers to the Patagonian Indians as "monsters" and "black-looking giants." Further on, when he is in daily contact with them, he verifies that they are tall, although he keeps insisting that their appearance is that of giants.

> In person they are large; on first sight, they appear absolutely gigantic. They are taller than any other race I have seen, though it is impossible to give any accurate description. The only standard of measurement I had was my own height, which is about five feet ten inches. I could stand very easily under the arms of many of them, and all the men were at least a head taller than myself. Their average height, I should think, is nearly six and a half feet, and there are specimens that could have been little less than seven feet high.[63]

The details about their size are accompanied by other descriptions that stress projected images of monstrosity.

> They exhibit enormous strength, whenever they are sufficiently aroused to shake off their constitutional laziness and exert it. They have large heads, high cheek-bones, like the North American Indians, whom they also resemble in their complexion, though it is a shade or two darker. Their foreheads are broad, but low, their hair covering them nearly to the eyes; eyes full, generally black, or of a dark brown, and brilliant, though expressive of but little intelligence [. . .]. They have deep heavy voices, and speak in guttural tones—the worst guttural I have ever heard—with a muttering, indistinct articulation, much as if their mouths were filled with hot pudding.[64]

A sailor with Patagonian Indians. From the book *Voyage Round the World,* by John Byron (1767).

Surprisingly, he describes the women as being rather short, adding something about dirtiness, which is strange in reference to Indians in that region, who generally bathed daily.

Guinnard was held captive by two different groups of Patagonians, the first of whom was the Poyuches. But being a curious and subtle observer, Guinnard distinguishes the following groups of Patagonian Indians: "the Payou-tchets, the Puel-tchets, the Caillihé-tchets, the Tchéouel-tchets, the Cangnecaoué-tchets, the Tchao-tchets, the Dilma-tchets, and the Yacanah-tchets."[65] He describes the Payou-tchets (Poyuches) as not very intelligent, grave of character, possessing fierce features, but kind in their demeanor. He makes no reference to their height, but does mention their hygiene: "Cold as these regions are for the greater part of the year, the Indians who inhabit them bathe every day before dawn, whatever may be the season, and without distinction of sex or age."[66] He considers the Tchéouel-tchets (Tehuelches) the most backward and poorest of the Patagonians, and inferior in size.

The second group with whom he lived were the eastern Patagonians. "In stature they appeared to me to approach six (French) feet; their type appeared to me to differ little from that of the Puelches. I found them slightly longer in the back, perhaps, compared with their height, and, seeing them on horseback, one might easily believe them to be taller than they are in reality."[67] Some Patagonians were taller than the average nineteenth-century European. If a traveler like Bourne, after three months of direct contact, insists on the Indians' gigantism, it is perhaps because he was aware that his narrative was meant for a potential reader who was eager to consume tales and fables of a world that was still exotic. From the earliest encounters, Europeans found it hard to separate their observations and make them compatible with their values and beliefs. The weight of strong traditions held sway in a continent which even after the discovery continued to export myths and legends. The step from the immeasurable to the measurable turned out to be too large a distance to cross.

An awareness of the reader, no doubt, influenced the writing of captivity narratives, texts made up of a variety of discourses. There are objective and classificatory descriptions, of which Guinnard and Bourne offer more than enough examples; value judgments that stress the savage and primitive appearance of the captors; fables extracted from the collective imagination. And there are also elements of suspense and surprise, which make the reading more attractive and occur disproportionately at the dramatic moment of capture and at different stages of the captive's escape or attempted escapes.

The Narrative of Santiago Avendaño

The only text by an Argentine written in the first person and published in the nineteenth century is Santiago Avendaño's. It appeared in the *Revista de Buenos Aires* in three parts, the first two in volume 14 (1867), under the title "La fuga de un cautivo de los indios," and the third, "Muerte del cacique Painé," in volume 15 (1868). In 1979 all three parts were collected into a book entitled *Cuestión de indios*, published by the Argentine Federal Police. Avendaño is of interest for several reasons. For one thing, it is obvious that the published articles were fragments of a larger text. The last of the three articles ended in an ellipsis, inviting the reader to a continuation that never came. Inquiries made by different researchers failed to discover the whereabouts of the original manuscript. In April of 1999 the entire text finally turned up. *Memorias del ex cautivo Santiago Avendaño* (Memoirs of the Ex-captive Santiago Avendaño) was edited and published by the scholar Father Meinrado Hux, who found the manuscript in the archives of the Museo de Luján, among the documents belonging to the writer Estanislao S. Zeballos. The discovery is of extraordinary significance, not only because the manuscript is valuable on its own, but because it answers some of the enigmas regarding the sources used by Zeballos to write his trilogy about the caciques of the pampas: *Callvucurá y la dinastía de los Piedra* (Callvucurá and the Dynasty of the Piedra) (1884), *Painé y la dinastía de los Zorros* (Painé and the Dynasty of the Zorros) (1886), and *Relmu, reina de los Pinares* (Relmu, Queen of the Pinares) (1887). A footnote by Zeballos in the first edition of *Calvucurá y la dinastía de los Piedra* reads: "This chapter is rigorously exact. I have taken the information pertaining to the period 1833 to 1861 from a most curious manuscript of 150 folios which in 1879 I found in el Desierto, in the midst of dunes, near what is today the town of General Acha."[68] Reading this, one can make the connection between the "most curious manuscript" and Avendaño's narrative.[69] The first version of my book was based on a series of hypotheses about Santiago Avendaño and his adventures in captivity that I formulated from the information in the three fragments published in the nineteenth century. The publication of *Memorias* has led me to restructure my book.

Memorias del ex cautivo Santiago Avendaño is a fundamental work for understanding the indigenous society of the *toldos*, the complexity of intertribal relations in the pampas, and the role played by the captives, *capitanejos,* and Creole renegades who spent their lives crossing the frontier back and forth. It also sheds light on a little-known historical fact, the role played by Indian tribes in the civil wars, when *unitarios* and *federales* clashed almost without interruption from 1820 to Roca's rise to the presidency in 1880. Both *federales* and *unitarios* constantly sought alliances with the Indians in order to further their causes. Indian *malones* were motivated on many occasions by the policy of harassment pursued by both factions.

Written from the sympathetic perspective of someone who knows the extraordinary complexity of the Indian world, *Memorias* is a pleasure to read. Avendaño writes: "I have read some writings, some articles which speak of the history and the customs of Indians without having known them up close. What they express is incomplete, insufficient and adulterated."[70] Avendaño spent seven years in the *toldos,* and dedicated the rest of his life to the cause of improving relations between the tribes and the government of Buenos Aires.

Avendaño's Captivity

Santiago Avendaño was born in the province of Mendoza on July 24, 1834. He was the youngest in a family of five children. He was taken captive at the age of seven during a *malón* in which the Ranquel caciques Painé and Pichún took part, as well as the renegade colonel cacique Manuel Baigorria, who sympathized with the cause of the *unitarios.* According to Hux, the *malón* might have been the result of "one of the actions in the civil war between *unitarios* and *federales,* which were common in the decade of the 40s."[71] Avendaño does not give many details about the incidents of the *malón;* he says only:

> I, Santiago Avendaño, was carried off by an invasion of Ranquilche Indians from a rural settlement in the south of the Province of Santa Fe, on March 15, 1842. I was then exactly 7 years, 7 months and 21 days, when I was torn from my parents. Papa's name was Domingo Avendaño and Mama, Felipa Lefebre. We were five brothers: Juan José, Andrés, Pepe, Fausto and I. My older brothers taught me to read because there was no school in the neighborhood. I was the

youngest of the boys. I was born July 24, 1834. On March 16 of 1842 the Ran-
quilche Indians dragged me with them to their *toldos*. Later I learned that the
invasion had been led by the caciques Coliqueo, Painé, Nahuelcheo, Anequeo,
Quechudéo, Caniú-Cal, Llemuel-hue, Llanquetruz, Güelé, Yanqué, Trolui-laf,
Calfuqueo, Güenu-vil, Güenu-Cal and others whose names I forgot.[72]

He was assigned to the Ranquel cacique Caniú, who brought him into his
family circle and treated him as his own son. Avendaño does not hide this; on
the contrary, he makes constant references to the love shown him by his adoptive father and other relatives, which turned his experience into a "happy captivity." At the age of twelve he showed signs of total adaptation, working as an
cowherd and caring for Caniú's one hundred dairy cows.

In 1846 a peace accord between the Ranqueles and the governor of
Buenos Aires, Juan Manuel de Rosas, included as a mark of good faith the return of ten captives on the part of the Indians. Cacique Pichuiñ, who had bro-
kered the accord, asked several caciques to contribute one captive as part of
the ransom demanded. Caniú, Pichuiñ's nephew, refused to include his
prized captive Santiago, despite strong pressure from his uncle. "We all have
an interest in peace," he said, "but we always see that we can't secure it. I have
a boy who is like a member of my family. He is the man of the house [*rucá*]
whenever I am gone. I find it impossible to cede him for the time being."[73]

The relative freedom his job afforded him—he had to herd the milk cows
to better pastures—allowed Avendaño to come into contact with other captives and with someone who would exert great influence in his life, Manuel
Baigorria. This man was an ex-colonel of the *unitario* army who, being pursued because of a warrant for his arrest, decided to seek refuge in the *tolderías* of the Ranquel cacique Painé, to whom he was related. He offered his
services to the Ranqueles, instructing them in military tactics, and took part
in numerous *malones*, more as an adviser than as a warrior. He had four wives:
a *china* (an Indian woman) and three captives.[74] He played a very important
role in relations between the Creoles and the Ranqueles, even after Rosas's
defeat in Caseros (1852). Baigorria belongs to that kaleidoscope of frontier
characters who dealt constantly with Indians, captives, merchants of any origin, military men, refugees, deserters, gauchos, and mediators. Borders were
vague lines, constantly crossed by this whirlwind of characters whose variable
relations made up a dense web of cultures in endless flux. Baigorria protected
the young Avendaño and encouraged him to escape, instructing him on the

best ways to do so. The opportunity arose when a *malón* was being planned against the settlements of San Luis. Caniú and other principal caciques were going to participate, which gave Santiago the chance to escape without being noticed. Baigorria urged him to take advantage of the opportunity.

> The invasion will be at San José del Morro. We have to go north in a straight line from this point on. Therefore, you can go straight toward the setting sun passing Los Loros Lake. There you can follow a trail that will lead you to *Chazileufú* (Desaguadero). When you get to the river you won't find any trail, just some paths which lead nowhere [. . .]. Continue always in a northerly direction [. . .]. I almost forgot to warn you, and this is the right moment to tell you what you need to do. In the first place, my son, don't implicate me [. . .]. You could be followed and they might catch up to you. In that case you should suffer the consequences of your crime without mentioning my name.[75]

Avendaño's *Memorias* are full of gratitude for Baigorria, and he defended him against the criticism of his contemporaries. The controversial deeds of this colonel, who became a *capitanejo,* were not easy to defend. Santiago gave him the opportunity to explain himself:

> Christians say that I am the cause of all the devastation. That I am the leader of the Indians. They consider me guilty of all the murders and robberies they commit. And that I am responsible for the suffering of so many wretches who have the bad luck to fall into captivity. My enemies say all this to warn people against me. But my conscience is far from considering me an accomplice in all these things. On the contrary, my conscience is clear because I have done everything I could, as a Christian, to help many. I have tried to lighten the misery of some, claiming them as my relatives. And I would have left them free in their homes, the moment I acquired them, but how many obligations would that have brought me?[76]

Santiago decided to flee. On November 1, 1849, he chose his best three horses and left at dawn. Seven years, seven months, and fourteen days had gone by since his capture, he tells us. From his detailed descriptions, it is obvious that he was familiar with the terrain. He describes each plant and animal, calling them by their Pampa names. "For sleeping I chose the shelter of a bush the Indians call *chayum,* which resembles rosemary because of its small leaves. In height it was about a yard and a half."[77] As in the case of other captives who escaped to the vast southern plains, the lack of water was his greatest enemy and the ultimate threat. Overcoming the obstacles of time,

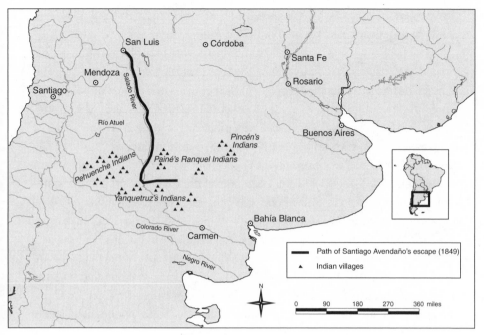

Map 8. Escape Route of Santiago Avendaño

distance, hunger, and thirst, Santiago Avendaño finally reached a ranch in the settlements on the outskirts of San Luis. He was able to warn the population about the Ranquel *malón* that had left the *toldos* at the time of his flight. "This good news made people in San Luis very grateful to me. The prominent members and families of their society sought permission to have me in their homes for a while. One after another they begged the governor to let them have the pleasure of seeing the 'captive child.' No one was denied the favor of having me visit for a while."[78]

His parents no longer lived in San Luis. They had moved to Guardia de Luján, in the province of Buenos Aires. Governor Juan Manuel de Rosas took an interest in the fugitive and helped him locate his family. Shortly after his return, however, another unexpected captivity began for Santiago. When he turned fifteen, he expressed a desire to follow the religious life, but was unable to do so for unexpected reasons. Because he refused to attend a military parade decreed by the provincial government, he was imprisoned in the garrison at Palermo for almost two years, until Rosas's fall in 1852. This incident was for the young Avendaño an authentic and terrible captivity, to which he devotes more space in his *Memorias* than to his captivity in the *toldos*. This part of the narrative is typical of anti-Rosas literature.

After he was set free, Avendaño wanted to devote himself to an activity that would serve the cause of the Indians and connect the two worlds he knew intimately. He was named "interpreter of the province of Buenos Aires." His job took him back to Salinas Grandes to negotiate with Calfucurá, who, disoriented by the fall of his ally Rosas, was preparing a great *malón* against the province. In 1859 Avendaño married Genoveva Montenegro, and they had seven children. He was promoted to lieutenant with the title of "interpreter of indigenous languages and chief of scouts of the First Division of the Southern Army in Azul." He continued to visit the *toldos* of Calfucurá and Catriel on different diplomatic missions until well into 1868. But he was mistrusted by Sarmiento's government, which dismissed him from his post and began a campaign to discredit him. Then he was offered the post of mayor of the Indians in the town of Azul. It was a difficult charge because it entailed both defending and controlling the Indians. His close friendship with Cacique Cipriano Catriel made the task easier, but also lead to his death. Avendaño became, in effect, the adviser to Catriel's Pampa Indians, who had been allies of the *unitarios* during Rosas's government. However, angered by the ingratitude of the new *unitario* government, Catriel sided with the Autonomistas in the fateful revolution of 1874. Defeated by troops loyal to the government, Catriel and Avendaño were taken prisoner. Handed over to Indian troops who had remained loyal to the government, they were publicly executed, their bodies pierced by lances.

Publication of Avendaño's Narrative

It is interesting to speculate on *La Revista de Buenos Aires*'s motives for publishing a mutilated text. The information in the two articles that appeared in 1867 and 1868 was confined to Avendaño's escape and a fragment of the chapter he wrote describing the funeral of Cacique Painé, when several of his wives were sacrificed in his honor. Besides the escape itself, little or nothing is revealed about the captive, his age, the names of his captors, dates, or any other interesting facts. The narrative centers fundamentally on the flight, with all its dramatic elements: unexpected dangers, exhaustion, despair, thirst, fear of being followed and captured, determination, hope, and the final liberation.

Perhaps it was the sympathetic attitude toward the tribes which emerges from the complete text that made the editors of the *Revista* decide to publish only selected passages and ignore the rest. There are chapters which possibly form part of Avendaño's project to write a history of the Indians, a project he never finished. The first chapters of the manuscript include information about Calfucurá's hegemony in the pampas, passages he entitles "Ranquel History," episodes about the deeds of the Pinchiras, and various chapters devoted to explaining the conduct of ex-colonel Manuel Baigorria. Tense relations with the tribes of the interior, at a juncture when the final offensives against the Indians were being prepared, made the complete narrative an embarrassing if not subversive text. This reservation did not, however, apply to his flight. The escape was another triumph of Creole society recovering one of its own from barbarism. It could be read as the exploit of a Christian youth (there are several references to the intervention of the Most High) who, evading the vigilance of his Indian captors, chose the spiritual benefits of Creole society, and in so doing became a hero of civilization. In the passages concerning his flight, there are no Indians or *tolderías*. The protagonist is set against a menacing landscape, personified in the first night's storm:

> [T]he wind began to blow hard, heralding a violent hurricane, which was not long in coming: water, stones and wind. As a precaution I got off the horse at the first signs of the storm [. . .]. The poor horses fought against the storm, they could not avoid the blows they received on their heads. Lighting struck with horrible frequency and so close that I and the horses were almost left unconscious.[79]

The stormy terrain, the saltwater lakes and streams, the ravines and irregularity of the land, and the predatory threat of a *tigre* (jaguar) create the proper backdrop. At times, the story is reminiscent of the best literature of the period, for example, key passages of Esteban Echeverría's *La cautiva*.

The Drama of Escape

Benjamin Bourne spent his three months of captivity thinking about being ransomed or escaping. He kept his captors in a constant state of expectation, promising more barrels of rum, sacks of tobacco, and other articles prized by the Patagonians if they would take him to be ransomed at one of the Christian settlements on the coast. The Indians well understood the value of their captive and guarded him accordingly. A Christian who did not speak their tongue, who was another mouth to feed, and who moreover was devoid of manly skills like guanaco hunting was of little value. If he was valuable, it was for the ransom he could bring. On one occasion, during long and complicated operations to ford a river, a task that took the whole tribe two days, Bourne saw an opportunity to escape. His master had remained on the other riverbank when night fell. Bourne thought of letting himself drift in the swift river current on an improvised raft and thus take the first step toward liberation. He approached the river when it was dark, but the constant barking of the dogs, who sensed his presence, raised suspicions and forced him to desist.

Desperate, he considered suicide if his situation did not improve. After months of constant insistence, his master decided to take him near Holland Island, where fishing schooners often put in. He was accompanied by three Indians. On the coast, the first day went by without their seeing any person or ship. They returned disappointed. The next day, luck smiled on them. Near the coast Bourne spied an approaching boat. Without a second thought, Bourne ran to the rocks on the beach, hurled himself into the bay's icy water, and swam vigorously toward the boat.

> My strength was fast failing me; the man at the helm, perceiving it, stretched out a rifle at arm's length. The muzzle dropped into the water, and arrested my feeble vision. Summoning all my remaining energy, I grasped it, and was drawn back towards the boat; a sense of relief shot through and revived me, but revived, also, such a dread lest the Indians should give chase, that I begged them to pull away,—I could hold on. The man reached down, and seized me by the collar, and ordered his men to ply their oars [. . .] and working my body up sufficiently to get one knee over the gunwale, I gave a spring, with what strength was left me, and fell into the bottom of the boat.[80]

During the following weeks Bourne was pursued by nightmares that brought back his anxiety that at any moment his captors would jump the barrier of the strait to recuperate their prized captive. These fears did not abandon him until he arrived, many months later, at his destination in California.

Auguste Guinnard found some stability in Calfucurá's tribe, where he spent the last stage of his three-year captivity. He enjoyed some liberty, his own room, and some freedom of movement. He had won the confidence of the Mapuche cacique.

> During the time of my misfortunes, I was never so happy as in the midst of this tribe, where, in my quality of *tchilca-tuvey* (writer to the grand cacique), I enjoyed general consideration and a certain credit. At my request, I was authorized by Calfoucourah [Calfucurá] to construct for myself a little cabin of canes near his tent. He took pleasure in watching me execute this work, the daily progress of which he followed.[81]

However, before he made it to Calfucurá's salt beds, Guinnard had had to escape his previous captors, a Pampa group, who accused him of betraying them and threatened his life. With them he had performed the tasks typically assigned to captives. He wasn't the only captive with that group. The narrative mentions many more and makes note of a large population of children of the captives, the result of continual miscegenation. "The most regular types may now very often be found among the Pampeans; these are the children of Indians and captives."[82] His stay with the Pampas was not a happy one. He complains of mistreatment, especially from the children, who amused themselves by throwing sharp objects at him and making him the constant butt of their jokes. He had two options: integration or flight. Guinnard did not reject the first option: "I might even have made out a kind of existence with my masters if the ill-treatment to which I was constantly exposed had not rendered my sufferings yet greater."[83] The second option, flight, constantly comes to his mind. Depressed, he also considers suicide.

Quite by chance, one day the Pampas discovered that they could make good use of their Christian. They found him reading some old papers, and they conjectured that if he knew how to read, he might know how to write. In this manner, he became their scribe, but bad luck pursued him and he was accused of having distorted messages dictated by the cacique.

> The first correspondence was carried to the frontier by Indians named by the cacique; one of them was my master. Some children accompanied them to carry the articles intended to be exchanged. Twelve or fifteen days after their departure, these children returned, exhausted by fatigue, terror in their faces, and uttering cries of distress. They related that after the dispatch had been read, the two envoys had been put in irons, awaiting death, and that it was certain I had betrayed the general confidence, and communicated some details of their

recent invasions. Naturally inclined to believe ill, these barbarians had no other intention than that of killing me.[84]

There was now no option but escape. He fled at night, after stealing a horse and stampeding the rest of the herd. As luck would have it, he was very close, a day's gallop, from the *toldos* of Calfucurá, who believed his story and defended him against the claims of his pursuers. The prestige of this centenarian, called Blue Stone, was unquestionable by this date. According to Guinnard, Calfucurá treated him with kindness and promised his support.

The degree of freedom he enjoyed in Calfucurá's camp allowed Guinnard to devote himself to observation of the Indians' customs. From time to time, the narrative is enriched by detailed descriptions of the complex world of the *toldos*. The depiction of the tenderness and solicitude with which he was treated—the proselytizing tendency of most tribes—is an element absent from travelers' narratives when they speak of captives, but it appears in accounts of those who lived among Indians.[85]

By the time of Guinnard's captivity, relations with the Indians who inhabited the vast territory of the pampas toward the south had worsened as land and cattle became progressively scarcer. The long confrontations, broken treaties, and unbroken series of *malones* had turned frontier neighbors into enemies. Nevertheless, Indians were aware of the need to inject new blood into their decimated tribes. The teaching, education, and care of captive children, youths, and women were tasks that Indians carried out when it was likely that acculturation and adaptation would be complete. Adult males were harder nuts to crack, but not hopeless cases. Guinnard repeatedly mentions this with respect to Calfucurá, although his experience with the other tribes with which he lived, Poyuches, Puelches, Patagonians, Pampas, and Salineros, was very different.

Despite the decidedly comfortable situation he had with Calfucurá's Salineros, Guinnard took the opportunity to escape offered by a celebration in the aftermath of a *malón*. Equipped with a lariat, bolas, and three horses, he undertook the uncertain nighttime escape. Thirteen days later, bearing the marks of his sufferings and thirst, Guinnard, accompanied by a single horse and a faithful dog, arrived at a ranch in Río Quinto where a Spanish family lived. The first stage of his escape had ended. On the ranch he recuperated as best he could and decided to ensure his liberty by crossing the Andes to Chile. The memory of his past misfortunes led him to opt for the mountain range, although the journey was longer and more complicated than via Buenos Aires.

On this second leg of the trip, Guinnard began to feel the first signs of depression.

> When I became convalescent, they seized every occasion to procure amuse-
> ment for me; but, in spite of their efforts, I remained in a feeble condition, my
> so long over-excited and tortured mind being unable to regain its quiet. I was
> constantly, as it were, under the influence of a terrible nightmare, in which all
> the horrible circumstances of my life of slavery, during which I had been night
> and day exposed to the chance of a tragic end, repassed before my eyes. Some-
> times it was the recollection of the many assassinations I had seen accom-
> plished by the Indians under my eyes, or, oftener, of circumstances under
> which I had been obliged to exercise the greatest coolness and energy in strug-
> gling with my murderers. When these horrible visions left my sight, and calm-
> ness returned to my exhausted senses, I felt incapable of speech or action. My
> weakness was such that the sound of my own voice caused me a sort of surprise
> and melancholy, for the use of speech was at least as new to me as the enjoy-
> ment of that dear liberty, after which I had sighed and wept so often.[86]

Modern psychiatry, psychoanalysis, and neurology have given the name post-traumatic stress disorder (PTSD) to the devastating effects that an extremely threatening or frightening experience can have on the human psyche. The trauma can produce hallucinations, insomnia, depression, and other uncontrollable symptoms: "As such, PTSD seems to provide the most direct link between the psyche and external violence and to be the most destructive psychic disorder."[87] Cathy Caruth argues that the trauma caused by these extreme situations is the effect not only of a destructive situation but also of the enigma of survival. The central idea of her argument is that only through the recognition of the relationship between destruction and survival can one understand the limits of these catastrophic experiences. In that sense, the experience of adult white males from a culture radically different from that of the Indians, and without previous contact with them—as was the case for several of the captives studied—fits well within this symptomatology. After crossing the Andes and reaching Valparaíso and Santiago, where he was well received and given every attention by friends and consuls who opened their homes to him and offered him work, Guinnard continued to experience the effects of post-captive trauma.

However, in spite of this wonderful change in my existence, my health was very much shattered, my nights were mostly restless and agitated by nightmares, which often disturbed the sleep of Monsieur Barthès, and made him very anxious on my account. When I was awake even, I could not shake off the distressing effects which any kind of surprise had upon me. The sudden appearance of anyone, or the unexpected sound of voices, shook my nerves and brought on a sort of convulsive trembling. My sudden change of food, instead of mitigating my liability to these attacks, seemed rather to augment it.[88]

The notes that close Guinnard's account help us to grasp the traumatic effects of three years of insecurity, fear, and unpredictable threatening situations. The narrative of his fascinating journey closes with these words, which are a subtle diagnosis.

As at Valparaiso, so it was on board the vessel that was bearing me to France, my mind, oppressed by long-continued misery, was absorbed by two conflicting emotions: the desire to return to France, and to all those whom I loved, and an incessant struggle with the reminiscences of my captivity.

Like Mungo Park, escaped from the tyranny of the Moors of the Great Sahara, I was a long time believing in my deliverance. It was with me as with that great traveller: I needed to cross the ocean, to return to my country, to the restorative calmness of the paternal hearth, to free my sleep from visions, and my brain from phantoms conjured up by the odious remembrance of the brigands of the desert.[89]

In time, Bourne and Guinnard resumed civil life, not without the benefits of the small degree of glory that their adventures earned for them. Their stories were well received by scientific societies and major newspapers. Meanwhile, in contrast, many ex-captives in the Río de la Plata suffered from ostracism and were rejected because of similar experiences. Their narratives were never written. Their lives were lost in anonymity. All that remains are concise depositions which time and dust devour on the shelves of historical archives.

Conclusion

It is nothing short of surprising that the two most complete narratives published about captives in the pampas and Patagonia in the nineteenth century were written by a Frenchman and a North American, and that, furthermore, they should be published in Paris and Boston, respectively. It is more striking when we consider that there were thousands of captives in eighteenth- and nineteenth-century Argentina. For Europeans, captivity was part of the exotic world rediscovered and redefined by the Enlightenment and the spirit of progress that was blowing through the continent. Scientific and literary societies were predisposed to study and propagate new knowledge about this world, while a growing market readily consumed its exotic products. In the case of New England, this spirit of renewal was reinforced, through a literature that had reached great heights of popularity, with the experience of those who had been captives of Indians in North America. It is not surprising that both markets happily received the narratives of Auguste Guinnard and Benjamin Franklin Bourne.

The reverse side of the coin can be seen in the coldness and lack of interest that captivity narratives faced in Argentina. The builders of the Argentine fatherland were not interested in stories that humanized Indians. Their *toldos* and *malones* represented serious political and economic problems that called for radical measures. There was interest in travel books, since, besides furnishing fascinating information about the geography of the nation and its expansive possibilities, they portrayed the life of the interior with a photographer's objectivity. The campaigns of the desert, whose purpose was to eradicate any Indian menace, were not compatible with the old project to save the noble savage—that is, if there were still noble savages. The only published Argentine text we have is Santiago Avendaño's, which centers on the flight of a fugitive who escapes from the Indians to return to the comforting hands of civilization.

⚔ FIVE ⚔

The Northern Frontier
From the Chichimecas to the Comanches

Andele got accustomed to this form of worship. He became an
expert and at last ventured one day to try to cure a wounded
man whom a Texas Ranger had shot. He gathered with the
crowd of medicine men around the man and began to sing the
buffalo song. This song is sung only over men who have been
wounded. It would be a sacrilege to sing it for mere amuse-
ment, or on other occasions than bloodshed. They shook buffalo tails over the man as they sang, and finally one of them
cried out, "I feel like my gods are all over me." He slapped his
sides, and shook himself, and roared in mimicry of the buffalo
bull, and began to spit red paint that he had in his mouth into
his hands and rub it upon Andele's face, and say to him, "There,
I give that to make you a great medicine chief." And Andele
verily thought that this would endow him with greater power.

—Methvin, *Andele: The Mexican-Kiowa Captive*

After the fall of Tenochtitlàn in 1521, there were several rapid movements
of territorial expansion. In the east Spaniards penetrated up to the legendary Pánuco River, and in the west into the arid lands of Baja California.
The adventures of Álvar Nuñez Cabeza de Vaca and his brave companions in
Florida and the Gulf of Mexico inspired the first major Spanish expeditions
north of the viceroyalty of New Spain, commanded by Father Marcos Niza,
Francisco Vázquez de Coronado, and Juan de Oñate, among others. In truth,
these expeditions were more like forays into a vast and unknown territory,
a kind of Pandora's box. Their fate was to reap some success and many fail-

ures, and they never established permanent settlements. Northern expansion brought administrative regulations that compartmentalized the new territories into the entities of Nueva Viscaya, Nuevo León, Nueva Galicia, Nuevo México, and eventually Texas, Pimería Alta, and California. In time, the deserts and mountains of the north would become a great frontier. Too extensive, unknown, hazardous, and mythical, this territory would prove difficult for settlers to possess. The history of northern Mexico is defined by a constant process of negotiation among new and old neighbors, adventurers, entrepreneurs, settlers, administrators, autochthonous Indians, and nomadic tribes. The study of this multiethnic frontier, and the Spanish failure to subjugate it due to the strong resistance of its inhabitants, is the subject of this chapter.

The scarcity of captivity narratives until well into the nineteenth century hampers the construction of our history. The data we have employed are taken from the letters and documents of governors and *adelantados* (frontier mayors), who were the agents of the difficult Spanish advance. In the early eighteenth century, the northern Mexican frontier was made problematic by the arrival of Apache and Comanche tribes who descended from the east and north of present-day Texas. The multidirectional activity of these tribes and their strong resistance to the European invasion resulted in the taking of many captives, some of whose narratives (only a few) have been preserved. Thanks to them, we have been able to trace, not without difficulties, the history of captivity along this frontier of tumultuous and endemic confrontations.

The Northern Advance: The Chichimecas

Rather than speaking of a frontier, perhaps we should speak of a series of juxtaposed minifrontiers. They acted in several directions, with multiple and contradictory energies, and shaped intense processes of assimilation and acculturation. This extensive territory, intuited but never well known, was a free land of promising riches and vertical mobility, not exempt from dangers that challenged the survival skills of its inhabitants. In this sense, several authors have found similarities between the experience of this frontier and the Anglo-American frontier.[1]

In his unusual journey, Cabeza de Vaca had observed the existence of numerous indigenous peoples who among themselves negotiated forms of coexistence and mutual influence. With the arrival of the Spanish and the introduction of horses, this fragile equilibrium slowly came apart. New invaders appeared—the Comanche, Ute, and Apache tribes—who made good use of the mobility the horse gave them. They came down to the territories of New Mexico and the valleys of the Río Grande, threatening and upsetting the frontier equilibrium as much as the expeditionary forces of the Spanish army and colonists. Their arrival precipitated wars of invasion, defensive skirmishes, surprise attacks, the breakup of communities, and the separation of peoples. All of which was punctuated by pillaging, massacres, and the taking of captives. In 1787 the general commander of the Provincias Internas (as they were called), Jacobo de Ugarte, informed the viceroy of New Spain in a letter about the many robberies, assaults, and kidnappings perpetrated in the region of Sonora, by bands formed by individuals of varied extraction: Taraumara Indians, mestizos, *palenques* (runaway slaves), mulattos, *coyotes* (wild Indians), *lobos* (Afro-Indians), white Indians, and some Apaches.[2] These transcultural bands lived off the robberies and depredations they perpetrated on frontier settlements, taking advantage of the instability and lack of protection in the zone. The existence of this human whirlwind defined the nature of the frontier. The absorption of whites, blacks, and mestizos into Indian communities, be they captives or renegades (white Indians), unquestionably had an impact on the process of miscegenation that was gradually taking shape. They brought new technologies, tools, customs, beliefs, ways of preparing and seasoning food, military strategies, and other basic knowledge which were gradually absorbed.

The nations or tribes that the first expeditionaries met on the northern frontier were fundamentally different from those of the cities and federations of the central valley of Mexico. With the exception of Pueblo Indians in New Mexico (the Zuñi, Acoma, and Hopi), who built their dwellings of adobe and organized their community around stable agricultural production, in the north the Spanish had to deal with nomadic tribes with a rudimentary level of material development. These tribes reacted to the Spanish invaders in two ways: either through passive resistance, compromise, and flight, or through different kinds of armed confrontations, perpetuating wars that refuted the supposed superiority of the Spanish army. The Mixtón Wars (1541–42) and the prolonged Chichimeca Wars (1550–1600) exemplify the steely indigenous resistance to the invader and the Spanish inability to resolve conflicts for which they were not adequately prepared.

The first great penetration into the territories of northern Mexico occurred as a result of the discovery of silver deposits in the zone of Zacatecas around 1540, in the kingdom of Nueva Galicia, founded in 1530 by the Spanish conquistador Nuño Beltrán de Guzmán. To this area came an avalanche of adventurers and settlers, following what Philip Powell has called "silver highways."[3] They set out on the hazardous journey accompanied by relatives and cattle, and they settled in places that until then had been the domain of nomadic Indians known as Chichimecas. The name Chichimeca had a double connotation: it referred to the northern tribes subjugated by Cortés's conquest, but it was also an insult meaning "dirty, uncivilized dog."[4] Numerous reports by the heads of Spanish expeditions mention these Indians' nakedness and their lack of a fixed domicile. Under the generic Chichimeca name were grouped four principal nations: Pames, Guamares, Zacatecos, and Guachichiles. Some more bellicose than others, these peoples shared a common stock and had taken part in the recent Mixtón Wars. The unstable peace, negotiated in 1542, was broken by the massive arrival of new white colonists, whose settlements near the mining centers threatened the habitat of the tribes. The reaction of the Indians was not long in coming. The violent Chichimeca Wars lasted from 1550 to 1600. The fierce reputation of Chichimeca warriors increased as the war of resistance wore on. The Chichimecas, later compared to the Araucanians for their tenacity and bellicosity, were formidable warriors, inured to the harshness of an arid environment and feared for their natural aggressivity and their reputation for cannibalism. "These nomads, who are the terror of the roads, cattle ranches and mining camps, fought constantly among themselves (war trophies—scalps, weapons and women—were their greatest glory), lived and fought in small groups called rancherías, almost without discernible and respectable leaders."[5]

The Chichimeca Wars were the longest wars between Europeans and Amerindians in the territory of North America. The first decade of the war was dominated by the Indians, to such an extent that they threatened the survival of the precarious mining colonies and the expulsion of the white population from the silver frontier. The feared Chichimeca warriors attacked the Spanish settlements inhabited by the racial kaleidoscope that characterized frontier society, made up of Spaniards, blacks, mulattos, mestizos, and Indian allies. The raiders stole the cattle, burned what remained on their way out, and murdered most of the inhabitants. On rare occasions they took captives. The prisoners were murdered in situ or tortured with refined techniques which increased the Chichimecas' fearsome reputation, not only among the Spaniards but also among the resident Indians subjugated to Spanish power.[6] The report written by Gonzalo de las Casas is very explicit in this respect.

> The warriors would also cut off the genitals and stuff them in the victim's mouth. They impaled their captives "as the Turks do." They removed various parts of the body, leg and arm bones and ribs, one by one, until the captive died; the bones were sometimes carried off as trophies. Some victims they threw over rough cliffs; some they hanged. They also cut open the back and tore out the sinews, which they used in tying arrow tips to shafts. Small children, not yet walking, were grabbed by the feet and their heads beaten against rocks until the brains squirted out.[7]

To these terrors one has to add the widespread belief in the man-eating practices of Guachichiles, mentioned in the reports of many governors and other officials, and which further terrorized the Spaniards and their allies. The psychological effect of these implicit threats had a great influence on the colonists and soldiers and defined the administration's policy of aggression in the northern territory. Indians captured in war were by decree made slaves and sold in the city of Mexico. In the slave market the going price for a Chichimeca warrior was eighty pesos and one hundred gold pesos for a young woman.[8] The uniqueness of the Chichimeca Wars consisted precisely in the breaking of the ideals of the *Leyes de Indias* (Laws of the Indies), which forbade the enslaving of Indians, a practice that was repeated, on a temporary basis, at the beginning of the seventeenth century in Chile. Slavery was authorized against rebellious Indians, although in practice it was used as a solution to the inability of viceregal authorities to recruit soldiers to serve on the frontiers. The ploy did not work because, according to some contemporary reports, many of the great Chichimeca leaders learned their military strategy while serving in the Spanish army or in Franciscan missions.[9] Insurgent Indians were also punished by hanging, the amputation of limbs, beheading, or burning at the stake, although slavery was the most common practice.

For their part, Chichimeca tribes took enemies captive as a form of resistance, but also to maintain a demographic balance. It was not a new practice; like most North American tribes, they had taken captives from their neighbors before the arrival of Europeans. Peter Stern concludes that "under the pressures of war and disease, Indians had to resort to replenishing tribal and band populations through raiding for captives."[10] The Chichimecas also captured pacified Indians from the zones of Guadalajara and Zacatecas who were allies of the Spanish. It can be argued that even among the civilizations of the valley of Mexico—Aztecs, Mexicas, and the cities of the Mexican confederation—captives were taken in wars in order to feed the supply of the cult that demanded sacrificial victims.[11] Accustomed as they were to the process of integration that had taken place in most of the cultures in the valley of Mexico, Spaniards were greatly surprised by the resistance of Chichimeca warriors.[12] As we saw in chapter 1, the previous instances of captivity in the territory known as Florida were accidental. During the Chichimeca Wars, whose impact was measured in great loss of life and property, the Spanish encountered for the first time the scourge of captivity used as a strategy of aggression and defense by indigenous societies.

In the Chichimeca Wars captivity followed the pattern observed in other parts of the continent. The Indians normally took young women and children who were not infants. Adult males, older women, and breast-feeding children were either ignored or killed in the act. Hernando de Vargas, in his report "Descripción de Querétaro," mentions the scarcity of women in the Gran Chichimeca (the area where the Chichimeca were active), which explains why they were valued prizes.[13] As the war wore on, the practice of taking captives became more common, motivated by their exchange value. Stern estimates that hundreds of captives were taken in the Chichimeca Wars.[14] According to Powell, "the damage inflicted upon Spaniard and Indian by the nomadic warriors greatly exceeded, in property as well as lives, directly and indirectly, any previous Spanish-Indian conflict on the mainland of North America."[15] Nevertheless, despite the high number of captives recorded in contemporary reports and the number of those who were rescued, in the official frontier reports we have only lists of names. Captives neither wrote nor were encouraged to write, a characteristic we have observed of all Spanish-Indian frontiers.

We can therefore conclude that the information captives might have provided was not considered valuable, either because it could equally be obtained from friendly Indians, the Indian slaves who served in the Spanish forces, or because the captives' testimony might challenge the alleged superiority of Spanish troops. Spaniards, like all Europeans, were so convinced of the superiority of Christian culture that the notion that a white person could elect to live among savages went beyond all established norms and was rejected with disbelief, especially if the savages in question were the primitive Chichimecas.

The long Chichimeca Wars came to an end at the beginning of the seventeenth century. The peace policy of the Spanish authorities had ultimately borne fruit, allowing the control of most tribes disseminated in the corridor between the viceregal capital and the isolated territories of Nueva Galicia.

This was not the end of northern expansion. A new frontier was opening farther north, in the kingdom of New Mexico, which was being colonized at that time. The experience of the Chichimeca Wars taught the Spanish administration several lessons, especially about methods of pacification. Nevertheless, control over indigenous communities and territorial stability were not guaranteed.

A New Way to the North

Five years before the definitive pacification of Nueva Galicia, in 1595, Juan de Oñate was given a royal grant to conquer and settle New Mexico. Three years later, he began an expedition made up of 130 soldiers, settlers accompanied by their families, a small group of Franciscan monks, and seven thousand head of livestock. Rumors about the fabulous wealth of the mythical cities of Cíbola had never died out, despite the failure of Vázquez de Coronado and Father Niza. The reports of Pedro Castañeda Nájera, chronicler of the Coronado expedition, cited the existence of seventy-one indigenous peoples in the valley of the Río Grande.[16] They were sedentary people, grouped in settlements with adobe houses and engaged principally in agriculture. They maintained a difficult equilibrium with the Apaches and Navajos who prowled the vicinity of their communities.[17] Oñate managed to settle in the area inhabited by these peoples and tried to carry out, without much success, different colonizing enterprises, although he spent most of his energy looking for minerals. The Franciscans were more successful, overcoming many difficulties in order to found several missions in the territory. It is estimated that in the 1630s about fifty missionaries were catechizing in the region, including Texas.[18]

This is the main reason why the kingdom was not abandoned, despite the suggestions of Viceroy Montesclaros. The lack of minerals, the aridity of the land, and the great distance from the capital of the viceroyalty made these territories a difficult enterprise to sustain, and a drain on the royal treasury. In addition, the initial hospitality of the Pueblo Indians soon turned to hostility. The triggering incident was the severe punishment that Oñate ordered in 1598 against the inhabitants of Acoma, the first village to rebel against the Spanish occupation, in response to the killing of eleven Spanish soldiers and Oñate's nephew Juan de Saldívar.[19] Oñate orchestrated a harsh reprisal against the village of Acoma, where Spanish troops attacked the defenseless inhabitants, destroying houses, murdering five hundred men and three hundred women, and taking captive some five hundred men, women, and children.[20] Oñate was punished for the brutal assault, but the initial harmony had turned into open hostility, leading years later to the great Pueblo Indian revolt in 1680. The administration's protection of the Indians and the paternalism of the missions could not compensate for the harsh reality: the Spanish colonists and their army needed Indian labor to survive in a difficult and alien environment.

The Pueblo Indian revolt of 1680 wiped out all vestiges of Spanish colonization. Settlements were destroyed, churches burned, missionaries murdered, and women and children taken captive. Pueblo Indians belonged to millenarian cultures, and despite their apparent hospitality they resented the profound transformations that the arrival of the Spanish had imposed on them, with their new gods, new techniques, different social relations, and heavy tax burdens. From the beginning, chiefs, but especially shamans and medicine men, were the principal leaders of the resistance against the white invaders.[21]

In the revolts, Pueblo Indians took women captive, the wives of colonists and soldiers, an uncommon practice among them. In the letters Diego de Vargas sent during the years of the reconquest and pacification of New Mexico, he mentions the recovery of captives taken thirteen years before during the revolt. Seventy-four were liberated by Indian allies in El Paso in 1691.[22] On the expedition to the village of Acoma, one of the most hostile to Spanish colonization, two members of the expedition, José Madrid and Martín Hurtado, recovered their sisters: Lucía Madrid, with two children she had in captivity, and Juana Hurtado, with two girls and a boy (one of the girls and the boy had Indian fathers).[23] Not all of the captives were Spanish. Among those liberated were some mestizos and Indians.

It is a bit surprising that during the revolt of 1680 Pueblo Indians would adopt practices that were in large measure alien to them. Traditionally, Pueblo Indians were the victims of the sporadic attacks of their neighbors, nomadic tribes from the east and west. *Genízaros* are a special case in the history of captivity in North America. Although there isn't total agreement about their origin, they are thought to be former Indian captives from a different origin, most of them Pueblo Indians, taken primarily by Apaches and Comanches and sold to the Spanish or liberated by them. *Genízaros* lived in independent communities on the periphery of villages, where they worked as servants and shepherds. Ironically, it was expected that they would be the first line of defense against hostile tribes.[24] In Arizona they were known as *nixoras,* and they were marginal beings, ambiguous products of the conflict-ridden frontier.

Thirteen years went by before the Spanish reestablished their abandoned bases in New Mexico. After the pacification of the territory by Diego de Vargas, some former colonists who had moved south of El Paso returned. The new phase of colonization was more secular in character. Missionaries went east and west to the zones inhabited by bands of nomadic Indians. To the west stretched the kingdom of Nueva Viscaya, which included the present Mexican states of Chihuahua, Durango, Sinaloa, and Sonora. Nueva Viscaya was conceived as the heart of the northwest frontier. In the seventeenth century it was the most densely populated zone north of the viceregal capital. Besides different Apache tribes, this area was inhabited by Conchos, Salineros, Janos, Masos, Tarahumaras, Sumas, and Pimas, who in turn suffered the sporadic hostilities of Comanches, Utes, and Navajos from the north. The arrival of the Spanish and their policy of "guerra a fuego y sangre" (war by fire and blood) complicated relations among these different tribes.[25]

Between 1640 and 1780 Spanish authorities established *presidios* (frontier garrisons) and imposed a policy of alliances with friendly Indians, whom they used as auxiliaries in campaigns against the tribes that resisted colonization. Under the impact of multiple encounters and the need to restructure the difficult ethnic and cultural equilibrium, new frontier relations evolved in which captivity, in several directions, became a routine practice. Indians took captives during their swift attacks on Christian settlements, and the Spanish took captives in the course of their campaigns against the "barbaric," non-Christian Indians. Bribes, ransoms, exchanges, barter, and payments were common practices that bore witness to the widespread character of the phenomenon. The 1680 Pueblo Indian revolt affected the neighboring territory, spreading like a wave to the west toward Sonora, in what has been called "the Great Northern Revolt."[26]

The first testimony we have dates from 1644–46 and describes the capture of Antonia Treviño and her children by Salinero and Cabeza Indians. Three of her children were murdered in her presence, and one her daughters was given as gift to a Salinero Indian. Antonia worked as a servant for several months until she was sold to Toboso Indians. She died among them during an epidemic.[27] In October of 1692 Diego de Vargas wrote that he had found a captive woman with three sons and a daughter, all born in captivity. She turned out to be Petrona Pacheco, wife of Cristóbal de Nieto, a resident of Sonora, captured during the 1680 revolt.[28] From the time of the Pueblo Indian uprisings until the truces of the 1720s, the number of Spanish held in captivity by Cabeza, Jojocome, Cocoyone, and Acoclame Indians increased. Numerous depositions speak of freed captives: whites, mestizos, mulattos, blacks, and even army captains. Generally they were young men, children, and women.

Each declaration presents a unique story, thwarting any attempt at generalization. In 1715 the declaration of two young men from the area states that they were captured by four Indians and a mulatto, whom they described as the most violent of the group. On the way, the captors killed a third captive because he complained of the cold and did not let them sleep. The deponents managed to escape.[29] In 1692 a seventeen-year-old ex-captive declared that he had passed from the hands of the Cabeza Indians into those of the Jojomes. The declaration concludes by saying that his last master "called him brother and treated him like a son, and never let him go barefoot or be mistreated by anyone."[30] In 1724 a fifteen-year-old boy, born in Guanaceví, declared that he had been captured with his mother, whom the Indians killed immediately. They took him to a camp where they planned to marry him to an Indian girl. He was able to escape at night. Two other Christian fugitives stated that in their captors' camp there were two assimilated Spaniards who refused to escape with them, alleging that among the Indians they didn't have to work and that they saw no reason to change their life.[31]

Reading the reports of governors, expeditionaries, and former captives, we deduce that the treatment accorded prisoners depended on the character of the captors. The bad reputation of Chichimecas and Comanches is not always supported by existing accounts. Stanley Noyes, an expert on Comanches, says that exceptions to the norm are more revealing than the norm itself.[32] Captives might be tortured, murdered, enslaved for the personal service of their captors or their wives; educated and incorporated into the tribe with full privileges and obligations; or, in the case of women, married and incorporated into a family. Governor Juan Bautista de Anza asserted that he had recovered captives in perfect health from the hands of Indians. On the other hand, the tragic fame of the Comanche chief Cuerno Verde II spread as a prototype of the tribe's cruelty. Lieutenant José María Sánchez y Tapia, artist and cartographer of the Comisión de Límites (Boundary Commission), wrote that Comanches "commit all manner of cruelties on their enemies [. . .]. Some prisoners are burned slowly for days; others they amputate parts of their body and apply glowing coals to their wounds, others are scalped and their heads held to the fire. They also use other terrible methods."[33]

Apaches, Comanches, Utes

After 1730 the threat of the Apache, Comanche, and Ute tribes and their allies spread through the kingdom. Comanches appeared in New Mexico at the time Vargas was reconquering the territory. Their arrival produced major adjustments in the difficult balance of intertribal relations. Raids and robberies were constant. They knew the territory, they moved swiftly, and they came armed with weapons acquired from the French.[34] The governor of Nueva Vizcaya, Felipe de Barri, asserted that, between 1771 and 1776, 1,763 persons had been killed in Indian fights, and 155 taken captive in the narrow corridor between the villages of El Gallo and Cuancamé.[35] The administration and the authorities viewed this worsening human drama with growing concern. Nevertheless, there was no efficient policy for ransoming captives until the arrival of Teodoro de Croix, whose administration lasted from 1776 to 1783. Worried about the loss of manpower, but also by the moral charge of abandoning prisoners to what he believed was a horrible fate, De Croix implemented a policy of recovering captives through ransoms and exchanges. He made compulsory the recovery of captives in Indian hands and urged the communities of *genízaros* in Sierra Blanca and Sonora to liberate the Apaches, which they in turn were holding captive.[36]

The main obstacle to the ransoming of captives was the absence of necessary funds, since most relatives lacked the resources. De Croix created a charitable fund for the redeeming of captives and encouraged the citizens of the kingdom to make contributions, which were collected through city halls and mayors. This initiative was not too successful, and in general donations to these funds were meager, despite the pressure exerted by families to recover their relatives. The most desirable products for which the Indians would barter were rifles, bullets, gunpowder, knives, shirts, underwear and blankets, cotton or linen cloth, tobacco, corn, and cattle. Exchange rates were not constant but varied in each transaction. One twelve-year-old boy was bartered for four knives, a sack of tobacco, two bushels of corn, four blankets, and six yards of woven cloth.[37]

The recovery of captives ran into additional problems. If the captives had spent a long time in captivity, their relatives might not be found because they had left the area. It was also difficult to identify liberated captives, especially when they had been carried off as young children. This was the case with a girl named Tomassa, who, after being returned by the Comanches in an exchange with the Mexican government, was never able to find her relatives. She was eventually handed over to a landowner as a servant.

The information we have is certainly too sparse to establish a sociology of captivity, but it helps us to understand the persistence of the phenomenon and the reaction of the authorities, which varied according to the period and the governors. Diego de Vargas, in 1692–93, affirmed that he had rescued 29 captives in New Mexico. Barri accounted for 155 in Nueva Vizcaya between 1771 and 1776. For his part, Felipe de Neve alludes to 152 captives recovered in 1784, in the territories of Texas, Louisiana, and New Mexico in negotiations with Comanches, and Gila and Mescalero Apaches.[38] The redemption of captives continued to be a common practice until the end of the nineteenth century, although documents become scarce after the truce of 1780.

The Northern Frontier in the
Nineteenth Century

The northern territories of the Spanish Empire were chronically unprotected for centuries. The northern frontier was of interest to the empire as long as it kept the promise of mineral wealth or as long as missionaries believed that the missions were a spiritual investment that compensated for the loss of life. When the Spanish period ended in 1821, after independence, the demographic map did not change appreciably. The north continued to be an inaccessible, remote frontier, peopled by pioneers and daring colonists and periodically overrun by bands of Comanches and Apaches who destabilized the territory. Before it seceded from Mexico, the population of Texas was only a third Mexican, the rest were Anglo-Saxons who came from the east. A difficult equilibrium was maintained between these settlers and the original inhabitants of the plains. The Comanches were a relatively manageable problem until the end of the war with Mexico in 1848, when the dimensions of their habitat gradually became reduced by the massive influx of settlers. Then their raids on the property of Mexicans and Anglos became more frequent and violent. Various sources tell of the alarming increase in Comanche attacks in the 1840s. Buffalo Hump, the famous Comanche chief, led raids into the territory of San Luis, Zacatecas, Chihuahua, Tamaulipas, Coahuila, and Nuevo León, at the head of more than eight hundred warriors.[39] In one of these attacks in Chihuahua, Comanches took a hundred and fifty captives. A Mexican who had spent many years in captivity told the Indian agent Robert S. Neighbors that the number of Mexican captives in some camps exceeded three hundred. In some reports, the numbers seem to exaggerate the magnitude of the problem. A Texan woman, exchanged by the Comanches, asserted that the number of captives in some camps was greater than the number of Indians.[40] Stanley Noyes maintains that the Comanche reputation as fierce Indians comes from that period, when the resources for survival dwindled as the United States expanded. Comanches and Apaches had no choice but to adapt to the new circumstances by stealing cattle and taking captives.[41]

Francisca Medrano was approximately four years old when she was taken from her father's house in New Mexico, together with a brother and a sister,

Coyotero Apache with Mexican captive.

by a band of Comanche marauders. Her parents died in the raid, and she never saw her brother and sister again. From the tranquility of the patio where she played, Francisca began a long journey full of emotional experiences. She lived to be a hundred (1831–1931). When she was old, she told her story to the Methodist missionary A. E. Butterfield, who transcribed it and had it published in a pamphlet entitled "Comanche-Kiowa and Apache Missions."[42] To judge from her narrative, Francisca doesn't seem to have any good memories of her time with the Comanches. She worked hard, like most captives, carrying water and firewood and serving her captors in everything they needed. Fortunately for her, she was sold to the Kiowas. During her life with them, she married a warrior and had three children.[43] None of the children survived. Francisca's narrative is evasive regarding these years. When her first Indian husband died, the Kiowas sold her back to the Comanches. With her new Comanche husband, she had a daughter, Margarita.

In 1869 the Federal Reserve Policy, established under the initiative of President Grant, placed Indian reservations under church control, hoping that religion would be a more effective overseer than the army. It was the same tactic followed by Catholic missions in Spanish America. As part of this initiative, a new series of reservations were established to serve as a curb to Indian raids, but also to help integrate the Indians who accepted the peace treaties that had been signed. To that end, in 1869 Fort Sill was founded in Oklahoma to give refuge to Indian families and help with the reintegration of former captives. The fort was built in the Wichita Mountains, an area of three and a half million acres. It is estimated that in the first years it sheltered more than five thousand Kiowa and Comanche Indians. Lawrie Tatum, a Quaker farmer, was appointed the first agent of the Kiowas in Fort Sill.[44]

Francisca decided to avail herself of the protection of the reservation. At Fort Sill, she was helped by a Mexican family and met a young Spaniard by the name of Abilene Medrano, who was a deserter from the Spanish army. Medrano protected her from the claims of her Comanche husband, who came to the fort, escorted by Comanche warriors, to demand her return. After some time, Francisca and Abilene were married and had three children, Louise, Juan, and Bonifacio. As part of the treaty with the U.S. Army, Francisca, who never considered herself Comanche, Kiowa, or Mexican but Aztec,[45] received 160 acres of land. Francisca and her husband made good use of the property and set to raising horses and cattle. They prospered and were able to leave their children an inheritance and property. Louise married an American army officer. Bonifacio, born when Francisca was fifty, was his mother's support after the death of his father in 1895.

In her account Francisca says little or nothing about her life among the Indians. She seems to rush through those years, like a fugitive. She doesn't mention the names of her Indian husbands, nor those of her dead children. Was she ashamed of her experiences in captivity? Was it a stigma to have borne the children of Indians? Curiously, her third marriage was to a Spaniard. Most of the narrative is devoted to her life at Fort Sill and especially to the work she did for the Methodist mission. She tells us that she never learned English, that she spoke Spanish and Comanche fluently, and that she never abandoned her Christian practices, even when she was married to Kiowa and Comanche warriors. Nevertheless, some Indian customs obviously did not leave her, because she never allowed herself to be photographed. She argued, according to the Comanche belief, that if she were photographed her spirit would leave her and she would die. She died on April 21, 1931.

The fact that Francisca's story was written by a Methodist minister certainly gives us much food for thought. The fact that he reduced to a minimum the part of her life devoted to the Indians and their practices, while dwelling on a detailed description of the former captive's contributions to the Methodist mission, is an unambiguous indication of the scribe's purpose. Furthermore, the narrative gives a full account of Francisca's conversion, which was the work of the pioneer Methodist missionary J. J. Methvin. It was he who was responsible for transcribing the stories of other ex-captives, Tomassa and Andrés Martínez (known as Andele). Methvin believed that the stories of these Indianized ex-captives, who had embraced the Christian faith, would serve as moral fables from which valuable lessons could be drawn. Speaking of the ex-captive as a model for all to follow, Methvin wrote: "His salvation and his development into a permanent and substantial civilization are as bright as the promises of God."[46]

Tomassa, Comanche Captive

There are many parallels between the stories of Francisca Medrano and Tomassa. The latter was born in Mexican territory in 1841, a time of radical change on the northern frontier. The Indian population, pressured from the east, was moving south. They had two options: they could either keep their nomadic freedom, or settle down on the reservations that had been set aside for them near army forts. At this time it was still possible to see bands of marauding Comanches, Apaches, and Kiowas on the outskirts of Chihuahua.[47] The kidnapping of several dozen women and children could be a question of survival for these tribes, considering the precariousness of these groups, always on the border of extinction.[48]

Tomassa had been carried off by Comanches and adopted into the group of the Carissa, who years later included her in an exchange negotiated with the Mexican government. Several months after the treaty of Guadalupe-Hidalgo, the Mexican government had not yet appointed an agent to oversee the exchange and reception of captives. Finally, under pressure from the U.S. government, an agency was installed in the city of El Paso, although it did not really begin to function until 1851.[49] When Tomassa arrived, no one in Mexico claimed her, and she wound up working as a servant for a rich family. Unhappy and missing her Comanche family, Tomassa decided to escape in the company of a boy who served in the same home and had arrived under similar circumstances. "The two children, possibly no more than ten or twelve years old, planned to return to the Comanches."[50] Finding her Comanche family, hundreds of miles away and in an unknown land, seemed virtually impossible. Tomassa was not cowed, however, and she thought through every detail of the flight.

> Stealthily hiding out food until a sufficient store had been accumulated, they left the hacienda or ranch one night, while a big party was being entertained and, taking a horse they fared forth on their return to the Comanches, hundreds of miles distant, with naught but the North Star as their guide. When their food gave out they killed the horse, dried the meat and took the hide along to use in making moccasins.[51]

Luck or destiny helped the two children overcome enormous difficulties. "When the last of the dried meat was gone and they were nearly famished, they stumbled into a Comanche camp, which providentially proved to be that of the very band with whom they had formerly lived."[52] Tomassa was reunited with her former family, with whom she spent the rest of her adolescence.

When it came time for her to marry, Tomassa refused to accept Blue Leggins, the man chosen by her mother. Once again she showed the rebellious spirit that had pushed her to flee from her Mexican employers years before. She argued that she wanted to marry Joseph Chandler, a mestizo with Chiroque blood, a merchant and owner of a small ranch, much older than she. Chandler was known to the Comanches because he raised horses and traded with Indian tribes. He spoke the Chiroque language fluently. To appease Blue Leggins he gave him three dollars and a rooster, thus acquiring rights to the girl. Tomassa and Chandler got married and settled near Fort Cobb, in Indian territory, where they raised the cattle they sold to the Comanches. They had a daughter and three sons. During the American Civil War, they were forced to emigrate, but they returned in 1868 and settled on a ranch near Fort Sill.

The end of the Civil War meant the end of slavery in the United States, but for Indian tribes of the West the options for survival did not improve. In Fort Sill, Tomassa worked as an interpreter. She spoke Spanish, English, Comanche, and Caddo. However, she often objected to the rules imposed on reservation Indians. She became an advocate of the Comanches, even of those who were not integrated into the reservation system. When Joseph Chandler died, Tomassa married George Canover, with whom she had three more boys. She accepted baptism and served the Reverend J. J. Methvin for the rest of her life. It was he who set down her story. A little before Tomassa died, she wrote a will which ended with a note that gives an excellent indication of the type of woman she was. "Wait, One more thing. My pony has pulled my buggy long time now, and he is old, and I want him to work no more, but let him have plenty good grass, and cared for, and fed plenty of corn and oats."[53] She died near Anadarko at the age of fifty-five.

Reverend Methvin's Compilations

One of the most complete narratives of a Spanish American captive, from the period before the territory was annexed by the United States, is that of Andrés Martínez, known to Indians as Andele. The adventure of his life and captivity with the Kiowas, among whom he became a warrior and a medicine man, is known to us thanks to Rev. J. J. Methvin, whom Andele served at the Methodist mission during the last years of his life. The fact that the narrative was transcribed by a Protestant minister links it to the tradition of captivity narratives from the North American continent. Richard VanDerBeets writes,

The earliest Indian captivity narratives published in America, those of the seventeenth and early eighteenth centuries, are straightforward and generally unadorned religious documents for the most part Puritan. [. . .] The captivity here takes on a typically symbolic and even typological value, reinforced by frequent scriptural citations.[54]

James F. Brooks is even more precise:

Andele's narrative seems closer in some respects to Puritan captivity narratives of the seventeenth century (like that of Mary Rowlandson, 1682) than many of its nineteenth-century contemporaries [. . .]. Like many Puritan narratives, it contains elements of spiritual autobiography, sermonizing, jeremiad, and the secular adventure story, but combines these with the ethnoexoticism of later captivity stories.[55]

While Rev. Methvin was instrumental in extracting from the captives who arrived at his mission the stories of their adventures, his hand is felt in every narrative, since he infuses them with a purpose that was perhaps not present in the original dictation. He insists on reminding us that, thanks to the work of evangelical churches, Indians and captives were saved from the destructive degeneration into which these "savage peoples" had fallen.

We know from the historian Robert Lowie that Andrés was aware of some errors in the narrative of his life as transcribed by Methvin.[56] It is hard to know whether they bothered him or not, especially the simplistic account of his conversion to Christianity and his supposed rejection of indigenous spiritual practices. Andrés's participation in peyote ceremonies seems rather to imply that he was looking for a synthesis of both systems of belief, the kind of syncretic religion so common among indigenous communities in Spanish America.

The lives of these three former captives, Francisca, Tomassa, and Andrés, and of others set down by Methvin are presented as a continuum, marked indelibly by a titanic struggle for survival. In the experience of the captives, the culmination of all efforts, the ultimate goal, is the revelation of Christian faith. At the conclusion of Andele's narrative, Rev. Methvin summarizes its meaning:

A most excellent trait in the character of Andele is his purpose to reach the very highest standard in whatever he undertakes. When E-ton-bo took him into her care and began teaching him Indians songs and customs of the tribe, he made such rapid proficiency that it provoked other boys to envy, and they were disposed to treat him roughly, but being the adopted grandson of the chief, he held prestige on that account, and soon conquered a place of high standing in the tribe.

This aspiration to excel has remained with him through all the years and when he became a Christian, his effort has been to be the very best and most efficient Christian. Religion, therefore, has been to him a real experience, deep and definite.

From the time he knelt at the altar in the little mission church in "old Anadarko," many years ago, down to the present he has never faltered.[57]

Rev. Methvin took his work very seriously, trying to control the Indians' polygamist tendencies and many other customs considered barbaric. With the aid of converts like Andrés, he tried to integrate Kiowa and Comanche children into the mission. In a symbolic initiation designed to "kill the Indian and save the Man," their hair was cut and they were given Western clothing. In this sense, the lives of Andrés and Tomassa were seen as perfect examples of Methvin's missionary efficacy. He writes:

Besides, God has a purpose in it all, for in the apparent calamity that had come to Andrés in his capture, God was overruling it all in preparing him for a life that should glorify him. We shall see as we read on.

God works in mysterious ways, and often His plans are many years in execution.[58]

In Andrés, Methvin found a disciple who served him not only as an interpreter with Comanches and Kiowas but also as a model on which to construct the future of his mission. Andele acted as adviser and as a "shepherd" to the Indians, visiting them in remote places. In addition, he was a model of adaptation to a settled and productive life. He worked the land assigned to him, prospered in his work, and got ahead. He built a house with his own hands near Anadarko, where he lived the rest of his life. At the end of his narrative, Methvin sums up what Andrés Martínez meant in terms of his ecumenical ends and his civilizing effort.

Together we have seen the transformation of Indian life—from the nomadic life to settled homes; from the tepee to the neat well kept cottage; from the fantastic paraphernalia of the Indian dress, to the well regulated dress of civilization; from the crude diet of the old days, served upon the ground, to meals of well cooked food by skilled cooks on tables spread with snow white linen and served with the delicacy of refined and cultured homes; from the wild discordant worship of nature, to the peaceful worship of nature's God; from the medicine tepee with its nightly orgies, to the well built church houses with the inspiring melody of Christian song. And as we contemplate the changes we can but exclaim, "Behold what God has wrought!"[59]

Rev. Methvin's missionary work acquired meaning from the trajectory of Andrés Martínez. The troublesome smudges that might have clouded the glory of the narrative were erased by the deft hand of the scribe who produced a revised and corrected text. Nonetheless, the narrative is of surpassing interest because it furnishes valuable information about the life of a captive of the Apaches and Kiowas in New Mexico and Texas. It is also a document of great human and social value, which sheds light on a crucial moment in the history of the frontier and the last indigenous tribes of the territory. Andrés Martínez's account offers firsthand information concerning the daily life of indigenous cultures, the rhythm of their life, values, socialization, and their death struggle to preserve a way of life. The story of Andrés allows us to follow the pulse of the Apaches and Kiowas in these last and definitive phases of profound intercultural transformation, when adaptable and obsolete elements were being sorted in a complicated process of survival.

The Story of Andrés Martínez (Andele)

Andrés Martínez was born into a Mexican family in New Mexico around 1855. He was the youngest of seven children. At the age of nine, while watching over his family's cattle, he was carried off by a Mescalero Apache patrol, together with his younger nephew Pedro.

> [T]hey were discovered by two Apaches, who, for some reason, had wandered from the main band, and who now ran upon the boys with a wild shout of delight. Rejoicing at the prospect of being chiefs, each singled out his boy, ran upon him, struck him with his spear and then claimed him as a captive.[60]

The first moments were extremely traumatic. Andrés witnessed how the Apaches brutally rid themselves of a Mexican peasant whom they had captured at the same time as the boys. The Mexican's body, bristling with arrows, was left on the dusty road. Days later they did likewise with Pedro, who,

Captive child with Apache children and adults.

terror-stricken and exhausted by the hardships of the flight, was proving to be a hindrance to the rapid pace imposed by the Indians.

> Pedro could go no further. He fainted away in his agony, but revived again and continued to cry piteously. The Indians stopped suddenly. A hurried and earnest consultation was held, when the Indian behind whom Pedro rode sprang from his horse carrying the little boy with him. The little fellow could with the greatest effort only stand upon his feet, strained in every limb, heartbroken, dying. Taking a spear from his belt, the Indian, standing behind Pedro, with a murderous grunt, thrust it through the body of the little sufferer.[61]

The journey to the Pecos River, where the rest of the group awaited them in a provisional camp, lasted twenty days, during which uncertainty hovered over Andrés and the road seemed to stretch on endlessly. Their arrival was greeted with joy, especially when the braves showed their victims' scalps as trophies of the expedition. "The names of the captors were on all lips, and a discordant song in their honor was made for the occasion, while each Indian of the marauding band was bragging about his own achievements."[62]

A new life was beginning for young Andrés. He was assigned to an Apache family, who put him to work carrying firewood and water. Unable to make himself understood, he was treated as a foreign object, especially by the Apache boys, who made him the target of their pranks and mockery: "It was an almost hourly occurrence for the Apaches boys to gather around him and hoot and jeer and throw stones at him, 'til his body was covered with bruises and festering sores."[63] The first family that adopted him treated him with disdain. He changed masters several times without improvement. Several weeks had passed when the tribe received the visit of some Kiowa braves who came to negotiate a peace treaty and a prisoner exchange with the Apaches. One of the visitors took an interest in Andrés and spoke to him in a combination of Spanish and Kiowa. He said his name was Santiago, and he turned out to be a Mexican captive who had grown up with a Kiowa tribe. He negotiated with the Apaches, and in exchange for a mule, two buffalo robes, and a red blanket, he got Andrés. Andrés followed Santiago and his Kiowa group on a three-month march to their permanent home to the northeast of Washita, Oklahoma. "With a glad heart leaving the Apaches, Andrés was soon established in the affections of the Kiowas."[64] When he arrived, he was assigned to E-ton-bo, daughter of Chief Heap O'Bears.

Andrés Martínez, whom the Kiowas called Andele because they could not pronounce his name, grew up among the Kiowas as one of them, participating actively in the phases and rites of passage his adoptive culture required. "Andrés watched everything with profound interest, and he took on the Kiowa ways very rapidly."[65] He took part in punitive expeditions against the Utes, their traditional enemies, and against white settlements to steal cattle and take captives. "Andele was active in his efforts to so learn the arts of Indian warfare that he might become a great chief."[66] He also took an interest in curative practices. He was convinced that he could acquire the powers of a shaman, although his interests were split between becoming a great warrior and devoting himself to curative and magical arts. He married three times. The first two marriages failed, the first because of incompatibility, the second because of a great difference in age.

In 1872 Napawat, successor to Heap O'Bears, decided to accept the protection of the U.S. Army on behalf of the Kiowas. During the first few years of their stay at the Fort Sill reservation they were able to keep their way of life, even carrying out raids against neighboring settlements, from which they stole cattle, mules, and crops. The Kiowas had a reputation for being unruly,

Ute Indian camp.

and they tenaciously resisted obeying certain reservation regulations.[67] If we can trust Rev. Methvin's account, the tribe's arrival at Fort Sill led to a strong identity crisis for Andele. At the reservation, he was noticed by the Indian agent, Lawrie Tatum, who took an interest in him. Tatum had recovered many Mexican and Anglo-American ex-captives under similar circumstances; it was part of his job. By then, Andele no longer spoke Spanish and could not understand the English of the American agents. "Agent Tatum tried to find out where he was captured, and about his people, but he could get no clue to his origin. The Kiowas could only tell that they bought him from the Apaches. Andele had some recollection of home and loved ones, but he dare not tell."[68] While working at the fort's smithy, Andele learned about mail, and wondered whether it could be used to locate his original family. Agent Tobin of the reservation offered to help him and wrote a letter with the return address: "Kiowa and Comanche U.S. Agency, Anadarko, Ind. Ter. January 6, 1883." The note was addressed to Dionisio Martínez (Andele's brother), Las Vegas, New Mexico. It read: "Dear Sir: Did you have a little brother stolen by the Indians many years ago, by name Andrés? The Indians call him Andele. If so, write me at once. He is here, and we think can be identified fully. Respectfully, Hugh Tobin, U.S. Physician."[69] After several failed attempts, one of the letters reached Dionisio's hands, who at the time was living in Colorado with his family. Before long he was in Anadarko to identify his long-lost brother. Andrés was dressed in full Kiowa regalia and his face was painted. Despite this, Dionisio, through the marks of time, recognized the face of his brother Andrés.[70]

Andrés asked permission of the Kiowa council to visit his mother, who was still alive, and his brothers. Twenty years had passed since his capture, and Andrés was a thirty-year-old Indian adult who dressed and thought like a Kiowa. He reached Las Vegas on March 19, 1885. "The white-haired mother, tottering under the weight of years, under the impulse of a mother's love, knew him as he entered the door, although he still wore some of the Indian paraphernalia. She could hardly endure the excess of joy as she hugged him to her heart, and called him her own little boy."[71] Andrés stayed four years with his family, after which he decided to return to the Kiowa reservation in Anadarko. In his absence, his last wife, Ti-i-ti, had passed away. Andrés resumed life on the reservation, worked at a lumber mill, and helped the Methodist church, which had started a new mission in the area.

In 1893 Andrés married Emma McWhorter, daughter of P. T. McWhorter, a Methodist preacher at the mission. He accepted baptism and devoted himself to pastoral duties, being instrumental in the conversion and catechizing of Indians on the reservation. He spoke Kiowa, Comanche, other Indian dialects, English, and the Spanish he had recovered during the four years he spent with his family in Las Vegas. Rev. Methvin describes Andrés as an exemplary Christian dedicated to evangelical labors among his Kiowa brothers. There are, however, other testimonies indicating that in 1923 Andele participated in a peyote ritual that finished with a reading from the Bible.[72] At the end of his life, he was an assiduous informant for scholars and anthropologists, expressing his pride in the history and culture of the Kiowas, his adopted people.

Captivity in Perspective

Andrés Martínez was one of many captives in the vast saga of the frontier between Mexico and the United States. Conservative estimates are that the number of Anglo-American and Mexican captives made up between 10 and 20 percent of the total Indian population. In the case of the Kiowas, it is calculated that by the year 1870, out of a population of 1,879, between 200 and 400 were captives or half-breed descendants of captives.[73] Studies carried out by the Ethnographic Field School of Santa Fe estimated that by 1933 70 percent of the descendants of Comanches were mestizos of Mexican extraction.[74]

What makes Andrés Martínez's story unique is that he went through not one but two processes of acculturation. As a nine-year-old torn from his parents' home he underwent the first process, which transformed him into a young brave, interested in Kiowa medicine. Methvin's pen does not sidestep the intensity with which Andrés gave himself over to the culture of his captors:

> Andele was looking on in astonishment, learning rapidly the Indian ways and absorbing fast the Indian superstitions. He watched Heap O'Bears, and wondered how it was possible for him to do so many wonderful things. He listened to the crowd of howling dancers and watched them as they leaped around in their nakedness before the idol.[75]

Three years after his capture, "Andele had become a veritable Indian with but little trace of civilized life left in him."[76]

On his arrival among the Kiowas he was adopted by Heap O'Bears's daughter, who treated him as her son. The process of integration turned him into a young initiate interested in learning the Kiowa's art of war so that one day he could become a great chief.[77] He was lucky to land in the bosom of a family at the top of the social scale, *ondei,* nobly born, generous warriors, which facilitated his social rise. Not all captives were this lucky. As a brave, he took part in many skirmishes with the U.S. Army and in raids on Anglo-American and Mexican settlements. These fights helped him understand the impact of Western civilization on the indigenous cultures of the continent, and he came to share their hatred for the white invader. At the end of one of the skirmishes with the U.S. Army, Methvin reports: "When the day dawned the soldiers had disappeared, but the battle field, or rather the slaughter pen, was a scene of horror, that gave Andele no good opinion of the white man or his God. Here were Cheyenne men, women and children, slaughtered and lying promiscuously in the snow stained with their own life blood."[78] Like any other Indian, Andele wanted vengeance against the white man. Totally integrated, he aspired to more. He was no longer a child and could make decisions about his future. He wanted to be a chief and a medicine man.

> Andele became completely Indianized. He took up his time in studying the Indians ways, for he had now come to believe all their superstitions, and engage in their worships. He had caught the spirit of their aspirations, and he hoped to be a great war chief. He thought the Indian idol, or "medicine," would pity him and help him, and so he cried to it, and often at night he would get up, go to the medicine man, worship, and offer a blanket or bit of property he possessed.[79]

The second and reverse process of acculturation and adaptation, to Anglo-Saxon culture, was slower and more painful, and subject to greater resistance. This makes sense, because Andrés was born in a Mexican, not an Anglo-Saxon, family. Furthermore, he was now an adult who had adopted Indian ways, and although the tribe under the leadership of Napawat had decided to accept the protection of the army, it continued to follow many of its old customs. The trip to Las Vegas to visit his family was fundamental in bringing about the change in Andele. During the four years he stayed with them, he shared the routine of daily life with his brothers and mother and regained the Spanish he had forgotten. In 1889 he decided to return to the Kiowas. After so many years of living together, he missed them. But his Indian wife had passed away, and he felt alone. He began to attend services at the Methodist church, built during his absence near the reservation, in which he was later baptized. It is hard to understand what impelled him to make this drastic change. Rev. Methvin's explanation, which interprets Andrés's decision as part of the divine plan, is not convincing. In any case, Andrés became part of the Methodist church as an active Christian. His life had made a 360-degree turn.

Andrés's narrative is set in the last independent years of the tribes of the Plains and the Southwest. Andrés witnessed the capture of Lone Wolf, the head chief of the Kiowas from 1866 to 1874, as well as that of Big Tree and Satanta. In exchange for the freedom of their chiefs, the Kiowas agreed to submit to the U.S. Council of Indian Affairs. The Kiowas had been known to the Spanish since the eighteenth century, and some had even been incorporated into Spanish society and received Catholic baptism. It is certain that captives played an important role in this process of assimilation. This is recognized today by many historians of the frontier in North America.

In Arizona, New Mexico, and Texas, even some members of warring tribes such as Apaches, Comanches, and Kiowas, became partly assimilated into Spanish society. In one extraordinary case in California, an Apache, Manuel González, was appointed alcalde of San José! The process of assimilation of individual Indians (a process quite different from that of the accommodations made by Pueblos and other tribes), usually began with women and children whom Spaniards had captured or ransomed and taken into their households to become Christians and to provide cheap labor.[80]

In 1807, in the governor's palace in Santa Fe, Kiowa chiefs approved treaties of peace and cooperation in exchange for "friends' gifts," that is, economic compensation. As time went on, North American expansion from the east and aftereffects of the Civil War destroyed the existing equilibrium in the zone. The incorporation of Andrés Martínez into Kiowa society took place at the moment when the power of the Kiowas and the other Indians of the Comanchería (Apaches, Utes, and Comanches) was vanishing.

Andrés's experience transports us to the world of the Kiowa tribe in the period before its dismemberment. We attend religious rituals, especially the Sun Dance, in which captive women played major roles, as well as the Scalp Dance and other matrimonial and mortuary practices. We learn of intertribal conflicts, especially with the Utes, at whose hands the great chief Heap O'Bears died, and we hear about battles against the U.S. Army. Social customs, games, and sports are described in detail. Of special interest is the description of Andrés's frustrated efforts to acquire the spiritual powers of a medicine man. "Often Andele engaged in this worship as above described, and sometimes in the early morning, after a night of anxiety, he would go and gather poles and build a sweat house, that he might worship in that way."[81] Finally, Andrés relates the surrender of the Kiowa chief Napawat to the government of the United States.

We must not forget that Andrés Martínez's story is a captivity narrative, and that therefore the adventure of the capture, the initial shock, and moments of surprise and anxiety are the fundamental material of the text. His story is not disappointing in this respect. It is told with an abundance of detail in which he itemizes the sufferings he endured after the trauma of being carried off. The murders of his nephew Pedro and the Mexican who were taken with him left a deep mark on him.

The narrative abounds in references to other captives he knew, who were taken in raids in which he took part or who were found in Indian villages. Before he was kidnapped by the Mescalero Apaches, Andrés and his nephew witnessed the captivity of a Mexican whom they saw arrive on the road with two burros loaded with flour. During the return journey, when the Apaches decided to get rid of little Pedro because he was hindering their progress, one of the Indians refused to kill him, alleging that he had Mexican blood in his veins: "My father was a Mexican. I can not kill him."[82] Santiago, the Kiowa brave who accompanied Chief Heap O'Bears and who wound up buying the rights to the boy, identified himself to Andrés as Mexican. Santiago "spoke to Andrés in Spanish, seeing that he was a Mexican. He himself was a Mexican, captured long years ago, when but a boy, and raised among them, and in ways and habits and dress was scarcely distinguishable from the real Indian."[83]

When he reached the Kiowa camp, Andrés met other captives, among them Somtottleti, also a Mexican, who became one of his best friends. On one of their marauding expeditions to Texas, the Kiowas attacked a frontier home where they killed all but one boy, whom they named Tahan, which means "Texan man." In 1872, when the Kiowas made one of their last attacks on the U.S. Army near Anadarko, "Tahan was about eighteen years old, and was as complete an Indian, in habits, customs, and superstitions, as the most extreme Indian, and was as bitter and cruel in purpose of bloodshed and plunder."[84] Years later, when the Kiowas, led by Napawat, decided to surrender to the army, one of the chiefs most wanted for his attacks and crimes, Zo-ko-yea, at first resisted for fear of being identified and punished. He didn't fear that any of the Indian braves would betray him, but he suspected that Tahan, because he had white blood, would do so, even though, according to Andrés, "there was not the least ground for suspicion, for Tahan hated white men as much as any Indian, and had proven it by the many bloody deeds committed upon them."[85] Nevertheless, the obsession of being betrayed tormented Zo-ko-yea to the point that he killed the young captive with his own hands and in cold blood.

In the first census taken at Fort Sill after the Kiowa surrender, fourteen white and twelve Mexican captives were counted. The last Kiowa chiefs died defending their liberties: Satank was killed at Fort Sill by a soldier under dubious circumstances; Satanta committed suicide in 1878 while in jail; Big Tree, after being freed from prison, converted to Protestantism and joined the Baptist Church.[86] With them ended an important era of the last Plains Indians.

Conclusion

In 1972 A. C. Green published *The Last Captive,* which contains the narrative of Herman Lehmann, a captive of the Apaches and Comanches from 1870 to 1879. This book, one of the most engaging of captivity narratives, ends with these words: "He was the last white captive to be released by the Comanches, but more than that, he remained a voluntary captive to their way of life for the remainder of his many days."[87]

From 1550–1600, when frontier commanders reported on the violent reprisals of the Chichimeca tribes, until 1870, the date of Herman Lehmann's capture, the history of Mexico's northern frontier changed slowly but steadily. Spain's advance to the north was thwarted time and again by tenacious Indian resistance. Many and varied were the protagonists of this human drama, which was written and rewritten on many stages.

At stake were the future of a vast territory and the way of life of its inhabitants. Most of the captives, of whom we know nothing beyond brief mentions in official reports, were mute protagonists. I refer to Estebanico, Alonso de Castilla, Lucía Madrid, Juana Hurtado, Petrona Pacheco, Antonia Treviño, Cristóbal Anaya, Juan Domínguez, and many others who are only names and who remain only names in the history of captivity. But beside them other names appear: Rosita Rodrigues, Francisca Medrano, Tomassa, and Andrés Martínez, or Andele. These people have not only names but stories full of anecdotes and drama. They have come down to us thanks to the efforts of Rev. J. J. Methvin, of the Methodist church, who for evangelical purposes collected and reworked their experiences in captivity. Francisca, Tomassa, and Andrés were of Mexican origin. They were born on Mexico's northern frontier, when the territory was being transformed under migratory pressure from the east of the continent. They witnessed the last era before the tribes of the Plains, Comanches, Kiowas, and Apaches, surrendered to U.S. authorities.

Their testimonies are invaluable. The story of Andrés Martínez is possibly one of the richest and most interesting narratives we have of a Mexican captive on the northern frontier. His descriptions of the Kiowas, their rituals for the adoption of a new member, their ways of hunting and trading, their raids and wars, internal conflicts, celebrations and cures, are of great ethno-graphical value. Of interest also are the different intracultural transfers through which Andrés Martínez passed, from his original Mexican culture, to adoption and integration with the Kiowas, through the recovery of his Mexican roots, to his return to the Fort Sill Kiowa reservation, and finally his assimilation into Anglo-Saxon culture through his conversion to Christianity in the Methodist Church.

⊰ SIX ⊱

From Helena Valero to Napëyoma
The Journey of a Captive

> Then I did start to run to the jungle. I was far but he was fol-
> lowing me. He shot another arrow at me, but it went over my
> head and hit a tree. I kept running. He stopped to adjust his
> bowstring. I took advantage of this to run farther and I disap-
> peared into the jungle. He wasn't able to find me. I remem-
> bered a place where there were rocks that could serve as a
> shelter and I went there. The mosquitoes gave me no rest. I
> spent the night swatting them and lamenting my fate [. . .].
> Crying and praying.
>
> —Helena Valero

The continent's arteries, the rivers of Amazonia, nurture the life of hundreds of cultures. They are the routes of communication which time and again cross invisible cultural borders. Helena Valero, her parents and brothers, were on one of those slow silent rivers when she was captured by the Kohoroshitari, one of the tribes of Yanomamö Indian stock. On another of those rivers traveled Helena, now Napëyoma, after a long captivity in the jungles of the Orinoco:

> When I returned from tending the crops, the woman told me that she had seen
> my brother. He came, in fact, on Sunday. They called me. He was sitting and I
> approached.
> "What's your name?" he said in Spanish.
> "Umbelina Helena Valero."
> "What's your father's name?"
> "Carlos Valero."

"Where did you live before?"

"In Nazarete, near Marabitanas."

Then he asked me my mother's name and those of my sisters, until I came to his name.

"And what's my name?"

"Your name is Anisio Enrique Valero."

"Then, it's really true. You are my sister." And he cried for a while. "I never thought I would ever see you again. I wouldn't have recognized you. When they took you we were so little."[1]

When Helena Valero was reunited with her brother, in October of 1956, twenty-four years had passed since her capture on November 26, 1932. Helena Valero now was called Napëyoma, and of her own free will she was returning with great difficulty to "civilization," in the company of her four children and her second husband, Akawë, a Yanomamö Indian. Helena Valero was thirty-seven years old. Hers had been an amazing journey through a vast territory located in Venezuela's south between the great valleys of the Orinoco and Negro Rivers. The Yanomamö inhabit a large area that extends from the valley of the high Orinoco and Negro Rivers, bathed by a series of tributaries: Siapa, Mavaca, Ocamo, and Matacunío. It is a tropical forest with constant rain and mountains that reach three thousand feet. Most of the lowlands are flooded during the rainy season, making difficult the Indians' frequent travels. Yanomamö villages are scattered irregularly over a vast area and connected by trails that in some cases are difficult to identify.[2] The distances between their villages vary from a few hours' travel to several days' journey. Visits from members of different villages are frequent, although they depend on political stability.

Helena Valero's captivity is remarkable for the adaptability and psychological strength of a woman who overcame the many extremely adverse situations in which she found herself. She fought for survival in a hostile environment that, in large measure, was foreign to her. At times, she lived completely alone in the heart of the Amazonian jungle, without weapons, tools, food, clothing, or fire to warm herself, and pursued by those who had taken her in. She suffered numerous wounds from arrows and cudgels, inflicted by abusive husbands or suitors, whose violence left permanent marks on her body. She also had to endure the aggressive jealousy of other wives, snakebites, bat attacks, and the threat of jaguars. She survived these trials with an exemplary courage that the Yanomamö themselves came to admire.

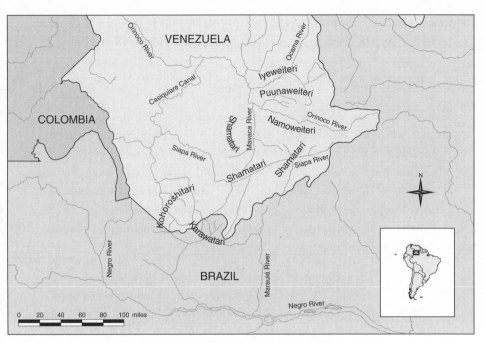

Map 9. Yanomamö Groups

By the time she returned, her parents barely remembered her. She returned with four of the six children she had conceived in captivity; the other two had died shortly after birth. Helena had to face the basic contradictions of a woman who had been forced to adapt to an alien culture during her formative years. Her return was a continuation of that journey, and not without obstacles. To her surprise, she discovered that adapting to the culture of her birth was no easy task. The joyful reception of her brother Anisio Enrique would not be the norm in the coming days. Her brothers accused her of being an Indian, they were ashamed of her and ostracized her. She was moved to tell the story of her captivity in order to clear up doubts about her story and to eliminate the threat of plagiarism.

Within the genre of captivity narratives, Helena Valero's story is an exceptional case. She endured a long captivity and retained a clear awareness of the process of acculturation she had undergone. She survived in an environment that was violent by Western criteria, and when it was necessary she took her fate in her own hands. She set down her experiences in an autobiographical work of exceptional literary and cultural value. Her long journey as a captive took her through the jungle and across cultural frontiers. Her round-trip from Helena Valero to Napëyoma and back again has no clear ending.

Capture

Helena Valero was captured by the Kohoroshitari, one of various Yanomamö groups, while her family was gathering fruit and fishing in the Marocoabi River, a tributary of the Negro River. They were preparing to go downriver when they felt the presence of a group of Indians observing them from the shore. "There they were, all of them naked with their member tied up; some painted black, others annatto; their heads shaved above like friars, around their heads some wore jaguar skin bands; others had armbands."[3] Before they knew it the Indians began to shoot arrows at them.

> "Get down!" my Dad shouted, and an arrow hit him in the head. Another hit him in the back. Tu, tu, tuku!, tu, tu, tuku! They fell like a cloudburst. One hit me in the belly, toward the right; it went under my navel, came out again on the left and stuck to my thigh, fastening my clothes to me. The arrowhead had curare![4]

Her mother felt the end was near. She had been hit by three arrows in the legs and buttocks. Unable to do anything, she shouted: "This is it, my daughter, the Macú are going to eat us!"[5] For his part, her father thought the best thing was to give their supplies to the Indians and jump in the water to get to the other shore. That is what they did, although the Indians did not give up the chase. Wounded, Helena asked her father to leave her on the way. "Twenty-four years later my father reminded me that I also said: 'Dad, save yourself and my brother. Someday we'll meet again.' After that I felt nothing."[6]

In the confusion of those moments, and despite her offering resistance, the Kohoroshitari took only Helena. Badly wounded as he was, they left her father, although it would have been easy to capture him. They weren't interested: a grown man would have been difficult to control, a hindrance on their long journey back to their *shabono* (communal dwelling).[7] Furthermore, the Yanomamö lacked social mechanisms for the assimilation of adult men. With Helena, it was a different matter. She was almost a girl; consequently, the acculturation process would not be so difficult. She would learn their language and customs, and in time she would be a mother and a prized exchange commodity. The wounds she suffered in the initial attack made her weak, and she fell into a drowsiness from which she did not revive until the next day. When she awoke, she was surrounded by Kohoroshitari Indians, who had quickly transported her to the first camp. It was the beginning of a journey that Helena could not have imagined even in dreams. "I woke up and I started to look around. I felt as if in another world: Indians everywhere, all naked, speaking another language [. . .]. It seemed a dream, but much too clear, much too evil."[8]

Helena was thirteen. She was no longer a girl, but not yet a woman. She was spared being raped by her captors because of her age and slenderness, which made her look younger than she was. From Helena's narrative we learn that captive Indian women were raped by all the Yanomamö men who took part in the capture, even those who remained behind in the *shabono*.[9] Napoleon A. Chagnon corroborates her testimony: "A captured woman is raped by all the men in the raiding party and, later, by the men in the village who wish to do so but did not participate in the raid. She is then given to one of the men as a wife."[10] None of the men claimed Helena as a wife, even though polygamy is the norm among the Yanomamö and a source of wealth for men. She was too young. They assigned her to some women who would care for her and educate her.

After a night's rest, the cacique ordered the raiding party back toward their *shabono*. "Women carried the things they had found in the houses of my uncles: clay and copper pots, pieces of graters, gourds, and cans. And in addition, *mapires* [baskets] full of *casabe* [cassava bread] which they had made. The men took three axes and four machetes they found."[11] Helena was wounded, in pain, and could not keep up. "Then they made Matohema, a young strong woman, carry me. She put on a majagua fiber band and carried me."[12]

At first, Helena thought only of escaping, although the possibilities were slim. She planned to lag behind and disappear into the dense vegetation. They wouldn't notice. She never found the opportunity. At last, they reached the *shabono*, where Helena was the object of general curiosity. "Many people gathered around me: old men, women, children [. . .]. All wanted to touch me. They pulled my hair [. . .]. I started to cry and to think: 'Now they're really going to kill and eat me.' I was full of fear. The old men talked and I didn't understand anything."[13] Helena's comment about being eaten is undoubtedly ironical. The scene is being described forty years after it happened.

Helena knew Yanomamö practices well, but she had also repeatedly heard the stories of the legendary cannibalism of savages. (The Yanomamö do practice a form of endocannibalism which consists in drinking the ashes of cremated relatives.)

Shortly after the commotion of her capture and the return trip, the Kohoroshitari were unexpectedly attacked by the Karawatari, their ancestral enemies.[14] The massacre that took place before her eyes was a baptism of blood for Helena and an introduction to the violence of the Yanomamö, which has been extensively described by experts on this society.[15] "As they gathered the women together, they took away their children and killed them. The older ones who tried to run away, they threw on the ground and pierced their bellies with their bows. How many children did they kill that time? My God."[16] She had to follow the Karawatari. "I cried, horrified."[17] It was the second episode in a series that would see her become a bone of contention between one group and another. It must be borne in mind that most confrontations between Yanomamö groups and even within a *shabono* have their root in disputes over women, infidelities, and abductions.[18]

The amount of time she spent with the Karawatari is uncertain. In general, her narrative lacks a clear chronology. Helena was not able to keep track of time during her years of captivity. The date was the first thing she asked her brother Anisio on the day of their reunion. What is certain is that the Karawatari were in turn attacked by the Shamatari, and this resulted in many other victims and, for Helena, another change of tribe.[19] The Patamanipweiteri tried to abduct her from the Shamatari, but when they failed, they decided to kill her so that, as they explained, no one else could have her.

On that occasion, as in later ones, Helena was forced to flee and live completely alone in the jungle. Finally, she came to the Wanitima-Theri, among whom she was chosen as a wife for Husiwë, their shaman and chief.

Surviving in the Jungle

The first years with the Yanomamö, from her capture to her marriage to Husiwë, were not easy for Helena. She was the constant victim of hostility. Her marginal status made her an easy prey. No man defended her, no family protected her, with the exception of some women who took pity on her and took her under their wing. However, it was also women who on occasion used her as a scapegoat. During those first years of adaptation and apprenticeship,

Helena thought constantly of escaping, returning, and finding her way back to her family. But she did not know how and was not able to flee because the environment was so foreign to her.

The rainforest where the Yanomamö live is a vast territory covered with trees and high underbrush whose lowlands are largely inaccessible during the rainy season. The Yanomamö are a seminomadic culture from the inner jungle, where they have plantings and groves. They have a hunting season, but they return to their plantings to harvest plantain, their main crop. When the groves decline, they migrate to new territories and begin the planting cycle again. Meanwhile they live as hunters and gatherers.

Several times Helena had to evade the unpredictable wrath of her captors, who threatened her with bows and arrows, gripped by an anger she did not understand. She survived by penetrating the great jungle, living there for long periods of time, completely alone, on one occasion for more than seven months. "My life of solitude had begun. I was determined to live this way until I found my freedom. I got up, packed my provisions, I hung them on my back and I left [. . .] with God and the Virgin Mary."[20]

In the jungle, Helena learned to survive by eating plants, wild fruit, reptiles, and river crabs. Her greatest enemy, more than loneliness or predatory animals, was the cold. At night, owing to the humidity produced by constant evaporation, the temperature drops. The Yanomamö do not wear clothes. A string around the waist onto which men knot their penis is their only garb. Feathers and bracelets are only for decoration. Alone and pursued, she never lost hope.

Later I began to wonder if there might be *dañeros* [witches] nearby. I got up a *dewapu* plant and began to shout. Nothing [. . .]. That's how I spent my first month of solitude. Since I liked *yoco* very much, and there was almost no other fruit, I moved near these plants. There I made my *tapirí* [shelter], similar to the previous one. I worked all afternoon on that. Later I lit my fire, ate a little *yoco*, prayed and went to sleep. It was about midnight when I heard the sound of a branch breaking. I turned to one side and saw a big, black shape, which was entering my *tapirí*. I jumped, grabbed a tree and climbed. From there I looked down. Another animal was following the first one. I think it was a black jaguar. I stayed up there trembling. When they disappeared, I came down, untied my hammock, took an ember and left. I went running down and ran up another side. There I sat. I cried and said, "Dear God, why didn't you let the jaguar find me sleeping and eat me once and for all?"[21]

Helena's loneliness during her extremely difficult times is moving. She was a fleeing prey, who had to learn quickly in order to survive. At such times, she demonstrated the courage, intelligence, and maturity to find the available resources and use them to her benefit. She read the signs of nature and adapted to them. However, it was impossible to go on this way; she saw her choices as either dying in the jungle or being murdered by Yanomamö men. To the amazement of the Yanomamö, she returned. They thought she was a ghost because, after so long, they had assumed she was dead. In the extreme loneliness to which her journey of captivity had brought her, she persisted in escaping from her captors, who at times did not know what to make of her. She neither spoke their language well, nor was she familiar with Yanomamö socialization mechanisms. The narrative is rich in episodes that, in full detail, demonstrate this woman's greatness.

From Helena Valero to Napëyoma

Helena's first rite of passage took place shortly after her arrival at her captors' camp. Men as well as women and children came to see and touch this novelty. She was the *napë* girl, the stranger, the civilized one, the one who was not like them, an identity that would produce differing reactions.[22] Next, she was stripped of her clothes, and her hair was cut with a bamboo splinter. "Then she took me to be bathed. Then she took annatto and painted almost all of my body."[23] The exterior transformation had been effected. Totally naked, like Yanomamö women, with a decorative string at her waist, shorn and painted with annatto, Helena was now Horehore prewë, which means "big flower." This was the first name given to her by the Kohoroshitari. Later they called her Napëyoma, which means "foreign woman."

The process of assimilation would take place in different phases, as Helena became familiar with Yanomamö customs and adapted to her physical surroundings. She would eventually pierce her lips, cheeks, ears, and nose with thorns and splinters, although she never liked being tonsured. Driven by necessity, she gradually learned their language: "When I didn't do what they told me because I didn't understand, they would hit my head."[24] Her clothes, a distinctive symbol of civilization, disappeared in shreds among the women of the *shabono*. Other symbols—her language, religion, and food—were the cultural baggage that Helena kept or negotiated in her long process of assimilation and rejection within Yanomamö society.

Yanomamö woman. (Photo by Dennis Woodruff; used with permission)

Her assimilation was slow and difficult, especially while she was single, be-fore Husiwë took her for his wife. To the Yanomamö, Helena was an oddity. She was whiter than they, and one of her sons was even born with blue eyes, for which they named him Miramawë, which means "the one with light-colored eyes." Some men found her attractive and wanted to possess her in order to have *napë* children. Others rejected her for the same reason. Helena complained that they did not treat her well because she was "other people." The idea that the Yanomamö have of the *napë* is related not to color but to a material culture they can differentiate. The *napë* wear clothes, they know the secrets of the manufacture of machetes and metal pots, they know how to swim, and they bury their dead instead of burning them. Her first husband, Husiwë, regretted that Napëyoma could not make machetes and metal pots, and he chastised her for this. Husiwë said that the *napë* do not respect the dead because they bury them underground, from where their souls cannot es-cape. On that occasion, Helena dared to do something no Yanomamö woman would do: answer back to her husband and contradict him. "You also don't know how to take care of your relatives. One of them dies? You immediately bring firewood and burn him. After he has suffered death, then you make him suffer more by roasting him."[25]

Napëyoma was always aware of her foreignness and explained it to her son Miramawë when he was old enough to understand the distinctive traits he had inherited from his mother:

"We are civilized people from the Negro River. My mother was civilized. My grandfather was white. He was from a place called Caracas, what they call a city. That is far away, I have never been there. We lived in Cucui, there between Venezuela and Brazil. Caracas is in Venezuela, but high up, above, far."

The boy looked past me, almost as if he did not understand. Later he asked: "Then if we are other people, why are we here?"

"Because I don't know where to go. Your brother is still too little. But someday we'll leave."[26]

This awareness of her foreignness might explain why Napëyoma held so tenaciously to her religious beliefs and worked hard to hold onto the language that she still spoke fluently after twenty-three years of not having had contact with anyone who spoke it. The times when her life was seriously threatened—which were many, especially in the first two years—she invoked her Christian God, prayed to Maria Help of Christians, Saint Barbara, and made vows to Saint Francis so that he would save the life of her sick son Kariyonawë. "Did I do my first holy communion to wind up here? Can it be that God has forgotten me? What bad luck I have! And I began to pray and later to sing the hymns we sang in the chapel at Taracuá. That filled me with emotion and made me cry."[27] Prayers appear throughout the narrative. Her first impulse after her reunion with her brother Anisio at the San Fernando Mission was to give thanks. "Before the painting of Maria Help of Christians I fell on my knees. I prayed and wept, I showed my children who had saved me. I remembered my sufferings, and my promises."[28] Language was another mechanism of identity that Helena did not lose. She spoke to her children in Spanish. When she returned, she could speak Spanish and Portuguese fluently: "I haven't forgotten Portuguese. You see, I always prayed in Portuguese."[29]

The fundamental step in her process of assimilation occurred when Husiwë, from the tribe of the Wanitima-Theri, took her as his fifth wife. "He had four others before me: Yepiami, the oldest, who was Tetehei-Theri; then came Shirikoma, who was Aramamisi-Theri; then Shapotama, Irota-Theri; his other wife was Toroam, a Patanowë. Then came I: Napëyoma."[30] Little by little she created a space for herself within the family clan. Although completely at the whim of her husband, like all Yanomamö women, at least she felt she belonged to a group and could seek consolation with other women. Yanomamö women respond immediately to the desires and demands of their husbands, even without waiting for his orders. Their dependency is total. When husbands return from hunting, they drop into their hammocks. Women have to quickly abandon anything they are doing and prepare their food. A small delay can provoke the wrath and violence of an irate husband. Women can find defense from an abusive husband in their brothers and relatives. Napëyoma had no such protection, but Husiwë in general turned out to be an understanding husband. She was diligent and hard-working, and maternity came to complete her process of integration.

She was fifteen or sixteen when she realized that she was pregnant for the first time. It was a day like any other in the middle of a trek through the jungle. "From there we went off again on a *wayumi* [trek]. We slept several nights by the great river. I was pregnant with my first child. I didn't like the idea of having children there because they would make it more difficult for me to escape."[31] Not long after that she had a girl. Her description gives a sense of distance, as if the childbirth were something alien to her body and also didn't have anything to do with Husiwë.

> That same night, I gave birth. Yepiami was ready. The two of us went out into the bush. She was carrying an ember and I [. . .] my belly ready to give birth. There the girl was born very small. Yepiami cut her umbilical cord with bamboo and went to put away the placenta in an armadillo hole. Later she was quiet. At dawn she was dead. I shook her but she wasn't breathing anymore. She was very small and did not survive the cold.[32]

With Husiwë, Napëyoma had found her place in the family group. Her husband brought game and cared about her, and his other wives respected her because of her great energy and courage. From time to time, she still had to endure Husiwë's fury, because like all Yanomamö men he had been raised to express his wrath at the least provocation, but little by little she earned a level of respect in the family *shabono.* "Watching my words, I got Husiwë to treat me well again."[33] Napëyoma's process of acculturation was never complete, but before Husiwë's death she probably reached the phase of greatest adaptation.

Witness to Violence

If any testimony stands out from the narrative it is the accounts of violence. Yanomamö society has long been considered a culture marked by the sign of violence. Chagnon calculates the total Yanomamö population to be approximately twelve thousand, distributed among groups that speak the same language and share modes of production and common cultural traits.[34] Violence is, in most cases, a regulated activity through which the different Yanomamö groups negotiate the distribution of the territory necessary to produce food (especially plantain), cotton, and tobacco, and to hunt. Balance between the population and available resources is fundamental to guarantee their survival, which explains the existence of conflicts between groups and the role they play. The abduction of women is common, and so are reprisals and acts of vengeance in response to offenses. Chagnon explains that boys are "are encouraged to be fierce and rarely punished by their parents for inflicting blows on them or on the hapless girls in the village."[35]

Helena's kidnapping by the Kohoroshitari was an act of violence followed by many others marking her life with the Yanomamö. As mentioned above, the attack perpetrated by the Karawatari on the Kohoroshitari on their way back to the *shabono* was noteworthy for its virulence. On that occasion Helena was both the victim of the violence and a witness to it.

Immediately they began to grab the women. The ones there were all young. The old women had run away [. . .]. Then they pulled out the first woman who was in my cave [. . .]. Another Karawatari followed the tracks of a woman, pushed aside a bunch of reeds that covered a hole and saw Yawarima. With his bow he threatened her and forced her to come out. He grabbed her and others came to take away her children. They grabbed the eldest and bashed him against a rock. The other women surrounded Yawarima to defend her youngest. "Don't kill him, don't kill him," they shouted. Some men loosened the women's arms, and took the boy and killed him by hitting him against a rock. His little head was torn to bits. The man who had killed Yawarima's children took her. All of them were grabbing women [. . .]. Later they saw she had a baby on her back. "It's a girl, let her be," one of them said. Later they fell on Yaayama. They took away her six-day-old baby and burst her against a rock [. . .]. The butchery done, the Karawatari began to taunt: "The Kohoroshitari are cowards. They ran away and abandoned their women and children. We killed their children and now we are taking their wives." [. . .]. I was horrified and cried.[36]

Especially during the first months after her capture, Helena had to face unfamiliar situations that shattered her preconceived notions of socialization. There were explosions of unwonted violence. On one occasion, a girl Helena was carrying during one of the constant Yanomamö migrations chewed some frog eggs that Helena had thrown away. The girl fell ill and died shortly afterward. The mother accused Helena of being the cause of her death: "Kill Napëyoma!" she screamed, "Let her die like my daughter!"[37] The next day at daybreak, Paurama, a female neighbor, advised her to flee because the men had agreed to the woman's petition and were going to shoot her: "Run to the jungle. That woman wants them to kill you. Those young men are putting curare on their arrowheads to kill you."[38] Helena decided to heed her advice and fled, but she returned after a few days, thinking that the initial anger had faded. She was wrong. The relatives of the dead girl were determined and sent several young men with poisoned arrows to kill her.

> I screamed. A curare arrowhead had stuck in my right thigh. It had pierced it and stuck in my left thigh. The arrow had fallen off. The criminal came running to pick up his arrow and left [. . .]. I became stiff, walking on the firewood, I dropped the ax, trembling. Then I looked at the arrowhead and I broke it between my legs. I took out the piece that had stuck in my left thigh, and leaving the other piece in my right thigh, I began to run to the jungle. I crossed the trail on which they had returned. I entered some highland, later I went down and stopped to take out the piece of arrowhead that remained. It was hard. I pushed from the inside and pulled. It wouldn't come out. I trembled. I invoked Saint Joseph, took the point with both hands and it came out. I tossed it. Then the blood began to flow. The other wound on the other leg was also bleeding, and the wound on the other side of this leg. With leaves I wiped the blood. If I left the blood on the trail they would find me and kill me. I kept running down. I found earthworm mud and covered my wounds with it to stop the bleeding. Later I ran like crazy, not knowing where, trembling. I climbed another hill, and up above I sat on a rock, I was as if drunk. My legs and arms were heavy, heavy, and I saw how all the trees were turning yellow on me, with a lot of smoke. The poison was taking effect. Blood was still flowing. It must have been around five when I heard the Indians coming. I couldn't move. I heard someone dragging a stick and saying, "My cudgel is so beautiful! If I find her, I'll smash her head with it."[39]

Helena was abducted because she was a woman. Women are prized as a source of labor and reproduction and, according to Chagnon, are the principal cause of wars and conflicts between the Yanomamö.[40] However, their subordination to men is absolute. Helena was the continual object of conjugal violence, which put her life in grave danger. Of her first husband, she says in an expression close to affection, "Deep down in his soul, Husiwë was good. Only when he was provoked did he become furious and do crazy things."[41] But he beat her many times at the beginning of the relationship, and even broke her arm in one of his angry fits. From her second husband, Akawë, she had to protect herself to the limits of her strength. Once, fed up with his unjustified attacks, she defended herself so forcefully that she almost killed him.

> At that point, I tripped him and tooon! He fell flat out, dropping the stick. I jumped on him, with one knee on either side of his body. With one hand I grabbed his balls and with the other his throat, and I squeezed and squeezed as hard as I could. He kicked around, but couldn't hit me hard. He screamed from the pain and called out, but I kept squeezing harder, choking his voice [. . .]. I squeezed harder, harder, harder, until he stopped shouting, his eyes turned, his tongue stuck out and he stopped moving.[42]

His relatives gave him up for dead. Fortunately, Akawë lived and followed her when she returned to the *napë* world. Similar passages are common throughout her narrative.

Yanomamö society has managed to channel violence through complicated rites or physical exercises. For example, there are regulated fistfights and fights with sticks that even describe the type of blow that is to be given and received. "War is only one form of violence in a graded series of aggressive activities. Indeed, some of the other forms of fighting, such as the formal chest-pounding duel, may even be considered as the antithesis of war, for they provide an alternative to killing."[43] The least offense, malicious rumors, jealousy, greed in commerce, accusations of cowardice, can lead to duels with sticks, fists, or arrows.

Helena lost her first husband as a result of his obsession with avenging an affront. A man who wants to keep his reputation must avenge any insult that questions his courage. The entreaties of Napëyoma and his other wives, and the advice of elders and relatives, were not enough to hold back the stubborn Husiwë, who finally—alone, because no one would go with him—attacked a *shabono* of the Pishaasi-theri and killed a boy. After this he had to undergo the purifications required of murderers. The response of the Pishaasi-theri was not long in coming, and Husiwë was riddled with poisoned arrows and died.

The reader may get the impression when reading Helena Valero's narrative that the book is filled with violence, both among the Yanomamö and toward her. However, it is important to realize that the narrative covers a period of twenty-four years and that, understandably, the narrator pays more attention to notable events, such as dangerous situations, wars, and escapes. It is not my purpose here to discuss the issue of violence in Yanomamö society and the social mechanisms it addresses.[44] It is important to stress that Helena was a victim of Yanomamö violence. The first violent act she suffered was her abduction, but its final manifestation was the difficulty she had in adapting to life when she returned to her original culture. This is what I wish to express by the metaphor of her "round-trip" between both cultures.

The Impossible Return to Civilization

"My family grew. Time passed and I found I was happier."[45] Nevertheless, her assimilation was never total. A desire to return was always alive in her, although it was dormant at times. Husiwë's death, lamented by Napëyoma, rekindled that desire. Before he died, when he felt he was mortally wounded, Husiwë advised her to return.

> "Take these children and go far away, far from here. Look for your relatives and take my children to them so that they can raise them." He squeezed their hands. "I feel I am going to die and leave them. Go and raise them with your people." As he said this he pressed the children's hands harder, as he looked at them, he breathed deeply, closed his eyes and was dead.[46]

Husiwë's death destabilized Napëyoma's life again. Who would take care of her now? she wondered. Without a husband, not only had she lost the protection of his group but, even worse, she had no one to take care of her body when she died. No one to take care of her ashes so that her soul would not get lost. She had no relatives except her small children. Once again she tried to revive the plan of returning, but she couldn't. She tried to live alone with her children, but that wasn't possible either. Single or by herself, there was no room for her in Yanomamö society. Her children, who were older now, also urged her to return to the nape, who have knives, axes, pots, and other artifacts coveted by the Yanomamö.

Although she didn't want to, she was forced to enter into a new and difficult relationship, with Akawë, her second husband. He mistreated all his wives and was incapable of sustaining his family by hunting. Napëyoma put up with this unwanted relationship and bore two other children, which made escape even more difficult. Akawë mistreated her and once threatened her with his bow. As we have seen, Napëyoma took charge of her fate and that of her children and defended herself against her abusive husband, almost killing him. This event was key in the evolution of her life among the Yanomamö.

The first chance she had, she and her children began to walk in the direction of the Ocamo River, a tributary of the Orinoco. Shortly after reaching the riverbank, they got news that a *napë* man had gone up the river with his ship six days before. They waited impatiently until Juan Eduardo, a Brazilian trader, returned. Then Napëyoma asked him to take them with him. Juan Eduardo agreed, and Napëyoma traveled downriver to search for her original family and her lost identity. She brought with her her four surviving children and Akawë, who had decided to join them at the last moment. The description of the return trip recalls the trip after her capture twenty-four years before.

> Soon we were in the middle of the river. There we heard the Indians shouting. They were Puunapiwei-theri and Witokaya-theri. They were all painted black and armed. Akawë greeted them with his hand. Then they shouted more and began to shoot arrows, but the arrows hit the water, owing to the wind and because we were already far.[47]

But now it was time for going home.

> It was October 15, 1956. That's what Juan Eduardo told me. Then I was able to count my years, because I had lost track of my age. Now I was thirty-seven. I thought: "I'm no longer a girl. If I don't find my parents, I'm not afraid. I'll find a place to live [. . .]." I was happy. The Orinoco River was all mine: it was the road to my home, the road to my freedom.[48]

The return to white society was usually not easy for female captives, especially those who had conceived children in captivity. They found a new obstacle when they returned that made difficult their incorporation into the society from which they came. Those women, like Helena, had had children with Indians, and their children were now considered Indians; worse yet, they themselves had been soiled by their carnal relations. Who were they now? Helena faced this dilemma shortly after her return. In the letter that her brother Luis sent their sister Antonia Rosalía he expressed the opinion that it would not be appropriate for Helena to go with her children to Manaus, where their mother now lived, because now she was an Indian and "he didn't want her to go there to dishonor the Valero family."[49] On that occasion, her father was on her side. Helena, however, felt rejected and disappointed. She thought of returning to the Yanomamö, as Akawë, her husband, did shortly after his arrival; alternatively, she could forget the incident and accept the destiny to which life had pushed her. "I could only cry. I had come from the jungle and that's why they thought I was Indian."[50] Encouraged by her father's reaction, Helena decided to go to Manaus and embrace her mother, whom she had not seen for twenty-four years, despite the continued opposition of her brothers, expressed in another letter, this time by Anisio Enrique. "He said he was astonished that I had dared to go to Manaus. He expected me to stay in Tapurucuara. He wrote that he looked on the house with contempt, because now I was there with my children, my Indians, and that he would never go to that house again."[51]

Helena's disillusionment was total, and her thoughts about white civilization reveal her disenchantment. "I spent 1957 in Manaus. My family's economic situation was not good. Civilization was not as good as I dreamed in the jungle."[52] Shortly after her return, her father died, but before he did, he advised her to leave, as years before her husband Husiwë had done: "You are here on my account. After I die, don't stay here suffering. Go far away, if possible. They can't stand to see your children and they don't love you. Go away; it's better."[53]

Placed in an ambiguous situation by the disdain of her relatives, Helena opted to stay in one of the Christian missions deep in Yanomamö territory. She took refuge at the mission, trying to blend in. The rumor spread that she had returned to the Yanomamö, which she denied. She explains the reason for her decision to go to the mission:

> It's not true that I have returned to the jungle, as some newspapers around have written, because I could not adapt to civilization. That is a big lie. Yes, in the jungle there are good things: game, plantain, fruit, honey [. . .] freedom. But [. . .] what about the arrows, beatings, jaguars, snakes, rays, ants, the *waka moshi* [. . .]. No, I never did get used to it. I adapted [. . .]. How I would love to have the means to buy a house in civilization and live with my children! [. . .] Don't ever say that I love to live with jaguars! [. . .] Twenty-four years of fear and bitterness is not a joke! I have returned to the jungle, yes, because there is no place for me in the city.[54]

184 ◁ Indian Captivity in Spanish America

Helena had suffered her family's disdain and that of the society into which she was born. The mission was a no-man's-land, an outpost of the West in unexplored territory. It was the spearhead of Christianity, and the citadel on which the European presence in the Americas rested for hundreds of years. Helena's encounter with the two cultures had turned her into a victim of both. The last words of her book capture well the meaning of her life:

> I have returned to the jungle, yes, because there is no place for me in the city. I am happy to stay near the Indians, because I want to teach them how they can be happy there. I want to teach them that in our civilization they could not be better off. For the rest, I continue to hope and have much faith in God. That's all. And that is the truth.[55]

This brave woman, who yearned to return to civilization, describes the disenchantment of her experience. The sweetness of her homecoming was elusive. Napëyoma, the wife of Husiwë and Akawë, returned with her mestizo children to be Helena Valero once more, the daughter of Carlos Valero. But she was not able or was not allowed to return. She had delved deeply into Yanomamö culture, and it had left deep marks in her. These marks were very visible to her brothers, who never accepted her. Her body, scarred by arrow wounds, beatings, and animals, was the painful image of a life spent in the struggle to adapt, looking for a place to be.

Today Helena continues to live at the mission in Ocamo, deep in Yanomamö territory. She works as a catechist. It is a frontier zone, an undefined place where both cultures meet and repel.

Her Autobiography

Helena Valero's autobiography is a human document that surpasses the limits of fantastic literature. With a wealth of details, Helena captures the story of her life among the Yanomamö, and sets it down with precision. More than a testimony of her captivity, her book is an insightful work of ethnography which none of the scholars of Yanomamö culture have challenged.[56] Certainly, Helena has an extraordinary memory, which allowed her to re-create with a profusion of detail twenty-four years of travel, pursuits, escapes, surprises, and daily routine. She did not write her memoirs herself, but she dictated them on several occasions. The first time was to the Italian anthropologist Ettore Biocca, who published the tape-recorded material in a book entitled *Yanomama* (1965), which appeared in French in 1968 and in English in 1970 with the title *Yanomama: The Narrative of a White Girl Kidnapped by Amazonian Indians*. Biocca hid Helena Valero's authorship and presented the text as his own. In response to criticism from the anthropologists J. Shapiro and Jacques Lizot, in the second French 1976 edition there is a transcription of a letter allegedly from Helena to Biocca in which she expresses the wish that her name not be mentioned in the book. Emilio Fuentes has researched the origin of this letter and asserts that it was not written by Helena but by her brother Luis, who represented her while she lived in Manaus, and who possibly benefited financially from the publication of the book.[57] Finally, Helena reluctantly told her story again. At first, she thought it wasn't worth it and that readers would laugh at her.[58] But she decided to do it, encouraged by René Agagliate, who did the recordings and helped with the organization of the material and with the transcription of numerous Yanomamö words and phrases, which Helena spoke better than Spanish or Portuguese. Emilio Fuentes edited the final version, which I have used in this study.

Yo soy Napëyoma: Relato de una mujer raptada por los indígenas yanomami (I Am Napëyoma: An Account of a Woman Captured by the Yanomami) (1984) is an autobiography in the vein of the best captivity narratives. It is important to consider the different elements that motivate the publication of an autobiographical text. I am referring to aspects of autobiography, like techniques of self-representation, which affect the production of the text and modify it. Sylvia Molloy, in her interesting book *At Face Value: Autobiographical Writing in Spanish America*, boldly advances certain hypotheses about the autobiographical genre in Spanish America. She rightly points to the tentative and ambivalent character of the best-known autobiographies, which are driven by the author's need for affirmation and search for recognition. "The vacillation between public persona and private self, between honor and vanity, between self and country, between lyrical evocation or factual annotation of the past are but a few manifestations of the hesitancy that marked (and even now may mark) Spanish American self-writing."[59] In effect, the fundamental factor determining the genre of many of the texts written in the Americas that are considered autobiographical—I am thinking of many of the chronicles of the conquest, letters of relation (*cartas de relación*), memorials, commentaries, and compilations, for example, the *Naufragios* of Cabeza de Vaca—is its addressee. What were the author's intentions? To inform an anonymous reader? To secure benefits? To inform posterity? To leave a record of unusual deeds and voyages? To satisfy a passion for writing? Any generalized answer to these questions is bound to be simplistic.

Valero's autobiography, for example, has unique characteristics. If, as Fuentes says, Helena ultimately chose to authorize the account of her life, she was motivated to do so by Biocca's undue appropriation of her story. In fact, her story attracted more than one author. In 1982 a book entitled *Shabono: A True Adventure in the Remote and Magical Heart of the South American Jungle,* was published. It was very well received by professional critics, and even *Newsweek* called it a fascinating work. The book tells the story of Florinda Donner, a graduate anthropology student who, while conducting field work in Venezuela, was supposedly adopted by a group of Yanomamö Indians with whom she lived for a while. In 1983 the book became controversial after the publication of an article in the journal *American Anthropologist* in which Rebecca B. de Holmes accused Donner of fraud and plagiarism: "Donner's fieldwork was not known among local anthropologists. Several phone calls to veteran Venezuelan anthropologists at the Instituto Venezolano de Investigaciones Científicas (IVIC) and the Universidad Central revealed that no one had heard of Donner or anyone of her description having done fieldwork among the Yanomamö."[60] Holmes accused Donner of using the English version of Helena Valero's narrative and manipulating it with fantasy elements very much in the manner of the works of Carlos Castaneda. Interestingly, Castaneda is quoted on the back cover of the book praising Donner's work. According to Mary Louise Pratt, many anthropologists who are experts on Yanomamö culture have agreed with Holmes that "Donner's whole book must be a fabrication and that Donner had probably never lived with the Yanomamö."[61]

But as Molloy writes, "Autobiography is always a re-presentation, that is, a retelling, since the life to which it supposedly refers is already a kind of narrative construct [. . .]. Autobiography does not rely on events but on an articulation of those events stored in memory and reproduced through rememoration and verbalization."[62] Many years separate Helena's first experiences from the time of the composition of her autobiography. It is unquestionable that she has an extraordinary memory that allows her to describe in detail the most minute past events and reconstruct the environment as if she were doing a documentary. A great deal of the book is devoted to the description of indigenous communities with valuable information about material, social, economic, political, and religious aspects of their life. Of special interest are Helena's descriptions of the physical environment, which she captures with precision. There is no doubt concerning the geographical features she describes. In addition, as Fuentes notes in the introduction to his edition, "The flights of an airplane over the High Orinoco (1941), the presence of the missionary Barker (1949), the journey of the Franco-Venezuelan expedition to the source of the Orinoco (1951), and other physical supports have helped to date the course of her life and estimate the ages of her children."[63] Various anthropologists who have lived with the Yanomamö agree on the narrative's accuracy and its organization as firsthand ethnographic material.

> The content of the narrative was compared with information provided by different Indians who knew Helena Valero or lived with her, with a view to greater exactitude, but this information really only served to corroborate what Helena said. No one better than she can present credentials as eloquent as the scars she bears from arrows or snakebites.[64]

Nevertheless, we note an imbalance in the text, which tends to remember certain episodes and rapidly gloss over others. For example, deliberately or not, Helena makes no mention of any affective contact with the Indians and on the contrary goes into great detail about their aggression, mistreatment, and dangerousness. It is interesting to observe that in the whole of Helena's long and meticulous narrative, which describes in great detail customs, rituals, trips, and relations, and becomes engrossed in animals, plants, and individuals, there is no reference to any type of affectionate contact with either of her two husbands. Husiwë takes her as his wife without any exchange of words. Her relations with men were distant and hard. With women she had a more harmonious relationship. Some protected her in moments of great danger, but distance seems to dominate the narrative. Napëyoma alone in the jungle, where she gradually adapted, seems to set the general tone. No doubt Helena selected the events she narrates and embellished them according to her recollection, which was influenced by emotive memory. This aspect might lead one to consider the narrative as a testimonial text. I feel that *Yo soy Napëyoma* does not follow the discourse of protest, accusation, or challenge typical of testimonial literature.[65] Helena's testimony contains elements of struggle and survival, which in part are the result of her captive status, but which are also part of the life of each and every Yanomamö living in a difficult and hostile environment. The great protagonist is the jungle. In the jungle, Yanomamö societies act to maintain ways of life and socialization proper to a culture adapted to its natural surroundings.

Conclusion

Helena Valero is a twentieth-century captive, a sample of an era in which existing frontiers fight to maintain the legitimacy of the cultures that inhabit them. She was a victim and a witness of that frontier, which to foreign eyes seems frozen in time. She traveled through the jungle with different Yanomamö groups, alone and as a fugitive. She returned by way of the Orinoco River to find her family. However, her great journey was the round-trip from Umbelina Helena Valero, daughter of Carlos Valero, to Napëyoma, the *napë* wife of Husiwë and Akawë. She crossed the cultural frontiers both ways, and was at given moments *napë* among the Yanomamö and Indian among the whites. Her coming and going turned her into a stranger, a foreigner, an "other" in both cultures and, as a consequence, the object of rejection and aggression.

For different reasons, and against her wishes, Helena recorded the story of her life with fascinating meticulousness of information and detail. One is amazed at the tremendous tenacity this thirteen-year-old girl needed to survive in a hostile, difficult environment that to a large degree was foreign to her. She resorted to certain cultural mechanisms to overcome the compelling difficulties of her existence. Religion, in her case, worked as a mechanism of identity which never left her. One wonders if Helena's adaptation would have been possible had she been older. Fuentes feels that "if she had been an adult, she probably would have succumbed to the harshness of life in the jungle. She would have been unable to adapt as she was at the age of thirteen."[66] Nonetheless, the history of captivity is the history of exceptions, not rules. There are as many models as there are cases, and we have knowledge of older captive women who survived captivity in extreme situations and adapted.

Helena's narrative is her autobiography. It follows the fundamental periods of her youth and maturity through formative years and profound changes. Like every autobiography, her narrative reflects the characteristics typical of the genre. An autobiography is, fundamentally, a story that we tell ourselves about ourselves, but with the awareness that an audience will read it. The autobiography of Helena Valero is a 539-page volume in which nothing is superfluous.

⊰ SEVEN ⊱

Captives in Literature

> It might be true, Siripo thought. He saw Lucía in a corner, amid the other terrified prisoners.
>
> To what race did she belong? Even with hands stained by a king's blood, she was unmoved?
>
> In the eyes of a savage, valor is worth a hundred times more than virtue. Siripo was perfidious, but not foolish and he felt restrained by that woman's greatness of soul.
>
> She and the others belonged to him, as spoils of war. He looked on all with disdain, all except Lucía Miranda, and he felt that the ambition to win her will and her love was born in his breast.
>
> —Hugo Wast, *Lucía Miranda*

Although the frontier as an independent entity developed over hundreds of years, a discourse about that new and changing entity did not find a growing medium until well into the nineteenth century. Before Spanish American independence, literature, with the exception of poetry, did not seem to wish to exploit the vast wealth offered by frontier characters and topics. With few exceptions, no novels, properly speaking, were written during the colonial period. The literature of that period was limited to poetry and drama. Literary output included hybrid forms that are difficult to classify: diaries, letters, reports, chronicles, commentaries, notices, natural histories, and travel books. This is not the place to enter into the debate over whether these hybrid texts belong to history or to literature.

Chronicles are texts, built on the fascinating narratives of the encounter between cultures. Although to some extent constrained by events, chronicles also bespeak a colonized imagination. It is not unusual to find in them codes belonging to different narrative discourses. In so-called historical texts, the original subjectivity of the author, in many cases, ends up blending fiction and reality.[1] In turn, literary discourse, of necessity, attempts to appropriate historical truth, protecting faithfulness to the referent, a mechanism more typical of history. Terry Eagleton reminds us that, in the eighteenth century and before, "the concept of literature was not confined as it sometimes is today to 'creative' or 'imaginative' writing. It meant the whole body of writing valued in society: philosophy, history, essays and letters as well as poems."[2] What is important to remember for the purposes of this work is the capacity of these colonial discourses to incorporate, consciously or unconsciously, elements of fiction, biblical myths, and medieval legends, decked out in the rhetoric of chivalric romances, hagiographies, and biblical texts.

Certainly, the conditions under which this literary corpus flourished were, in the best of cases, difficult. The Consejo de Indias (Council of the Indies) and the Inquisition regulated and controlled the production and the distribution of books in the Americas. Writings critical of the conduct of peninsular authorities (I refer specifically to *Cautiverio feliz*) met with disapproval. It is sufficient to bear in mind that Bascuñán's extensive manuscript was not published until the middle of the nineteenth century. Cabeza de Vaca's *Naufragios* was luckier. Even though it brushes the limits of the proscribed, loaded, as it is, with equivocal elements such as disillusionment, failure, uncontrolled ambition, cannibalism, shamanism, magic, and mystery—subjects too controversial to be glossed over by censors—the manuscript was published in 1542. It was the chronicle of an unexplored continent appearing at a time when relations with the indigenous peoples were marked by the innocence and expectation of the first encounters. *Naufragios* impressed readers on the Peninsula and apparently met with the monarch's approval.[3] Who knows what other reasons fostered its publication? What sets these captive texts, and most of the ones studied in this book, apart from the vast historical and literary production of the colonial period is their testimonial character, which imparts a sense of unquestionable authenticity. Let us remember the desire of many chroniclers (Bernal Díaz del Castillo among them) to legitimize their histories on the basis of their unique status as witnesses of the deeds described.

Independence promoted the development of genres that were more in accord with the vision that the new republics wished to project. Andrés Bello,

José Lastarria, and Bartolomé Mitre, among others, stressed the urgent need to produce a literature that would express the ideas, the idiosyncrasy, and the creative spirit that were deemed desirable for the newly emerging republics. Mitre felt that the novel was "the highest expression of the civilization of a people; it is the fruit of a tree that has reached full maturity."[4] Basically, it was expected that narrative would be the means by which the liberal creed's ideas of progress and modernity would spread. The choice of themes in postindependence prose and poetry is therefore not surprising. In general there was no interest in the monarchical period and colonial times. The literature of the frontier was passed through a sieve in a process of meticulous selection. Certain themes, types, and settings were selected; others were scorned. There is no doubt about Domingo F. Sarmiento's influence on the way frontier types were perceived. His *Facundo,* was, throughout the century, the dictionary for the description of national characters, specifically frontier characters. The depiction of Indians and frontier life in Argentine nineteenth-century literature is clearly tendentious.[5]

In the nineteenth century, the subject of captivity is practically absent from all Spanish American literatures with the exception of Argentina's. Isolated works appeared in other parts of the continent, without ever forming a corpus. In Argentina, the topic was treated more frequently, although never reaching the popularity attained by captivity narratives in North America.[6] If not important in terms of quantity, these works certainly were in terms of their significance. The ideological content of these works is shamelessly obvious: they idealize the captive woman as they animalize the Indian. Specifically, the instrument of this ideological manipulation was the body of the abducted woman. Her body was transformed into a symbol that inverted the terms of the process of dispossession. In this formulation, it was not Europeans who stole land from Indians and deprived them of their natural way of life. Instead it was Indians who brutally deprived whites of their most prized possession. "The violence perpetrated by Indians on captive women, in and of itself justified any violence against the captor."[7]

It would seem that captivity and ideology are inseparable. In Spain, captivity literature has a long tradition harking back to the captives in Algiers at the time of the Christian resistance to Turkish Mediterranean invasions. Even earlier, the subject was treated in Greek and Byzantine novels.[8] The body of the captive was transported to America, from the Chilean chronicles of Alonso González de Nájera (1614) to the Río de la Plata chronicles of Ruy Díaz de Guzmán (1612), the better to serve the cause of Spanish expansionism and the plundering of America's riches. Abduction is an act of violence that results from the radical confrontation between two societies. The captive, male or female, functions as a victim of latent violence. Therefore the person of the captive becomes the object of contention, over which vengeance and negotiation are plotted. It also becomes the political-ideological rationale to justify future repression.

The present chapter studies the range and purposes of fictive writing about captives in the Spanish American context. It must be kept in mind that this is not a closed subject, since Spanish American literature, which in the last two decades has shown a clear inclination for historical subjects, has returned to the topic of captives in recent novels such as Juan José Saer's *El entenado* (The Witness) (1983), and César Aira's *Ema, la cautiva* (Ema, the Captive) (1981).

Captivity in Colonial Epics

Captivity narratives began to appear in the sixteenth century as part of longer chronicles, but their inclusion did not seem to indicate an awareness of their uniqueness. Anonymous or unknown shipwrecked people, lost expeditionaries and captives, appear in the pages of the chronicles, adding their adventures to the vast collection of colonial anecdotes. The texts of Álvar Núñez Cabeza de Vaca, Francisco Núñez de Pineda y Bascuñán, Juan Falcón, Father Ávila, and Hernando de Escalante y Fontaneda are the exception rather than the rule. Their narratives were written in prose and in the first person, at a time when no one seemed interested in these peculiar episodes in the otherwise triumphal march of conquest. For the rest, captive stories before independence were written in the third person by a chronicler who had direct or indirect knowledge of the episode. The possibility for fictionalization in these cases is great, as we shall see in the case of the captivity of Lucía Miranda and Sebastián Hurtado, which appeared in Ruy Díaz de Guzmán's chronicle *La Argentina,* published in 1612. Practically all the chroniclers of the kingdom of Chile mention captives, some in more detail than others. The official chronicler Gonzalo Fernández de Oviedo heard these fascinating stories and repeated them in his great work, *Historia general y natural de las Indias* (General and Natural History of the Indies).[9] Named and unnamed, captives appear in this chronicle as anecdotes in the great colonial adventure. There are touches of ambiguity in the stories which reflect Fernández de Oviedo's awareness of the changing attitude of the Spanish Crown toward Indians during the first part of the sixteenth century.

Colonial epic poetry, especially in the kingdom of Chile, took on subjects that were considered suitable. Spanish Golden Age epic poetry felt a strong attraction to history. The prestige of epic poetry was such that it was frequently consulted as a source of reference. This was the case with poems like Alonso de Ercilla's *La Araucana* (*The Araucaniad*) (1569), and Diego de Arias de Saavedra's *Purén indómito* (Purén Untamed).[10]

La Araucana is, without question, the epic poem with American subject matter that had the greatest historical and literary impact. Critics elevated it to the rank of the first literary monument that dealt with the conquest. Nonetheless, the real interest of the poem derives from the ambiguity in its depiction of the characters and of the war between Spaniards and Araucanians. The poem can be read as an attempt to vindicate the noble character of the Indians. Ercilla achieved this through the creation of a series of Araucanian heroes whose verisimilitude is questionable. The heroism and haughtiness of Lautaro and Caupolicán are meant to excuse the Spanish army's failure to pacify the kingdom. At the same time, Ercilla's depiction of Araucanian heroic invincibility established a model of indigenous resistance to the invasion.

> Never has a king subjected
> Such fierce people proud of freedom,
> Nor has alien nation boasted
> E'er of having trod their borders;
> Ne'er has dared a neighboring country
> Raise the sword and move against them;
> Always were they feared, unshackled,
> Free of laws, with necks unbending.[11]

Thanks to Ercilla, Araucanians live on in history, their deeds engraved in golden letters, while universally no notice is taken of the continuous, and no less heroic, resistance of other peoples to the European invasion. The deeds of other Amerindians were considered the barbaric acts of savages. Not so in the case of the Araucanians. In this sense, it can be said that not all the indigenous peoples of the continent had the good fortune of finding a poet to remember and save them from historical silence. Ercilla sang the deeds of the Araucanians, comparing them to the glorious infantry regiments of Castile. His work sculpted models and immortalized them. His influence on historians and on his literary imitators was vast. Maxime Chevalier believes that the poem was read and imitated by all Creole authors who wrote epics.[12] The popularity of *La Araucana* lasted until the Romantic period. The translation of the poem by Robert Southey in the nineteenth century was widely read in Europe and inspired numerous poems on the topic of the noble savage.[13]

Canto 3, which tells of the first great revolt of the Araucanians against Spanish aggression, introduces the character of Lautaro, a captive Indian in the service of Governor Pedro de Valdivia. Lautaro, like many Mapuches who had been *encomendados* (placed in servitude by the Spanish), went over to the Indians, and his actions were instrumental in the Araucanian victories over the Spanish troops. Ercilla's portrayal of Lautaro turns him into a mythical figure, claimed by writers of the nationalist period and even later. The other heroic character he created was Caupolicán, whose stature equals that of the bravest Spanish commanders. Pedro de Valdivia was the first Spanish captive in Araucania whose death was reinvented time and again by chroniclers and poets.

> Chief Caupolicán was joyous,
> Seeing him alive and humbled.
> With a conqueror's voice and gesture,
> Threats he made, and posed him questions.
>
> Then Valdivia, wretched captive,
> Answered, lowly and obedient,
> Begging that he be not murdered,
> Swearing future peace and freedom.[14]

However, neither Alonso de Ercilla nor Pedro de Oña (*Arauco domado* [Arauco Tamed], 1596) paid particular attention to the subject of Christian captives. They were more interested in the numerous Indian captives of the Spaniards, the so-called *Indios amigos*. These were in fact ladinos made to serve the Spanish enemy, and like Lautaro, they rebelled against Spanish oppression. Diego de Arias y Saavedra, in his long poem *Purén indómito*, was the writer who paid greatest attention to Christian captives, especially through the figure of the captive white woman.[15] In canto 19, devoted to the sacking of the city of Valdivia, we read:

> Some Indians took two, others three, or four, and even six women
> and held them by their blond hair,
> laden with gold, and silver, and their other belongings,
> mistreated, weeping, sorrowful women . . . [16]

Arias de Saavedra introduces the theme of the Indians' lascivious desire for white women, here configured as victims, while their bodies acquire a growing symbolic function. There is no historic basis for the Mapuches' alleged special attraction for white women, but this belief was instrumental in spurring and justifying the violence of conquest.

> But to the greater sorrow of the women
> those uncivil Indians ordered that they cease
> their weeping, mourning, tears, and laments,
> and that the women should make merry and clap,
> and they made all widows and maidens
> doff their garments
> and then dress in accordance to Indian custom:
> with short dresses and loose hair;
>
> And because they refused to undress,
> owing to their great chastity and shame,
> with barbarous fury they were uncoiffed,
> no locks or braids were spared;
> their clothes also without pity they took
> with great insolence and shamelessness,
> and in place of their dainty tunics,
> they were given coarse woolen ones instead . . .
>
> Oh, sad mourning! Oh, unfortunate fate!
> Oh, cruel, unheard of shame!
> Oh, insufferable and pitiless pain!
> Oh, bitter death, bitter living death!
> Oh, adverse predicament, monstrous and ill-starred!
> Oh, unequalled, unbound sorrow,

> that noble and modest ladies
> should be subject to idolatrous barbarians![17]

There are numerous similarities, poetic, thematic, and intentional between *Purén indómito* and *La Araucana*. Both are also close to the arguments
advanced by most of the chroniclers of the kingdom of Chile. The view they
present of the war is pessimistic and moralizing, dwelling on the bad reputation and inept conduct of the Spanish administration. Arias de Saavedra considers the Spanish military disasters to be divine punishment for moral devi-
ations and conduct improper to Christian rulers. As an example, he cites the
punishments to which rebellious Indians were subjected: the amputation of
hands and other body parts, and various physical tortures. The general tone
of the poem is pessimistic and depressing, without room for heroism. Some
critics have even felt that this aspect calls into question the epic character
of the poem, so few are the heroes and so many the villains.[18] Outstanding
among the villains are the priest, Juan Barba, a renegade and idolater, who
went over to the enemy and took part in atrocities and sacked churches, and
the nobleman Jerónimo Bello, also a traitor. Nor do the Indians fare better.
They are portrayed as pagans inclined to evil by nature. Scenes of the abduction and rape of white women are countless.

> Three were raping a virgin
> in public, without remorse or shame,
> and the noble maiden was screaming,
> her hands tied with her braid;
> but, when Friar Pedro saw the unmentionable
> insolence and so much shamelessness,
> he came and like a Catholic Christian,
> restrained the barbarous villain;
>
> because of this and because he preached a sermon
> exhorting the unfortunate women
> to die with love for He who made them,
> rather than being by barbarians ravished,
> from a massive poplar
> with spreading branches and a smooth base,
> the Indians had him hanged, and left in the shade
> so that he would not preach against them anymore . . .

> One hundred and fifty comely virgins,
> more beautiful than lilies and flowers,
> fair, noble, graceful, and lovely to behold
> these perfidious traitors brought.
> And in the celebration of their feast,
> oh, crude, unreasoning, deflowerers!
> none was left who was not raped,
> nor matron left unravished.[19]

In this episode and others, the white woman's body acquires significant symbolic connotations. The nakedness of the noble, pure ladies described by Arias de Saavedra expresses the intimacy of the body social of Christian culture, which seems far superior to that of the Indians. Although authors like Ercilla and Arias maintain that the prolonged wars of Arauco and their consequences were due fundamentally to the bad administration of the kingdom, the superiority of Christian culture is not questioned.

Saavedra inaugurates a clearly instrumental formula that will be repeated unchanged in fictive literature about captives. The captive woman is presented as a victim through whose body a complicated relationship between Europeans and Indians is articulated. Indeed, this clear, unequivocal treatment appears in another chronicle of the period, the episode of the captivity of Lucía Miranda, included in *La Argentina* (1612), by Ruy Díaz de Guzmán.

The Legend of Lucía Miranda

The legend of Lucía Miranda is a fictionalized history hidden in the folios of a long chronicle, *La Argentina,* which gave symbolic expression to the conflict arising from the difficult relations between Christian and indigenous populations in the Río de la Plata area. Ruy Díaz de Guzmán, a Creole mestizo whose father was a Spanish nobleman and whose mother was a Guaraní Indian, was born in Asunción, Paraguay, between 1558 and 1560. He rose to be governor. The chronicle is based on several extant narratives of the principal expeditions of discovery in the Río de la Plata. The work of Díaz de Guzmán is that of a compiler more than an eyewitness chronicler. He covers the expeditions and governorships of Díaz de Solís, Sebastián Gaboto, Pedro de Mendoza, and Álvar Núñez Cabeza de Vaca.

The lack of trustworthy information and the many contradictions in the episodes about Lucía Miranda have raised doubts about its authenticity. According to Díaz de Guzmán's version, Lucía Miranda and her husband, Sebastián Hurtado, were part of Sebastián Gaboto's expedition. After founding Fort Corpus Christi, Gaboto returned to Spain to report on his discoveries. Captain Nuño de Lara remained in command of the fort. Relations between the Spaniards and the neighboring Indians had been good in the early days of the conquest, especially with the Timbúes, with whom the Spaniards lived and traded. Díaz de Guzmán writes that the Spanish "were welcomed and treated with hospitality by the inhabitants of that province."[20] Later on, the excessive demands imposed by the Spaniards on the Indian population strained relations and led to a series of conflicts, one of which was the context for the Lucía Miranda incident.

The narrative describes the relations of the Spanish with the Timbúes, "people of good will and nature," and their two brother caciques, "one named Mangoré and the other Siripó, both young men about thirty or forty, brave and experts in war."[21] The year was 1532. The drama began when the older brother, Mangoré, "took a fancy to a Spanish woman who was in the fortress, by name Lucía Miranda, married to a certain Sebastián Hurtado, both from Ecija," and made amorous advances.[22] She rejected him, invoking the fidelity she owed her husband. Mangoré then planned to take his desired prey by force and, taking advantage of the absence of Sebastián, who was upriver on a voyage of discovery, organized an assault on the Spanish fort. The fort was destroyed, "not leaving a man alive, except five women, who were there together with the greatly desired Lucía and some three or four boys, who because they were children were not killed but taken prisoner and made captives."[23] Mangoré lost his life in the attack. His younger brother Siripó, first out of devotion for his brother and later seduced by her beauty, abducted Lucía, "who when she found herself in his power, could not hide her feeling of great misery, with tears in her eyes, and although she was treated well and served by Siripó's servants, that in no way kept her from feeling disconsolate, seeing herself possessed by a barbarian."[24]

Upon his return, Sebastián Hurtado was informed of the awful events and decided to head out alone in search of his wife. He was captured, but at Lucía's pleading his life was spared. In their forlorn captivity, the loving spouses sought each other in the darkness of the night. Learning of these furtive encounters, and driven by jealousy, Siripó "had a great bonfire made to burn the goodly Lucía," while Sebastián was handed over to "many young men, who bound his feet and hands, and tied him to a carob tree, where he was shot with arrows by those barbarians, until his life left him."[25]

The authenticity of this account is doubtful. Norberto Ras asserts that "the names of the Spaniards mentioned by Díaz de Guzmán, like Sebastián Hurtado, Nuño de Lara and others, are invented and apparently there were no caciques named Mangoré or Siripó."[26] There is no confirmation that there was any woman on Gaboto's expedition. *La Argentina* includes several stories of dubious truthfulness. The episode of La Maldonada, for example, saved from a lioness after escaping her captors, seems extracted from the Bible. Enrique de Gandía feels that Díaz de Guzmán's chronicle "contains two novels: that of Lucía Miranda and that of La Maldonada."[27]

It is interesting that although captivity was a daily reality recorded in many sources, a female captive's narrative should be written using fictional material. The inclusion of the story in Díaz de Guzmán's chronicle can be explained by ideological reasons. In 1612, the date he finished writing his chronicle, the process of disenchantment regarding the promise of the explored area of the Río de la Plata had reached rock bottom. No gold had been found. The legend of the Caesars, which had fostered so many southern expeditions, was never more than a legend, and conflicts with the indigenous inhabitants were on the rise. Díaz de Guzmán, like other mestizo chroniclers, had to face his personal conflicts and in addition had to justify the actions of the conquistadores in a zone of Indian resistance. Given this context, we can understand the usefulness of the legend of Lucía Miranda. Cristina Iglesia and Julio Schvartzman explain it in the following manner:

> In the midst of the chronicle's discourse, a mythical episode emerges which condenses all the moves necessary to justify the conquest. If myth is a language chosen by history, this episode will become a model of the complicities and betrayals that tug at history's relation with literature.[28]

The legend of Lucía Miranda voices the Spanish reaction to the Indians after the first phases of the conquest, which were marked by a certain tone of admiration and surprise. Her captivity and sacrifice bring together all the attributes of the white female captive, and consequently define the characteristics of her captors. Lucía, forced into a union against her will, defends her honor as the ultimate good. In the process she takes on a particular role that we shall see repeated in nineteenth-century works. We have seen how Arias de Saavedra, through Fray Pedro, exhorts Spanish female captives "to die with love for He who made them / rather than being by barbarians ravished."[29] Lucía is burned at the stake like Saint Lucy, her namesake. Her husband, Sebastián, is shot with arrows, just like Saint Sebastian, whose martyrdom added to the glory of the Church. Thus both are linked to Christian martyrology. By contrast, the Indian is represented as a barbarian possessed by an uncontrollable lust that makes him break all treaties with the Christians. The female captive, more than the male captive, will serve to implement, at a certain level, the contradictory mechanisms of the civilizing discourse in its relation with indigenous peoples. "The myth of Lucía Miranda, that is to say, an Indian's fatal desire for a white woman, served at first to justify the violence of the conquest. Later, during the last quarter of the nineteenth century, it would become an ideological support in the campaign to exterminate the Indian."[30]

In the *Historia de la conquista del Paraguay, Río de la Plata y Tucumán*, (History of the Conquest of Paraguay, Río de la Plata and Tucumán), published in 1745, Pedro Lozano returned to the myth of Lucía Miranda. Modified and adapted, the story was presented as a paradigm of the struggle between good and evil. Good, of course, is identified with Christianity and evil with the Timbúes. Moreover, Lozano reworked the interracial love conflict and used it as the basis for several conclusions about the Indian. In the version in *La Argentina*, Siripó offers Lucía marriage; he doesn't want her as a slave but as his wife. However, the door is shut. There is no possibility for an amorous relationship between a white woman and an Indian. Cultural differences cannot be bridged. Honor, bravery, and goodness adorn this mythical heroine. Díaz de Guzmán mentions many more Indian captives of the Spaniards whose fate seems to have improved in captivity. Iglesia and Schvartzman remark that "the captive white woman, in our literature, is born on top of the overwhelming reality of the captive Indian woman."[31]

The novelistic potential of the episode eased its transformation into the stuff of fiction. Díaz de Guzmán's narrative is devoid of even minimal ethnographical information, and we learn nothing about the Timbúes, although such deficiencies should not come as a surprise. Before the nineteenth century, the informative narratives of Cabeza de Vaca and Núñez de Pineda y Bascuñán are the exception rather than the rule. Fiction worked to further cloud the picture, imposing literary codes or referring to legends imported from European traditions. The Indians and captives of *La Araucana, Purén indómito,* and *Arauco domado* seem extracted from the classical Greco-Roman tradition, or are framed by scenes of unmistakable Renaissance design.[32] In *Arauco domado* the episode of Tegualda, daughter of Cacique Brancol, and her unfortunate husband, the captive Crepino, recalls the story of Isabella and Zerbino in *Orlando Furioso.*

Be that as it may, the captive drama of Lucía Miranda impressed the public, and the many imitations that appeared in the nineteenth century and later are proof of it. In 1789 Lavardén wrote a tragedy in three acts entitled *Siripó,* which was performed in Buenos Aires. Some years later, a drama with the title *Siripó y Yara* premiered, although it might be the same play.[33] In 1864 a drama entitled *Lucía Miranda* was performed, and several novels based on the same episode were published: *Lucía Miranda,* by Eduarda Mansilla de García, the sister of Lucio V. Mansilla, serialized in 1860 and published in book form in 1883; and *Lucía Miranda* (1860), by Rosa Guerra. More recent are Alejandra R. Canepa's *Lucía Miranda,* published in Barcelona in 1918, and Hugo Wast's 1929 version, of the same title.[34]

The Popularity of the Subject in Other Literatures

In areas most affected by Indian attacks, like southern Chile, stories about captives were daily anecdotes of colonial life. Some of them, as we have seen with Lucía Miranda and Juan Barba, had become legends. However, in neither high culture nor the oral tradition of the Americas did the theme of captivity have an impact comparable to what it had in the Spanish Golden Age. With the exception of certain anecdotal connections, it is impossible to establish a direct influence in the treatment of the subject on either side of the Atlantic. It is true that the equation Indian = Moor appears in certain passages by colonial authors. Indians are called Moors in some Argentine chronicles and traditional ballads. In her novel *Lucía Miranda,* Eduarda Mansilla transforms the Timbúe chiefs Mangoré and Siripó into North African princes.

On the Iberian Peninsula, Miguel de Cervantes gave a great boost to a tradition that descended from classical and Byzantine literature with a drama called *Los tratos de Argel* (The Traffic of Algiers), and a novel, *El cautivo* (The Captive), the first modern novel about the subject. Later he continued to cultivate this thematic vein in a series of dramas: *Los baños de Argel* (The Bagnios [Prisons] of Algiers), *El gallardo español* (The Gallant Spaniard), and *La gran Sultana* (The Great Sultana); and several short novels, including *El amante liberal* (The Liberal Lover) and *La galatea*. "With these plays, Cervantes filled the Spanish stage with a most varied collection of captives, renegades, Moors and Turks."[35] Cervantes had been a captive in Algiers himself, an experience that, doubtless, marked his life. He sees captivity as an awful trial for the Christian. The temptations to which the captive is exposed are many, and they measure the captive's virtue. In the second part of *El Ingenioso Hidalgo Don Quijote de la Mancha*, there are references to the sexual perversions of the Moors and the danger faced by young Christian women who fell into the power of Turks. Cervantes was not the only one to practice this genre. The story "El Abencerraje" and the novel *Ozmín y Daraja*, by Mateo Alemán, are great antecedents. Within the Spanish tradition of frontier ballads (*romances fronterizos*), in turn, hundreds of ballads about captives had become vastly popular and much imitated.[36]

The almost total absence of fictive narratives in Spanish America during the colonial period has already been mentioned. There are some rare exceptions to the rule. *El cautiverio feliz*, considered a novel by some critics, seems to have inspired the composition of a play that was first performed in 1634 in Lima with a good deal of success.[37] The play, put on by the Lima company Los Conformes, deals with a Spanish soldier captured by Araucanian Indians. In captivity, he falls in love with the daughter of a Mapuche cacique, and an intense romance begins.[38] In the end, the lovers are reunited in Christian territory after the soldier has been ransomed and his lover captured by Spanish troops. The public of Lima received the play with enthusiasm. Perhaps in the construction of the interracial romance we can establish some significant connections between both literatures. One constant is the blossoming of a romance that unites a Christian captive with a beautiful Moorish woman. In Cervantes's *El cautivo*, the beautiful Zoraida betrays her father and enables the flight of the Christian prisoner. During his own captivity, Cervantes had heard a popular Algerian legend which inspired him: the legend of the Moorish beauty Zahara—daughter of a rich Algerian renegade, Agi Morato—who, instructed in Christianity by a female slave, falls in love with a Christian captive, helps him escape, and flees with him. It is almost impossible to trace the dissemination of a legend. Legends and myths have a life of their own, and their channels of dissemination are often unfollowable. Nevertheless, we can't help but point to the consistency with which this aspect of the plot was repeated in other latitudes. Both in the chronicles and in fiction we find the story of an Indian woman who, moved by love or compassion, at the last minute saves the life of a captive or allows him to escape.

In the Anglo-American tradition, this became one of the legends that most influenced the captivity narrative: the story of Captain John Smith and Pocahontas. Told for the first time by Smith in his *General Historie of Virginia, New England, and the Summer Isles* (1624), it has since been the inspiration for novels, stories, plays, films, poems, paintings, and sculptures, and has become an icon of popular culture. The veracity of the story has never been proven and its evolution reveals incongruities.[39] In Spanish America the legend was adopted by El Inca Garcilaso, Fernández de Oviedo, Mariño de Lobera, and Diego Rosales, among others.

This particular subject apart, I am inclined to think that the two traditions, the one that developed in Golden Age Spain and the one that evolved in Spanish America, parted company. While Spain settled comfortably into fiction, Spanish America was not able to escape the influence of the chronicles and certain epic poems.

In New England literature, the theme of the captive reached extraordinary dimensions and served to harden established beliefs into the cultural stereotypes of the period. These included the beliefs that Indians were savages and instinctively cruel, that the European expansion toward the interior of the continent was a mission driven by manifest destiny, and that women, guardians of family honor, were the sacrificial victims on whom Indians vented their animal instinct. Narratives by or about captives became best sellers. According to Richard VanDerBeets, "As the frontier pushed westward under continuing conflict, the tales of Indian captivity accompanied it, gradually becoming our first literature of catharsis in an era when native American fiction scarcely existed."[40]

The first works of fiction involving captives in New England date from the last decades of the eighteenth century, and they continued to appear regularly throughout the nineteenth century. In time, several features came to define the genre. The actions of frontier heroes seemed to follow a pattern copied from ballads, poems, and stories. The public identified with them in a process of symbiotic recognition. The characters were daring. These heroes faced unfavorable circumstances, such as the physical and numerical superiority of their captors, but thanks to their superior ingenuity and intelligence they overcame the odds. Unexpected dangers and dramatic escapes provided tension. Later, certain characteristics of the escapes allowed readers to associate the fugitive with legendary characters such as David Crockett and Daniel Boone.

Drama, exclusively American exotic surroundings, and the risks associated with the constant westward expansion shaped an artistic current of considerable force. The physical frontier gave way to the imagined frontier. Captivity invited the imagination to cross to the other side of a frontier full of unexpected threats and marvelous worlds. Among the pioneering works of the genre, we must mention Ann Eliza Bleecher's sentimental novel *The History of Maria Kittle* (1797), and Charles Brockden Brown's gothic novel *Edgar Huntly or Memoirs of a Sleepwalker* (1799). Nelson Baker went back to one of the best-known captive episodes, John Smith's rescue by the young Pocahontas, and turned it into the play, *The Indian Princess; or, La Belle Sauvage* (1808). But it was James Fenimore Cooper's *Leatherstocking Tales* that definitively captured the attention of the greater reading public.[41] Leatherstocking is a frontier hero in the tradition of Daniel Boone. In *The Last of the Mohicans* (1826), Cooper returned to the topic in a novel which David Haberly calls "the most influential early nineteenth-century American novel."[42] The novel's impact went far beyond the simple definition of a particular genre; it contributed to the shaping of an idea of America which had profound consequences in Europe and Latin America.[43] At a time when the urge to erase any trace of savage Indians was boiling over, Cooper's challenge was to strike a balance. On the same map, Cooper managed to include the great enterprise of westward expansion, the noble savage, and the other savage Indians whose atrocities smothered captivity narratives. Cooper found the formula to effect this compromise in the multifaceted character of the female captive.

It seems that neither Cooper nor the many practitioners of the genre in North America had much of an impact on their peers in Spanish America. Fiction about captives was not produced with the same regularity and fervor in Spanish America, with the exception of the Río de la Plata.[44] There are very

Juan Mauricio Rugendas, *El rapto: Rescate de una cautiva*
(The Abduction: Rescue of a Female Captive), 1848.

few works treating this theme in other countries of the continent. Remarkable among these are *Cumandá,* by the Ecuadorian Juan León Mera; *Tabaré,* by the Uruguayan Juan Zorrilla de San Martín; and "Inámi o la Laguna de Ranco," a poem by the Chilean Salvador Sanfuentes.

From *La cautiva* to Martín Fierro

In Argentina, daily exposure to captivity familiarized the population with a reality that did not require the further stimulus of fantasy. Most of the settlements of the interior had suffered the scourge of captivity. However, the Argentine government was debating what policy to adopt with regard to the Indian. It is at this point that fiction comes in, advancing thanks to its power of representation, dramatizing episodes, and ultimately tipping the balance to one side of the issue. The Dantesque vision depicted in the first part of *La cautiva* (1837), by Esteban Echeverría, or the infernal passage that launches the second part of *Martín Fierro* (1878), by José Hernández, exudes the heavy ideological charge with which it was written. Nineteenth-century Argentina, which was undergoing a rapid process of expansion, was in a hurry to resolve the Indian problem.

The captive woman functions as a metaphor for the antagonism between two societies in their struggle for survival. Echeverría opposes that frontier culture which created so many theoretical problems for writers of his generation, unable, as they were, to adopt a middle ground in the Manichaean conflict between civilization and barbarism. Echeverría's white captive María is a sublime woman who escapes from the horrors of barbarism, among them the possibility of miscegenation, which in Romantic eyes implied the loss of purity. That purity was to serve as the foundation of the new nation, a nation that would be ethnically and culturally white. María embodies civilization, and she fights to the death to defend her virtue against the onslaught of the savage. This formulation represents perfectly the Romantic idealization of the *Joven Generación Argentina* (Young Argentine Generation). María fights to rescue her husband, but fundamentally she fights to save her purity. Her son is no mestizo, he is Brian's son (note the English name), and he is the symbol of the new independent Argentina. Free from the barbaric horrors of the *toldos*, this new Argentina aspires to be admitted with full privileges to the gathering of civilized nations. The poem reaches its climax when, after a nocturnal orgy in the Indian camp, María summons all her depleted strength and sinks a knife into her captor's breast.

> A body grunts and pants,
> And turns; but she
> Plucks up spirits and courage,
> And in the breast of the savage
> plunges the keen knife.[45]

María departs from the standard model of Romantic heroines and adopts an active role. More than honor is at stake; Echeverría will not compromise. The horrible descriptions of life in the *tolderías,* isolated from the socioeconomic context that explains them, formulate a political ideology and a plan of action.

> Then begins the pandemonium,
> And the tremendous ululation
> The infernal shrieking
> And the pitiful voices.

> While disconsolate weep
> The miserable *cautivas*,
> And so too their tender children
> Seeing that their mothers cry.
> All the while bonfires
> In the darkness blaze,
> And to the painted countenances
> And to the long hair
> Of those besotted Indians
> Give such a sinister cast
> So strange a color,
> A mien so terrible and ugly,
> That sprung from the abyss they seem
> A loathsome, hell-bound, breed,
> Rapt in the oafish pleasure
> Of their warlocks' feast.[46]

The infernal scenery constructed by Echeverría contrasts with images of the noble savage promoted by European Romantics. It is certainly true that the indigenous pampas presented concrete problems that had nothing to do with the scenery imagined by Romanticism on the other side of the Atlantic. Echeverría's Indian is not at one with his surroundings, but an alien being in the exotic environment of nature created by the hand of God. Postindependence Creole society had to find solutions to the problems posed by frontier tribes.

Besides *La cautiva,* whose reputation has endured even to our day, Echeverría wrote another poem on the same subject which has come down to us in incomplete form. In "Los cautivos" the hope of liberation depends on divine intervention.

> Death and captivity awaits them,
> The fiercest slavery
> Among those stupid savages
> Tears and bitterness without consolation;
> If the compassionate heavens
> Send no one to avenge their outrages.[47]

José Hernández, in *Martín Fierro,* treats the topic in an unusual manner. The first part of the poem (1872) can be read as a treatise on frontier culture from the perspective of the gaucho. The central character, Martín Fierro, is a disillusioned renegade who abandons so-called civilization and seeks the protection of the Indian *tolderías:* "I know that the chiefs over there / will give shelter to Christians."[48] Martín Fierro, the *payador* (an improvisational singer), tells or sings that he lived with his wife and children in a *pago* (small farm), tilling the earth, that he was forcibly recruited to serve on the frontier, and that when he returned, he had lost his wife, children, and humble possessions. He laments:

> In my part of the land, at one time,
> I had children, cattle, and a wife;
> but my sufferings began,
> they pushed me out to the frontier—
> and when I got back, what was I to find!
> a ruin, and nothing more.[49]

The character is based on the countless Martín Fierros who endured similar frontier experiences. In the Archivos de la Nación (National Archives) in Buenos Aires, there are numerous declarations by renegades or simply farmers whose dramas recall that described by Hernández. José Ylario Funes's 1780 petition to the viceroy seems a copy of Fierro's story, even though it was written one hundred years earlier.

I, Joseph Ylario Funes, bring to the attention of Your Excellency, with the greatest respect, that being in a farm in the Alto Redondo near La Matanza, and living there in a house with my wife Juana Josepha Andrade and three sons, having come one day, last week, to the city to sell some chickens in the plaza. When I returned home, I found it unoccupied and at the discretion of anyone who would want to steal from me what was in it. Seeking to know the whereabouts of my family, I learned that they had been taken away by Lieutenant Don Joseph Antonio Diaz to the Guardia de la Laguna del Monte. Apparently he had orders to take them to this place of bad living and where out of laziness people do not devote themselves to work. I not being of that class of people, bring it to the attention of Your Excellency. So that justice may be served, please have him restore my wife and children to me, because remaining in my place of domicile, devoted to working the land with many obligations, this is a notable hurt to me. I ask Your Excellency to have him hand over my wife and to allow me to stay in the part I have settled, quiet and in peace as before.[50]

Miguelito, whom Lucio V. Mansilla meets in the *toldos* of Mariano Rosas, is also a replica of Martín Fierro.[51]

Enrolled in the frontier army, Fierro endures the abuses of the army and experiences Indian *malones*. Abuse, corruption, the absence of any kind of organization, and lack of pay kill Fierro's faith. He deserts from the army to become a gaucho *matrero* (an outlaw gaucho). Much later, he seeks shelter in the *tolderías* as a lesser evil.

> Setting out to cross the desert
> as if you were a criminal,
> and leaving behind you here
> forsaken—as we did then—
> your wife in someone else's arms
> and your young children gone.
>
> How many times during the crossing
> of that vast plain—
> remembering your unhappy state
> so far from those you love—
> you lie down among the desert weeds
> and give way to bitter tears.[52]

The hardships of frontier forts were a daily reality, as were the number of renegades who crossed the frontier line and went over to the Indian *tolderías*. These men, who lived in a zone of continual exchange and traffic, knew the Indians well. Sometimes they met them in battle, and many other times they traded with them. The frontier, in this sense, played an ambiguous role, it was a no-man's-land and an everyman's land, a place of fusion and encounter. The rancor in Hernández's characterization of the Pampa Indians in the second part of the poem is, therefore, surprising:

> Out there, there's no mercy
> nor any kind of hope:
> the Indian's opinion is
> that it's always right to kill—
> since whatever blood he doesn't drink
> he likes to watch run out.[53]

Although Fierro and his companion Cruz go to the *toldos* as renegades, the Indians take them captive in order to hold them for ransom. Hernández's detailed description of the *tolderías* couldn't be more tendentious. But the most violent moment is in the passage about the white captive, whose precarious situation makes Fierro react.

> Later, I learned from her
> just how things had been.
> An Indian raiding-band had come
> to her part of the country—
> they had killed her husband
> and carried her off prisoner.
>
> Two years, she'd been there
> in that cruel captivity.
> She kept beside her
> a little child she'd brought with her. . . .
> The Indian woman hated her
> and used her as a slave.[54]

In this episode, the captive, whose name is not revealed, is accused by one of her Indian husband's other wives of having bewitched another woman and caused her death. The husband's fury is unleashed on the defenseless captive, whose passivity seems to feed the savage's wrath.

> The Indian took her out of sight
> and started threatening her
> saying she had got to confess
> if it had been sorcery,
> or else he was going to punish her
> by beating her to death . . .
>
> And the cruel savage
> went on lashing her—
> every time he hit her
> he grew more and more furious,
> and the wretched woman fended off
> the blows, as well as she could.
>
> And he shouted at her, raging,
> *"You no want confess!"*
> he knocked her down with a backhand blow
> and to complete her agony

> he cut the throat of her little child
> there, at her feet.[55]

After cutting the child's throat, a mestizo child he had had with the captive, the Indian ties the mother's hands with the little one's guts and prepares to finish the job. This is the last straw for Fierro. He jumps on the Indian and, after a titanic combat, kills him.

The violence of these passages reveals a virulent antagonism matched only by Juan Cruz Varela in an 1827 poem entitled "En el regreso de la expedición contra los indios bárbaros, mandada por el Coronel D. Federico Rauch" (On the Return of the Expedition against the Barbarous Indians, Commanded by Colonel Don Federico Rauch). In that poem, Indians are depicted as alienated from nature and in a state of extreme dehumanization. Colonel Rauch, a German officer, has come to Argentina to kill Indians "to exterminate the blood-thirsty race / of the fierce tigers of the desert."[56]

In Hernández's poem, Martín Fierro helps the woman and decides to return to the other side of the frontier. Before them is the desert and the unknown dangers of the flight. The poem then resumes its descriptive realism:

> It's a very serious danger
> to cross the desert on the run;
> a great many have died from hunger,
> because running that kind of risk
> you can't even make a fire
> in case you'll be found out.
>
> Only a man's good judgment
> can help him to survive;
> there's no hope of being rescued,
> only God can come to your aid. . . .
> It's a rare thing, in the desert,
> for a man to come through alive.[57]

Without exchanging one word or taking an interest in her future fate, Fierro's misogyny closes the scene of the escape. Woman appears in the poem as victim. She is the spark that makes Fierro react at key moments. He becomes an outlaw gaucho because of his wife, and for the captive's sake he kills the Indian and escapes from the *tolderías*, but neither woman is allowed to have her own voice. They are only secondary characters. When they reach the sierra, without a word Fierro abandons the captive and continues on his uncertain way.

> Right there, I said goodbye
> to my sad companion.
> I told her, "I'm off, it's no matter where,
> even though the Government gets me—
> taking hell for hell, I'd rather have
> the one at the frontier."[58]

It is important to remember that the second part of the poem was written in 1878, five years after the first, and the political situation in the country and in Hernández's life had changed substantially in that time. In the interior, the expansion into Indian territory was a reality. Confrontations with frontier tribes had intensified as cattle ranchers became a powerful group and incorporated gauchos into their estancias as a labor force. Furthermore, negotiations with the tribes of the interior had not reached the desired results. Hernández, who had been a political émigré, was now a senator of the republic. The program of incorporation into society through work, education, and religion, which Fierro recommends to his sons and Picardía in the second part of the poem, excludes Indians. With the episode of the captive, Hernández passes sentence on the future of the indigenous population and shuts the door to any possibility of dialogue.

> The tribes have been disbanded—
> the proudest of the chiefs
> are dead or taken captive
> with no hope to rise again,
> and of all the braves and their followers
> there are very few now left alive.[59]

Considering the widespread success of the poem, which went through several editions in a brief span of time, it is not surprising that its vision of the Indian was also accepted. In a letter to Hernández, his editor, José Puig y Clavera, wrote that between January and August of 1878 he has sold all eight thousand copies of the first edition. A note accompanying the fourteenth edition, in 1897, reads: "This edition of two thousand copies makes for an astonishing total of sixty-two thousand copies sold, an unprecedented figure in American countries and also extremely rare in European Latin countries."[60] León Barski, who has studied the book's impact, writes: "It isn't surprising that the orders of *pulperos* [owners of general stores in the interior] to city whole-sale dealers, included, besides yerba maté, sugar, wine, and *caña* (brandy made from sugar cane), large numbers of copies of *Martín Fierro*. It was clearly, a popular consumer item, a unique event in Argentine literature."[61]

Literary Captives

It is true that, in the eighteenth and nineteenth centuries, captivity in Chile, Argentina, and northern Mexico generated a series of concrete social, economic, and political problems that frontier societies had to face. There was no fiction there. Fiction comes from the hard models that were projected onto literature, models that varied according to the rhythm of a society confronting profound changes. In the case of Argentina, Indians did not fit into the civilizing plans of the foundational state, so shortsighted in its social analysis. After Roca's campaign in the desert in 1884, the raiding tribes disappeared into Patagonia, leaving room only for the elegy of a people who had fought to the end for its survival. This explains the appearance, at the end of the century, of poems like *Lin-Calel* (written in 1885, published in 1910) and *Pehuén Mapu*, which present a nostalgic vision of the Indian.

A great deal of the information we have about the territories of the interior, the life of the Indians, society, and geography was obtained by travelers who crossed the Americas and carried out what some critics have called "the rediscovery of America."[62] These travelers, some of whom were scientists— biologists, geographers, topographers—and military men, described the Río de la Plata interior in detail according to their own interests. Some on their own account, others commissioned by the government, carried out expeditions to Indian territory and described, in profuse detail, the habitat of the indigenous peoples. They tend to describe the Indian *tolderías* with a combination of fascination and disdain. Among the many travelers in this group, one deserves special mention: Estanislao S. Zeballos, the author of a series of works that are difficult to classify because they straddle journalism and the novel.

Zeballos was a typical representative of his generation, devoted to multiple professional activities and many intellectual interests. His works are hard to define and could easily be considered travel books, anthropological essays, or historical narratives. His first essays adhere to Santiago Arcos's thesis justifying the war of aggression as the best defense against Indian *malones*. In *La conquista de quince mil leguas: Estudio sobre la traslación de la frontera sur de la República al Río Negro* (The Fifteen Thousand League Conquest: A Study of the Moving of the Southern Frontier of the Republic to the Negro River) (1878), Zeballos advocates a policy aimed at forcing, by armed means, the southerly retreat of tribes to the Negro River. His later books are more conciliatory, and one can perceive the attempt to approach the other, the Indian misunderstood by Echeverría and his generation. *Painé y la dinastía de los zorros* (Painé and the Dynasty of the Zorros) (1886) and *Relmu, reina de los pinares* (Relmu, Queen of the Pine Groves) (1887) belong to narrative fiction but have a great anthropological charge. *Callvucurá y la dinastía de los piedra* (Callvucurá and the Dynasty of the Piedras) (1884), on the other hand, resembles the historical chronicles.

Zeballos describes the frontier as a picturesque world, full of contrasts, a complex social panorama of violence, poverty, and ethnic blending. In the frontier of Zeballos's books, Christian *capitanejos* coexist with Indian warriors, caciques with officers exiled from the regular army, gauchos and *chinas* (Indian women) with captives, in social formations in which racial distinctions are hard to detect. His attitude is conciliatory: he refers to Ranquel society as "a mysterious and unknown primitive civilization."[63] Zeballos's literary world is pretty faithful to contemporary chronicles and travel books. In *Painé y la dinastía de los zorros*, Panchita, a character for whom the narrator feels a special attraction, is introduced. "Who is she? Born in a southern village of the province of Córdoba, she grew in the bosom of a Creole family who owned a fortune. Her father was the owner of an estancia and was once an authority in his district."[64] Abducted in a *malón*, Panchita lives as a captive and as Cacique Painé's favorite, although she never erases from her mind the passion she felt for a lieutenant in Córdoba. In *Relmu, reina de los pinares*, the plot begins with the escape of the narrator, Liberato Pérez, who had crossed the frontier to evade the pursuit of the troops of the governor of Buenos Aires, Juan Manuel de Rosas. Cacique Painé protects him, and when the cacique dies, Liberato Pérez escapes in the company of Panchita, thereby gratifying the frustrated desire of the previous novel. The intricacy of the love stories makes one think that Zeballos's characters are based on people he met in the *toldos*. Zeballos liked to boast that he had personally met Calfucurá and had read his extensive correspondence.

Ángel della Valle, *La vuelta del malón* (Returning from the Raid), 1892.

We have already remarked that flight is one of the common themes of captivity narratives. Its dramatic potential is obvious, and a fictional captivity narrative without an escape is very rare. The dangers of flight, with the vast desert threatening the almost impossible escape, create the necessary tension through a series of unforeseen events and emotions. There are escapes or attempted escapes in *La cautiva, Martín Fierro, Lin-Calel,* and *Pehuén-Mapu,* and in Zeballos's and Mansilla's stories. Beset by many dangers and overwhelmed by dreams and nervous excitation, the fugitive captive in *Relmu* still has time to feel guilty and bemoan the fact that by escaping he betrays the Indian who showed him so much affection during his captivity.

In 1873 the Academia Argentina de Ciencias y Letras was founded to bring together representatives of the sciences and humanities. The generation of 1880 was well represented in the Academia. Among its members were the poets Rafael Obligado and Martín Coronado, and Eduardo Ladislao Holmberg, a naturalist and a great reader of Dickens, whom he translated. One of his works, *Dos partidos en lucha* (Two Parties at War), goes into Darwin's theories, which were much in vogue among positivists. Holmberg was also the author of a poem that, though long and tedious, is of great interest to our study,

Lin-Calel. If *La cautiva* and *Facundo* had foregrounded nature and its inhabitants but warned of their unlimited risks, Holmberg's verse invokes them in grandiose tones. In his empire of nature, the Indian rules.

Holmberg began to write *Lin-Calel* in 1885. In 1886 the Uruguayan José Zorrilla de San Martín published *Tabaré*, whose aim, to exalt the history of an extinct race, coincides with Holmberg's. It is important to stress the unequivocal Christian message in both works. The protagonists of both poems, Lin-Calel and Tabaré, are second-generation captives. They are characters who, in the civilizing discourse, represent the ethnic and cultural blend that the new times were beginning to accept. *Lin-Calel* was published, as "an homage to his country," on May 25, 1910, the centenary of Argentine independence. The Pan-American Conference, which had centered largely on the problem of the Indian, had just taken place. Some of the scholars who participated were Cañas Pinochet, Holmberg, and José Toribio Medina.

In Holmberg's poem, Lin-Calel is the beautiful daughter of Cacique Tromen-Cura and a Christian captive who has passed on her religious beliefs and taught Spanish to her daughter. Lin-Calel's father has promised her in marriage to Auca-Lonco, the principal cacique of the sierra, who has sent the young warrior Reukenám to escort back his future wife. On the journey back, love develops between the mestiza and the Indian, who feel the anguish of their future separation the closer they get to Auca-Lonco's *tolderías*, where she must be handed over. In despair, the lovers decide to flee to a mountain, at which point Lin-Calel drops to her knees and implores God's help. Horrified to learn that his beloved is the daughter of the hated *huincas* (Christians), Reukenám throws himself into a gorge. Reukenám's death is propitiatory in the poem because the sacrifice liberates the soul of the warrior so that he can be admitted to the heaven of the new nation, Argentina.

> "*Huinca!* You are a *huinca!* Lin-Calel, my life
> you, all my heart, all that is in me!
> You, a *huinca,* Lin-Calel! Curse you!
> Keep in your bosom the soul of my race,
> and in that abyss where I will hurl my body
> look for my heart which no longer loves you!"
> And he sprung, with a terrible jump
> Reukenám flung himself into the gorge
> cursing his love, but leaving behind

a seed of courage and vigor,
the evolving archetype which in its softness
will become the masses. . . .
Hail, oh seed, of the uncertain future!
Hail, wonder of the love of country!
That is the star that will guide your steps!
You will give your blood to the blue and white,
because that love gave you life,
because that light will mold your race![65]

The Charrúa Indians of *Tabaré* had disappeared from the Río de la Plata map much earlier than the Pehuenches of *Lin-Calel*. In his poem, Zorrilla takes on a semi-archaeological task. In this respect, the opening verses of the poem, which suggest an exhumation, are significant: "Here I will lift the cover from a tomb."[66] Later, the elegiacal purpose of the poem is declared:

And among moans, and laughs, and savage cries,
The ghost arose of an extinguished race:

Shade of that nomad and barbarian tribe,
Which long ago dwelt in my native land,
Like echoes of a prayer that no one heard,
That on its way to heaven the winds bore off.[67]

The main character of *Tabaré* is also the mestizo offspring of a captive and a Charrúa chief. Blue-eyed and aloof, Tabaré lives in silence, pining for the love of Blanca, the daughter of a Spanish officer and the image of her mother. Zorrilla's Tabaré is a man misunderstood. He does not fit into the fashionable taxonomies of this period when social Darwinism vied with positivism and other scientific and pseudoscientific theories, like phrenology. Note Zorrilla's characterization:

Strange being this! What race's lineaments
Have left their impress on that slender form?
His skull has room enough for thoughts to lodge,
And his broad brow has space for genius.

That line Charrúa is; that other . . . human.
The look, that in his eyes shows, tender is . . .
Is there not, in the depth of those blue orbs,
Another being hid, with eyes of black?

> The soft pelt of a tiger of the woods
> Covers the body of the graceful youth;
> No paint his face disfigures, and his lips
> Are not pierced by the warrior's ornaments.
>
> Pallid he is, and sad; and in his look,
> And in the ghastly aspect of his face,
> Something mysterious is, that moves the heart
> To love, disquiet, sorrow and sympathy.[68]

That character, who is uncomfortable among the pale Spaniards and marginalized by the Charrúa "savages," attracts the attention of the white Blanca, who, paradoxically, turns out to be an olive-skinned Andalusian with curly jet hair. The plot, after their encounter, is simple. Blanca is taken captive by the raiding Indians of Cacique Yarandú. Tabaré goes to Blanca's rescue and carries her back to the Spanish camp. During the return trip, love blossoms. When they approach the camp, Gonzalo, Blanca's brother, taking Tabaré for her captor, kills him with his sword.

Tabaré is a totally fictional character who belongs to neither history nor legend. He has been created for the purpose of forging a type who will reconcile, in the love of country, the dual cult of the aboriginal peoples and the Hispano-Christian tradition. According to Alberto Zum Felde, this character did not exist in Uruguay's historical tradition, Zorrilla invented him. The closest thing to a mestizo is not Tabaré "but the coarse gauchos who have fought in our wars and done chores in our estancias, when they haven't been outlaws or soldiers."[69]

Zorrilla, like Holmberg, assumes the anachronistic task of giving voice to the silenced throats of the vanished Indians. Both resort to a mawkish nostalgia that lacks any serious political content. This does not mean that the poems in question are not carefully researched. They demonstrate a considerable knowledge of both Charrúa and Pehuenche culture. The disappearance of these peoples is presented as unavoidable, a consequence of racial evolution and the expansion of Christian civilization. This is how Zorrilla sees it. In an elegiac tone and Romantic vein, he intones a requiem for the extinct race, showing, nevertheless, the inevitability of their disappearance:

> Come with me to your home. The Indian then
> Will go back to the forest's fastnesses;
> His race is dead; their home fires long ago
> Have sunk to ashes on their forest hearths.[70]

Although *Lin-Calel*'s tone is epic, one can detect the influence of the dominant scientific or pseudoscientific discourse of the era. The realism of some descriptions is combined with the dithyramb, and there are notable similarities with *La Araucana*. The poem could even be considered subversive, were it not for the fact that by the time Holmberg published it, there were no Indians left to hear the message. In the context of Indianist literature, *Lin-Calel* appears as a posthumous poem, and as a precursor. It closes the chapter on a literature that justified military actions that pushed frontier tribes to an unrecognizable south, and it initiates a new Indianist literature marked by a badly assimilated sense of guilt. The security with which Creole society had established its supremacy at the end of the nineteenth century facilitated making peace with the Indian past.

An Attractive Subject for the Romantics

The subject of the female captive was not cultivated in the nineteenth century with the frequency one would have expected, since it contained all the ingredients attractive to a Romantic sensibility: contrasts, strong emotions, exoticism, and human drama. Several authors, however, embraced the subject and gave it life. Echeverría, Ascasubi, Hernández, Blanco, Guerra, Eduarda Mansilla, Holmberg, Mera, Sanfuentes, Zorrilla de San Martín, and almost all those who wrote about the topic in the nineteenth century were Romantics. One could say that there were captives of the Indians and captives of literature, since fiction created stereotypes and fixed them in the popular imagination. It is not surprising that the legend of Lucía Miranda was recovered and reworked by several writers who discovered its great Romantic potential.

The theme of the female captive was enlisted in other literatures of the continent to different purposes. The approach taken by the Ecuadorian Juan León Mera in his 1879 novel *Cumandá* is of great interest. As a conservative, Catholic writer, Mera struck a difficult balance between life in the wilds of eastern Ecuador and Catholic dogma. The novel's focus on the eastern jungle has a double intention: to stake out a claim on this new state, which was in dispute between Ecuador and neighboring Peru, and to establish Ecuadorian nationalism on a Catholic foundation.[71]

The novel's protagonist is Cumandá, a beautiful Indian girl who falls in love with Carlos, son of Father Domingo Orozco, a character based on the historical Fray Bartolomé de las Casas. Orozco had been a landowner and *encomendero* until the Indians rebelled against his abuses and burned the hacienda and murdered most of his family. Orozco understood this act as retribution for his evil deeds and resolved to atone for his guilt. He abandoned the sierra, accepted the Dominican habit, and founded a mission in the remotest part of the jungle. His small daughter, Julia, had been saved by a nurse and sold as a captive to a family of Tongana Indians, by whom she was raised and given the name Cumandá. Cumandá is a strong and ambiguous character. She adapts to the jungle and acquires the strength of a man and a rugged character, but she retains the sweetness, innocence, and intelligence proper to a girl, "white as ivory" and with a soul that clearly differs from that of the members of her Tongana family: "A combination of sweetness and arrogance, timidity and fire, love and disdain; [. . .] she was all simplicity and vivacity, innocence and vehemence, the sweetness of passionate love and the bitterness of pride; she was all soul and all heart; a noble soul, but uncultured; a heart that was Christian in origin, in the breast of a savage."[72] What explains Cumandá's character and her spiritual superiority is not the mere fact that she is a white captive, but that before her captivity she had been baptized. Faith has injected that different touch that makes her superior to all around her. Among the Indians of Father Orozco's mission who have accepted baptism, one can also observe the vivifying impact of religion:

> Christian regeneration had sweetened the customs of the Indians without diminishing their character. It had inclined their heart to good, and was gradually awakening their intelligence and preparing them for a more active life, for a vaster stage, for contact, mixing and fusion with the outer world, where passions boil, and errors and vices appear that are unknown to savages, but where also the beneficent power of civilization bubbles and spills over everything.[73]

With realist precision, Mera describes the geography of eastern Ecuador, but simplifies to a grotesque degree the characteristics of the various indigenous groups of the region: the Jíbaros, Záparos, Zamoras, Logroños, Moronas, and Tonganas. Some are violent and bloodthirsty, others meek and hospitable, and these characteristics are determined by how close they live to a missionary center. The author laments the ills unleashed by the unfortunate expulsion of the Jesuits in 1787: "More than a century ago, the tireless constancy of missionaries had begun to bring some gusts of shining civilization to these barbarous peoples."[74] The Ecuadorian civilization the writer proposes is Christianity integrated into a culturally homogenous combination.

The plot, which owes much to Chateaubriand's *René*, thickens when the two lovers, Cumandá and Carlos, discover, in the final anagnorisis, that they are brother and sister. However, the passage that is of interest to us is that of Cumandá's betrothal to the elderly Yahuarmuqui, chief of the Palora Indians, "fierce savages, and barbarous infidels." Cumandá, who is a virgin, has accepted the marriage arranged by her adoptive parents, but resists its consummation because of her love for Carlos. Cumandá takes advantage of the darkness of night and Cacique Yahuarmuqui's drunkenness to escape through the jungle, which, reflecting her state of mind, closes over the lovers' dark destiny. She flees to save her virginity, to reclaim her love for Carlos, and to avoid the consummation of her marriage with the infidel Palora chief. Cumandá's death puts an end to this Romantic tragedy, sublimating the impossible love between Carlos and Cumandá in the indispensable sacrifice of the protagonist, who dies before mixing her blood with the Indian's.

The outcome seems to repeat the tragedy of María in *La cautiva* or of Lin-Calel. In none of these stories do the captive heroines, or daughters of female captives, mix their blood with an Indian. It is as if the authors were trying to reverse the process of miscegenation that was already a reality in the nineteenth century. If the new scientific theories insisted on a hierarchy of races, what could be done about a continent created on the basis of ethnic and cultural *mestizaje*? The subject of the captive explored this inherent concern, and it did so from the very heart of the matter.

Captivity and Identity

In the back room of captivity fiction lies the subject of identity. Various authors have studied Bascuñán's *Cautiverio feliz* as a text of an emerging Creole consciousness. Captives were assimilated through an inevitable process of acculturation. The mechanisms of transculturation inherent in the phenomenon, studied in previous chapters, were excluded from the discourse of literary history. What it retained was the opposite phenomenon, that of the female captive's resistance to assimilation through marriage and maternity, which would entail the loss not only of her purity but also of her identity. The topic's fascination lay precisely with the West's inability to accept the fact that captives might choose life among their captors. This was especially hard to accept because the ideological framework of the Spanish monarchy dictated that the Indian was in a natural and spiritual state of complete inferiority. As was argued in the sixteenth-century debates at the University of Salamanca, his state ought to be that of natural slavery.

The first two cases of captivity on the continent about which we have information clearly exemplify this dilemma. They are the captivities of Jerónimo de Aguilar and Gonzalo Guerrero, found by Hernán Cortés on the Yucatán coast in 1518. Jerónimo de Aguilar represents the ethnocentric stance. He rejoiced to be reunited with his companions and marched off with them on the expedition to Mexico. Guerrero, on the other hand, refused to return, alleging that he had a family with the Indians and was happy to remain with them. Guerrero and the others who chose to stay, and there were many, are the paradigm that subverts the civilizing discourse's claims to superiority. Those who remained never told their version of the story. However, recent works of fiction have tried to fill this gap, by reconstructing scenarios using the few existing bits of information and a great deal of imagination. *Gonzalo Guerrero* (1980), by Eugenio Aguirre, and *Gonzalo Guerrero: Memoria olvidada: Trauma de México* (1995) (Gonzalo Guerrero: Forgotten Memory: Mexico's Trauma), by Carlos Villa Roiz, are two recent Mexican novels that attempt to recapture the greatness of the Spanish soldier turned Maya warrior.

By deciding to stay, Guerrero earned a place in the pantheon of Mexican heroes, together with Cuauhtemoc and other Aztec warriors. Villa Roiz's novel ends with an elegy by Guerrero's son in which he accepts without reluctance his early *mestizaje*. "I seek myself inside his story, I find memories; to learn more about myself, I need to see myself reflected in others and the best mirror to understand my *mestizo* blood, the first one in this part of the world, is the life of my father: Gonzalo Guerrero."[75] Gonzalo Guerrero's great contribution, according to Eugenio Aguirre, was not leading Maya troops against the Spanish conquistadores but being the father of the first mestizo.

Let song rise in your honor, let the trail of the jungle be blazed, let the gods be perfumed with incense. They who guided your steps and who opened their sanctuaries to receive your offering, the gifts of an old world which spilled blood and ashes to sketch the profile of these lands, of these men who now belatedly honor you and engrave your name Gonzalo Guerrero or Gonzalo de Aroca or Gonzalo Marinero, with deep pride in the parchment of their conscience.[76]

Ethnicity and nationalism are the common denominator of a great many of the works we have studied from the end of the nineteenth and beginning of the twentieth centuries. *Tabaré* is a patriotic poem which, despite its guilty conscience, justifies Spanish conquest and, more importantly, the establishment of Christian culture. Zorilla de San Martín's poem appeared in the midst of raging polemics between Catholics, rationalists, and fervent followers of the new positivist creed. The author played a fundamental role in that polemic by creating national symbols.[77] The poem, written while he was exiled in Argentina, was soon accepted and elevated to the category of the national poem of Uruguay. In *Lin-Calel*, Reukenám, incapable of embracing the religion of his lover, commits suicide. The poet makes certain to write his epitaph, which seems to metaphorically join the Indian's blood to the "blue and white" of the national flag, while crediting him with being a "seed of the uncertain future" and a "wonder of the love of country."[78]

Reevaluation of the Topic in the Twentieth Century

Leopoldo Lugones, a *modernista* poet but a practitioner of conservative regionalist outlook, delved into frontier topics, chiefly in a volume of ballads published shortly after his death in 1938. The book is entitled *Romances del Río Seco*. The collection contains a poem about captives, "El rescate" (The Rescue), which is without precedent. The captive taken in Villa María, a frontier town founded by Viceroy Sobremonte, is the statue of the Virgin Mary venerated in the town. A *malón* made up of Guyacurú and Mocoví Indians razes the city, burning barns and sacking houses. Unable to take any female captives, the Indians enter the church and abduct the statue of the Virgin.

> Greedily they grabbed
> Whatever they could carry,

And even the Virgin
They took from the altar.

Sated from pillage,
They began to hurry,
They wrapped her with her jewels
In the altar cloth.

Amid booty and junk,
An Indian threw her in his sack,
And the satisfied horde
Headed for their camp.[79]

This act by the Indians provokes a collective cry for reprisal. The captivity of their Virgin moves the townspeople much more than the fate of any other captive. Who will protect the town from droughts and other disasters, now that their patron saint has been stolen? A massive posse is rapidly organized to follow the *malón* on the way to the *toldos*. They catch up to the Indians by nightfall and are amazed to observe a sudden sad look on the face of the statue of the Virgin.

Standing there in the mud
For some unexplained reason
She seems to be sad
And seems to have become smaller.[80]

The fury of the townspeople falls on the Indians and culminates with the collective cutting of their throats, blessed by the presence of the holy image.

I'm not saying
It was a miracle,
I just tell you
What I saw.

It's certainly true that for a long time
People talked about that story,
And the massacre certainly
Brought the *caris* much glory.[81]

From the same period are two stories by Jorge Luis Borges, "Historia del guerrero y la cautiva" ("Story of the Warrior and the Captive Maiden") and

"El cautivo" ("The Captive"). In the first of these stories, Borges resorts to one of his typical literary strategies and situates the female captive in the context of universal history. To do so, he establishes a comparison between three characters: a white English woman captive, his grandmother, and the barbarian warrior Droctulft, who abandoned his own people to fight for Ravenna. The blue-eyed captive told Borges's grandmother, who was also English, that she had been taken in a *malón* and was the wife of a *capitanejo*, to whom she had borne two children. She said that her life was spent among "the horsehide tents, the campfires fueled by dung, the feasts of meat singed over the fire or of raw viscera, the stealthy marches at daybreak; the assault of living in the dirt, the shouting and the sacking, the making of war, the thundering roundup of stock by naked horsemen, the polygamy, the stench, and the sorcery."[82] Moved, his grandmother offered to mediate on her behalf. "The other woman answered that she was happy, and she returned that night to the desert."[83] The grandmother was then able to understand her own fate. In some way, she too was the captive of "an implacable continent." The next time his grandmother saw the former captive, she was drinking the warm blood of a slaughtered sheep. Was she doing it to reaffirm her Indian identity or because it was an acquired custom? The dividing line between being and wanting to be, Borges says, is personal, mysterious, and comes from an individual's intimate depth and not from established categories. Droctulft rejects Aryanism to defend Rome and dies in the effort. The English captive renounces all the material advantages of civilization to die in the savagery of the *toldos*. The two stories could be antagonistic, but Borges, to the contrary, shows us the similarity of the intimate energy that guided them.

Two recent novels return to the subject of captives with the desire, shared by many writers today, to reread, rewrite, and demythify parts of the continent's history, and to question hegemonic interpretations. Never before has the history of the continent claimed the attention of Spanish American writers with the intensity seen in the last twenty years. The list of titles and authors is immense, and it would be superfluous to mention them all here.[84] What is of interest to us is that the subject of captives has been recovered and reworked by two Argentine authors, Juan José Saer and César Aira.

Saer's *El entenado* (The Witness) tells the story of a Spanish adolescent orphan traveling as a cabin boy with Juan Díaz de Solís's Río de la Plata expedition in 1515. Just as the Spaniards reach the American coast and are disembarking, the expedition is attacked by Indians. They take the young cabin boy captive, in an almost surreal episode, and take him swiftly to an Indian village, where he will live through a ten-year adventure. *El entenado* repeats many of the traditional stereotypes about Indians: they practice cannibalism, sodomy, and other sins of the flesh; they sink into orgies of alcohol and hallucinogenic drugs, then fall exhausted into deep depressions, followed by a return to normal life, defined by monotony and the purest chastity and abstinence. Many of the descriptions given by the protagonist when he returns to Spain at a mature age seem taken from classic texts. Descriptions of the physical appearance of Indians recall Columbus's *Diary,* while the orgies and cannibalistic practices betray the influence of one of the continent's first captives, Hans Staden, who wrote about his captivity among the Tupi of Brazil in 1554.[85] Despite these similarities, the novel does not dwell on ethnographic references. The action, therefore, could be occurring in any tropical part of the continent, and the captors are American Indians installed in a time out of time. Amaryll Chanady comments:

> Instead of a historiographic fiction (or historiographic metafiction, to use Linda Hutcheon's term), the novel appears to be a postmodern "historiophagous" fiction in which texts are systematically decontextualized, reassembled in a heterogeneous collage, and reworked in a homogeneous style, in order to constitute a Borgesian distillation of the global text.[86]

The description of the captivity and of the processes of assimilation and marginalization take up two-thirds of the novel. But the originality of *El entenado* lies in Saer's treatment of the former captive's reintegration into Spanish society after his rescue. First he seeks peace in a convent, later he goes off with a troupe of actors trying to re-create his experiences. Writing in the last years of his life, he attempts to exorcise present ills and reconcile them with the past he cannot let go of.

> I can honestly say that, in its own way, my whole body remembers those years of intense, carnal life which seem to have penetrated it so deeply that it has grown insensible to any other experience. Just as the Indians from some of the neighboring tribes used to trace an invisible circle in the air to protect themselves from the unknown, my body, wrapped in the skin of those years, now lets nothing in from the outside. Only what resembles it is acceptable.[87]

The former cabin boy is a man captured by the contradictions of a dichotomy he experienced in his own flesh. Unable to understand and accept the otherness of the first experience, he is also unable to effect a complete reincorporation into his own culture. Perhaps that is the final purpose of Saer's text, to depict the range of incommunication and let us understand that it was a constant during the long years of contact, conquest, frontier, and captives.

Aira's text, *Ema, la cautiva,* is not as interesting. It is a postmodern fantasy that does not do justice to history. From an initial realistic description of the crossing of the arid pampas where Ema is abducted by a *malón,* the novel devolves into spheres of pointless fantasy where the *toldos* resemble the luxurious and sensual oases of the most fervid orientalist imagination. In the same postmodern vein, we would have to include the work of another Argentine writer, Abel Posse, who in a recent novel, *El largo atardecer del caminante* (The Traveler's Long Dusk) (1992), re-creates Cabeza de Vaca's *Naufragios.* In an attempt to fill in the gaps in Cabeza de Vaca's text, Posse allows himself a great deal of poetic license, describing an imaginary love affair of the shipwrecked Cabeza de Vaca in the Isla del Mal Hado, and the existence of children who will keep the memory of their shining father.

Conclusion

The extraordinary role played by the subject of the female captive in fiction is unquestionable. Captives were the product of the internal confrontations of frontier societies concerned with resolving fundamental conflicts of coexistence and growth. History and fiction went hand in hand as ideological tools that justified political and military programs—among them, territorial expansion. The subject of male and female captives attracted nineteenth-century writers, especially because of its potential for fiction, but also because it allowed them to give voice to a problem of great concern. It was not by chance that fiction chose to employ the body of the female captive ideologically, and to endow it with a strong symbolic charge. Seventeenth-century authors had already done it. The captive woman represented the raped body of Christian civilization. Her immaculate purity was used to construct a discourse that denied or attempted to deny the possibility of transculturation. If anything is clear about the phenomenon of captivity, it is that through captives a slow process of transculturation began which would have profound repercussions for frontier societies. The theme of the female captive appears in fiction as an accident, as an infection that invades the body social and leads to gangrene. Even those authors disposed to question the actions of Spaniards (Ercilla, Arias de Saavedra) cannot justify captivity, and least of all the captivity of a white woman.

Romanticism revived interest in the subject, shaping it according to the tendencies of liberal discourse, which was generally programmatic and foundational. Indians, gauchos, and caudillos, real characters of nineteenth-century society, were the protagonists of many works of fiction and essays of a sociological bent. Alongside the official discourse, a popular frontier literature emerged that dealt with similar topics, but did so through popular poems. It is in the Río de la Plata, where, for certain sociopolitical reasons, the topics of the frontier, among them captivity, were treated most frequently. We have only to trace the development of the *poesía gauchesca* (poetry about gauchos) in Argentine letters to get an idea of the dimension of the phenomenon. Indians, gauchos, female captives, and other frontier characters look out from their pages, instilling them with life. However, even these popular manifestations, the poems and the environment they re-create, are impregnated with a strong ideological content. The subject of captivity was so linked to the problem of the Indian that its trajectory evolved according to the national debate about this problem.

What was being debated were fundamental aspects affecting the existence and survival of the nation, and that therefore touched deeply on the subject of national identity. In the Manichaean worldview of the authors of the independence period (Sarmiento, Echeverría, Mármol, and Mitre), there is no doubt that the subject of the Indian was framed as a basic problem of survival for both cultures.

Forced to face the phenomenon of captivity, Río de Plata society had to consider the problem of the other, and his right to coexist. We must bear in mind that the Indian has been the ignored subject of Argentine history, where even the myth of his origin was denied, as Susana Rotker correctly states.[88] The so-called Indian question was an ample debate in which different sectors of society participated. The works we have studied, from the legend of Lucía Miranda to *Martín Fierro*, help us to understand the evolution of the debate. The stance of late nineteenth-century authors became more conciliatory as the tribes were pushed farther south, to the edge of total eradication. The victorious expansion of Creole society allowed a reevaluation of the Indian from a nostalgic perspective. He was no longer a threat to Creole expansionism, but a memory, and therefore belonged to literature.

Another current of the genre owes its existence to the thematic potential of captivity. Captivity offered sufficient exotic elements—Romantic passion, simple characters, dramatic contrasts, and action—to guarantee its popularity among a growing and avid reading public. The series of sentimental novels written about the legend of Lucía Miranda are true daughters of coarse, conservative Romanticism. *Salvaje* (Savage) (1891), by Blanco, seems to gather all of Spanish American Romanticism's sullied stereotypes concerning Indians. In *Salvaje* Arturo, the son of a Spanish mother and a Mapuche father, witnesses the extermination of his father's tribe, embraces Christian civilization, and is transformed into a prominent Buenos Aires lawyer.[89] *Cumandá* uses a drama among savages only to underscore the indisputable advantages of Christian civilization as a mechanism of cultural integration.

Borges introduces ambiguity as a theme and universality as a measure. Borges's proposal presents both sides of the coin. Who is a captive of whom? The stories of Droctulft and the English woman captive can be the same story. Postmodernity attempts to deconstruct the patriarchal rigidity of discourses. In the recuperation effected by literature in the last decades, the theme of captivity appears as one of many historical subjects in which the new historical narrative has shown an interest.

⊰ EPILOGUE ⊱

Since the first stages of my research for this project, captivity stories have continued to appear here and there, one by one, unexpectedly, as if they wanted to be part of history. It had to be. Captives are the victims of hostile frontier relations, and the field that produces this rare breed is still a fertile cultural and geographical reality. In Amazonia, a multitude of largely deserted frontiers are negotiated every day, between nature with its multiple needs, the original tribes, and the West, represented by ranchers, *seringueiros* (rubber tappers), and seekers after gold and fortune.

The captivity of Manuel Córdova-Ríos bears witness to the existence of this problematically negotiated, ultimate frontier. Córdova-Ríos was born in Peru in 1887 and was fifteen when he was captured by Amahuaca or Huni Kui Indians in the vast frontier zone between Peru and Brazil, at the head of the Jurúa River. His captivity, was, if not a happy one, an ordinary one, insofar as Córdova-Ríos underwent all the phases of adaptation to the new society without trauma. He endured all the rites of passage of the Amahuacas and acquired much knowledge about his adoptive society, especially the identification and preparation of medicinal and hallucinogenic plants. He was elected to succeed Chief Nixi Xuma Waki upon his death. Bad omens and a way of life that was under constant threat led him to return at an advanced age. Córdova-Ríos's narrative was published in 1971 by F. Bruce Lamb, a North American forestry specialist, with the title *Wizard of the Upper Amazon: The Story of Manuel Córdova-Ríos*. The first edition rapidly sold out. At the prodding of Andrew Weil, who knew Lamb, a second and a third edition were published. For reasons that had nothing to do with the history of captivity, Weil was interested in this narrative. He wrote in the introduction to the third edition: "For many readers the most compelling sections of the book will be the descriptions of the use of *Banisteriopsis caapi*, the *yagé* or *ayahusca* of the Amazon forests. This powerful hallucinogen has long been credited with the ability to transport humans beings to realms of experience where telepathy and clairvoyance are commonplace."[1]

Weil's comments seem to be in line with some new readings of captivity literature. The popularity of Carlos Castaneda's books and of movies like *The Emerald Forest* (1985), directed by John Boorman, point to the existence of a new sensibility, inclined to see on the other side of the frontier exotic experiences that exert a strong attraction on our insatiable appetite for novelty. There is an interest in the ability of healers and shamans to make us experience unexplored mental and spiritual capacities through magic or the use of drugs and herbs. Ettore Biocca's interest in the story of Helena Valero is along these lines. His text *Yanomama: The Narrative of a White Girl Kidnapped by Amazonian Indians* dwells on the descriptions of rites associated with the use of hallucinogenic drugs or shamanic practices.

The subject of captivity has always entailed the added feature of the exotic. From the total otherness of the first sixteenth-century encounters, there was an evolution toward a reformulation of the concept of the Native American. Certain human aspects aside, the subject of captivity attracted attention because of its association with issues that the dogmatic Christian mentality considered delicate or difficult to define. One of the attractions for readers of Hans Staden's *The True History of His Captivity*, published for the first time in 1557, was the morbid detail with which Staden relates the many cases of cannibalism he claims to have witnessed. This aspect was stressed time and again by the editors of the book's numerous editions.[2] The myth of cannibalism associated with American Indians has never ceased to reappear in captivity narratives. Other myths related to the dark aspects on which the West projected its colonizing imagination. Otherwise, of what use were the beliefs in the chronic sodomy of savages; their insatiable sexual appetite, especially for white women; polygamy; their natural cruelty; their consumption of unclean foods; their physical superiority due to a culture adapted to the harshness of the natural environment, and their chronic state of savagery?

Despite the advances of cultural anthropology and relativist discourse, despite our better understanding of man and his mysteries, the unknown regions of the continent's wilderness areas seem to draw us with a sensual force that goes beyond the limits of rational knowledge. In this unavowed space, the stories of captives reappear. *The Emerald Forest* begins with a text informing us that the film is based on the real story of the abduction of a seventeen-year-old boy by Amazonian Indians. As always in fiction, the story departs from ethnographic data when it introduces dramatic elements. The final product is a patchwork in which many elements common to captivity literature are interwoven. I don't know whether the film was successful in Latin America. As we have seen in this book, for various reasons, captive narratives were never a popular genre in the culture of Spanish America. I have suggested several reasons that might explain this phenomenon. One of the most important is the impact of censorship on the culture in general, its concern with selecting books that would edify readers. When fiction about captives makes its appearance in nineteenth-century Río de la Plata, it serves a political cause, the displacement and consequent extermination of Indians. Never before had the subject of captives, which was the account of the Indians' struggle for survival, been of such great interest. Let's not forget that the stories of Manuel Córdova-Ríos and the different versions of Helena Valero's life among the Yanomamö were brought to light by North American and European scholars.

The great challenge of this book has been to find the sources, data, narratives, stories, the ignored voices, from the other side of the frontier. On occasion, there were promising bits of information, which when followed proved no more than vanishing traces. For example, we know that the Guahibos of the Llanos de Nueva Granada, today Llanos de Casanare in Colombia, had the practice of taking captives and that it became the modus vivendi of this nomadic tribe.[3] At times the Guahibos and the Caribs cooperated with the Spanish territorial administration in the exchange of captives from neighboring tribes.[4] In his *Historia de la conquista de Itzá* (1701), Juan de Villagutierre mentions numerous attacks by Itzá and Lanzador Indians who carried off captive women. Nevertheless, despite many references found in chronicles and the documents of colonial officials, the narratives are conspicuous by their absence. Were they never written? Have they not been found? Perhaps this is one of the tasks remaining for future research.

Notes

1. Álvar Núñez Cabeza de Vaca and Florida Captives in the Sixteenth Century

1. La Florida was said to encompass all the lands extending to the west of the actual peninsula as far as the Río Panuco, as well as those extending to the north without limit.

2. Weber, *The Spanish Frontier in North America*, 46.

3. Ferrando, introduction to *Naufragios y comentarios*, 27–28.

4. Fernández de Oviedo, *Historia general y natural de las Indias*, vol. 4.

5. My interpretation of the term "frontier" is that it represents both place and process, inextricably joined. Frontiers existed in a constant process of negotiation even before the arrival of the Spaniards. But their arrival forced numerous adjustments, owing, principally, to the impact that domesticated animals had on the tribes of the continent.

6. El Inca Garcilaso de la Vega was born in Cuzco, in 1539, of a Spanish father and an Inca mother. He was the author of important chronicles written from a mestizo perspective, among which of particular note are the following: *Comentarios reales* (1609), a fundamental document for understanding the Incas; *Historia general del Perú* (1617), which recounts the first years of the Spanish presence in the Andes; and *La Florida del Inca* (1606), devoted to the failed expedition of Hernando de Soto.

7. Vega, *La Florida del Inca*, 120.

8. Hudson, *Knights of Spain, Warriors of the Sun*, 33.

9. Escalante Fontaneda, *Memoir of D. d'Escalante Fontaneda respecting Florida*, 25–35.

10. For the compostion of his chronicle *La Florida del Inca,* El Inca Garcilaso made use of diverse sources: the oral testimony of Gonzalo Silvestre and Diego Tapia, who were his chief informants; a memoir in manuscript form entitled "Peregrinaciones," the work of the soldier Alonso Carmona; and the unedited account of one Juan Coles, which El Inca Garcilaso found in Córdoba. All of these informants were survivors of Hernando de Soto's expedition (see Durand, "La redacción de *La Florida del Inca*"). A brief mention of Juan Ortiz appears in Fernández de Oviedo, *Historia general y natural de las Indias*, 2:155.

11. Vega, *La Florida del Inca*, 115.

12. Ibid., 116.

13. Ibid., 117.

14. Ibid.

15. Ibid., 117–18.

16. Ibid., 118.

17. Ibid., 123.

18. Ibid., 450.

19. Ibid., 159.

20. Ibid., 288.

21. June Namias writes that captivity was a tactic of war usually employed by the tribes of northeast and southeast North America (Namias, *White Captives,* 3).

22. Vega, *La Florida del Inca,* 332.

23. Ibid., 333.

24. Ibid., 460.

25. Axtell, *The European and the Indian,* 175.

26. Vega, *La Florida del Inca,* 332.

27. Solís de Meras, *Pedro Menéndez de Avilés y la conquista de la Florida,* 113.

28. True, introduction to *Memoir of D. d'Escalante Fontaneda respecting Florida,* 21.

29. Letter of Menéndez de Avilés, October 20, 1566, cited in Lyon, *The Enterprise of Florida,* 148.

30. True, introduction to *Memoir of D. d'Escalante Fontaneda respecting Florida,* 12.

31. In the edition that I have used there is a version in Spanish and an English translation, by Buckingham Smith, which notably facilitates the comprehension of the text.

32. True, introduction to *Memoir of D. d'Escalante Fontaneda respecting Florida,* 19.

33. Escalante Fontaneda, *Memoir of D. d'Escalante Fontaneda respecting Florida,* 35.

34. Ibid.

35. Ibid.

36. Solís de Meras, *Pedro Menéndez de Avilés y la conquista de la Florida,* 124.

37. Namias, *White Captives,* 3.

38. Ibid.

39. See Oré, *The Martyrs of Florida,* 89–90.

40. Ibid., 92.

41. Ibid.

42. Vega, *La Florida del Inca,* 123.

43. Ibid., 124.

44. Axtell, *The European and the Indian,* 175.

45. Vega, *La Florida del Inca,* 252.

46. Ibid., 128.

47. Ibid., 129.

48. Axtell, *The European and the Indian,* 170.

49. Vega, *La Florida del Inca,* 347.

50. Ibid.

51. Ibid., 451.

52. Ibid., 453.

53. Cabeza de Vaca, *Naufragios y comentarios,* 49.

54. Ibid.

55. Vega, *La Florida del Inca*, 455.

56. Pánfilo de Narváez is a tragic figure in this era of the great expeditions. His early career was tied to that of Diego Velázquez, governor of Cuba, whom he met in 1509, and who commissioned him to pursue Hernán Cortés in Mexico and bring him back to Cuba to be tried for insubordination. The plan backfired. Cortés's men defeated Narváez and put him in chains. Narváez returned to Spain, where he managed to get himself appointed "Adelantado and Conqueror of Florida." He did not survive the expedition.

57. Cabeza de Vaca, *Naufragios y comentarios*, 68–69.

58. Weber, *The Spanish Frontier in North America*, 51.

59. Pagden, *The Fall of Natural Man*, 81.

60. Cabeza de Vaca, *Naufragios y comentarios*, 87.

61. Ibid., 75.

62. Ibid.

63. Ibid., 77.

64. Ibid., 89.

65. Pagden, *The Fall of Natural Man*, 87.

66. Ibid.

67. Cabeza de Vaca, *Naufragios y comentarios*, 72.

68. Ibid., 62.

69. Ibid., 48.

70. Ibid., 54.

71. Ibid., 57.

72. Ibid., 61.

73. Ibid., 62.

74. Ibid., 51.

75. Ricklis, *The Karankawa Indians of Texas*, 6.

76. Cabeza de Vaca, *Naufragios y comentarios*, 71. The existence of giants is another of the medieval myths that made a great impression on the men of this era. Time and again, conquistadores and captives refer to having been held captive by giants, or mention nearby villages where giants live. Cabeza de Vaca, who was more realistic, explained that the men's fear altered their perceptions of reality, although he also uses the word "giants": "All the Indians we came across since Florida used bows and arrows, and since their bodies are well developed and they go naked, at a distance they look like giants" (ibid., 58).

77. Ibid., 76.

78. See Chipman, "In Search of Cabeza de Vaca's Route across Texas"; Krieger, "The Travels of Alvar Núñez Cabeza de Vaca in Texas and Mexico"; Pupo-Walker, "Los Naufragios de Álvar Núñez Cabeza de Vaca"; and Pilkington, "The Journey of Cabeza de Vaca."

79. Cabeza de Vaca, *Naufragios y comentarios*, 73.

80. Ibid., 78.

81. Ibid., 99.

82. Ibid., 95.

83. Ibid., 79.

84. Ibid.
85. Ibid., 125.
86. Ibid., 98.
87. Ibid.
88. Ibid.
89. Ibid.
90. Ibid., 79.
91. Ibid.
92. Ibid., 106.
93. Ibid., 123.
94. Salisbury, *Manitou and Providence*, 35.
95. Cabeza de Vaca, *Naufragios y comentarios*, 101.
96. See Pupo-Walker, "Pesquisas para una nueva lectura de los Naufragios"; and Pastor, *Discursos narrativos de la conquista*.
97. Weber, *The Spanish Frontier in North America*, 55.
98. Escalante Fontaneda, *Memoir of D. d'Escalante Fontaneda respecting Florida*, 70.
99. See Hilton, introduction to *La Florida del Inca*, 26.
100. The chronicle of El Inca is in line with the Renaissance concept of history, in the sense that only dignified events are worthy of being set down as history, and for that reason there is silence about those events not worthy of mention. He writes: "It is not known why the angry Pánfilo de Narváez committed the offenses which because they were so hateful are not discussed" (*La Florida del Inca*, 114–15).
101. Ibid., 129.
102. Geiger, bibliographical introduction to *The Martyrs of Florida*, xiii.
103. Oré, *The Martyrs of Florida*, 93.

2. *Malocas* on the Araucanian Frontier

1. Valdivia, *Cartas de Pedro de Valdivia*, 37.
2. Mariño de Lobera, *Crónica del Reino de Chile*, 337.
3. "Meanwhile, the Indians made a fire in front of him, and with the shell of a clam, which they call *pello* in their language, they cut off his biceps. Although they had swords, daggers, and knives, they did not use them, in order to cause him greater pain, and they roasted and ate them in his presence" (Góngora y Marmolejo, *Historia de todas las cosas que han acaecido en el Reino de Chile*, 115).
4. Rosales, *Historia general de el Reino de Chile*, 79–80.
5. Ras, *Crónica de la frontera sur*, 79.
6. Ibid., 76.
7. Jara, *Guerra y sociedad en Chile*, 149.
8. See the following works: Jara, *Guerra y sociedad en Chile*; Pinto Rodríguez, *Misioneros en la Araucanía*; Leiva, *El primer avance a la Araucanía*; Armond, "Frontier Warfare in Colonial Chile"; León Solís, "La corona española y las guerras intestinas";

Anadón, *Pineda y Bascuñán, defensor del araucano;* Villalobos, *Relaciones fronterizas de la Araucanía;* and Zapater, *Los aborígenes chilenos a través de cronistas y viajeros.*

9. The terms "Araucanian," "Araucania," and "Araucanian culture" have more significance if they are applied to present-day Chilean aborigines rather than to the indigenous peoples encountered by the Spaniards in the sixteenth century. Those latter groups were made up of different tribes that shared certain cultural traits—among them, language. For the Spaniards, the differences were more military than ethnic. The use of the suffix *-che* (meaning "people"), along with the location of the different groups, allows us to make a distinction between the Picunche ("People of the North") and the Huilliche ("People of the South"), all of whom belong within the Mapuche, or Araucanian, group, this latter term given and used by the Spaniards. For the purposes of this work I will use the terms "Mapuche" and "Araucanian" interchangably to refer to the Chilean Indians, and the terms "Picunche," "Pehuenche," and "Huilliche" to refer to specific groups among them.

10. González de Nájera finished writing his book in 1614, but the manuscript remained unpublished until 1866. The advocates of a defensive strategy did not view the appearance of this work favorably.

11. González de Nájera, *Desengaño y reparo de la Guerra del Reino de Chile,* 42.

12. Góngora y Marmolejo, *Historia de todas las cosas que han acaecido en el Reino de Chile,* 72.

13. Ercilla, *The Araucaniad,* trans. Lancaster and Manchester, 37.

14. The success of the first installment of *La Araucana* explains, in part, the widespread dissemination of the myth of Arauco. Marcos A. Moriñigo and Isaías Lerner remark that four editions of the first part of the poem were published before the second part appeared (see Mariñigo and Lerner, introduction to *La Araucana*). On the other hand, the great importance attached to a work written in verse conferred a greater historical verisimilitude to the chronicle. Ercilla unquestionably had an extraordinary impact on the creation and popularization of the Araucania myth.

15. Sergio Villalobos writes, "It is a commonplace of the Chilean mentality to think that the Araucanians were a 'military race' and that their characteristics have been passed down to their mestizo descendants" (Villalobos, *Relaciones fronterizas de la Araucanía,* 23).

16. Of great interest is the historical periodization of the advance into Araucania traced by Sergio Villalobos in his work *Araucanía: Temas de historia fronteriza.*

17. Sergio Villalobos points to the great demographic disparity between Indians and Spanish Creoles as a fundamental factor in the long and vigorous Araucanian resistance (Villalobos, *Relaciones fronterizas de la Araucanía,* 24).

18. Núñez de Pineda y Bascuñán, *Cautiverio feliz,* 21.

19. It is accepted that the manuscript was finished in 1673, although it was not published until 1863. Francisco's point of view as a Spanish Creole is an aspect that has been extensively debated, and several authors agree about the special political significance of the Creole stance assumed by Bascuñán in articulating his criticism of the Spanish administration in Chile. His critique centers on the policy of the Council of the Indies that discriminated between Creoles and Peninsulars when it came to the assignment of government

jobs and privileges. See Bauer, "Imperial History, Captivity, and Creole Identity in Francisco Núñez de Pineda y Bascuñán's *Cautiverio feliz*".

20. One finds many Americanisms in the text, such as *maloca* (raid), *maloquear* (to raid), *chacra* (farm), *cacique* (Indian chief), *macana* (war mace), *papas* (potatoes), *porotos* (beans), etc.

21. Núñez de Pineda y Bascuñán, *Cautiverio feliz*, 46.

22. Ibid.

23. Ibid.

24. Ibid., 67.

25. Bengoa, *Historia del pueblo mapuche*, 18–19.

26. Núñez de Pineda y Bascuñán, *Cautiverio feliz*, 142.

27. Ibid., 142–43.

28. León Solís, *Maloqueros y conchavadores en Araucanía y las Pampas*, 98.

29. Alvaro Jara refers to the organization of the Araucanians into family groups, called *rehue* or *lov*, and to a certain connection among them by means of alliances of mutual defense, called *ailla-rehue*. The most important pacts were made in times of war, which would occasion the naming of temporary chiefs, whose prestige depended on their personal status, the number of relatives they had, and the amount of animals and moveable goods they owned. On the other hand, before the appearance of the Spaniards, these tribal groups had faced few threats, with the exception of sporadic intertribal conflicts. This benign circumstance did not favor the development of a confederation, which would appear later (see Jara, *Guerra y sociedad en Chile*, 49).

30. Padden, "Cultural Adaptation and Militant Autonomy among the Auracanians of Chile," 70.

31. Zapater, "Parlamentos de paz en la guerra de Arauco (1612–1626)," 69.

32. See Beltrán, "La organización de los parlamentos de indios en el siglo XVIII," 115.

33. Núñez de Pineda y Bascuñán, *Cautiverio feliz*, 26.

34. Ibid., 27.

35. Slavery was declared legal in 1608. However, Álvaro Jara has collected testimony that shows this practice existed before that date (Jara, *Guerra y sociedad en Chile*, 151). Slavery represented a great source of commerce for the Spanish forces, who entered Indian territory and took Indians of all ages whom they would later sell at great profit in the cities of Chile and in Peru. Since that time, and as a direct result of this practice, the controversy between those who advocated slavery and a war of extermination and those who advocated a policy of defensive warfare had filtered into every sector of society. Bascuñán defended the second position, and a great part of his *Cautiverio feliz* is devoted to combating the abuse of the Indians, citing the bad policies followed by many of the colonial authorities and governors as the cause for the wars (Núñez de Pineda y Bascuñán, *Cautiverio feliz*, 30).

36. Núñez de Pineda y Bascuñán, *Cautiverio feliz*, 27.

37. Ibid., 29–30.

38. Ibid., 30.

39. Ibid., 31.
40. Ibid., 36.
41. Ibid., 76.
42. Jara, *Guerra y sociedad en Chile*, 84–85.
43. In canto 3 of part 1 of the epic, Lautaro appears, exhorting his compatriots to rebel:

> There a well-known chieftain's scion
> Who as a page once served Valdivia,
> Long caressed by him, and favored
> In the time of peaceful service,
> Saw his kin to flight succumbing;
> Moved and fired with love of country,
> He enkindled them to courage,
> Shouting words to chide and challenge:
> [. . .]
> Thereupon he charged, and brandished
> Fibred lance at Lord Valdivia,
> Hoping by this ostentation
> To add force to stern persuasion;
> Thus he dashed 'midst steel of Spaniards,
> As the thirsty hind in summer
> Flings himself in cooling waters
> To expel the fires that seer him.
>
> > Ercilla, *The Araucaniad*, 54–55

44. Núñez de Pineda y Bascuñán, *Cautiverio feliz*, 37.
45. Ibid.
46. Ibid., 39.
47. González de Nájera and other chroniclers refer to the cannibalistic rituals associated with the idea of reprisal: "And these are not enemies who are only satisfied with killing, no matter how much the youthful age or physical condition of a victim, or their sad pleading, might move them to compassion, but rather they take great delight in excessive cruelty, as they gradually roast and eat the pieces they cut from a victim, as the victim watches, and they also consume the rest of the flesh that remains on their bodies when they are finally dead" (González de Nájera, *Desengaño y reparo de la Guerra del Reino de Chile*, 54).
48. Alvaro Jara has referred to the deeply ritual meaning of the ceremonial sacrifices, which were meant to seek protection before important battles: "It seems that this procedure narrated by Pineda had a double magical meaning" (*Guerra y sociedad en Chile*, 54).
49. Núñez de Pineda y Bascuñán, *Cautiverio feliz*, 40.
50. Ibid., 41.
51. Zapater, "Testimonio de un cautivo," 316.
52. Villalobos, *Relaciones fronterizas de la Araucanía*, 24.

53. Núñez de Pineda y Bascuñán, *Cautiverio feliz,* 71.

54. Ibid., 95.

55. Ibid., 103.

56. Jara, *Guerra y sociedad en Chile,* 146.

57. Núñez de Pineda y Bascuñán, *Cautiverio feliz,* 93.

58. González de Nájera, *Desengaño y reparo de la Guerra del Reino de Chile,* 166.

59. León Solís, *Maloqueros y conchavadores en Araucanía y las Pampas,* 25.

60. González de Nájera, *Desengaño y reparo de la Guerra del Reino de Chile,* 81.

61. Alvaro Jara writes: "The best prey, in greatest demand, fastest selling, and at the best prices, were the war Indians, and especially their women and children. In the previous chapters we have already seen the imperative need for labor in the Kingdom, and if one considers also the purchasing possibilities of the Peruvian market, the enslavement of Indians was the best complementary source of income to which the members of the army that fought in Arauco could aspire" (Jara, *Guerra y sociedad en Chile,* 145).

62. Góngora y Marmolejo, *Historia de todas las cosas que han acaecido en el Reino de Chile,* 116.

63. González de Nájera, *Desengaño y reparo de la Guerra del Reino de Chile,* 60.

64. Zapater, "Testimonio de un cautivo," 314.

65. Jones, "Calfucurá y Namuncurá," 175–86.

66. See Pinto Rodríguez, "Frontera, misiones y misioneros en Chile y la Araucanía."

67. Núñez de Pineda y Bascuñán, *Cautiverio feliz,* 171.

68. Ibid., 150.

69. Ibid., 124.

70. Ibid., 124–25.

71. Ibid., 162.

72. Ibid., 183–84.

73. See Anadón, *Pineda y Bascuñán, defensor del araucano.*

74. Picón-Salas, *De la conquista a la independencia,* 119.

75. Núñez de Pineda y Bascuñán, *Cautiverio feliz,* 20.

76. Ibid., 193.

77. For an review of this debate, see Garrote Bernal, "El *Cautiverio feliz* de Núñez de Pineda y Bascuñán."

78. Zapater, "Testimonio de un cautivo," 314.

79. Ibid., 314.

80. Ibid., 317.

81. Ibid.

82. Ibid., 323.

83. Ibid., 315.

84. Ibid.

85. Ibid., 317.

86. See Correa Bello, *El cautiverio feliz en la vida política chilena del siglo XVII.*

87. Zapater, "Testimonio de un cautivo," 315–16.

88. Núñez de Pineda y Bascuñán, *Cautiverio feliz*, chap. 10.

89. Zapater, "Testimonio de un cautivo," 323.

90. Ibid., 320.

91. See Guarda Geywitz, "Los cautivos en la guerra de Arauco," 93–157.

92. Ibid., 71.

93. Ibid., 70.

94. Ibid., 99.

95. Ibid.

96. González de Nájera, *Desengaño y reparo de la Guerra del Reino de Chile,* 68.

97. Diego de Rosales tells the story of Gaspar Álvarez, a deserter from the army of Arauco, much appreciated among the Indians because of his skills as a hatter, "a craft unknown among the Indians and for which they held him in high esteem" (see Rosales, *Historia general de el Reino de Chile,* 176).

98. González de Nájera, *Desengaño y reparo de la Guerra del Reino de Chile,* 54.

99. Guarda Geywitz, "Los cautivos en la guerra de Arauco," 107.

100. Ibid., 71.

101. Núñez de Pineda y Bascuñán, *Cautiverio feliz,* 168.

102. Herren, *Indios carapálidas,* 131.

103. González de Nájera, *Desengaño y reparo de la Guerra del Reino de Chile,* 55.

104. Ibid., 192.

105. Ibid., 117.

106. Góngora y Marmolejo, *Historia de todas las cosas que han acaecido en el Reino de Chile,* 74–75.

107. Ibid., 69.

108. Herren gives information about the numerous deserters in the lands of Chile, whose number seems to be greater than in other areas of the frontier. Some, like the Spaniard Juan Sánchez, distinguished themselves by leading large armies of Indians. Herren seeks an explanation for this apparent epidemic of desertions in Chile in the "disenchantment with an arbitrary and oligarchical society determined to prosecute a long and sterile war" (*Indios carapálidas,* 130).

109. León Solís, *Maloqueros y conchavadores en Araucanía y las Pampas,* 60.

110. See Armond, "Frontier Warfare in Colonial Chile."

111. Guarda Geywitz, "Los cautivos en la guerra de Arauco," 123.

112. Ibid., 124.

113. See Armond, "Frontier Warfare in Colonial Chile," 117.

3. Captives in the Río de la Plata Region

1. In no other part of the continent did captivity reach the massive proportions it acquired in the Río de la Plata.

2. On the subject of captivity in the Río de la Plata, the works of Carlos A. Mayo deserve special attention.

3. Jones, "Calfucurá y Namuncurá," 179.

4. Ibid., 178.

5. Ras, *Crónica de la frontera sur,* 381.

6. See Tapson, "Indian Warfare on the Pampa during the Colonial Period."

7. Jones, "Calfucurá y Namuncurá," 184.

8. For Carlos Martínez Sarasola, the self-denominated "Conquest of the Desert" was in reality the culmination of a campaign of extermination and cultural disintegration that had been systematically carried out from the first decades of the nineteenth century. Certain conciliatory opinions in the debate on the "Indian question" had done nothing except postpone temporarily this tragic end.

9. See the periodization put forth by Carlos Mayo and Amalia Latrubesse in *Terratenientes, soldados y cautivos;* see also Walther, *La conquista del desierto.*

10. Walther, *La conquista del desierto,* 84.

11. León Solís, "Las invasiones indígenas," 77.

12. Ras, *Crónica de la frontera sur,* 219.

13. Walther, *La conquista del desierto,* 88.

14. *Copia de la carta, escrita por un misionero de la Compañía de Jesús del Paraguay, al Padre Juan Joseph Rico, Procurador General de dicha Provincia en esta Corte, en que le refiere el estado presente de aquella provincia, y sus Misiones, así antiguas como nuevas, entre Christianos, y Gentiles,* Brown University Library, p. 464.

15. See Saignes, "La guerra 'salvaje' en los confines de los Andes y del Chaco."

16. Walther, *La conquista del desierto,* 88.

17. Mayo and Latrubesse, *Terratenientes, soldados y cautivos,* 18.

18. See Adrien, "The Noticias secretas de América."

19. Walther, *La conquista del desierto,* 97.

20. As a result of repeated Indian attacks, Governor Andonaegui, with the approval of the *cabildo* of Buenos Aires, created a regular corps of salaried militia, who were called *blandengues* (Mayo and Latrubesse, *Terratenientes, soldados y cautivos,* 44).

21. For an in-depth study of the lines of defense, see Viñas, *Indios, ejército y frontera;* Mayo and Latrubesse, *Terratenientes, soldados y cautivos;* Walther, *La conquista del desierto;* Portas, *Malón contra malón;* and Ras, *Crónica de la frontera sur.*

22. For a periodization of Indian raids on the settlements to the north and south of Buenos Aires, see the works of Mayo and Latrubesse (*Terratenientes, soldados y cautivos*) and León Solís (*Maloqueros y conchavadores en Araucanía y las Pampas*).

23. Martínez Sarasola, *Nuestros paisanos los indios,* 26.

24. Ras, *Crónica de la frontera sur,* 194.

25. *Acuerdos del extinguido cabildo de Buenos Aires,* 17.

26. Walther, *La conquista del desierto,* 87.

27. Mayo and Latrubesse, *Terratenientes, soldados y cautivos,* 61.

28. Ibid., 56.

29. Ebélot, *Relatos de la frontera,* 27.

30. Declaración, December 8, 1786, Archivo General de la Nación, Buenos Aires, Argentina (hereafter cited as AGN), IX, 1-5-3.

31. Ibid.

32. Declaración, January 12, 1781, AGN, IX, 1-4-6.

33. Declaración, February 23, 1781, AGN, IX, 1-6-2.

34. Ibid.

35. See Jones, "Comparative Raiding Economies, North and South."

36. Ibid., 182.

37. See Mayo, "El cautiverio y sus funciones en una sociedad de frontera."

38. This subject is studied in greater detail in chapter 4.

39. Avendaño, *Memorias,* 160.

40. Declaración, December 8, 1786, AGN, IX, 1-5-3.

41. Declaración, December 8, 1786, AGN, IX, 1-5-3.

42. Mayo, *Fuentes para la historia de la frontera,* 13.

43. Declaración, October 3, 1780, AGN, IX, 1-4-6.

44. Declaración, April 6, 1779, AGN, IX, 1-6-2.

45. The edition I consulted was Ernesto J. Fitte and Julio A. Benencia, eds., *Juan Manuel Rosas y la redención de cautivos en su campaña al desierto (1833–1834).*

46. Typical responses of the captives were recorded on this order of detail (see Fitte and Benencia, *Juan Manuel Rosas*):

> 127. Josefa Espinosa. From Punta, from El Morro, 10 years old; daughter of Juan Francisco and María Cabrera. She was captured 3 years ago on her farm.
>
> 188. Gervacia Allende. Porteña from Guardia de Luján, 16 years old, single; daughter of Marcelino Allende and Josefa Gorrea. She was captured at a young age on the frontier.
>
> 208. Basilia Debia. Porteña from Guardia de Rojas, twenty-three years old: black hair, eyes the same, dark complexion, large mouth, regular nose. Does not remember the names of her parents. She was captured fifteen years ago on the outskirts of her town. She is somewhat pock-marked and speaks Spanish.
>
> 218. José. Porteño, from Salto, 16 years old, curly black hair, black eyes, dark complexion, large mouth, broad nose; son of Inés. He was captured 13 years ago in his own town. Does not speak Spanish.

47. Fitte and Benencia, *Juan Manuel de Rosas,* 20.

48. Susan M. Socolow has analyzed this data thoroughly in her article "Spanish Captives in Indian Societies."

49. "Residencia del Colonel Don Juan Victorino Martínez de Tineo," 1764, Audiencia de Buenos Aires, Archivo General de las Indias, Seville, Spain, p. 49.

50. The expedition of Colonel Pedro Andrés García was commissioned by the govern-

ment for the purpose of securing a lasting peace with the tribes south of the Río Salado (see García, "Diario," 4:562–63).

51. León Solís, "Las invasions indígenas," 97.

52. Declaración, February 20, 1787, AGN, IX, 1-4-3.

53. Declaración, December 1783, AGN, IX, 32-3-4.

54. Socolow, "Spanish Captives in Indian Societies," 123.

55. See Mandrini, *Los araucanos de las pampas en el siglo XIX*.

56. Félix San Martín writes: "The Puelches were polygamous and they could have as many women as they could feed. The social rank of the men was measured by the number of wives they had" (San Martín, *Neuquén*, 131).

57. Mandrini, *Los araucanos de las pampas en el siglo XIX*, 12.

58. González Arili, *Los indios pampas*, 35.

59. See Jones, *"La cautiva."*

60. See Avendaño, "Muerte del cacique Painé."

61. Martínez Sarasola, *Nuestros paisanos los indios*, 227.

62. González Arili, *Los indios pampas*, 35.

63. Declaración, July 27, 1788, AGN, IX, 21-2-5.

64. Declaración, February 23, 1781, AGN, IX, 1-6-2.

65. Declaración, 1804, AGN, IX, 35-5-8.

66. Declaración, December 16, 1788, AGN, IX, 1-6-3.

67. Avendaño, *Memorias*, 155.

68. Declaración, December 24, 1749, Archivo Histórico de Tucumán, Argentina, vol. 2, folio 245.

69. Socolow, "Spanish Captives in Indian Societies," 123.

70. Declaración, December 13, 1777, AGN, IX, 12-9-13.

71. Declaración, December 13, 1777, AGN, IX, 12-9-13.

72. Hernández, "Diario," 4:144.

73. García, "Diario," 4:565.

74. The "Indian Question," as it was called, divided those who advocated an offensive policy of extermination and those who favored defensive strategies and negotiation (see Arcos, *Cuestión de indios;* Viñas, *Indios, ejército y fronteras;* Aníbal Portas, *Malón contra malón;* Walther, *La conquista del desierto;* and Martínez Sarasola, *Nuestros paisanos los indios*).

75. See Ebélot, *Relatos de la frontera*.

76. Mansilla, *Una excursión a los indios ranqueles*, 180.

77. Ibid., 198. Mariano Rosas was the son of the cacique Painé. He had been taken prisoner as a youngster by forces from Buenos Aires and jailed. Juan Manuel de Rosas brought him to one of his estancias, educated him, and had him baptized, giving him his own last name. Years later, Mariano escaped with some other Indians and inherited the *cacicazgo* from his father. According to what Mansilla says, he retained "the most pleasant memory of veneration for his godfather" (ibid., 180).

78. Ibid., 322.

79. I take up this case in the next chapter.

80. Mandrini, *Los araucanos de las pampas en el siglo XIX,* 15.

81. The term "Auca" was used to refer to tribes of Araucanian origin.

82. Declaración, May 21, 1792, AGN, IX, 1-4-6.

83. Later in his declaration, Barquero seems to have doubts about the indentity of the cacique-priest. "He never had the sense that he was a Jesuit, but he could have been. What is certain is that he heard from the Indians who had him captive that this cacique doesn't allow the Indians to cross the frontier to harm Christians" (Declaración, May 8, 1772, AGN, IX, 1-5-6).

84. Declaración, August 20, 1783, AGN, IX, 1-4-6.

85. Declaración, August 26, 1783, in Mayo, *Fuentes para la historia de la frontera,* 25.

86. Ebélot, *Relatos de la frontera,* 128–29.

87. Service in the first rural militias was obligatory, on a call-up basis, and unpaid. Later, the militias were more regulated and salaries were established, which when they came, came late. A captain earned 50 pesos a month, an *alférez* [lieutenant?] 25, sergeants received 16 pesos, corporals 12, and foot soldiers 11 (Mayo and Latrubesse, *Terratenientes, soldados y cautivos,* 20).

88. Ibid., 47.

89. Mansilla, *Una excursión a los indios ranqueles,* 289–90.

90. Informe, November 24, 1803, AGN, IX, 1-2-4.

91. Mayo and Latrubesse, *Terratenientes, soldados y cautivos,* 53.

92. Declaración, March 21, 1788, AGN, IX, 1-6-3.

93. Declaración, January 30, 1788, AGN, IX, 1-6-3.

94. Declaración, December 14, 1789, AGN, IX, 1-6-3.

95. Declaración, September 25, 1788, AGN, IX, 1-6-3.

96. Declaración, March 8, 1794, AGN, IX, 1-5-3.

97. Baigorria, *Memorias.*

98. Mayo, *Estancia y sociedad en la Pampa.*

99. Declaración, November 27, 1803, AGN, IX, 1-2-4.

100. Informe, 1790, AGN, Tribunales, legajo 227, expediente 17.

101. Expediente, October 7, 1800, AGN, IX, 24-3-1.

102. Declaración, 1791, AGN, IX, 24-2-1.

103. Declaración, May 9, 1809, AGN, IX, 23-7-7.

104. Cédula Real, January 23, 1790, AGN, IX, 24-2-1.

105. Declaración, February 22, 1781, AGN, IX, 1-7-4.

106. Declaración, June 14, 1752, in Mayo, *Fuentes para la historia de la frontera,* 5.

107. Declaración, December 9, 1780, AGN, IX, 1-4-3.

108. Declaración, October 10, 1784, AGN, IX, 1-7-4.

109. Declaración, March 24, 1787, AGN, IX, 1-4-3.

110. Declaración, February 23, 1781, AGN, IX, 1-6-2.

111. Ibid.

112. See Malossetti Costa, *Rapto de cautivas blancas.*

113. León Solís uses the term "guerra chica" to refer to the *malocas* or *malones* indigenous to Chile and Argentina, respectively (see León Solís, "Las invasions indígenas").

114. See Saignes, "La guerra 'salvaje' en los confines de los Andes y del Chaco."

4. Accounts of Captives in the Pampas and Patagonia

1. Levernier and Cohen, *The Indians and Their Captives*, xiii.

2. Ibid., xxvi.

3. VanDerBeets defines the stages of this voyage of initiation: the first is marked by capture and separation; the second, transforming, stage is adaptation and survival, or voluntary adoption; and the third is the return, accompanied by a symbolic rebirth and moral growth (see VanDerBeets, *The Indian Captivity Narratives*).

4. Ibid., xii.

5. Levernier and Cohen, *The Indians and Their Captives*, xv.

6. Ibid., xix.

7. Ibid., xx.

8. This was true for Mary Rowlandson: *Sovereignty & Goodness of God*, published in 1682, went through thirty editions. *Redeemed Captive: Returning to Zion* (1707), by John Williams, was reissued twenty times (see Namias, *White Captives*, 9).

9. Juan Luis Alborg, in the introduction to the Spanish edition, points out the profound differences between the first and second French editions. The first edition, more spare, is really no more than a superficial synopsis of the journey. In the second edition, chapters were added and the writing was improved substantially (Alborg, introduction to *Tres años de esclavitud entre los patagones*, 1123–24).

10. Guinnard, *Tres años de esclavitud entre los patagones*, 1126.

11. Ibid., 1125.

12. Pratt, *Imperial Eyes*, 31.

13. Guinnard, *Tres años de esclavitud entre los patagones*, 1127.

14. Guinnard, *Three Years' Slavery among the Patagonians*, 40. Unless otherwise noted, all subsequent quotations are from the 1871 English-language edition, translated from the third French edition by Charles S. Cheltnam.

15. Ibid., 32–33.

16. Ibid., 12.

17. Martínez Sarasola notes the existence of small parties of Indians, not connected to the better organized groups, whose activities consisted in picking up the trails of other *malones* so as to take whatever had been left behind (Martínez Sarasola, *Nuestros paisanos los indios*, 229). Guinnard wrote in his diary: "They often devote themselves to the sacking of farms, from which they plunder a great number of horses and cows."

18. Guinnard, *Three Years' Slavery among the Patagonians*, 32.

19. Ibid., 76, 94.

20. Ibid., 221.

21. Bourne, *The Captive in Patagonia*, 18.

22. Ibid., 206.

23. García, "Diario."

24. Martínez Sarasola, *Nuestros paisanos los indios,* 153–54.

25. Ibid., 222.

26. Ibid.

27. Jones, "Calfucurá y Namuncurá," 179.

28. Ibid., 184.

29. Sarmiento quoted in Viñas, *Indios, ejército y frontera,* 53.

30. Ibid., 57.

31. Ibid., 56.

32. See Operé, "Cautivos de los indios," 62–63.

33. Bourne, *The Captive in Patagonia,* 39.

34. García, "Diario," 4:635.

35. Juan and Ulloa sent the king a clandestine volume in which they informed him about other critical aspects regarding the viceroyalty; this volume was edited and published in 1826 by the Englishman David Barry, with the title *Noticias secretas de América.* The censorship or covering up of important aspects of the colonies had been a Spanish royal tendency since the first years of discovery in the lands of La Florida (see Adrien, "The *Noticias secretas de América*").

36. A precursor to these foreign travelers was the English priest Thomas Falkner, who made journeys of great value and wrote about them in some of his most pertinent works, *Derrotero de los Césares* and *A Description of Patagonia and the Adjoining Parts of South America,* published in English in 1774.

37. Viedma, "Diario."

38. Villarino, "Diario."

39. Hernández Cornejo, "Diario."

40. Cruz, "Viaje."

41. Azara, "Diario."

42. Rosas, "Diario."

43. García, "Diario," 4:564–65.

44. Sosnowski, preface to *Una excursión a los indios ranqueles,* ix.

45. Ibid., xvii.

46. Mansilla, *Una excursión a los indios ranqueles,* 195.

47. Ibid., 322.

48. Ebélot, *Relatos de la frontera,* 28–29.

49. Ibid., 25.

50. Pagden, *European Encounters with the New World,* 3.

51. Letts, introduction to *The True History of His Captivity, 1557,* by Hans Staden 9.

52. Padgen, *The Fall of Natural Man,* 83.

53. There were various American cultures that practiced cannibalism. Perhaps the best known are the Aztecs, whose rituals we know from numerous sources, but principally from the works of the Franciscan missionary Bernardino de Sahagún, who describes them in

extraordinary detail. Cannibalism was also practiced in Mesoamerica, by the Xiximes, Chichimecas, and Mayas of the Yucatán. In South America, there are numerous references to cannibalism among the Tupi-Guaraní.

54. Bourne, *The Captive in Patagonia*, 46.

55. Ibid., 73–74.

56. Ibid., 87.

57. Ibid.

58. Ibid., 121.

59. Guinnard, *Three Years' Slavery among the Patagonians*, 36.

60. Ibid., 49–50.

61. Gandía, *Historia crítica de los mitos de la conquista americana*, 29.

62. Díaz de Guzmán, *La Argentina*, 61.

63. Bourne, *The Captive in Patagonia*, 54–55.

64. Ibid., 55.

65. Guinnard, *Three Years' Slavery among the Patagonians*, 41. These groups are today known as the Poyuches, Pulliches, Calliches, Tehuelches, Cañecahuelches, Chauches, Huilliches, Dilmaches, and Yacanaches.

66. Ibid., 52.

67. Ibid., 77.

68. Zeballas, *Callvucurá y la dinastía de los Piedra*, 29.

69. P. Meinrado Hux, who edited Avendaño's mansucript, wonders whether part of the original manuscript has been lost, since certain references of the author's do not appear in the text, including the fact that Avendaño refers to the existence of some chapters that were not found in the archives (Avendaño, *Memorias*, 10).

70. Ibid., 90.

71. Ibid., 12.

72. Ibid., 89.

73. Ibid., 163.

74. Baigorria, *Memorias*, 112.

75. Avendaño, *Memorias*, 190–91.

76. Ibid., 187–88.

77. Ibid., 215.

78. Ibid., 245.

79. Avendaño, "La fuga de un cautivo de los Indios," 35.

80. Bourne, *The Captive in Patagonia*, 164.

81. Guinnard, *Three Years' Slavery among the Patagonians*, 255.

82. Ibid., 114.

83. Ibid., 89–90.

84. Ibid., 218–19.

85. James Axtell has written about the proselytizing tendencies and educational power of the North American Indians (see Axtell, *The European and the Indian*, 175).

86. Guinnard, *Three Years' Slavery among the Patagonians*, 303–4.

87. Caruth, *Unclaimed Experience*, 58.

88. Guinnard, *Three Years' Slavery among the Patagonians*, 353–54.

89. Ibid., 370–71.

5. The Northern Frontier

1. Silvio Zavala has dealt with this subject in his article "The Frontier in Hispanic America." See also Thomas D. Hall, "The Río de la Plata and the Greater Southwest."

2. Stern, "The White Indians of the Borderlands," 280.

3. Powell, *La guerra chichimeca*, 32.

4. Ibid., 48.

5. Ibid., 9–10.

6. Powell, *Soldiers, Indians, and Silver*, 50.

7. "Informe de Gonzalo de las Casas," cited in ibid., 65.

8. Powell, *Soldiers, Indians, and Silver*, 120.

9. "Informe del virrey Enríquez a su sucesor de fecha 26-9-1580," cited in Powell, *Soldiers, Indians, and Silver*, 181.

10. Stern, "The White Indians of the Borderlands," 266. Others who have studied the subject have reached the same conclusion; see Noyes, *Los Comanches*; Heard, *White into Red*; Kenner, *History of New Mexican–Plains Indian Relations*; VanDerBeets, *The Indian Captivity Narratives*; Rister, *Border Captives*; Namias, *White Captives*; McNitt, *Navajo Wars*; Brooks, "Captives and Cousins"; Salisbury, *Manitou and Providence*; Demos, *The Unredeemed Captive*; Griffen, *Apaches at War and Peace*; Jones, "Rescue and Ransom of Spanish Captives"; and Axtell, *The European and the Indian*.

11. See Sahagún, *Historia general de las cosas de Nueva España*.

12. See Baudot, *Utopía e historia en México*; and Gibson, *Tlaxcala in the Sixteenth Century*.

13. Stern, "The White Indians of the Borderlands," 267.

14. Ibid.

15. Powell, *La guerra chichimeca*, 66.

16. Espinosa, *Crusaders of the Río Grande*, 8.

17. See Kenner, *History of New Mexican–Plains Indian Relations*.

18. Espinosa, *Crusaders of the Río Grande*, 12.

19. Weber, *The Spanish Frontier in North America*, 85.

20. Ibid., 86.

21. Espinosa, *Crusaders of the Río Grande*, 218.

22. Letter of Diego de Vargas to the Viceroy, dated El Paso, January 10, 1692, cited in Espinosa, *Crusaders of the Río Grande*, 87.

23. Espinosa, *Crusaders of the Río Grande*, 105.

24. Jones, "Rescue and Ransom of Spanish Captives," 132–33.

25. Ibid., 131.

26. Weber, *The Spanish Frontier in North America*, 137.

27. Jones, "Rescue and Ransom of Spanish Captives," 133.

28. Ibid., 139.

29. Ibid., 135.

30. Bancroft Library, 1693b, cited by Griffen, *Apaches at War and Peace*, 12.

31. Griffen, *Apaches at War and Peace*, 136.

32. Noyes, *Los Comanches*, 70.

33. Ibid., 73.

34. Thomas, *The Plains Indians and New Mexico*, 17.

35. Jones, "Rescue and Ransom of Spanish Captives," 137.

36. Ibid., 142.

37. Ibid., 147.

38. Ibid.

39. Rister, *Border Captives*, 49.

40. Ibid., 50.

41. Noyes, *Los Comanches*, 5.

42. In Corwin, *The Kiowa Indians*.

43. The Kiowas were a tribe from the area of present-day Kansas and Oklahoma. They made constant trips to the west to trade with Comanche and Apache bands.

44. Cutler, "Lawrie Tatum and the Kiowas Agency."

45. Corwin, *The Kiowa Indians*, 7.

46. Methvin, *Andele*, 25.

47. Corwin, *The Kiowa Indians*, 14.

48. Stern, "The White Indians of the Borderlands," 281.

49. Rister, *Border Captives,* 57.

50. "Tomassa," in Corwin, *The Kiowa Indians*, 105.

51. Ibid.

52. Ibid.

53. Ibid., 110.

54. VanDerBeets, *The Indian Captivity Narratives*, ix.

55. Brooks, introduction to *Andele*, 15.

56. Lowie, "Societies of the Kiowa," cited in Brooks, introduction to *Andele*, 15.

57. Methvin, *Andele*, 128–29.

58. Ibid., 120.

59. Ibid., 133.

60. Ibid., 32.

61. Ibid., 38.

62. Ibid., 42.

63. Ibid., 43.

64. Ibid., 49.

65. Ibid., 55.

66. Ibid., 86.

67. Cutler, "Lawrie Tatum and the Kiowas Agency," 232–33.

68. Methvin, *Andele*, 93.

69. Ibid., 117.

70. Ibid., 119.

71. Ibid., 119–20.

72. Brooks, introduction to *Andele*, 13.

73. Ibid., 5.

74. Ibid., 17n8.

75. Methvin, *Andele*, 60.

76. Ibid., 65.

77. Ibid., 86.

78. Ibid., 71.

79. Ibid., 77.

80. Weber, *The Spanish Frontier in North America*, 307.

81. Methvin, *Andele*, 78.

82. Ibid., 33.

83. Ibid., 46.

84. Ibid., 87.

85. Ibid., 92.

88. Cutler, "Lawrie Tatum and the Kiowas Agency."

87. Green, *The Last Captive*, 160.

6. From Helena Valero to Napëyoma

1. Valero, *Yo soy Napëyoma*, 529.

2. See Chagnon, *Yanomamö: The Fierce People*.

3. Valero, *Yo soy Napëyoma*, 25.

4. Ibid., 24–25.

5. Ibid., 25.

6. Ibid.

7. The *shabonos*, the communal dwellings of the Yanomamö, are formed by a series of constructions of wood and thatch laid out in a circle. The construction of a *shabono* requires a great collective effort and is the most complicated and intense task in Yanomamö culture. They usually last about two years, after which the thatch begins to deteriorate and rot owing to the effects of climate and insects (see Chagnon, *Yanomamö: The Fierce People*, 52).

8. Valero, *Yo soy Napëyoma*, 26.

9. Helena mentions that many women were raped repeatedly when they got to the *shabonos* (ibid., 466).

10. Chagnon, *Yanomamö: The Fierce People*, 175.

11. Valero, *Yo soy Napëyoma*, 31.

12. Ibid.

13. Ibid., 34.

14. Chagnon, *Yanomamö: The Fierce People*, 175.

15. See Cocco, *Iyëwei-theri;* and Harris, "The Yanomamö and the Causes of War in Band and Village Societies."

16. Valero, *Yo soy Napëyoma*, 49.

17. Ibid.

18. Chagnon, *Yanomamö: The Fierce People*, 7–8.

19. Valero, *Yo soy Napëyoma*, 70.

20. Ibid., 101.

21. Ibid., 106.

22. The term *napë* can be translated as "enemy," "stranger," "foreigner," or "not Yanomamö."

23. Valero, *Yo soy Napëyoma*, 33.

24. Ibid., 40.

25. Ibid., 174.

26. Ibid., 314.

27. Ibid., 104.

28. Ibid., 529.

29. Ibid., 532.

30. Ibid., 161.

31. Valero, *Yo soy Napëyoma*, 199–200. A *wayumi* is a period of time spent in one or two places in the jungle during which the Yanomamö subsisted on hunting, fishing, and gathering wild fruit.

32. Ibid., 200.

33. Ibid., 173.

34. Chagnon, *Yanomamö: The Fierce People*, 1.

35. Ibid., 115.

36. Valero, *Yo soy Napëyoma*, 48–49.

37. Ibid., 91.

38. Ibid.

39. Ibid., 97–98.

40. Chagnon, *Yanomamö: The Fierce People*, 176.

41. Valero, *Yo soy Napëyoma*, 317.

42. Ibid., 492.

43. Chagnon, *Yanomamö: The Fierce People*, 170.

44. Brian Fergusson has refuted Chagnon's interpretation, pointing out that during the period Chagnon did his fieldwork, Yanomamö society was suffering from increased aggression from outsiders, generated by the invasion of settlers and an alarming reduction in the group's living space, and that these factors could have exacerbated tensions among the Yanomamö groups during the period studied by Chagnon (see Fergusson, *Yanomami Warfare*).

45. Valero, *Yo soy Napëyoma*, 313.

46. Ibid., 354.

47. Ibid., 524.
48. Ibid.
49. Ibid., 531.
50. Ibid.
51. Ibid. 535.
52. Ibid.
53. Ibid., 538.
54. Ibid. 538–39.
55. Ibid., 539.
56. Valero's text coincides fundamentally with the best ethnographies of the Yanomamö people, among them the works of Chagnon and Cocco, already mentioned, as well as that of Jacques Lizot ("Poisons yanomami de chasse, de guerre et de pêche").
57. Fuentes, introduction to *Yo soy Napëyoma,* 10.
58. "Don't go and laugh and think it's all lies. Everything, just as it happened, the complete truth is here in this book. I don't want you to laugh, because I didn't have a good time at all" (Valero, *Yo soy Napëyoma,* 18).
59. Molloy, *At Face Value,* 4.
60. Holmes, "Shabono."
61. Pratt discusses aspects related to the controversy provoked by this book in her article "Field Work in Common Places" (29).
62. Molloy, *At Face Value,* 4.
63. Fuentes, introduction to *Yo soy Napëyoma,* 11.
64. Ibid.
65. I subscribe to many of the ideas expressed in Jara and Vidal, *Testimonio y literatura.*
66. Fuentes, introduction to *Yo soy Napëyoma,* 14.

7. Captives in Literature

1. For a discussion of this subject, see Pupo-Walker, *La vocación literaria del pensamiento histórico en América;* and Rodríguez Fernández, introduction to *Purén indómito.*
2. Eagleton, *Literary Theory,* 17.
3. In Enrique Pupo-Walker's opinion, the biographical material and its presentation betray no significant disagreement with the framework of institutional values advanced by the Spanish Crown (see Pupo-Walker, "Pesquisas para una nueva lectura de los Naufragios," 517).
4. Mitre, *Soledad,* 15.
5. Indians, for Sarmiento, were "savages avid for blood and plunder" (Sarmiento, *Facundo,* 14).
6. Many scholars have studied the North American captivity narrative; see, e.g., Ebersole, *Captured by Texts;* Fitzpatrick, "The Figure of Captivity"; Haberly, "Captives and Infidels," and "Women and Indians"; Pearce, "The Significances of Captivity Narrative"; and VanDerBeets, *The Indian Captivity Narratives.*

7. Malosetti Costa, *Rapto de cautivas blancas,* 9.

8. See Camamis, *Estudios sobre el cautiverio.*

9. It is interesting to note the inclination to revisit certain of the topics of captivity, some of the most prevalent of which are the cannibalism of the Indians, the sacrificing of captives, and the recurrent allusion to the daughters of Indian caciques who intercede for the life of an unfortunate captive. The captivity of Juan Ortiz in La Florida exemplifies this modality, as does that of Francisco Martín in Venezuela's interior, cited by Fernández de Oviedo. Not only was Martín saved from being roasted alive by an Indian woman, but like Cabeza de Vaca he was indoctrinated by the Indians in their curing practices (Fernández de Oviedo, *Historia general y natural de las Indias,* 3:28).

10. Although the exact date is unknown, Arias de Saavedra's manuscript dates from the first years of the seventeenth century.

11. Ercilla, *The Araucaniad,* 37.

12. Chevalier's list of those influenced by Ercilla's work includes Pedro de Oña, Juan de Mendoza Monteagudo, Juan de Castellanos, Antonio de Saavedra Guzmán, Martín del Barco Centenera, Hernando Álvarez de Toledo, Gaspar Villagrá, and Melchor Xufré de Ávila (Chevalier, "Los lectores de la epopeya," 219).

13. See Franco, *Historia de la literatura hispanoamericana,* 21.

14. Ercilla, *The Araucaniad,* 57.

15. Arias de Saavedra's manuscript, dating from the beginning of the seventeenth century, was not published until 1862, by Barros Arana.

16. Arias de Saavedra, *Purén indómito,* canto 19.

17. Ibid.

18. See Rodríguez Fernández, introduction to *Purén indómito.*

19. Arias de Saavedra, *Purén indómito,* canto 19.

20. Díaz de Guzmán, *La Argentina,* 85.

21. Ibid., 95–96.

22. Ibid., 96.

23. Ibid., 99.

24. Ibid.

25. Ibid., 101.

26. Ras, *Crónica de la frontera sur,* 27.

27. Gandía, introduction to *La Argentina,* 25.

28. Iglesia and Schvarzman, *Cautivas y misioneros,* 41.

29. Arias de Saavedra, *Purén indómito,* canto 19.

30. Rotker, "*Lucía Miranda:* Negación y violencia del origen," 118.

31. Iglesia and Schvarzman, *Cautivas y misioneros,* 52.

32. *Arauco domado* (Arauco Tamed) was written by Pedro de Oña (1570?–1643?), and published in 1596.

33. See Gutiérrez, *Estudios biográficos y críticos.*

34. See Lichtblau, "El tema de Lucía Miranda en la novela argentina," 23–31.

35. Camamis, *Estudios sobre el cautiverio,* 54.

36. See Domínguez, introduction to *Tres novelas moriscas*.

37. See Bauer, "Imperial History, Captivity, and Creole Identity in Francisco Núñez de Pineda y Bascuñán's *Cautiverio feliz*."

38. The play has not come down to us, although we do have references to the impact its performance had in its day (see Lohmann, *El arte dramático en Lima durante el Virreinato*). Of interest also is the work of Monica L. Lee, in which she looks at the opposite phenomenon, that is to say, the influence of the Araucanian War on the Spanish stage of the Golden Age (see Lee, "De la crónica a la escena").

39. Levernier and Cohen, *The Indians and Their Captives*, 12.

40. VanDerBeets, *Held Captives by Indians*, xix.

41. Levernier and Cohen, *The Indians and Their Captives*, xxviii.

42. Haberly, "Captives and Infidels," 8.

43. See the excellent work of David T. Haberly, "Women and Indians: The Last of the Mohicans and the Captivity Tradition."

44. For a study of the subject in Argentina, see Operé, "Cautivos de los indios, cautivos de la literatura."

45. Echeverría, *La cautiva*, 606.

46. Ibid., 603.

47. Echeverría, "Los cautivos," 976.

48. Hernández, *The Gaucho Martín Fierro*, 168–69.

49. Ibid., 22–23.

50. Declaración, June 23, 1780, AGN, IX, 1-7-4.

51. Mansilla, *Una excursión a los indios ranqueles*, chaps. 27–31.

52. Hernández, *The Gaucho Martín Fierro*, 192–93.

53. Ibid., 196–97.

54. Ibid., 246–47.

55. Ibid., 250–51.

56. See Varela, *Poesías*, 221–36.

57. Hernández, *The Gaucho Martín Fierro*, 274–75, 276–77.

58. Ibid., 278–79.

59. Ibid., 224–25.

60. Barski, *Vigencia del Martín Fierro*, 84.

61. Ibid., 83.

62. Pratt, *Imperial Eyes*.

63. Zeballos, *Painé y la dinastía de los Zorros*, 72.

64. Ibid., 62.

65. Holmberg, *Lin-Calel*, 307–8.

66. Zorrilla de San Martín, *Tabaré*, 2–3. All subsequent Spanish- and English-language quotations from *Tabaré* are from the bilingual edition, translated by Walter Owen.

67. Ibid., 10–11.

68. Ibid., 94–97.

69. Zum Felde, "Tabaré," 429.

70. Zorrilla de San Martín, *Tabaré*, 300–301.

71. Operé, "*Cumandá*," 77–87.

72. Mera, *Cumandá, o un drama entre salvajes*, 54.

73. Ibid., 69.

74. Ibid., 49.

75. Villa Roiz, *Gonzalo Guerrero*, 568. The last chapter of the novel reproduces the 1536 document "Carta de Andrés Cereceda, Gobernador de Honduras, dando cuenta de la muerte de Gonzalo Guerrero" (Letter of Andrés Cereceda, Governor of Honduras, giving an account of the death of Gonzalo Guerrero).

76. Aguirre, *Gonzalo Guerrero*, 224.

77. See Malosetti Costa, *Rapto de cautivas blancas*.

78. Holmberg, *Lin-Calel*, 308.

79. Lugones, *Romances del Río Seco*, 132.

80. Ibid., 138.

81. Ibid., 139.

82. Borges, *Collected Fictions*, 210–11.

83. Ibid.

84. For the Argentine case, see Giardinelli, *El país de las maravillas*, 186–90.

85. Staden's text, *The True History of His Captivity, 1557*, was published in Germany in that year.

86. Chanady, "Saer's Fictional Representation of the Amerindian in the Context of Modern Historiography," 681.

87. Saer, *The Witness*, 146–47.

88. Rotker, "*Lucía Miranda:* Negación y violencia del origen," 17.

89. The captivity of Teofania re-created by Blanco seems to have been inspired by the captivity of Elisa Bravo, who was shipwrecked in 1849 in Chilean Araucania. The episode, reported in the newspapers of the time, had a great reverberation, and it inspired the French painter Raymond Monvoisin, who produced two paintings: *Elisa Bravo in the Shipwreck* and *Elisa Bravo in Captivity*.

Epilogue

1. Weil, introduction to *Wizard of the Upper Amazon*, vi.

2. There were three German editions in 1557, and subsequent ones in 1558 and 1559. The first French edition is from 1559, and the first Flemish edition is from 1558. A Latin edition appeared in 1593, and a Dutch one in 1563, followed by many others. The English and Portuguese editions date from 1874 and 1893, respectively.

3. See Rausch, *The Llanos Frontier in Colombian History*, 9.

4. See Rausch, *A Tropical Plains Frontier*, 44.

Bibliography

Archival Sources

Archivo General de las Indias (AGI), Seville, Spain
Archivo General de la Nación (AGN), Buenos Aires, Argentina
Archivo Histórico de Tucumán (AHT), Argentina

Other Sources

Acevedo, Edverto Oscar. "De intérpretes y cautivos." *Boletín de la Academia Nacional de la Historia* 62–63 (1989–90): 597–605.

Acuerdos del extinguido cabildo de Buenos Aires, vol. 1, bk. 1. Buenos Aires: Talleres de la Penitenciaría Nacional, 1907.

Adorno, Rolena. "The Negotiation of Fear in Cabeza de Vaca's *Naufragios.*" In *New World Encounters,* edited by Stephen Greenblatt. Berkeley: University of California Press, 1993.

Aguirre, Eugenio. *Gonzalo Guerrero.* Mexico City: Editorial Diana, 1991.

Aira, César. *Ema, la cautiva.* Buenos Aires: Editorial de Belgrano, 1981.

Alborg, Juan Luis. Introduction to *Tres años de esclavitud entre los patagones: Relato de mi cautiverio,* by Augusto Guinnard. Madrid: Espasa Calpe, 1941.

Alonso, Carlos J. "Civilización y barbarie." *Hispania* 72, no. 2 (1989): 256–63.

Alvarez, Gregorio. *Pehuén Mapu: Tierra de la Araucaria: Tragedia esotérica del Neuquén.* Buenos Aires: Editorial Pehuén, 1954.

Anadón, José. *Pineda y Bascuñán, defensor del araucano: Vida y escritos de un criollo chileno del siglo XVII.* Santiago: Editorial Universitaria, 1977.

Andrien, Kenneth J. "The *Noticias secretas de América* and the Construction of a Governing Ideology for the Spanish Empire." *Colonial Latin American Review* 7, no. 2 (1998): 175–92.

Angelis, Pedro de, comp. *Colección de obras y documentos relativos a la historia antigua y moderna de las Provincias del Río de la Plata.* 8 vols. Buenos Aires: Editorial Plus Ultras, 1969–72.

Arcos, Santiago. *Cuestión de indios.* N.p., 1979.

Arias de Saavedra, Diego. *Purén indómito* [Purén Untamed]. Edited by Mario Rodríguez Fernández. Concepción: Universidad de Concepción, 1984.

Armond, Louis de. "Frontier Warfare in Colonial Chile." In *Where Cultures Meet: Fron-*

tiers in Latin America History, edited by David J. Weber and Jane M. Rausch. Wilmington, DE: Scholarly Review Books, 1994.

Ascasubi, Hilario. *Paulino Lucero. Aniceto el Gallo. Santos Vega.* Edited by Jorge Luis Borges. Buenos Aires: Editorial Universitaria de Buenos Aires, 1969.

Avendaño, Santiago. "La fuga de un cautivo de los Indios: Narrada por el mismo." In *Cuestión de indios.* N.p.: Policía Federal Argentina, 1979.

———. *Memorias del ex-cautivo Santiago Avendaño, 1834–1874.* Edited by P. Meinrado Hux. Buenos Aires: Elefante Blanco, 1999.

———. "Muerte del cacique Painé." In *Cuestión de indios.* N.p.: Policía Federal Argentina, 1979.

Axtell, James. *The European and the Indian: Essays in the Ethnohistory of Colonial North America.* New York: Oxford University Press, 1982.

Azara, Félix de. "Diario de un reconocimiento de las guardias y fortines que guarnecen la línea de frontera de Buenos Aires para ensancharla." In vol. 8A of *Colección de obras y documentos relativos a la historia antigua y moderna de las Provincias del Río de la Plata,* compiled by Pedro de Angelis. Buenos Aires: Editorial Plus Ultras, 1972.

Baigorria, Manuel. *Memorias.* Buenos Aires: Solar/Hachette, 1975.

Bannon, John Francis. *The Spanish Borderlands Frontier, 1513–1821.* Albuquerque: University of New Mexico Press, 1974.

Barros, Álvaro. *Fronteras y territorios federales de las Pampas del Sur.* Buenos Aires: Librería Hachette, 1975.

Barski, León. *Vigencia del Martín Fierro.* Buenos Aires: Editorial Boedo, 1977.

Baudot, George. *Utopía e historia en México: Los primeros cronistas de la civilización mexicana (1520–1569).* Madrid: Espasa-Calpe, 1983.

Bauer, Ralph. "Imperial History, Captivity, and Creole Identity in Francisco Núñez de Pineda y Bascuñán's *Cautiverio feliz.*" *Colonial Latin American Review* 7, no. 1 (1998): 59–82.

Beltrán, María Luz. "La organización de los parlamentos de indios en el siglo XVIII." In *Relaciones fronterizas en la Araucanía.* Santiago: Ediciones Universidad Católica de Chile, 1982.

Bengoa, José. *Historia del pueblo mapuche: Siglos XIX y XX.* Santiago: Ediciones Sur, 1985.

Biocca, Ettore. *Yanomama: The Narrative of a White Girl Kipnapped by Amazonian Indians.* Translated by Dennis Rhodes. New York: E. P. Dutton, 1970.

Blanco, C. M. *Salvaje: Novela argentina.* Buenos Aires: Casa Editora Franco-Española, 1891.

Borges, Jorge Luis. "El cautivo." In *El hacedor.* Madrid: Alianza Editorial, 1972.

———. *Collected Fictions.* Translated by Andrew Hurley. New York: Penguin Books, 1998.

———. "Historia del guerrero y la cautiva." In *El Aleph.* Madrid: Alianza Editorial, 1972.

Bourne, Benjamin Franklin. *The Captive in Patagonia; or, Life among the Giants: A Personal Narrative.* Boston: D. Lothrop Company, 1880.

Brooks, James F. "Captives and Cousins: Violence, Kinship, and Community in the New Mexico Borderlands, 1660–1880." Ph.D. diss., University of California at Davis, 1995.

————. Introduction to *Andele: The Mexican-Kiowa Captive*, by J. J. Methvin. Albuquerque: University of New Mexico Press, 1996.

Burns, E. Braford. *The Poverty of Progress: Latin America in the Nineteenth Century.* Berkeley: University of California Press, 1980.

Cabeza de Vaca, Alvar Núñez. *Naufragios y comentarios.* Edited by Roberto Ferrando. Madrid: Historia 16, 1984.

Camamis, George. *Estudios sobre el cautiverio en el Siglo de Oro.* Madrid: Editorial Gredos, 1977.

Carreño, Antonio. "*Naufragios,* de Alvar Núñez Cabeza de Vaca: Una retórica de la crónica colonial." *Revista Iberoamericana* 53, no. 140 (1987): 499–516.

Caruth, Cathy. *Unclaimed Experience: Trauma, Narrative, and History.* Baltimore: John Hopkins University Press, 1996.

Chagnon, Napoleon A. *Yanomamö: The Fierce People.* New York: Holt, Rinehart, and Winston, 1983.

Chanady, Amaryll. "Saer's Fictional Representation of the Amerindian in the Context of Modern Historiography." In *Amerindian Images and the Legacy of Columbus,* edited by René Jara and Nicholas Spadaccini. Minneapolis: University of Minnesota Press, 1992.

Chang-Rodríguez, Raquel. *Violencia y subversión en la prosa colonial hispanoamericana, siglos XVI y XVII.* Madrid: Ediciones José Porrúa, 1982.

Chevalier, Maxime. "Los lectores de la epopeya en los siglos XVI y XVII." In *Historia y crítica de la literatura hispanoamericana: Época colonial,* edited by Cedomil Góic. Barcelona: Editorial Crítica, 1988.

Chipman, Donald E. "In Search of Cabeza de Vaca's Route Across Texas: An Historiographical Survey." *Southern Historical Quarterly* 91 (1987): 127–48.

Clendinnen, Inga. *Ambivalent Conquests: Maya and Spaniard in Yucatan, 1517–1570.* New York: Cambridge University Press, 1987.

Cocco, Luis. *Iyëwei-theri: Quince años entre los Yanomamös.* Caracas: Librería Editorial Salesiana, 1972.

Colón, Hernando. *Historia del Almirante.* Edited by Luis Arranz. Madrid: Historia 16, 1985.

Coña, Pascual. *Testimonio de un cacique mapuche.* Santiago: Pehuén Editores, 1973.

Correa Bello, Sergio. *El cautiverio feliz en la vida política chilena del siglo XVII.* Santiago: Editorial Andrés Bello, 1965.

Cortázar, Augusto Raúl. *Indios y gauchos en la literatura argentina.* Buenos Aires: Instituto de Amigos del Libro Argentino, 1956.

Cortés, Hernán. *Cartas de relación de la conquista de México.* Madrid: Espasa-Calpe, 1970.

Cortés, José. *Views from the Apache Frontier: Report on the Northern Provinces of New*

Spain. Edited by Elizabeth A. H. John; translated by John Wheat. Norman: University of Oklahoma Press, 1989.

Corwin, Hugh D., ed. *The Kiowa Indians: Their History and Life Stories.* Lawton, OK, 1958.

Cruz, Luis de la. "Viaje a su costa del alcalde provicional del Ilustre Cabildo de la Concepción de Chile." In vol. 2 of *Colección de obras y documentos relativos a la historia antigua y moderna de las Provincias del Río de la Plata,* edited by Pedro de Angelis. Buenos Aires: Editorial Plus Ultras, 1972.

Cutler, Lee. "Lawrie Tatum and the Kiowas Agency, 1869–1873." *Arizona and the West* 13, no. 3 (1971): 221–44.

Demos, John. *The Unredeemed Captive: A Family Story from Early America.* New York: Alfred A. Knopf, 1994.

Derounian-Stodola, Kathryn Zabelle. *Women's Indian Captivity Narratives.* New York: Penguin Books, 1998.

Díaz de Guzmán, Ruy. *La Argentina.* Edited by Enrique de Gandía. Madrid: Historia 16, 1986.

———. *Relación de la entrada a los Chiriguanos.* Edited by Ch. de Crozefon. Santa Cruz de la Sierra: Fundación Cultural Ramón Darío Gutiérrez, 1979.

Díaz del Castillo, Bernal. *Historia verdadera de la conquista de Nueva España.* Edited by Joaquín Ramírez Cabañas. Mexico City: Editorial Porrúa, 1974.

Domínguez, Ivo. Introduction to *Tres novelas moriscas.* Montevideo: Instituto de Estudios Superiores, 1975.

———, ed. *Tres novelas moriscas.* Montevideo: Instituto de Estudios Superiores, 1975.

Donner, Florinda. *Shabono.* New York: Delacorte Press, 1982.

Doucet, Gaston Gabriel. "Sobre cautivos de guerra y esclavos indios en el Tucumán: Notas en torno a un fichero documental salteño del siglo XVIII." *Revista de Historia del Derecho* 16 (1988): 59–152.

Durand, José. "La redacción de *La Florida del Inca:* Cronología." *Revista de Historia* (Lima) 21 (1954): 288–302.

Dutton, Bertha P. *American Indians of the Southwest.* Albuquerque: University of New Mexico Press, 1983.

Eagleton, Terry. *Literary Theory: An Introduction.* Minneapolis: University of Minnesota Press, 1985.

Ebélot, Alfred. *Relatos de la frontera.* Edited by Alicia D. Carrera. Buenos Aires: Editorial Solar/Hachette, 1968.

Ebersole, Gary L. *Captured by Texts: Puritan to Postmodern Images of Indian Captivity.* Charlottesville: University Press of Virginia, 1995.

Echeverría, Esteban. *La cautiva.* In *Obras completas,* edited by José P. Barreiro. Buenos Aires: Antonio Zamora, 1951.

——— "Los cautivos." In *Obras completas,* edited by José P. Barreiro. Buenos Aires: Antonio Zamora, 1951.

Ercilla, Alonso de. *La Araucana.* Edited by Marcos A. Morínigo and Isaías Lerner. 2 vols. Madrid: Clásicos Castalia, 1983.

——— *The Araucaniad.* Translated by Maxwell Lancaster and Paul Thomas Manchester. Nashville: Vanderbilt University Press, 1945.

Escalante Fontaneda, Hernando de. *Memoir of D. d'Escalante Fontaneda respecting Florida.* Translated from the Spanish with notes by Buckingham Smith, Washington, 1854; edited by David O. True. Coral Gables, FL: Glade House, 1945.

Espinosa, Manuel. *Crusaders of the Río Grande: The Story of Don Diego de Vargas and the Reconquest and Refounding of New Mexico.* Salisbury, NC: Documentary Publications, 1977.

Falkner, Thomas. *A Description of Patagonia and the Adjoining Parts of South America.* Edited by Arthur E. S. Neumann. Chicago: Armann and Armann, 1935.

Fergusson, Brian. *Yanomami Warfare: A Political History.* Santa Fe: School of American Research Press, 1995.

Fernández de Oviedo, Gonzalo. *Historia general y natural de las Indias* [A General and Natural History of the Indies]. Edited by Juan Pérez de Tudela Bueso. 5 vols. Madrid: Atlas, 1959.

Fernández Retamar, Roberto. "Algunos usos de civilización y barbarie." *Casa de las Américas* 17, no. 102 (1977): 29–52.

Ferrando, Roberto, ed. Introduction to *Naufragios y comentarios,* by Alvar Núñez Cabeza de Vaca. Madrid: Historia 16, 1984.

Fitte, Ernesto J., and Julio A. Benencia, eds. *Juan Manuel de Rosas y la redención de cautivos en su campaña del desierto (1833–1834).* Buenos Aires: Academia Nacional de la Historia, 1979.

Fitzpatrick, Tara. "The Figure of Captivity: The Cultural Work of the Puritan Captivity Narrative." *American Literary History* 3, no. 1 (1991): 1–26.

Franco, Jean. *Historia de la literatura hispanoamericana.* Madrid: Editorial Ariel, 1985.

Fuentes, Emilio. Introduction to *Yo soy Napëyoma: Relato de una mujer raptada por los indígenas yanomami,* by Helena Valero, edited by Emilio Fuentes. Caracas: Fundación La Salle de Ciencias Naturales, 1984.

Gandía, Enrique de. *Historia crítica de los mitos de la conquista americana.* Buenos Aires: Juan Roldán y Cia., 1929.

———. Introduction to *La Argentina,* by Ruy Díaz de Guzmán. Madrid: Historia 16, 1986.

Garasa, Delfín Leocadio. "Una literatura de Frontera." *Logos: Revista de la Facultad de Filosofía y Letras* 15 (1979): 253–70.

García, Pedro Andrés. "Diario de la expedición de 1822 a los campos del sur de Buenos Aires desde Morón hasta la Sierra de la Ventana." In vol. 4 of *Colección de obras y documentos relativos a la historia antigua y moderna de las Provincias del Río de la Plata,* compiled by Pedro de Angelis. Buenos Aires: Editorial Plus Ultras, 1972.

Garrote Bernal, G. "El *Cautiverio feliz* de Núñez de Pineda y Bascuñán, entre la crónica de Indias y la doctrina político-moral." *Analecta Malacitana* 13, no. 1 (1990): 49–68.

Geiger, Maynard. Bibliographical introduction to *The Martyrs of Florida (1513–1616),* by Luis Gerónimo de Oré. Edited and translated by Maynard Geiger. New York: Joseph F. Wagner, 1936.

Giardinelli, Mempo. *El país de las maravillas: Los argentinos en el fin del milenio.* Buenos Aires: Editorial Planeta, 1998.

Gibson, Charles. *Tlaxcala in the Sixteenth Century.* Stanford: Stanford University Press, 1967.

Gil, Juan. *Mitos y utopías del descubrimiento.* 3 vols. Madrid: Alianza Editorial, 1992.

Góic, Cedomil, ed. *Historia y crítica de la literatura hispanoamericana: De romanticismo al modernismo.* 2 vols. Barcelona: Editorial Crítica, 1988.

Góngora, Mario. "Vagabundaje y sociedad fronteriza en Chile (Siglos XVII a XIX)." In *Estudios de historia de las ideas y de historia social.* Valparaiso: Ediciones Universitarias de Valparaíso, 1980.

Góngora y Marmolejo, Alonso de. *Historia de todas las cosas que han acaecido en el Reino de Chile y de los que lo han gobernado (1536–1575)* [A History of All the Things that Have Happened in the Kingdom of Chile and of Those Who Have Governed]. Edited by Alamiro de Avila Martel and Lucía Invernizzi Santa Cruz. Santiago: Ediciones de la Universidad de Chile, 1990.

González Arili, Bernardo. *Los indios pampas: Bandoleros a medio vestir.* Buenos Aires: Editorial Stilcograf, 1960.

González de Nájera, Alonso. *Desengaño y reparo de la Guerra del Reino de Chile* [The Detection of Errors and Reflections on the War in the Kingdom of Chile]. Santiago: Editorial Andrés Bello, 1971.

Green, A. C., ed. *The Last Captive.* Austin: Encino Press, 1972.

Griffen, William B. *Apaches at War and Peace: The Janos Presidio, 1750–1858.* Albuquerque: University of New Mexico Press, 1988.

Guarda Geywitz, Gabriel. "Los caciques gobernadores de Toltén." *Boletín de la Academia Chilena de Historia* 35, no. 78 (1968): 40–56.

———. "Los cautivos en la guerra de Arauco." In *Visión de los otros y visión de sí mismos: ¿Descubrimiento o invención entre el Nuevo Mundo y el Viejo?* Madrid: Consejo Superior de Investigaciones Científicas, 1995.

Guerra, Rosa. *Lucía Miranda.* Buenos Aires: Editora Universidad de Buenos Aires, 1956.

Guinnard, Auguste. *Three Years' Slavery among the Patagonians: An Account of His Captivity.* Translated from the 3rd French edition by Charles S. Cheltnam. London: R. Bentley and Son, 1871.

———. *Tres años de esclavitud entre los patagones: Relato de mi cautiverio.* Edited by Juan Luis Alborg. Madrid: Espasa Calpe, 1941.

Gutiérrez, Juan María. *Estudios biográficos y críticos.* Buenos Aires: Imprenta del Siglo, 1865.

Guy, Donna J., and Thomas E. Sheridan, eds. *Contested Ground: Comparative Frontiers on the Northern and Southern Edges of the Spanish Empire.* Tucson: University of Arizona Press, 1998.

Haberly, David T. "Captives and Infidels: The Figure of the *Cautiva* in Argentine Literature." *American Hispanist* 4, vol. 12 (1978): 7–16.

———. "Women and Indians: *The Last of the Mohicans* and the Captivity Tradition." *American Quarterly* 28, no. 4 (1976): 430–43.

Hall, Thomas D. "The Río de la Plata and the Greater Southwest: A View from World-System Theory." In *Contested Ground: Comparative Frontiers on the Northern and Southern Edges of the Spanish Empire*, edited by Donna J. Guy and Thomas E. Sheridan. Tucson: University of Arizona Press, 1998.

Hanisch Espíndola, Walter. "Esclavitud y libertad de los indios de Chile, 1608–1696." *Historia* 16 (1981): 5–65.

Harris, Marvin. "The Yanomamö and the Causes of War in Band and Village Societies." In *Brazil, Anthropological Perspectives: Essays in Honor of Charles Wagley*, edited by Maxine L. Margolies and William E. Carter. New York: Columbia University Press, 1979.

Heard, Norman J. *White into Red: A Study of the Assimilation of White Persons Captured by Indians.* Metuchen, NJ: Scarecrow Press, 1973.

Hennessy, Alistair. *The Frontier in Latin American History.* London: Edward Arnold, 1978.

Hernández, José. *The Gaucho Martín Fierro.* Bilingual ed. English version by C. E. Ward; annotated and revised by Frank G. Carrino and Alberto J. Carlos. New York: State University of New York Press, 1967.

———. *Martín Fierro.* Edited by Eleuterio F. Tiscornia. Buenos Aires: Editorial Losada, 1976.

Hernández, Juan Antonio. "Diario que el capitán D. Juan Antonio Hernández ha hecho, de la expedición contra los indios teguelches, en el gobierno del señor D. Juan José Vértiz gobernador y capitán general de las provincias del Río de la Plata, en 1 de octubre de 1777." In vol. 4 of *Colección de obras y documentos relativos a la historia antigua y moderna de las Provincias del Río de la Plata*, compiled by Pedro de Angelis. Buenos Aires: Editorial Plus Ultras, 1972.

Hernández Cornejo, Juan Adrián. "Diario de la primera expedición al Chaco emprendida en 1780." In vol. 7 of *Colección de obras y documentos relativos a la historia antigua y moderna de las Provincias del Río de la Plata*, compiled by Pedro de Angelis. Buenos Aires: Editorial Plus Ultras, 1972.

Herren, Ricardo. *Doña Marina, La Malinche.* Barcelona: Editorial Planeta, 1992.

———. *Indios carapálidas.* Barcelona: Editorial Planeta, 1992.

Hilton, Sylvia. Introduction to *La Florida del Inca,* by Garcilaso de la Vega. Madrid: Historia 16, 1986.

Holmberg, Eduardo Ladislao. *Lin-Calel.* Buenos Aires: L. J. Rosso y Cía., 1910.

Holmes, Rebecca B. de. "Shabono: Scandal or Superb Social Science?" *American Anthropologist* 85 (1983): 664–65.

Howard, David A. *Conquistador in Chains: Cabeza de Vaca and the Indians of the Americas.* Tuscaloosa: University of Alabama Press, 1997.

Hudson, Charles. *Knights of Spain, Warriors of the Sun: Hernando de Soto and the South's Ancient Chiefdoms*. Athens: University of Georgia Press, 1997.

Hux, Meinrado. *Coliqueo: El indio amigo de los Toldos*. Buenos Aires: Eudeba, 1980.

Iglesia, Cristina, and Julio Schvartzman. *Cautivas y misioneros: Mitos blancos de la conquista*. Buenos Aires: Catálogos Editora, 1987.

Jara, Álvaro. *Guerra y sociedad en Chile: La transformación de la guerra de Arauco y la esclavitud de los indios*. Santiago: Editorial Universitaria, 1971.

Jara, René, and Hernán Vidal, eds. *Testimonio y literatura*. Minneapolis: Institute for the Study of Ideologies and Literature, 1986.

Johnson, Julie Greer. *Satire in Colonial Spanish America: Turning the New World Upside Down*. Austin: University of Texas Press, 1993.

Jones, Kristine J. "Calfucurá y Namuncurá: Nation Builders of the Pampas." In *The Human Tradition in Latin America: The Nineteenth Century*, edited by Judith Ewell and William H. Beezley. Wilmington, DE: SR Books, 1989.

———. "*La cautiva:* An Argentine Solution to Labor Shortage in the Pampas." In *Brazil and the Rio de la Plata: Challenge and Response*, edited by Luis Felipe Clay Méndez and Lawrence W. Bates. Proceedings of the Sixth Annual Conference of the Illinois Conference of Latin Americanists. N.p., 1983.

———. "Conflict and Adaptation in the Argentine Pampas, 1750–1880." Ph.D. diss., University of Chicago, June 1984.

———. "Comparative Raiding Economies, North and South." In *Contested Ground: Comparative Frontiers on the Northern and Southern Edges of the Spanish Empire*, edited by Donna J. Guy and Thomas E. Sheridan. Tucson: University of Arizona Press, 1998.

Jones, Oakah L. *Nueva Vizcaya: Heartland of the Spanish Frontier*. Albuquerque: University of New Mexico Press, 1988.

———. "Rescue and Ransom of Spanish Captives from the *Indios Bárbaros* on the Northern Frontier of New Spain." *Colonial American Historical Review* (Spring 1995): 129–48.

Kelly, Fanny. *Narrative of My Captivity among the Sioux Indians*. Edited by Clark and Mary Lee Spence. Stanford: Longmeadow Press, 1990.

Kenner, Charles J. *History of New Mexican–Plains Indian Relations*. Norman: University of Oklahoma Press, 1969.

Kestler, Frances Roe, ed. *The Indian Captivity Narrative: A Woman's View*. New York: Garland Publishing, 1990.

Kicza, John E., ed. *The Indian in Latin American History: Resistance, Resilience, and Acculturation*. Wilmington, DE: Scholarly Resources, 1993.

Krieger Alex, D. "The Travels of Álvar Núñez Cabeza de Vaca in Texas and Mexico, 1534–1536." In *Homenaje a Pablo Martínez del Río en el vigésimo aniversario de la primera edición de "Los orígenes americanos."* Mexico City: Instituto Nacional de Antropología e Historia, 1961.

Lagmanovich, David, "Los naufragios de Álvar Núñez como construcción narrativa." *Kentucky Romance Quarterly* 25, no. 1 (1978): 27–37.

Lamb, Bruce F. *Wizard of the Upper Amazon: The Story of Manuel Córdova-Ríos*. Berkeley: North Atlantic Books, 1974.

Lancaster, Maxwell. "The Happy Captivity of Francisco Núñez de Pineda y Bascuñán." *Valderbilt Studies in Humanities* 1 (1951): 161–73.

Landa, Diego de. *Relación de las cosas del Yucatán*. Edited by Miguel Rivera. Madrid: Historia 16, 1985.

Lázaro Avila, Carlos. "Los cautivos en la frontera araucana." *Revista Española de Antropología Americana* 24 (1994): 191–207.

———. "Las visiones condicionadas de Falcón y Pineda: Dos cautivos europeos ante la sociedad araucana." In *Visión de los otros, visión de sí mismos: ¿Descubrimiento o invención entre el Nuevo Mundo y el Viejo?* edited by Fermín del Pino and Carlos Lázaro. Madrid: Consejo Superior de Investigaciones Científicas, 1995.

Lee, Mónica L. "De la crónica a la escena: Arauco en el teatro del Siglo de Oro." Ph.D diss., University of British Columbia, 1993.

Leiva, Arturo. *El primer avance a la Araucanía: Angol, 1982*. Santiago: Ediciones Universidad de la Frontera, 1984.

León Solís, Leandro. "La corona española y las guerras intestinas entre los indígenas de Araucania, Patagonia y las Pampas, 1760–1806." *Nueva Historia* 2, no. 5 (1982): 31–67.

———. "Las invasiones indígenas contra las localidades fronterizas de Buenos Aires, Cuyo y Chile, 1700–1800." *Boletín Americanista* 36 (1986): 75–104.

———. *Maloqueros y conchavadores en Araucanía y las Pampas, 1700–1800*. Temuco: Ediciones Universidad de la Frontera, 1991.

Levernier, James, and Hennig Cohen, eds. *The Indians and Their Captives*. Westport, CT: Greenwood Press, 1977.

Letts, Malcolm. Introduction to *The True History of His Captivity, 1557*, by Hans Staden. New York: Robert M. McBride and Co., 1929.

Lichtblau, Myron I. "El tema de Lucía Miranda en la novela argentina." *Armas y Letras* 2 (1959): 23–31.

Lizot, Jacques. *Tales of the Yanomami: Daily Life in the Venezuelan Forest*. Cambridge: Cambridge University Press, 1985.

———. "Poisons yanomami de chasse, de guerre et de peche." *Antropologica* 31 (1972): 3–20.

Lohman, Guillermo. *El arte dramático en Lima durante el Virreinato*. Madrid: Estades, 1945.

López de Gómara, Francisco. *La conquista de México*. Edited by José Luis de Rojas. Madrid: Historia 16, 1987.

Lozano, Pedro. *Copia de carta escrita por un misionero de la Compañía de Jesús del Paraguay, al Padre Juan Joseph Rico, Procurador del General de dicha Provincia, y sus misiones, assi antiguas, como nuevas, entre Christianos y Gentiles*. Córdoba, 1740.

Lugones, Leopoldo. *Romances del Río Seco*. Córdoba: Alción Editora, 1984.

Lullo, Orestes di. *Reducciones y fortines*. Santiago del Estero, 1949.

Lyon, Eugene. *The Enterprise of Florida: Pedro Menéndez de Avilés and the Spanish Conquest of 1565–1568.* Gainesville: University of Florida Press, 1976.

Malosetti Costa, Laura. *Rapto de cautivas blancas: Un aspecto erótico de la barbarie en la plástica rioplatense del siglo XIX.* Buenos Aires: Universidad de Buenos Aires, Facultad de Filosofía y Letras, 1994.

Mandrini, Raúl. *Los araucanos de las pampas en el siglo XIX.* Buenos Aires: Centro Editor de América Latina, 1984.

Mansilla, Lucio V. *Una excursión a los indios ranqueles.* Edited by Saúl Sosnowski. Caracas: Biblioteca Ayacucho, 1984.

Mansilla de García, Eduarda. *Lucía Miranda.* Buenos Aires: J. C. Rovira, 1933.

Mantegazza, Pablo. *Viajes por el Río de la Plata y el interior de la Confederación Argentina.* Buenos Aires: Casa Editora Coni Hermanos, 1916.

Mariño de Lobera, Pedro. *Crónica del Reino de Chile.* Madrid: Atlas, 1960.

Martínez Estrada, Ezequiel. *Radiografía de la Pampa.* Edited by Leo Pollman. Buenos Aires: Colección Archivos, 1993.

Martínez Sarasola, Carlos. *Nuestros paisanos los indios: Vida, historia y destino de las comunidades indígenas en la Argentina.* Buenos Aires: Emecé Editores, 1992.

Mayo, Carlos A. "El cautiverio y sus funciones en una sociedad de frontera: El caso de Buenos Aires (1750–1810)." *Revista de Indias* 45, no. 175 (1985): 235–43.

———. *Estancia y sociedad en la Pampa, 1740–1820.* Buenos Aires: Editorial Biblos, 1995.

———, ed. *Fuentes para la historia de la frontera: Declaraciones de cautivos.* Mar del Plata: Universidad Nacional del Mar del Plata, 1985.

Mayo, Carlos A., and Amalia Latrubesse. *Terratenientes, soldados y cautivos: La frontera (1736–1815).* Mar del Plata: Universidad Nacional del Mar del Plata, 1986.

McNitt, Frank. *Navajo Wars: Military Campaigns, Slave Raids, and Reprisals.* Albuquerque: University of New Mexico Press, 1972.

Mera, Juan León. *Cumandá, o un drama entre salvajes.* Madrid: Espasa-Calpe, 1976.

Methvin, J. J. *Andele: The Mexican-Kiowa Captive.* Edited by James F. Brooks. Albuquerque: University of New Mexico Press, 1996.

Mitre, Bartolomé. *Soledad.* La Paz: Ediciones Camarlinghi, 1968.

Molloy, Sylvia. "Alteridad y reconocimiento en los *Naufragios* de Álvar Núñez Cabeza de Vaca." *Nueva Revista de Filología Hispánica* 35, no. 2 (1987): 425–49.

———. *At Face Value: Autobiographical Writing in Spanish America.* Cambridge: Cambridge University Press, 1991.

Montagne, Víctor. *Cuentos cuyanos.* Buenos Aires: Agencia General de Librería y Publicaciones, n.d.

Mora, Carmen, ed. *Las siete ciudades de Cíbola: Textos y testimonios sobre la expedición de Vázquez de Coronado.* Seville: Ediciones Alfar, 1992.

Moriñigo, Marcos A., and Isaías Lerner. Introduction to *La Araucana,* by Alonso de Ercilla. Madrid: Clásicos Castalia, 1983.

Musters, George Chaworth. *Vida entre los patagones: Un año de excursiones por tierras no frecuentadas desde el estrecho de Magallanes hasta el Río Negro.* Edited by Raúl Rey Balmaceda. Buenos Aires: Ediciones Solar/Hachette, 1964.

Namias, June, ed. *White Captives.* Chapel Hill: University of North Carolina Press, 1993.

"Noticias de Juan de Candelaria de esta villa de San Francisco de Albuquerque de edad de 84 años nació el año 1692." *New Mexico Historical Review* 4, no. 3 (1929): 273–97.

Noyes, Stanley. *Los Comanches: The Horse People, 1751–1845.* Albuquerque: University of New Mexico Press, 1993.

Núñez de Pineda y Bascuñán, Francisco. *Cautiverio feliz y razón individual de las guerras dilatadas del Reino de Chile.* Edited by Alejandro Lipschutz and Alvaro Jara. Santiago de Chile: Editorial Universitaria, 1973.

Oatman, Lorenzo D., and Olive A. Oatman. *The Captivity of the Oatman Girls among the Apache and Mohave Indians.* Edited by Lindley Bynum. New York: Dover Publications, 1994.

Ollier, María Matilde, and Leandro de Segastizábal. *Tu nombre en mi boca: Historias argentinas de la pasión y del amor.* Buenos Aires: Editorial Planeta, 1994.

Oña, Pedro de. *Arauco domado* [Arauco Tamed]. Obra impresa en Lima, por Antonio Ricardo de Turin en 1596, y ahora editada en facsímil. Madrid: Ediciones Culturas Hispánicas, 1944.

Operé, Fernando, ed. *Cautivos.* Buenos Aires: Ediciones del Instituto Movilizador de Fondos Cooperativos, 1997.

———. "Cautivos de los indios, cautivos de la literatura: El caso del Río de la Plata." *Hispamérica* 26, no. 76–77 (1997): 49–76.

———. "*Cumandá:* La novela ecuatoriana entre la cruz y la espada." *Crítica Hispánica* 20, no. 1–2 (1998): 77–87.

———. "El discurso natural y moral en Hispanoamérica: De la Colonia a la Independencia." *Letras de Deusto* 27, no. 70 (1996): 145–67.

Oré, Luis Gerónimo de. *The Martyrs of Florida (1513–1616).* Edited and translated by Maynard Geiger. New York: Joseph F. Wagner, 1936.

Padden, Robert C. "Cultural Adaptation and Militant Autonomy among the Araucanians of Chile." In *The Indian in Latin American History: Resistance, Resilience, and Acculturation,* edited by John E. Kicza. Wilmington, DE: Scholarly Resources, 1993.

Pagden, Anthony. *European Encounters with the New World.* New Haven, CT: Yale University Press, 1993.

———. *The Fall of Natural Man: The American Indian and the Origins of Comparative Ethnology.* Cambridge: Cambridge University Press, 1986.

Pastor, Beatriz. *Discursos narrativos de la conquista: Mitificación y emergencia.* Hanover, NH: Ediciones del Norte, 1988.

Pearce, Roy Harvey. "The Significances of Captivity Narrative." *American Literature* 19 (1947): 1–20.

Picón-Salas, Mariano. *De la conquista a la independencia.* Mexico City: Fondo de Cultura Económica, 1980.

Pigafetta, Antonio. *Primer viaje alrededor del mundo.* Edited by Leoncio Cabrero. Madrid: Historia 16, 1985.

Pilkington, William T. "The Journey of Cabeza de Vaca: An American Prototype." *South Dakota Review* 6 (1980): 73–82.

Pinto Rodríguez, Jorge. "Frontera, misiones y misioneros en Chile y la Araucanía (1600–1900)." In *Misioneros en la Araucanía, 1600–1900,* edited by Jorge Pinto Rodríguez. Temuco: Universidad de la Frontera, 1988.

———, ed. *Misioneros en la Araucanía, 1600–1900.* Temuco: Universidad de la Frontera, 1988.

Portas, Julio Aníbal. *Malón contra malón: La solución final del problema del indio en la Argentina.* Buenos Aires: Ediciones de la Flor, 1967.

Posse, Abel. *El largo atardecer del caminante.* Buenos Aires: Emecé Editores, 1992.

Powell, Philip W. *La guerra chichimeca (1550–1600).* Mexico City: Fondo de Cultura Económica, 1996.

———. *Soldiers, Indians, and Silver: The Northward Advance of New Spain, 1550–1600.* Berkeley: University of California Press, 1969.

Pratt, Mary Louise. "Field Work in Common Places." In *Writing Culture: The Poetics and Politics of Ethnography,* edited by James Clifford and George E. Marcus. Berkeley: University of California Press, 1986.

———. *Imperial Eyes: Travel Writing and Transculturation.* New York: Routledge, 1997.

Puiggrós, Rodolfo. *De la colonia a la revolución.* Buenos Aires: Ediciones Cepe, 1974.

Pupo-Walker, Enrique. "Los Naufragios de Álvar Núñez Cabeza de Vaca: Notas sobre la relevancia antropológica del texto." *Revista de Indias* 474 (1987): 755–76.

———. "Pesquisas para una nueva lectura de los Naufragios, de Álvar Núñez Cabeza de Vaca." *Revista Iberoamericana* 53, no. 140 (1987): 517–39.

———. *La vocación literaria del pensamiento histórico en América: Desarrollo de la prosa de ficción: Siglos XVI, XVII, XVIII y XIX.* Madrid: Editorial Gredos, 1982.

Ras, Norberto. *Crónica de la frontera sur.* Buenos Aires: Editorial Hemisferio Sur, 1994.

Rausch, Jane M. *The Llanos Frontier in Colombian History, 1830–1930.* Albuquerque: University of New Mexico Press, 1993.

———. *A Tropical Plains Frontier: The Llanos of Colombia, 1531–1831.* Albuquerque: University of New Mexico Press, 1984.

Ricklis, Robert A. *The Karankawa Indians of Texas: An Ecological Study of Cultural Tradition and Change.* Austin: University of Texas Press, 1996.

Riley, Glenda. *Women and Indians on the Frontier, 1825–1925.* Albuquerque: University of New Mexico Press, 1984.

Riobó, Carlos. "Cuerpos y voces de cautivos: Los espacios discursivos en el corpus argentino." *Romance Quarterly* 46, no. 2 (1999): 112–23.

Rister, Carl Coke. *Border Captives: The Traffic in Prisoners by Southern Plains Indians, 1835–1875.* Norman: University of Oklahoma Press, 1940.

Rodríguez Fernández, Mario. Introduction to *Purén indómito*, by Diego Arias de Saavedra. Concepción: Universidad de Concepción, 1984.

Rosales, Diego de. *Historia general de el Reino de Chile, Flandes Indiano*. Edited by Alfonso Calderón. Santiago: Editorial Universitaria, 1969.

Rosas, Juan Manuel de. "Diario de la comisión nombrada para establecer la nueva línea de frontera al sur de Buenos Aires bajo la dirección del Señor Coronel Juan Manuel de Rosas con las observaciones astronómicas practicadas por el Señor Senillosa miembro de la commission." In vol. 8A of *Colección de obras y documentos relativos a la historia antigua y moderna de las Provincias del Río de la Plata*, compiled by Pedro de Angelis. Buenos Aires: Editorial Plus Ultras, 1972.

Rotker, Susana. "*Lucía Miranda:* Negación y violencia del origen." *Revista Iberoamericana* 63, no. 178–79 (1997): 115–27.

Sáenz, Jimena. "Las cautivas." *Todo Es Historia* 36 (1970): 75–83.

Saer, Juan José. *El entenado*. Buenos Aires: Alianza Editorial, 1992.

———. *The Witness*. Translated by Margaret Jull Costa. London: Serpent's Tail, 1990.

Sahagún, Bernardino de. *Historia general de las cosas de Nueva España*. 2 vols. Madrid: Alianza Universitaria, 1988.

Saignes, Thierry. "La guerra 'salvaje' en los confines de los Andes y del Chaco: La resistencia chiriguana a la colonización europea." *Quinto Centenario* (Universidad Complutense, Madrid) (1985).

Salisbury, Neal. *Manitou and Providence: Indians, Europeans, and the Making New England, 1500–1643*. New York: Oxford University Press, 1982.

Sanfuentes, Salvador. *Obras dramáticas*. Santiago: Imprenta de los Tribunales, 1850.

San Martín, Félix. *Neuquén*. Buenos Aires: Taller Gráfico de Luis Bernard, 1930.

Sarmiento, Domingo F. *Facundo: Civilización y barbarie: Vida de Juan Facundo Quiroga*. Edited by Raimundo Lazo. Mexico City: Editorial Porrúa, 1966. Translated by Kathleen Ross as *Facundo: Civilization and Barbarism: The First Complete English Translation*, with an introduction by Roberto González Echevarría (Berkeley: University of California Press, 2003).

Slatta, Richard. *Comparing Cowboys and Frontiers*. Norman: University of Oklahoma Press, 1997.

———. *Cowboys of the Frontiers*. New Haven, CT: Yale University Press, 1990.

———. *Gauchos and the Vanishing Frontier*. Lincoln: University of Nebraska Press, 1983.

Socolow, Susan Migden. "Spanish Captives in Indian Societies: Cultural Contact along the Argentine Frontier, 1600–1835." *Hispanic American Historical Review* 72, no. 1 (1992): 73–99.

Solís de Meras, Gonzalo. *Pedro Menéndez de Avilés y la conquista de la Florida (1565)*. Oviedo: Grupo Editorial Asturiano, 1990.

Sorensen, Diane Goodrich. *Facundo and the Construction of Argentine Culture*. Austin: University of Texas Press, 1991.

Sosnowski, Saúl. Preface to *Una excursión a los indios ranqueles*, by Lucio V. Mansilla. Caracas: Biblioteca Ayacucho, 1984.

Staden, Hans. *Hans Staden: The True History of His Captivity, 1557.* Edited and translated by Malcolm Letts. New York: Robert M. McBride and Co., 1929. First published 1557.

Stern, Peter. "The White Indians of the Borderlands." *Journal of the Southwest* 33, no. 3 (1991): 263–81.

Tapson, Alfred J. "Indian Warfare on the Pampa during the Colonial Period." *Hispanic American Historical Review* 42, no. 1 (1962): 1–28.

Thomas, Alfred B. *Forgotten Frontiers: A Study of the Spanish Indian Policy of Don Juan Bautista de Anza, Governor of New Mexico, 1777–1787.* Norman: University of Oklahoma Press, 1969.

———. *The Plains Indians and New Mexico, 1751–1778: A Collection of Documents Illustrative of the History of the Eastern Frontier of New Mexico.* Glendale, CA: Arthur H. Clark Co., 1940.

True, David O. Introduction to *Memoir of Do. d'Escalante Fontaneda respecting Florida,* by Hernado de Escalante Fontaneda. Translated from the Spanish with notes by Buckingham Smith, Washington, 1854; edited by David O. True. Coral Gables, FL: Glade House, 1945.

Turner, Frederick Jackson. *History, Frontier, and Section: Three Essays by Frederick Jackson Turner.* Edited by Martin Ridge. Albuquerque: University of New Mexico Press, 1992.

Valdivia, Pedro de. *Cartas de Pedro de Valdivia, que tratan del descubrimiento y conquista de Chile.* Madrid: Atlas, 1960.

Valero, Helena. *Yo soy Napëyoma: Relato de una mujer raptada por los indígenas yanomami.* Edited by Emilio Fuentes. Caracas: Fundación La Salle de Ciencias Naturales, 1984.

VanDerBeets, Richard, ed. *Held Captives by Indians: Selected Narratives, 1642–1836.* Knoxville: University of Tennessee Press, 1994.

———. *The Indian Captivity Narratives: An American Genre.* Lanham, MD: University Press of America, 1984.

———. "A Surfeit of Style: The Indian Captivity Narratives Penny Dreadful." *Research Studies* 39 (1971): 297–306.

Varela, Juan Cruz. *Poesías.* Buenos Aires: L. J. Rosso, 1942.

Vega, Garcilaso de la. *La Florida del Inca.* Edited by Sylvia Hilton. Madrid: Historia 16, 1986.

Vidal de Battini, Berta. "La lucha con el indio de la Pampa en la tradición popular." *Logos: Revista de la Facultad de de Filosofía y Letras* 15 (1979): 247–51.

Viedma, Antonio de. "Diario de Viedma" and "Descripción de la costa meridional del sur llamada vulgarmente Patagonia." In vol. 7B of *Colección de obras y documentos relativos a la historia antigua y moderna de las Provincias del Río de la Plata,* compiled by Pedro de Angelis. Buenos Aires: Editorial Plus Ultras, 1972.

Vigil, Ralph H., Frances W. Kaye, and John R. Wunder. *Spain and the Plains: Myths and*

Realities of Spanish Exploration and Settlement on the Great Plains. Niwot: University Press of Colorado, 1994.

Villagutierre, Juan. *Historia de la conquista de Itzá.* Edited by Jesús M. García. Madrid: Historia 16, 1985.

Villalobos, Sergio R. *Los Pehuenches en la vida fronteriza.* Santiago: Ediciones Universidad Católica de Chile, 1989.

———, ed. *Relaciones fronterizas de la Araucanía.* Santiago: Ediciones Universidad Católica de Chile, 1982.

———. *Vida fronteriza en la Araucanía: El mito de la guerra del Arauco.* Santiago: Editorial Andrés Bello, 1995.

Villalobos, Sergio R., and Jorge Pinto, eds. *Araucanía: Temas de historia fronteriza.* Temuco: Ediciones de la Universidad de la Frontera, 1985.

Villarino, Basilio. "Diario de la navegación del Buen Suceso y el desagüe del río Colorado." In vol. 7B of *Colección de obras y documentos relativos a la historia antigua y moderna de las Provincias del Río de la Plata,* compiled by Pedro de Angelis. Buenos Aires: Editorial Plus Ultras, 1972.

Villa Roiz, Carlos. *Gonzalo Guerrero: Memoria olvidada: Trauma de México.* Mexico City: Plaza y Janés, 1995.

Viñas, David. *Indios, ejército y frontera.* Mexico City: Siglo XXI Editores, 1982.

Vivar, Jerónimo de. *Crónica de los reinos de Chile.* Edited by Angel Barral Gómez. Madrid: Historia 16, 1988.

Wakefield, Sarah F. *Six Weeks in the Sioux Tepees: A Narrative of Indian Captivity.* Edited by June Namias. Norman: University of Oklahoma Press, 1997.

Walther, Juan Carlos. *La conquista del desierto.* Buenos Aires: Editorial Universitaria de Buenos Aires, 1970.

Wast, Hugo. *Lucía Miranda.* Buenos Aires: Editores de Hugo Wast, 1929.

Weber, David J. *The Spanish Frontier in North America.* New Haven, CT: Yale University Press, 1992.

Weber, David J., and Jane M. Rausch, eds. *Where Cultures Meet: Frontiers in Latin American History.* Wilmington, DE: SR Books, 1994.

Weil, Andrew. Introduction to *Wizard of the Upper Amazon: The Story of Manuel Córdova-Ríos,* by Bruce F. Lamb. Berkeley: North Atlantic Books, 1974.

Zapater, Horacio. "Parlamentos de paz en la guerra de Arauco (1612–1626)." In *Araucanía: Temas de historia fronteriza,* edited by Sergio R. Villalobos and Jorge Pinto. Temuco: Ediciones de la Universidad de la Frontera, 1985.

Zapater Equioiz, Horacio. *Los aborígenes chilenos a través de cronistas y viajeros.* Santiago de Chile: Editorial Andrés Bello, 1973.

———. *La búsqueda de la paz en la guerra de Arauco: Padre Luis de Valdivia.* Santiago de Chile: Editorial Andrés Bello, 1992.

———. "Testimonio de un cautivo: Araucanía, 1599–1614." *Historia* 16 (1988): 296–325.

Zavala, Silvio. "The Frontiers of Hispanic America." In *Where Cultures Meet: Frontiers in Latin America,* edited by David J. Weber and Jane M. Rausch, 42–50. 3rd ed. Wilmington, DE: SR Books, 1994.

Zeballos, Estanislao S. *Callvucurá y la dinastía de los Piedra.* Edited by Roberto F. Giusti. Buenos Aires: Ediciones Solar, 1994.

————. *Painé y la dinastía de los Zorros.* Edited by Luis V. Sommi. Buenos Aires: Editorial Universitaria de Buenos Aires, 1964.

————. *Relmu: Reina de los Pinares.* Buenos Aires: Librería Hachette, 1955.

Zorrilla de San Martín, Juan. *Tabaré: An Indian Legend of Uruguay.* Translated by Walter Owen. Washington, D.C.: Pan American Union/UNESCO, 1956.

Zubizarreta, Carlos. *Capitanes de aventura: Cabeza de Vaca, el infortunado; Irala, el predestinado.* Madrid: Ediciones Cultura Hispánica, 1964.

Zum Felde, Alberto. "Tabaré." In *Historia y crítica de la literatura hispanoamericana: Del romanticismo al modernismo,* edited by Cedomil Góic. Barcelona: Editorial Crítica, 1991.

Index

Italicized page numbers refer to illustrations.